I0896694

Management Strategies and Business Models for Circular Economy Transformation

Mohamad Saad El Dine Knio
https://orcid.org/0000-0001-9074-8618
Lebanese International University, Lebanon

Najib Bou Zakhem
Lebanese International University, Lebanon

IGI Global
Scientific Publishing
Publishing Tomorrow's Research Today

Vice President of Editorial Melissa Wagner
Director of Acquisitions Mikaela Felty
Director of Book Development Jocelynn Hessler
Production Manager Mike Brehm
Cover Design Jose Rosado

Published in the United States of America by
IGI Global Scientific Publishing
701 East Chocolate Avenue
Hershey, PA, 17033, USA
Tel: 717-533-8845 | Fax: 717-533-7115
Website: https://www.igi-global.com E-mail: cust@igi-global.com

Library of Congress Cataloging-in-Publication Data

CIP DATA PENDING

ISBN13: 9798337376554
Isbn13Softcover: 9798337376561
EISBN13: 9798337376578

British Cataloguing in Publication Data
A Cataloguing in Publication record for this book is available from the British Library.

Table of Contents

Detailed Table of Contents

Purpose – This study examines the impact of AI utilisation on workforce size and productivity, and its implications for the circular economy in the Turkish banking sector. Design/methodology/approach – Data from five private banks (2014–2023) were analysed using correlation and regression methods. Workforce size was measured by employee count; productivity was based on internal performance scores. Findings – AI use significantly affects both variables. AI-driven services tend to reduce workforce size while boosting productivity. Interestingly, a positive correlation was observed between complaint rates and productivity. Discussion – AI supports sustainability via digitalization and resource efficiency, aligning with circular economy principles. However, the decline in workforce size reflects concerns in literature about AI-driven unemployment, requiring strategic planning.

This chapter examines support mechanisms and policies for advancing circular entrepreneurship in Lebanon taking into account the country's economic, environmental, and infrastructural challenges hindering its development. Reflecting on comparative policy frameworks applied in countries such as Finland, the Netherlands, Scotland, and South Africa, key lessons are identified enabling a suggestion of a tailored roadmap relevant to the Lebanese context. The roadmap constitutes three phases along with a defined time frame for developing the essentials like policies, institutional coordination, and operational capacity, while highlighting the role of entrepreneurship, civil society, academia, and international actors in supporting the transition. The chapter also formulates performance metrics and monitoring frameworks while establishing mechanisms for accountability. It concludes by arguing that circular entrepreneurship is still showing high resilience and hope for economic regeneration despite all the constraints and limitations.

The circular economy has emerged as a compelling alternative to the traditional linear "take-make-dispose" economic model, gaining significant traction across academia, industry, and policymaking (Geissdoerfer et al., 2020). This shift is primarily driven by an increasing awareness of the environmental impacts associated with linear systems, especially the rapid depletion of resources and growing waste production (Henry et al., 2020). At the heart of this transformation, circular business models offer innovative solutions that decouple economic growth from resource depletion by prioritizing closed-loop systems and enhancing resource efficiency (Adam et al., 2017).In this section, the chapter will define circular economy business model (CEBM) in precise terms. The circular business model notion is based on two underlying concepts: the circular economy and business model innovation. This section will introduce the circular economy, business model innovation and circular business models topics. The researchers will conduct a literature review of the circular business models.

The concepts of circular economy is gaining momentum in addressing global issues in the areas of waste management, climate change, product life-cycle design and supply chain management. Leaders have significant impact on the strategic directions of their organizations and dedication to the circular economy goals. The chapter examines how the transformational, ethical, participative, and adaptive leadership influence sustainable resources use in circular economies (CE). The chapter used a descriptive analysis based on exploring an update of existing literature and articles and a peek on real world insights. The chapter aims at giving readers an insight at how leaders can effectively support the shift towards circular economies while maintaining their commitment to sustainability initiatives, and highlighting existing

Preface

The global economy faces unprecedented challenges, from resource depletion and environmental degradation to social inequalities exacerbated by linear "take-make-dispose" models. The circular economy (CE) offers a transformative framework to address these issues by prioritizing resource efficiency, waste reduction, and regenerative systems. *Management Strategies and Business Models for Circular Economy Transformation* explores how businesses, policymakers, and leaders can adopt circular principles to foster sustainable development across diverse contexts. This book integrates interdisciplinary perspectives, drawing on case studies, theoretical frameworks, and innovative policy proposals to provide actionable insights for circularity in industries, economies, and societies.

From leveraging artificial intelligence in banking to mobilizing diaspora networks for entrepreneurship, the chapters address critical dimensions of the circular economy, including workforce dynamics, leadership styles, policy frameworks, and cultural transformation. By examining global best practices alongside context-specific challenges, particularly in emerging economies like Lebanon, this book underscores the universal relevance of circularity while acknowledging the socio-economic and environmental barriers that shape its implementation. It is intended for business leaders, policymakers, academics, and sustainability professionals seeking to navigate the complexities of transitioning to a circular economy, offering rigorous analysis and forward-thinking recommendations to inspire a regenerative future.

CHAPTER OVERVIEW

Chapter 1 examines the impact of AI on workforce size and productivity in the Turkish banking sector, highlighting its alignment with circular economy principles through digitalization and resource efficiency. It analyzes data from private banks (2014–2023) and discusses the trade-offs between AI-driven productivity gains and workforce reduction, emphasizing the need for strategic planning to address unemployment concerns.

Chapter 2 proposes a policy framework to advance circular entrepreneurship in Lebanon, considering its economic and environmental challenges. It draws lessons from global case studies (e.g., Finland, Netherlands) to develop a phased roadmap, incorporating performance metrics and stakeholder collaboration to foster resilience and economic regeneration.

Chapter 3 defines circular business models (CBMs) and traces their evolution from linear economic systems. It explores the principles of closed-loop systems and resource efficiency, grounded in a literature review, to highlight how CBMs decouple economic growth from resource depletion and promote sustainable innovation.

Chapter 4 investigates how transformational, ethical, participative, and adaptive leadership styles drive sustainable practices in circular economies. Through descriptive analysis and real-world insights, it highlights leadership's role in supporting sustainability initiatives and overcoming challenges in waste management, product design, and supply chains.

Chapter 5 explores the neurobiological dimensions of leadership decision-making in circular economies, emphasizing the interplay of cognitive reasoning, emotions, and physiological responses. It argues that balancing these elements enhances adaptive and authentic leadership, proposing a reconsideration of traditional decision-making models.

Chapter 6 analyzes the hospitality industry's shift toward sustainability through circular business models. It addresses resource use and waste challenges, advocating for systemic changes to balance eco-friendly operations with service quality and aligning with Sustainable Development Goals for long-term value creation.

Chapter 7 discusses transforming business models to integrate social, economic, and environmental goals through circularity. It emphasizes resource efficiency, stakeholder engagement, and change management, using the AIDA model to guide cultural shifts toward sustainable practices and long-term value creation.

Chapter 8 proposes leveraging the Lebanese diaspora to promote circular economy entrepreneurship as a pathway for post-crisis recovery. It presents a three-pillar policy framework, supported by international case studies, to harness diaspora expertise and capital for sustainable innovation and resilience in Lebanon's fragile context.

CONCLUSION

The circular economy represents a paradigm shift that transcends traditional economic models, offering a pathway to reconcile economic prosperity with environmental and social sustainability. The chapters in this book collectively illuminate the multifaceted strategies required to achieve this transformation, from leveraging cutting-edge technologies like AI to redefining leadership and policy frameworks. They highlight the importance of context-specific solutions, as seen in Lebanon's resilience amid crises, while drawing on global best practices to inform scalable approaches. The integration of circular business models, stakeholder engagement, and innovative governance underscores the potential for systemic change across industries and societies.

Looking forward, the transition to a circular economy demands sustained collaboration among businesses, policymakers, academia, and communities. Challenges such as workforce displacement, cultural resistance, and infrastructural limitations must be addressed through adaptive leadership, robust policy frameworks, and inclusive innovation. By embracing the principles of circularity—resource efficiency, waste minimization, and regeneration—this book envisions a future where economic systems are resilient, equitable, and aligned with the planet's ecological boundaries. It calls for continued research, policy experimentation, and global cooperation to realize the full potential of the circular economy, paving the way for a sustainable and prosperous future.

Chapter 1
AI Utilization, Workforce Dynamics, and Productivity in Turkish Banking Implications for the Circular Economy

Begum Al
https://orcid.org/0000-0001-8839-4478
Marmara University, Turkey

ABSTRACT

Purpose – This study examines the impact of AI utilisation on workforce size and productivity, and its implications for the circular economy in the Turkish banking sector. Design/methodology/approach – Data from five private banks (2014–2023) were analysed using correlation and regression methods. Workforce size was measured by employee count; productivity was based on internal performance scores. Findings – AI use significantly affects both variables. AI-driven services tend to reduce workforce size while boosting productivity. Interestingly, a positive correlation was observed between complaint rates and productivity. Discussion – AI supports sustainability via digitalization and resource efficiency, aligning with circular economy principles. However, the decline in workforce size reflects concerns in literature about AI-driven unemployment, requiring strategic planning.

DOI: 10.4018/979-8-3373-7655-4.ch001

1. INTRODUCTION

The 21st-century's banking sector has been undergoing profound digital transformation (Yıldırım, 2006). This transformation is mainly moving away from traditional branch-centred models to technology-driven services model. At the first look it may be seen as a shift for increasing operational efficiency as well as increasing customer satisfaction. Nevertheless, this is a part of a broader push for sustainability and systemic change (Işkın, 2010).

In fact, in global discussions on sustainability, the concept of the circular economy has emerged as a framework for redesigning economic activities to be more regenerative and resource-efficient (Lu and Serafim, 2023). A circular economy entails moving from the linear and traditional "take-make-dispose" model toward one where resources are continuously reused, waste is minimised, and value is maintained within the system (Lu and Serafim, 2023). Achieving this transition requires rethinking how industries operate. This includes service industries like banking to improve resource efficiency, reduce waste, and leverage innovation for sustainable growth (Meena & Ganesan, 2020; Szeiner & Balázs, 2023). Digitalisation and AI play a crucial role in this process. Indeed, they are increasingly recognised as enablers that can decouple economic activity from physical resource use since it allows more output to be obtained with fewer material inputs (OECD, 2023). Indeed, both private and public sectors are called to transform their operations to address climate change, cut pollution, and improve resource efficiency, and the financial sector in particular has a central role in shifting from a linear, wasteful economy toward one that embeds circularity in finance (ConnectEarth, 2025). This context underlines that the modernisation of banking through AI and digital tools should be seen as part of a systemic sustainability transition rather than seen alone as a technological upgrade (Annisa et al., 2024).

Within the banking industry, the adoption of AI and other digital technologies has already redefined how value is delivered to the customers (Bueno et al., 2024). In this manner, banks have increasingly digitised their products and services through using internet and mobile banking to AI-driven chatbots and analytics (Gartner, 2020; McKinsey, 2019). This effectively dematerialising many banking processes that once relied on physical infrastructure. Dematerialisation in finance refers to the substitution of physical documents, cash, and in-person services with digital equivalents (Annisa et al., 2024). This trend aligns with circular economy principles by reducing the need for physical resources such as paper, branch energy use, and physical storage and rationalisation processes for greater efficiency (FasterCapital, 2025). For example, shifting to online banking and electronic statements lowers paper consumption and cuts down on the carbon footprint associated with printing and transporting documents (FasterCapital, 2025). Similarly, AI-supported digital workflows can optimise operations which leads banks to use less energy and materials. Accordingly, this contributes creating a smaller environmental footprint for offered services. When look at the issue from this point it can be said that the banking sector's digital transformation is yielding a form of digital sustainability. Because banks leverage AI to automate and innovate and as a result, they have the opportunity to operate more efficiently while consuming fewer physical resources. Accordingly, this not only improves operational cost-effectiveness but also resonates with society's expectations for greener more responsible business practices.

Furthermore, the increased use of AI is enabling banks to develop new products such as personalised financial planning tools or algorithmic lending platforms and business models such as fintech partnerships that could support sustainable finance innovations (Bloomberg, 2024).

Early evidence even suggests that adopting circular economy strategies in finance can help in increasing the operational profits. For example, the sustainable finance market such as green bonds, ESG investments, etc. is growing rapidly and the move toward circular economy models is seen as a strategic opportunity for financial institutions to achieve both profitability and sustainability goals (ConnectEarth, 2025). The intersection of AI-driven banking modernisation with circular economy ideals thus presents a timely arena for research, promising insights into how technology can drive win-win outcomes in economic and environmental performance. At the same time, these digital advancements bring new challenges and considerations. Banks are optimising their workforce and processes through AI. This raises concerns about job displacement, skill gaps, and organisational change. There is a growing debate on the net impact of AI on employment. In this manner, some experts highlight AI's potential to augment human productivity and create new roles, while others warn of significant displacement of workers by automation. In practice, many banks have reported downsizing or retraining staff as AI systems take over routine tasks, from customer service inquiries to back-office processing. Notably, recent analyses have pointed out that companies often conceal the extent of layoffs attributable to AI to avoid public backlash. This underscores a need for transparency and proactive management of workforce transitions in the era of AI (Karyağdı, 2022). Beyond workforce issues, there is the question of maintaining service quality and inclusiveness. Because banks pursue efficiency, they must ensure that automated services do not alienate less tech-savvy customers or compromise customer satisfaction (Shabir et al., 2023). However, early signs of tension are evident (Apendi et al., 2025). In fact, higher productivity achieved through AI can coincide with higher customer complaint rates, as it decreases customer experiences. All these dynamics illustrate that AI adoption in banking is not just a technical evolution (Apendi et al., 2025). Thus, it is a societal transformation, touching on economic, social, and sustainability dimensions. Framing this transformation within circular economy principles provides a valuable perspective. Considering these, this study examines the relationship between AI utilisation, workforce dynamics, and productivity in the Turkish banking sector, with a view toward understanding how these trends align with or challenge the goals of a sustainable, circular economic transition. The findings are used to derive insights and policy recommendations for achieving an inclusive and efficient digital transformation in banking that supports long-term sustainability.

1.1. Definition of Artificial Intelligence

Artificial intelligence (AI) refers to the ability of machines to perform behaviors that are considered intelligent when performed by humans, or it can be defined as a theory that demonstrates how the human mind functions (Pirim, 2006). AI is a general term for information technologies that can perform tasks typically unique to humans, such as visual perception, speech recognition, decision-making, and language translation by imitating human intelligence (Yıldız, 2023).

In general, the concept of AI implies that technological entities possess the ability to perceive a complex matter and make appropriate decisions regarding it (Ersoy, 2017). AI can be described as a package of programs or an individual program that can replicate certain aspects of human behavior (Smith, 2018). In essence, it is a technology designed to mimic human judgment and cognitive skills and to respond to environmental cues (Munoko et al., 2020). Therefore, AI requires high-quality data to learn what actions to take (Gotthardt et al., 2020).

Another definition of AI frames it as the field of computer science concerned with machines that behave in a way that would be deemed intelligent if exhibited by humans (Negnevitsky, 2005). AI involves creating machine learning systems, decision-making mechanisms based on data, and autonomous management capabilities. It analyses data with mathematical and logical models that simulate human consciousness, aiming to make the most accurate predictions and decisions (Serçemeli, 2018).

In simpler terms, AI refers to intelligent behavior mimicked by a machine (Hegde, 2019). When it comes to AI, it operates on models that align directly with human consciousness, focusing on tasks such as speech recognition, learning, visual perception, recognition, and strategy formation (Gültekin, 2021). Particularly in recent years, AI has made its presence increasingly felt in sectors like marketing, finance, and healthcare (Bingöl, 2023).

In the banking sector, AI applications are used to gather market intelligence, deliver banking services to customers, and enhance communication. These AI applications are employed to strengthen the bank's image, retain existing customers, attract new ones, reduce the workload of branches, and provide faster services by directing customers towards internet and mobile banking (Gümüş et al., 2020).

Indeed, in an effort to keep pace with the times and accurately address customer demands by collaborating with customer experience offices, the dynamically evolving banking sector has undergone significant digital transformations. Banks have started to offer their products and services via technologies such as Interactive Voice Response (IVR), internet banking, mobile banking, QR code systems, and chatbots. As part of this digital transformation process, banks are utilising AI, a key component of the Fourth Industrial Revolution, to deliver the right product or service to the appropriate customer, manage business processes optimally, predict customer demands, enhance financial consulting, and improve their reliability and security, thereby steering towards new-generation banking solutions (Akbaba and Gündoğdu, 2021).

1.2. The Impact of Artificial Intelligence on Productivity and Employment

According to the data published by PwC in 2024, artificial intelligence (AI) is already enhancing employee productivity. Sectors exposed to AI have seen nearly a fivefold increase in productivity. This rise in productivity is one of the most critical factors driving economic growth and improving living standards (PwC, 2024). According to the 2024 Global CEO Survey, 84% of CEOs whose companies have adopted AI believe that this technology will boost the productivity of their employees during working hours. Increased productivity does not only mean that tasks will be completed faster but also that new, AI-supported ways to create value will be discovered. Additionally, 70% of CEOs think that AI will significantly transform how their companies create and deliver value within the next three years (PwC, 2024).

According to a report by Google, the widespread use of generative AI in Turkey could add approximately 5% to Turkey's annual GDP within the next decade. This translates to an additional 1.2 to 1.4 trillion Turkish lira (50-60 billion USD). These gains stem from three sources: contributions to productivity from individuals working with generative AI, time saved from tasks automated by generative AI, and the reallocation of that time to other value-added activities.

The same report predicts that in Turkey, 55% of jobs will involve working alongside generative AI, while 41% of jobs are expected to remain unaffected by generative AI. Jobs expected to be highly impacted by AI constitute only 4% of existing jobs in Turkey. In an AI-supported economy, it is anticipated that new jobs created due to automation will replace those that are eliminated, leading to no significant change in unemployment levels (Thelle et al., 2024).

Approximately 70% of the economic potential of generative AI is expected to come from sectors such as trade, transportation, tourism, manufacturing, construction, energy, and water. The most significant relative increase in added value is anticipated in information-intensive business services. Despite Turkey having a strong operational environment for the widespread use of AI, it lags behind in terms of strategy, infrastructure, and fundamental innovation dynamics. To fully harness the benefits of AI, Turkey needs to retrain its workforce, equip it with new AI-related skills, increase R&D activities, and accelerate commercial breakthroughs. The adoption of artificial intelligence tends to increase productivity and may have non-negative or even positive effects on employment at the firm level (Saam, 2024; Shen & Zhang, 2024), although aggregate effects on the economy are still emerging (Saam, 2024).

The literature on the impact of AI on unemployment continues to expand, emphasising the need to focus more on AI's complex role in the automation process. Two key effects are particularly noteworthy: the substitution effect and the displacement effect. The substitution effect, supported by empirical and theoretical studies, posits that AI has the potential to negatively impact the labor market by creating unemployment. However, it is believed that governments can mitigate this adverse effect through appropriate redistribution policies (Mutascu, 2021).

The impact of technological innovations on employment can be analysed under two main headings: the displacement effect, which causes workers to move away from their current tasks, and the productivity effect, which increases labor demand by creating new job areas (Petropoulos, 2018). When examined historically, automation's impact on the labor market has shown fluctuations, but it has not resulted in long-term increases in unemployment rates (Autor, 2015).

Frey and Osborne (2013) note that technological advancements have both disruptive and creative effects, with productivity growth leading to the creation of new jobs. Acemoglu and Restrepo (2018) discuss how factors such as productivity, capital accumulation, and the deepening of automation influence labor demand. Automation, particularly in capital-intensive production, drives productivity increases and, therefore, boosts labor demand.

Two distinct perspectives on AI emerge in the literature. The optimistic view argues that AI enhances human capabilities and increases demand for skilled workers, while the pessimistic view suggests that AI will replace workers, leading to increased unemployment (Huang et al., 2019).

1.3. AI Adoption, Banking Transformation and the Circular Economy

While banking is not traditionally seen as a resource-intensive industry in the same way as manufacturing or agriculture, the principles of the circular economy are highly relevant as the sector transforms digitally (Bueno et al., 2024). A circular economy model emphasises designing systems that eliminate waste and keep resources in use through strategies like reuse, recycling, and efficiency improvement (Lu and Serafim, 2023). In the context of banking, the "resources" in question extend beyond physical materials to include digital infrastructure, human skills, customer data, and financial capital (Lu and Serafim, 2023). AI adoption can influence how all these resources are managed and optimised. Following are some examples of this:

Dematerialisation of Services: One of the most important ways that AI and digitalisation contribute to circular economy goals in banking is through the dematerialisation of financial services. Dematerialisation, in this context means to the reduction or elimination of physical materials in delivering products and services. In banking, examples of dematerialisation include a shift from paper-based statements to electronic records. In addition, from cash to digital payments, and from in-person transactions at branch offices to mobile or online banking can be seen as a dematerialisation. By transitioning from physical to digital channels, banks reduce their consumption of paper, plastics and even the energy associated with operating through large branch networks. This transition aligns with the circular principle of using fewer virgin resources and generating less waste. Research on digital finance highlights that this kind of dematerialisation not only helps in cutting costs. In fact, it also supports sustainability. Indeed, online and mobile banking reduce the need for physical infrastructure and travel and which in turn lowers carbon emissions and resource usage (Lu and Serafim, 2023). For example, every customer who opts for e-statements and digital signatures in place of mailed paper statements directly contributes to conservation of trees and reduction of waste, while the bank saves on printing and postage costs. AI comes into play by improving digital service delivery. For example, intelligent chatbots handle customer inquiries that might otherwise require paper forms or face-to-face visits. In addition, AI-driven fraud detection replaces manual, paper-heavy auditing processes and machine learning algorithms can optimise data centre operations for energy efficiency. However, it is also important to acknowledge the digital infrastructure's footprint. In this manner, running AI systems and data centres consumes electricity and hardware, which means banks must also focus on renewable energy use and e-waste recycling to ensure net environmental benefits. On balance, though, the banking sector's digital shift represents a move toward "doing more with less" providing financial services with significantly lower material input. This dematerialisation trend supports a decoupling of service growth from resource consumption, echoing the circular economy's core tenet of decoupling economic activity from environmental impact (OECD, 2023).

Efficiency and Resource Productivity: The productivity gains associated with AI in banking can be interpreted through a circular economy lens as improvements in resource productivity. In circular economy discourse, a key goal is to maximise the utility obtained from a given amount of resources. In this context, AI technologies enable banks to increase output per unit of input. Here, inputs include physical resources. Nevertheless, it also includes human labour hours and capital.

By automating routine processes and augmenting human capabilities, AI allows banks to serve more customers, process more transactions, and manage more data with the same or fewer resources than before. This is analogous to improving the yield of a better service delivery and financial intermediation achieved with streamlined operations. From a circular perspective, this means the sector is able to generate more economic value for each unit of labour and infrastructure invested. This effectively increases the resource efficiency of banking operations. Such efficiency gains are critical to sustainability. Because, they imply that the economy can grow without a commensurate increase in resource use or waste generation. In fact, the OECD has noted that digitalisation can help decouple economic growth from resource use and the banking sector's AI-led efficiency is a prime example of this decoupling (OECD, 2023). Moreover, efficiency in banking can translate to broader sustainability impacts. For example, if AI reduces operational costs and increases profitability, banks might have better capacity to invest in sustainable initiatives or offer lower interest rates on green loans. Customers benefit from faster and more reliable services. This potentially increase trust in digital channels and further reduce reliance on resource-intensive branch banking. However, it should be noted that pure efficiency focus can sometimes lead to unintended effects. In a circular economy framework, efficiency must be balanced with system resilience and quality. This should ensure that short-term productivity gains do not create new problems. Therefore, banks need to pursue AI-driven efficiency within a holistic strategy that also values customer experience and employee well-being.

Innovation and New Business Models: AI is a catalyst for innovation in banking since it spurs new products, services, and even business models. Its should be noted that many of these innovations can support circular economy objectives in finance. One concept from circular economy literature is the shift from selling products to providing services or Product-Service Systems (PSS) as a way to optimise resource use. In banking, parallel move can be seen towards banking-as-a-service and platform-based models. In here, banks leverage technology including AI to offer financial services in an on-demand, modular fashion. This can lead to more shared infrastructure and industry collaboration, reducing duplication of efforts and resources across the financial system. For example, consider how multiple banks might share a blockchain-based trade finance platform or how AI-powered credit scoring services can be outsourced to fintech providers that serve many institutions at once. These arrangements create a more circular use of digital resources and knowledge, as opposed to each bank expending resources to develop similar solutions in silos. Additionally, AI allows for innovative financial products that incentivise sustainable behaviour. In this manner, some banks are now using AI algorithms to analyse environmental, social, and governance (ESG) data and create "green credit scores" or tailor interest rates based on a borrower's sustainability performance. Such products encourage borrowers and investees to adopt circular practices. The integration of big data and AI also helps in tracking and tracing resources in supply chains, which banks can use in trade finance to ensure that materials are recycled or sourced sustainably, thereby directly supporting circular supply chain financing (Apendi et al., 2025). Moreover, AI can enable dynamic pricing and usage-based financial services. For example, insurance premiums that adjust based on real-time behaviour data, or "pay-as-you-use" models in lending, aligning with the circular economy idea of paying for performance rather than owning assets outright. This can lead to more mindful consumption of financial resources. In essence, the banking sector's transformation fuelled by AI is opening opportunities to develop financial practices and instruments that reinforce circular economy outcomes, from funding renewable energy and recycling projects to encouraging customers towards sustainable choices. Scholars have noted that emerging digital technologies like AI, when combined with business model innovation, are seen as providing solutions to many challenges in implementing the circular economy (Shabir et al., 2023). In fact, AI and the Internet of Things (IoT) are identified as key enablers of the circular transition across industries. In banking, this enabling role means AI makes existing processes more efficient. However, it also allows the conception of new forms of financial intermediation that could directly support a circular, sustainable economy.

Systemic and Human Capital Considerations: A true circular economy transition is system-wide, requiring consideration of social and human factors alongside technology and environment. AI-driven transformation in banking brings to the forefront the importance of human capital as a resource that should not be wasted. In a circular approach, just as materials are recycled and given a new life, the workforce must be "recycled" in terms of reskilling and upskilling. However, AI utilisation tends to reduce workforce size. This highlights a potential social challenge since it may decrease the number of workforce. In other words it could lead to unemployment and inequality. Outcomes at odds with the inclusive ethos of sustainability. However, circular thinking would urge that these displaced or transitioning employees be retrained and redeployed rather than discarded. In other words, banks and policymakers should treat employee skills and experience as a valuable resource to be replenished and repurposed, much like circulating assets in a closed loop (Apendi et al., 2025). This could involve large-scale investment in continuous learning programs, AI literacy training, and the creation of new career pathways within banks. By doing so, the banking sector ensures that human talent is retained in the economic cycle, analogous to keeping materials in circulation instead of sending them to landfill. Such an approach may mitigates the social impact of AI. Nevertheless, it can also enhance the long-term adaptability and resilience of the banking workforce. From a policy standpoint, this alignment of AI adoption with a circular use of human capital may involve partnerships between banks, educational institutions, and government agencies to facilitate workforce transformation.

1.4. Research on Banking Sector

According to Bratişanu (2017), it has been proven that AI-supported innovative advancements have revised the business model of finance. Recently, it has been noted that customers and the traditional banking structure are benefiting from automation and social media connection technologies. Models that integrate the automation of customer relations, advanced analytics, and AI software enhance the customer experience and increase the efficiency of the risk management process (Yıldız, 2023).

Votintseva et al. (2019), in the context of Russia's Digital Economy program, divided their research into three main categories: the operational areas of financial actors, platforms and technologies for effective customer-oriented services, and the development of information platforms. They conducted a survey and found that technological banking applications had positive effects on the country's economy.

Gümüş et al. (2020) addressed the transactions made through AI-based alternative distribution channels in banks in Turkey in their study, examining the correlation between AI usage and demographic characteristics in terms of trust. A survey was conducted with 500 participants, and the results showed that the ways in which AI is used differ based on factors such as age, gender, occupation, and income distribution. The study found that as age, income, and education levels of the participants increased, their trust in AI also increased. Additionally, they concluded that the effective use of AI in the financial sector provided significant convenience for users.

In essence, developments in AI have had a transformative effect on the banking sector. AI advancements have increased the cost-effectiveness of banks. Through electronic and mobile payment systems, enhanced credit techniques, and online and mobile access channels, additional cost savings have been achieved (Yıldız, 2023). In their research, Jaksic and Marinc (2015) identified improvements in key areas such as communication, decision-making, automation, and empowerment for bank customers, reshaping how bank clients interact with financial institutions through AI developments.

There have also been significant developments and changes in audit mechanisms. For example, in March 2016, KPMG, one of the leading financial audit firms, announced its collaboration with IBM Watson to apply cognitive computing technology to its professional service offerings (Özçetin, 2022). The idea was to use Watson to help auditors analyse large volumes of financial data to detect anomalies. For instance, in the commercial mortgage loan portfolios of banks, cognitive technology scaled human skills and judgments, enabling auditors to gain a more detailed and comprehensive understanding of potential audit exceptions based on loan files and credit ratings (Issa et al., 2016). Another auditing firm, Deloitte, has partnered with Kira Systems Inc., which offers a contract analysis system, to develop cognitive models that assist auditors in the complex task of document review by extracting and structuring textual information for better analysis (Issa et al., 2016). This AI application, known as "Kira Systems," is also used to enhance Deloitte's security activities (Gacar, 2019).

2. METHODOLOGY

The purpose of this research has been determined as examining the impact of Artificial Intelligence Utilisation on Workforce Size and Productivity in the context of the banking sector in Turkey. In this study, five private banks operating in Turkey were selected. Each bank was chosen based on a specific criterion. The criterion is either the data to be examined in this research was published by the selected bank, or the necessary data could be obtained by the researcher from the bank. Accordingly, five private banks operating in Turkey were selected using a purposive sampling method. The names of these private banks will be kept confidential.

The data used in the research were obtained from the annual financial reports of the selected banks, and missing data were completed by directly contacting the banks. The values between 2014 and 2023 were used in the study. The data and their descriptions used in the research are presented below:

Between 2014 and 2023, six types of data were used to determine Artificial Intelligence Utilisation:

- AI-based financial product diversity: Changes in the number of AI-based products and services offered by banks between 2014 and 2023.
- Customer complaint rates: Changes in customer complaints between 2014 and 2023.
- AI-based customer service interactions: Usage rates of systems providing customer services using AI (chatbots, virtual assistants, or digital channels) between 2014 and 2023.
- Number of AI-based services: Changes in the number of AI-supported services (chatbots, virtual assistants, risk analysis systems, etc.) offered by banks between 2014 and 2023.
- Total R&D expenditures on AI technologies: R&D expenditures for innovation and AI solutions in the banking sector between 2014 and 2023.

- Annual investment in AI projects: Resources allocated by banks to AI projects between 2014 and 2023.

In the research, workforce size was examined based on the changes in the number of employees in the selected banks between 2014 and 2023, and productivity was evaluated in terms of the productivity score achieved by the banks internally during the same period.

First, the correlation between the six sub-factors constituting Artificial Intelligence Utilisation and both workforce size and productivity was examined. Subsequently, a regression analysis was conducted to investigate the impact of Artificial Intelligence Utilisation on workforce size and productivity using the same six sub-factors.

3. FINDINGS

Table 1. Correlation Matrix

		Variety of AI-based financial products	**Customer complaint rates**	**AI-based customer service interactions**	**Number of AI-based services**	**Total R&D spending on AI technologies**	**Annual investment in AI projects**	**Workforce Size**	**Productivity**
Variety of AI-based financial products	Pearson Correlation	1							
	Sig. (p)								
Customer complaint rates	Pearson Correlation	.345	1						
	Sig. (p)	.230							
AI-based customer service interactions	Pearson Correlation	.456	.465	1					
	Sig. (p)	.248	.146						
Number of AI-based services	Pearson Correlation	.367	.356	.143	1				
	Sig. (p)	.003	.433	.342					
Total R&D spending on AI technologies	Pearson Correlation	.123	.245	.340	.324	1			
	Sig. (p)	.045	.272	.022	.244				
Annual investment in AI projects	Pearson Correlation	.376	.234	.343	.326	.365	1		
	Sig. (p)	.291	.454	.002	.245	.002			
Workforce Size	Pearson Correlation	**-.253****	.345	.462	.323	**-.134****	**-.438****	1	
	Sig. (p)	**.004**	.125	.098	.127	**.001**	**.015**		
Productivity	Pearson Correlation	**.344****	**.386****	**.356****	**.234****	**.450****	**.364****	.342	1
	Sig. (p)	**.010**	**.018**	**.002**	**.002**	**.023**	**.005**	.126	

According to the correlation analysis results, there is a negative and statistically significant relationship between "variety of AI-based financial products" and "workforce size" (Pearson correlation= -.253; p= .004<0.05). However, there is a positive and statistically significant relationship between "variety of AI-based financial products" and "productivity" (Pearson correlation= .344; p= .010<0.05).

There is a positive and statistically significant relationship between "customer complaint rates" and "productivity" (Pearson correlation= .386; p= .018<0.05). Between "AI-based customer service interactions" and "productivity", there is a positive and statistically significant relationship (Pearson correlation= .356; p= .002<0.05). There is also a positive and statistically significant relationship between "number of AI-based services" and "productivity" (Pearson correlation= .234; p= .002<0.05).

There is a negative and statistically significant relationship between "total R&D spending on AI technologies" and "workforce size" (Pearson correlation= -.134; p= .001<0.05). However, there is a positive and statistically significant relationship between "total R&D spending on AI technologies" and "productivity" (Pearson correlation= .450; p= .023<0.05).

There is a negative and statistically significant relationship between "annual investment in AI projects" and "workforce size" (Pearson correlation= -.438; p= .015<0.05). However, there is a positive and statistically significant relationship between "annual investment in AI projects" and "productivity" (Pearson correlation= .364; p= .005<0.05).

Table 2. Regression Analysis Results

	R^2	β	Sig *(p)*
*** Workforce size ← Variety of AI-based financial products**	**.234**	**-.353**	**.004**
Workforce size ← Total R&D spending on AI technologies	.143	-.355	**.002**
Workforce size ← Annual investment in AI projects	.245	-.498	**.016**
* Productivity ← Variety of AI-based financial products	.135	.324	**.010**
Productivity ← Customer complaint rates	.257	.246	**.020**
Productivity ← AI-based customer service interactions	.346	.435	**.002**
Productivity ← Number of AI-based services	.134	.332	**.002**
Productivity ← Total R&D spending on AI technologies	.257	.421	**.024**
Productivity ← Annual investment in AI projects	.296	.347	**.005**

* Dependent variable: Workforce size
* Dependent variable: Productivity

According to the regression analysis results, the "variety of AI-based financial products" (β= -.353, p= .004<0.05), "total R&D spending on AI technologies" (β= -.355, p= .002<0.05) and "annual investment in AI projects" (β= -.498, p= .016<0.05) have negative and statistically significant effect on "workforce size".

The "variety of AI-based financial products" has a positive and statistically significant effect on "productivity" (β= .324, p= .010<0.05). Similarly, "customer complaint rates" (β= .246, p= .020<0.05) and "AI-based customer service interactions" (β= .435, p= .002<0.05) have positive and statistically significant effect on "productivity". The "number of AI-based services" has also a positive and statistically significant effect on "productivity" (β= .332, p= .002<0.05). The "total R&D spending on AI technologies" has a positive and statistically significant effect on "productivity" (β= .421, p= .024<0.05). And finally, "annual investment in AI projects" has a positive and statistically significant effect on "productivity" (β= .347, p= .005<0.05).

Figure 1. Productivity - Time Series Analysis

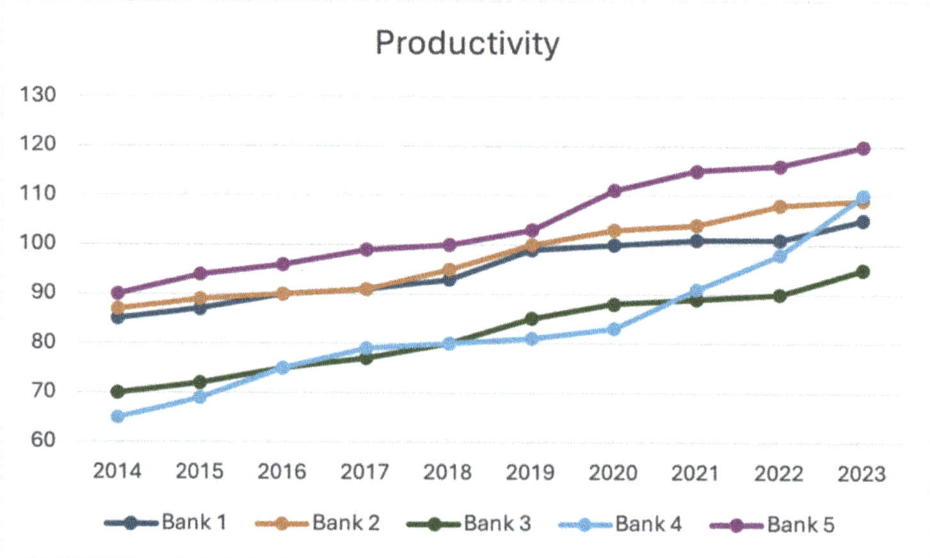

The values above reflect the productivity levels of banks between 2014 and 2023. According to the figure, all 5 banks show a steady upward productivity trend during this period. Notably, Bank 5 experienced a significant increase in 2019, while Bank 4 saw a substantial rise in 2020.

Figure 2. Workforce Size - Time Series Analysis

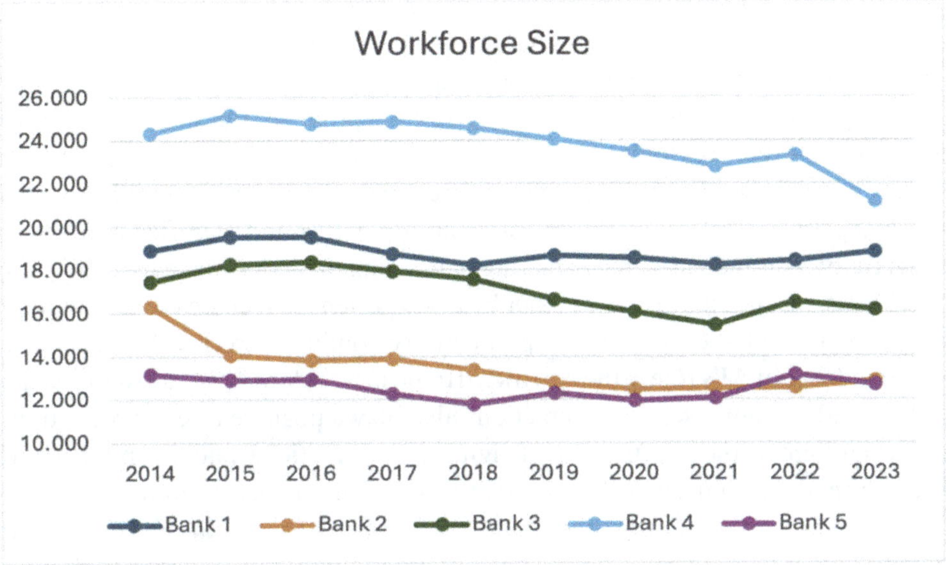

The figure above shows the values related to the workforce size of banks between 2014 and 2023. According to the figure, all banks except Bank 5 exhibit a declining trend in workforce size during this period. Notably, Bank 2, Bank 3, and Bank 4 show a significant decrease in workforce size. In contrast, the workforce size at Bank 5 appears to have remained stable.

4. CONCLUSION AND DISCUSSION

The purpose of this research has been determined as examining the impact of Artificial Intelligence Utilisation on Workforce Size and Productivity in the context of the banking sector in Turkey. In this study, five private banks operating in Turkey were selected using a purposive sampling method. In the research, workforce size was examined based on the changes in the number of employees in the selected banks between 2014 and 2023, and productivity was evaluated in terms of the productivity score achieved by the banks internally during the same period. First, the correlation between the six sub-factors constituting Artificial Intelligence Utilisation and both workforce size and productivity was examined. Subsequently, a regression analysis was conducted to investigate the impact of Artificial Intelligence Utilisation on workforce size and productivity using the same six sub-factors.

The results of correlation and regression analyses showed that AI utilisation has a significant impact on workforce size and productivity in the Turkish banking sector. According to the findings, the increase in AI-based products and services generally tends to reduce the workforce size, but greatly increases productivity. In particular, "variety of AI-based financial products" and "annual investment in AI projects" have a negative effect on workforce size but a positive and significant effect on productivity. This indicates that banks are optimising their workforce for efficiency.

With the exception of Bank 5, other banks experienced a decrease in workforce size between 2014 and 2023, while productivity continued to rise. This serves as strong evidence of AI's role in the downward trend in workforce size across the banks.

AI-based customer service interactions also play a positive role in productivity levels, highlighting the effectiveness of digital transformation strategies in enhancing efficiency and reducing costs. The positive correlation between customer complaint rates and productivity on the other hand showed an existence of unexpected and negative situation. Normally, an increase in productivity is associated with more efficient and effective processes, leading to improved customer satisfaction. However, there could be several potential explanations for a positive correlation in this context. The methods used to increase productivity (such as automation or cost-cutting measures) might negatively impact the customer experience. For example, increased use of automation in customer service (i.e. chatbots) may reduce personal interaction, causing customers to file more complaints.

As banks grow rapidly and increase their productivity, the surge in customer numbers or the growing demand for services might negatively affect service quality. This situation could lead to more complaints while also achieving high operational efficiency. Banks may become more efficient in their operations but fail to focus sufficiently on customer expectations. As a result, even though internal processes become more efficient, customers may not be satisfied with these changes, leading to an increase in complaints. Such a positive correlation indicates the risk of neglecting customer experience and satisfaction in the pursuit of productivity gains. These findings highlight the need for smoother conceptual transitions across sections, ensuring that the interplay between workforce reduction, productivity gains, and customer satisfaction is analysed as an integrated whole rather than as isolated observations. In this respect, it suggests that businesses must balance the optimisation of processes with the goal of improving customer satisfaction.

Moreover, R&D spending on AI technology show a negative impact on workforce size but a positive impact on productivity. This suggests that banks are able to achieve higher productivity with fewer employees, providing a critical insight into how automation and digitisation may reshape future workforce demands. For example, Bank 5 saw the highest positive impact of AI on productivity in 2019, while Bank 4 experienced a noticeable increase in productivity in 2020 despite a drop in workforce size. These findings suggest that digitalisation and AI adaptation not only save costs but also optimise productivity.

In conclusion, when examining the effects of AI on workforce size and productivity in the banking sector, it can be said that digitalisation and automation tend to reduce human labor while significantly improving productivity. This indicates that future labor demands will be shaped by the advantages AI offers.

When evaluated in the context of the literature review, the findings of this research reveal that AI-supported innovative advancements have indeed revised the business model of finance within Turkey's banking sector, as noted by Bratişanu (2017). Both customers and the traditional banking structure are benefiting from automation and social media connection technologies (Bratişanu, 2017). The results show that developments in AI have had a transformative effect on the banking sector, as AI advancements have significantly increased the cost-effectiveness of banks. In particular, investments in AI technologies, such as electronic and mobile payment systems, enhanced credit techniques, and online and mobile access channels, have led to additional cost savings (Yıldız, 2023).

The findings related to productivity improvements align with the propositions of Işkın (2010) and Yıldırım (2006), suggesting that AI has a positive impact on the efficiency of banking operations. In this sense, the banking sector is enhancing its operational efficiency and gaining a competitive advantage by offering more value to its customers (Karyağdı, 2022). These results also support Google's projection that the widespread use of generative AI in Turkey could add approximately 5% to Turkey's annual GDP within the next decade.

However, the findings also indicate that AI investments are leading to a reduction in workforce size, corroborating Bloomberg's (2024) analysis, which highlights "a striking truth that companies are concealing layoffs caused by artificial intelligence." In this regard, the results of this research align with the pessimistic view in the literature, which suggests that AI will replace workers, leading to increased unemployment (Huang et al., 2019).

From a broader perspective, these findings also underscore the potential of AI-driven transformations in the banking sector to contribute meaningfully to sustainability and the transition toward a circular economy. As banks increasingly digitise their operations and reduce their reliance on physical infrastructure, they inherently support dematerialisation and improved resource efficiency. Two core principles of circular economy models. By minimising paper-based processes, optimising energy use through digital workflows, and leveraging AI for leaner operations, financial institutions can lower their environmental footprint while maximising value creation. However, for this transition to be truly sustainable, it is essential that social dimensions particularly workforce impacts are addressed alongside environmental considerations. Thus, aligning AI implementation with circular economy principles requires not only operational efficiency but also strategic investments in human capital, ethical governance, and inclusive innovation. In particular, introducing targeted reskilling and workforce adaptation strategies would help mitigate the negative employment effects of AI utilisation, thereby enhancing both the social inclusiveness and the practical relevance of the findings. This integrative approach can ensure that AI technologies serve not only economic and technological goals but also the broader objectives of social equity and ecological responsibility.

Building on this, it is suggested that future research should focus on the demographic characteristics of those who are forced to leave their jobs as a result of AI utilisation. This is important because understanding the age, education level, gender, and professional background of displaced workers can provide deeper insights into the specific groups most affected by AI-driven automation. Such insights could help policymakers and organisations develop targeted strategies for reskilling and workforce reintegration, thereby mitigating the negative impacts of AI on employment.

REFERENCES

Acemoglu, D., & Restrepo, P. (2018). Artificial intelligence, automation and work. *Working Paper Series (National Bureau of Economic Research)*, •••, 24196.

Akbaba, A. İ., & Gündoğdu, Ç. (2021). Bankacılık hizmetlerinde yapay zekâ kullanımı. *Journal of Academic Value Studies*, *7*(3), 298–315.

Annisa, S., Siahaan, E., & Lumbanraja, P. (2024). Impact of digital transformation on banking employee performance with self-efficacy as a mediator. *Problems and Perspectives in Management*, *22*(4), 523–531. DOI: 10.21511/ppm.22(4).2024.39

Apendi, D. A. O., Li, K., Pea-Assounga, J. B. B., & Bambi, P. D. R. (2025). Investigating the Impact of E-Banking, Employee Job Security, Innovativeness, and Productivity on Organizational Performance: Perspectives from South Africa. *Sustainable Futures : An Applied Journal of Technology, Environment and Society*, •••, 100605.

Autor, D. (2015). Why are there still so many jobs? *The Journal of Economic Perspectives*, *29*(3), 3–30.

Bingöl, Ç. (2023). Yapay zeka destekli uygulamalı eğitim platformu-bankacılık simülasyonu. [PABD]. *Parion Akademik Bakış Dergisi*, *2*(1), 1–22.

Bloomberg, H. T. (2024). AI is driving more layoffs than companies want to admit, 8 February 2024, https://www.bloomberg.com/news/articles/2024-02-08/ai-is-driving-more-layoffs-than-companies-want-to-admit (Access date: 24 September 2024).

Bratişanu, V. (2017). Digital innovation the new paradigm for financial services industry, *Bucharest 'University of Economic Studies*, Speacial Issue, 84-93.

Bueno, L. A., Sigahi, T. F., Rampasso, I. S., Leal Filho, W., & Anholon, R. (2024). Impacts of digitization on operational efficiency in the banking sector: Thematic analysis and research agenda proposal. *International Journal of Information Management Data Insights*, *4*(1), 100230.

Ersoy, Ç. (2017). *Robotlar, Yapay Zeka ve Hukuk*, 2. Bs., İstanbul, On İki Levha Yayıncılık.

FasterCapital. (2023). *Online Banking: The Role of Dematerialization in Modern Finance*. Available at: https://www.fastercapital.com/content/Online-Banking--Online-Banking--The-Role-of-Dematerialization-in-Modern-Finance.html#:~:text=Dematerialization%20in%20finance%20refers%20to,physical%20resources%20and%20%2013

Frey, C. B., & Osborne, M. A. (2013). *The Future of Employment: How Susceptible are Jobs to Computerisation?* University Martin School.

Gacar, A. (2019). Yapay zekâ ve yapay zekânın muhasebe mesleğine olan etkileri: Türkiye'ye yönelik fırsat ve tehditler. *Balkan Sosyal Bilimler Dergisi*, *8*, 389–394.

Gartner. (2020). *Top trends in banking and investment services for 2020*. https://www.gartner.com/en/documents/3984417

Gotthardt, M., Koivulaakso, D., Paksoy, O., Saramo, C., Martikainen, M., & Lehner, O. (2020). Current state and challenges in the implementation of smart robotic process automation in accounting and auditing. *ACRN Journal of Finance and Risk Perspectives*, *9*(1), 90–102.

Gültekin, A. (2021). *Spinoza Ontolojisi Bağlamında Yapay Zekânın İmkânı*. Doktora Tezi, İnönü Üniversitesi Sosyal Bilimler Enstitüsü.

Gümüş, E., Medetoğlu, B., & Tutar, S. (2020). Finans ve bankacılık sisteminde yapay zekâ kullanımı: Kullanıcılar üzerine bir uygulama. *Bucak İşletme Fakültesi Dergisi*, *3*(1), 28–53.

Hegde, A. G. (2019). Artificial intelligence and law. *Pen Acclaims*, *7*, 1–10.

Huang, M. H., Rust, R., & Maksimovic, V. (2019). The feeling economy: Managing in the next generation of artificial ıntelligence (AI). *California Management Review*, *61*(4), 43–65.

Işkın, S. (2010). *Türk Bankacılık Sisteminde Alternatif Dağıtım Kanalları (Elektronik Bankacılık)*. Hizmetlerinin Riskleri ve Denetimi. Marmara Üniversitesi Bankacılık ve Sigortacılık Enstitüsü.

Issa, H., Sun, T., & Vasarhelyi, M. A. (2016). Research ideas for artificial intelligence in auditing: The formalization of audit and workforce supplementation. *Journal of Emerging Technologies in Accounting*, *13*(2), 1–20.

Jaksic, M., & Marinc, M. (2015). The future of banking: The role of information technology. *Bancni vestnik: Bankıng Sector At The Crossroads: Challenges For. Future*, *64*(11), 68–73.

Karyağdı, N. G. (2022). Bankacılık sektöründe dijital dönüşümün verimliliğe olan etkileri: TRB2 bölgesinde nitel bir çalışma. *Kahramanmaraş Sütçü İmam Üniversitesi Sosyal Bilimler Dergisi*, *19*(2), 852–870.

Munoko, I., Brown Liburd, H. L., & Vasarhely, M. (2020). The ethical implications of using artifcial iin auditing. *Journal of Business Ethics*, *167*, 209–234.

Mutascu, M. (2021). Artificial intelligence and unemployment: New insights. *Economic Analysis and Policy, 64*, 653–667.

Negnevitsky, M. (2005). *Artificial Intelligence: A Guide to Intelligent Systems*, 2. Ed., England: Pearson Education Limited.

OECD. (2023). *Digitalisation for the transition to a resource efficient and circular economy*. OECD Publishing. Available at: https://www.oecd.org/en/publications/digitalisation-for-the-transition-to-a-resource-efficient-and-circular-economy_6f6d18e7-en.html#:~:text=Digital%20transformation%20is%20increasingly%20recognised,way%20to%20scaling%20up%20circular

Özçetin, N. (2022). Muhasebe denetiminde yapay zekâ. *Uşak Üniversitesi Uygulamalı Bilimler Fakültesi Dergisi*, *2*(1), 29–41.

Petropoulos, G. (2018). The Impact Of Artificial Intelligence On Employment, Neufeind M., O'Reilly J. and Ranft F. (Eds.), *Praise for Work in the Digital Age*, Rowman & Littlefield International, 119-132.

Pirim, H. (2006). Yapay zeka. *Journal of Yasar University*, *1*(1), 81–93.

PwC. (2024). PwC's 2024 AI Jobs Barometer: How will AI affect jobs, skills, wages, and productivity? https://www.pwc.com.tr/tr/Hizmetlerimiz/dijital-hizmetler/ai-jobs-barometer.pdf (Access date: 20 September 2024).

Saam, M. (2024). The Impact of Artificial Intelligence on Productivity and Employment–How Can We Assess It and What Can We Observe? *Inter Economics*, *59*(1), 22–27.

Serçemeli, M. (2018). Muhasebe ve denetim mesleklerinin dijital dönüşümünde yapay zekâ. *Electronic Turkish Studies*, *13*(30), 369–386.

Shabir, M., Jiang, P., Wang, W., & Işık, Ö. (2023). COVID-19 pandemic impact on banking sector: A cross-country analysis. *Journal of Multinational Financial Management*, *67*, 100784.

Shen, Y., & Zhang, X. (2024). The impact of artificial intelligence on employment: The role of virtual agglomeration. *Humanities & Social Sciences Communications*, *11*(1).

Smith, S. S. (2018). Digitization and financial reporting – How technology innovation may drive the shift toward continuous accounting. *Accounting and Finance Research*, *7*(3), 240–250.

Szeiner, Z., & Balázs, K. (2023). The impact of digitalization on working and job roles in the banking sector. *Acta Oeconomica Universitatis Selye*, *12*(1), 68–78. DOI: 10.36007/Acta.2023.12.1.6

Thelle, M. H., Lundberg, A. T., Hovmand, B. E., Woltmann, H. H., Virtanen, L., Tranholm-Mikkelsen, N., Pedersen, S. T., & Oure, A. J. (2024). The economic opportunity of AI in Türkiye. Implement Consulting Group Study, May 2024, https://cms.implementconsultinggroup.com/media/uploads/articles/2024/The-economic-opportunity-of-generative-AI-in-T%C3%BCrkiye/The-economic-opportunity-of-generative-AI-in-Turkiye.pdf (Access date: 21 September 2024).

Votintseva, L., Andreeva, M., Kovalenin, I., & Votintsev, R. (2019). Digital Transformation Of Russian Banking Institutions: Assessments And Prospects. *IOP Conference Series. Materials Science and Engineering*, *497*(1).

Yıldırım, H. U. (2019). *Bankacılık Sektöründe Yazılım Projelerinin Değerlendirilmesi ve Uygulamaya Yönelik Birer Örnek*. İstanbul Üniversitesi Sosyal Bilimler Enstitüsü İşletme Anabilim Dalı Muhasebe Bilim Dalı.

Yıldız, M. (2023). *Yapay Zekâ ve Yeni Sayı Sistemlerinin Muhasebe ve Finans Alanında Uygulaması*. İksad Yayınevi.

Chapter 2

A Policy Framework for Enabling Circular Entrepreneurship in Emerging Economies: The Case of Lebanon

Sarah Chahine
https://orcid.org/0000-0001-5109-130X
Lebanese International University, Lebanon

Mabelle Al Haddad
https://orcid.org/0009-0001-3741-5010
Lebanese International University, Lebanon

Ola Talal Masry
https://orcid.org/0009-0006-8924-298X
Lebanese International University, Lebanon

ABSTRACT

This chapter examines support mechanisms and policies for advancing circular entrepreneurship in Lebanon taking into account the country's economic, environmental, and infrastructural challenges hindering its development. Reflecting on comparative policy frameworks applied in countries such as Finland, the Netherlands, Scotland, and South Africa, key lessons are identified enabling a suggestion of a tailored roadmap relevant to the Lebanese context. The roadmap constitutes three phases along with a defined time frame for developing the essentials like policies, institutional coordination, and operational capacity, while highlighting the role of entrepreneurship, civil society, academia, and international actors in supporting

DOI: 10.4018/979-8-3373-7655-4.ch002

the transition. The chapter also formulates performance metrics and monitoring frameworks while establishing mechanisms for accountability. It concludes by arguing that circular entrepreneurship is still showing high resilience and hope for economic regeneration despite all the constraints and limitations.

SECTION 1: INTRODUCTION

The economic development model of circular entrepreneurship presents an alternative structure that moves away from resource-intensive systems to focus on sustainable regeneration. The circular entrepreneurship model diverges from traditional extraction-use-disposal methods by promoting business strategies that maintain material value while protecting ecosystems and supporting permanent economic and environmental stability (Geissdoerfer *et al.*, 2017). The strategic implementation of circular entrepreneurship serves as a development tool for low- and middle-income countries to achieve inclusive regenerative development while creating employment opportunities in areas with environmental degradation and economic instability (Ababio et al., 2024).

There is significant untapped potential in promoting circular economy practices in several resource-constrained countries with limited infrastructure for applying this economic model. In Finland, circular economy practices have increased economic development, national cohesion, sustainability, and the feeling of collective ownership for development (Hinsa et al., 2025). In the Netherlands, such practices improved material efficiency, promoted societal participation and cross-sector collaboration and spatial inclusivity (Block, 2019). In Scotland, sustainable practices led to synergy among public and private sectors and increased economic and environmental resilience (Haris et al., 2024).

The economic situation of Lebanon makes it an ideal location to study circular entrepreneurship possibilities. Lebanon currently faces a multi-faceted crisis that combines economic breakdown, political stagnation, regular power outages, and unresolved waste management issues (World Bank, 2021b; UNDP, 2022). For instance, *the country grapples with a vulnerable banking system, a depreciated national currency, regulatory limitations, joblessness and brain drain, as well as electricity and water scarcities.* Despite these numerous obstacles, it still possesses an energetic entrepreneurial culture and well-educated young people, together with an extensive network of expatriates. These resources possess potential value, which can be maximized through strategic efforts to develop localized circular innovation. Some initiatives highlight the tendency towards green and circular entrepreneurship within the constrained ecosystem, lubricating the transition to circular entrepreneurship (Rosenbaum and Kehdy, 2022). In fact, the actual situation makes circular entrepreneurship transform from a sustainability aspiration into a necessary socio-economic requirement.

Lebanon is experiencing an obvious absence of regulations accompanied by notable deficiencies in institutional support mechanisms and policy gaps, all hindering the existence and potential development of novel business models targeting economic development with efficiency in resource consumption (Chaarani and Raimi, 2021). This highlights the need to create a clear and detailed national plan that includes circular economy principles in Lebanon, while focusing on important areas like entrepreneurship, innovation, resource efficiency, and waste reduction to achieve a circular economy and support circular entrepreneurship.

This chapter investigates the expanding field of circular economy policy by studying both the opportunities and constraints that exist in Lebanon and similar weak national systems. Most present discussions about circular economy derive from high-income countries that possess strong institutions and stable infrastructure systems to support circular initiatives (Ruiz-Real et al., 2018; Wiedenhofer et al., 2024; Muñoz and Navia, 2021). This chapter investigates the process of designing circular policies in areas characterized by weak state capabilities and sensitivity to outside disturbances (OECD, 2020a). The chapter devotes special attention to two essential pillars that ensure successful implementation: effective stakeholder alignment and the development of monitoring and evaluation frameworks that consider local needs. The circular economy strategies lack sufficient development in many cases, especially when emerging economies face institutional barriers alongside insufficient data infrastructure that hinders meaningful advancement.

The chapter links conceptual theories to pragmatic policy knowledge by presenting the current economic, environmental, and entrepreneurial scene in Lebanon in the upcoming section, introducing the concepts of circular economy and circular entrepreneurship in the third section, and showcasing several successful cases where circular economy policies are implemented, namely Finland, the Netherlands, Scotland, and South Africa. After that, an evaluation of stakeholder roles and responsibilities is presented, highlighting the need for collective work focusing on governmental bodies, local authorities and municipalities, entrepreneurs, academia, research institutions, civil society organizations and NGOs, donors, the private sector, *etc.* The section afterwards introduces needed metrics that guarantee the successful implementation of a circular economy in the country. The chapter exemplifies complete entrepreneurship transformation through its ability to institutionalize change and societal progress while promoting environmental protection.

SECTION 2: SITUATING LEBANON: ECONOMIC, ENVIRONMENTAL, AND ENTREPRENEURIAL REALITIES

1. Overview of Lebanon's Socioeconomic Challenges

Economic crisis and currency collapse

The Lebanese banking system has encountered substantial challenges since 2019 due to poor financial governance and the devaluation of the national currency, which endured a drastic 81% value loss. Particularly, capital controls, a default on euro bonds, and a radical decrease in customer trust have caused an escalation in informal financial activities. Baz (2025) highlights that such activities are fueled by remittance-driven informal banking—since citizens are becoming more dependent on informal means for transferring money—currency pegs, and sovereign debt exposure. Additionally, practices related to financial engineering have escalated the crisis, resulting in withdrawal limits and failure to meet Central Bank liabilities (Rizkallah, 2022). Many Lebanese investors were directed toward cryptocurrencies as a substitute for the Lebanese pound, demonstrating skepticism toward traditional banking systems (El-Chaarani, 2023).

The surge in regulatory restrictions, informal remittances, economic instability, corruption, and tax evasion, as well as the rise in unprecedented events like the Beirut port explosion and the COVID-19 pandemic (Islam, 2021), has caused higher reliance on informal labor markets, specifically by refugees and other marginalized communities (Ltaif, 2024). Since Lebanon lacks the proper infrastructure (e.g., fast internet connections, power, *etc.*), several attempts to promote digital livelihoods failed. According to Shibli (2023), several initiatives were presented to overcome the crisis through sustainable online work in an attempt to provide refugees and minorities with digital skills to bypass local and economic barriers, ultimately reaching a dead end, forcing individuals to revert into informal sectors. Consequently, people embraced entrepreneurship to mitigate hardships by establishing their businesses as an attempt to endure the crisis. Entrepreneurial activity has then played a pivotal role in strengthening economic stability (Boustani, 2023).

2. Unemployment and brain drain

The aforementioned factors, along with the shortage of decent employment opportunities, pushed the youth to seek regional and international job opportunities, further aggravating Lebanon's brain drain (Omar, 2025). The skilled workforce is drastically decreasing in the country as doctors and other healthcare workers are fleeing, diminishing the effectiveness of essential services (Islam, 2021). Structural barriers include the disparity between employment and academia, insufficient information about the labor market, economic stagnation, and sectarian patronage networks (Majed, 2018; Cieslik *et al.*, 2022; Palalić *et al.*, 2021).

3. Public service breakdown:

Lebanon also suffers from shortages in electricity and water, where the electricity sector has experienced a systematic breakdown and the water supply has been significantly reduced. The country vastly relies on private generators or solar energy, which recently emerged as a viable economic option (Fayssal *et al.*, 2024), as well as on tankers and other polluted sources as the main water supply (Islam, 2021).

Environmental Pressures and the Failure of the Linear Economy

In 2015, garbage protests surged across Lebanon, underscoring the failed waste management in the country. Several reports by UNDP and Human Rights Watch stress the pressing need for decentralized waste management systems to substitute the insignificant centralized recycling infrastructure (Abbas *et al.*, 2017), which is hindered by several technical and financial challenges (Ahad *et al.*, 2020). On the other hand, poorly managed landfill management extends the contamination of groundwater and increases air pollution (Ozbay and Koc, 2022). Additionally, Lebanese rivers and coasts are also polluted as a result of the discharge of untreated sewage and industrial waste disposal. Immediate sustainable practices are recommended as solutions (Bozorg-Haddad *et al.*, 2020).

Entrepreneurial Landscape in Lebanon

Resilience has surged in the Lebanese entrepreneurial ecosystem despite decreasing international investments. Local entrepreneurial ventures remain successful and thriving, specifically in agriculture and tech (Bouzakhem *et al.*, 2023). Agriculture, according to the World Bank (2021a), is an essential sector in Lebanon's entrepreneurial ecosystem, and differentiated support should be directed to the agriculture sector to embed our practices within a circular economy (World Bank, 2021a). Nonetheless, the limited formal support mechanisms obstruct structured entrepreneurial efforts (Chaarani and Raimi, 2022). For instance, financial support, whether from banks, VCs, or angel investors, is limited and sometimes reflects nepotism, as it is offered to select members (Chahine, 2018), which hinders innovation. Startup infrastructure pertaining to legal and regulatory infrastructure, support structures, mentorship, human capital, *etc.*, is lacking, weakening the formal startup ecosystem (Hamzah, 2025).

Furthermore, despite Lebanon being one of the MENA countries with comparatively high-level Total early-stage entrepreneurial Activity (TEA) of 24.8 (GEM, 2018), entrepreneurship is vastly necessity-based considering low employment opportunities, the deteriorating socio-economic situation (Boustani, 2023), and the decline in foreign investments (Bouzakhem *et al.*, 2023). Female necessity entrepreneurship is also escalating considering the limited availability of resources as well as the enhanced culture of empowering women (Mouzaen and Hernández-Lara, 2023). Necessity entrepreneurship prevails in sectors like retail and consumer service, taking advantage of low barriers to entry (Boustani, 2023). Although several negative consequences of necessity-based entrepreneurship are recorded, specifically limited innovation, low development potential (Ivanović-Đukić *et al.*, 2022), negative impact on sustainable development (Huđek and Hojnik, 2020), creation of vulnerable entrepreneurs, *etc.*, this type of entrepreneurship has at least helped in decreasing unemployment rates in the country (Annan and Haidoura, 2023).

Financial Mechanisms for Entrepreneurship in Lebanon

Entrepreneurship in Lebanon is impeded by financial challenges generated by the ongoing economic and socio-political crises in the country. Yet the emergence of innovative financial mechanisms such as blended finance and diaspora funding represents potential opportunities to support circular entrepreneurship that emphasizes sustainability and resource efficiency.

Blended finance is a financially innovative tool that addresses the financing gap in Lebanon's entrepreneurial ecosystem. The essence of blended finance is its ability to combine public and private funding to mitigate investment risks and mobilize other private actors' capital for high-impact projects that utilize public resources in some way, including high-impact projects that align with circular economy principles. It often involves public-private partnerships that enhance capacity building, technology transfers, and infrastructure to incentivize circular entrepreneurship. In addition, blended finance may involve risk mitigation tools to attract private capital, such as insurance products and guarantees, to mobilize the private sector. Identifying subsidies specifically targeted to circular business models may also encourage businesses to engage in sustainable circular practices (Cuesta-González and Morales-García, 2023).

Diaspora funding is another important source of funding. Lebanon has a large diaspora that is economically active in the country, and those have contributed to the economy through remittances as well as investments in different sectors. Diaspora bonds can be issued to Lebanese expats to mobilize funding specifically for circular economy projects. Diaspora crowdfunding platforms can actively connect diaspora investors with local entrepreneurs and contribute to the global economy. Diaspora-oriented networking events can also identify potential opportunities to support circular entrepreneurship in Lebanon and mobilize resources (Stel, 2013).

A number of tangible measures will need to be undertaken to institute these financial mechanisms. Entrepreneurs will need capacity building in relation to their ability to engage with and manage funds, particularly if it is their first time engaging in blended finance or diaspora funding. Policy reform is another significant consideration to create a supportive environment for blended finance and diaspora investment as part of a sustainable financing model. NGO collaborations can be important because they provide technical assistance and mentoring so that entrepreneurs have the capacity and support to build a successful business model for their circular businesses (Chaarani, 2021).

Integrating both blended finance and diaspora funding in Lebanon's entrepreneurial ecosystem will address the systemic obstacles and create the support networks to develop a vibrant circular entrepreneurial ecosystem. Both funding mechanisms will address urgent funding challenges as well as lay the foundations for sustainable economic development.

Positioning for Circular Economy Transition

Although circular economy efforts have gained global recognition and support, they have seen minimal progress in Lebanon. Institutional support for circular economy efforts remains limited, which constrains entrepreneurs due to a lack of resources needed to foster innovation (Rosenbaum, 2022). Additional barriers to circular startups exist, such as shortages in local knowledge and mentorship and dependence on donor aid, further challenging business model development and the potential for scaling and sustaining such startups (Lit *et al.*, 2024; Elmustapha and Hoppe, 2020). Conversely, customer mistrust and negative perceptions can impede the success of circular economy initiatives. Studies show that although young Lebanese consumers would prefer sustainable purchasing, the "consumer acceptance" of circular products and services in Lebanon remains limited; this discrepancy is largely attributed to a combination of socio-psychological, cultural, and informational barriers reflected in purchasing choices. While many individuals claim environmental concern, only a small proportion actively seek sustainable products or engage with circular options (Nasreddine et al., 2014).

There is considerable unrealized potential in fostering community-based entrepreneurship and decentralized economic models in Lebanon. In 2015, entrepreneurs adopted innovative approaches to dealing with the garbage crisis (Dapp, 2018). Furthermore, decentralized virtual power plants encourage households to support green local power solutions, enabling individuals to distribute excess energy to neighbors, in turn offering monetary incentives for adopting renewable energy (Ncube *et al.*, 2023). Beyond addressing the systemic collapse of the electricity sector, this approach is also facilitating a shift among entrepreneurs toward circular economy models.

In several instances, NGOs have played a pivotal role in bridging the support gaps circular startups are facing. They facilitate the success of social enterprises by fulfilling some of their psychological and environmental needs through training, access to resources, *etc.* (Chaarani and Raimi, 2021).

These programs continue to face challenges in being integrated into national policies and regulatory frameworks, which significantly limits their impact on the broader entrepreneurial ecosystem. Additionally, such initiatives fail to address key factors like education, team composition, and leadership, which suggests that more integrated, comprehensive, and formal approaches are needed to effectively support social entrepreneurs in the circular economy, addressing their diverse and evolving needs.

SECTION 3: UNDERSTANDING CIRCULAR ENTREPRENEURSHIP

Defining the Circular Economy

The linear economic model is inherently extractive, relying on a one-way flow of resources—a "take-make-dispose" model, which exacerbates resource depletion and environmental harm. In contrast, circular economies advocate for a regenerative approach that emphasizes resource efficiency, waste minimization, and environmental sustainability. Moreover, linear economy practices contribute to increased waste by placing excessive emphasis on disposables rather than prioritizing designs that support recyclability and repairability, as well as increased energy consumption.

The circular economy revolves around five main core principles that promote sustainable practices by employing efficient resources, reducing waste, and restoring natural systems. The first principle, designing out waste, is aimed at minimizing environmental impact across production and consumption phases by employing strategies (Velenturf and Purnell, 2021) such as dematerialization and the utilization of renewable bioproducts like bacterial cellulose to replace conventional synthetic inputs. Keeping materials in use is another core principle focusing on prolonging product life cycles through circular strategies such as reuse and material recovery (Ramakrishna and Jose, 2022). For instance, solar panel remanufacturing, e-waste management, *etc.*

Additionally, the circular economy is also focused on regenerating natural systems through reviving natural ecosystems while minimizing environmental impacts, such as in sustainable architectural approaches (Mangaroska, 2024). Providing economic benefits is another core principle inspiring innovative practices, the establishment of new business models, and employability (Aiguobarueghian *et al.*, 2024). Lastly, global supply chain integration links circular practices to the supply chain to further adopt efficient use of resources and decrease waste.

The numerous socioeconomic constraints in Lebanon pose challenges to the applicability of these principles. As the waste management system in the country is inadequate, the effective implementation of designing out waste strategies is hampered. Limited public awareness, suitable regulatory frameworks, and the absence of incentives for businesses also obstruct the employment of keeping materials in use. Furthermore, countries such as Lebanon tend to prioritize pressing economic and societal issues over environmental regeneration and rehabilitation efforts. Achieving economic benefits is also contingent upon substantial infrastructure and technological investment, which currently constitutes a major barrier. On the other hand, overreliance on imports and poorly integrated supply chains also adds complexity to integrating global supply chains.

Circular Entrepreneurship

Circular entrepreneurship encompasses establishing ventures that align with the principles of circular economy, prioritizing public policy frameworks and green supply chain management (Vecchio *et al.*, 2021), as well as decreasing inputs and waste outputs while promoting both sustainable outcomes and financial gains (Cullen and De Angelis, 2020). Circular venture approaches create economic, societal, and environmental value (Mohapatra *et al.*, 2024), embracing open innovation and cross-sector collaboration (Dantas *et al.*, 2022). Circular entrepreneurship is rooted in moving away from the "take-make-dispose" model to align with reformative models focusing on resource efficiency and longevity.

The overarching characteristics of circular entrepreneurship directly align with those of circular economies. The focus here is on closed-loop systems of production that encourage waste minimization and circular use of materials, developing eco-friendly alternatives to scarce natural resources. Additionally, circular entrepreneurship embraces a philosophy that prioritizes environmental impact before the production, use of raw materials, and disposal of products—aligning closely with the core goals of the circular economy (Solomon *et al.*, 2024).

Circular entrepreneurship offers unique business models like product-as-a-service, which allows businesses to provide customers with access to certain products instead of buying them (Lüdeke-Freund *et al.*, 2019); the sharing economy model, which necessitates the pooling of resources (Netter *et al.*, 2019); the repair and use model, which focuses on prolonging the life of products through upcycling, refurbishment, and other distinctive approaches (Lüdeke-Freund *et al.*, 2019); and industrial symbiosis, which employs waste from one industry as inputs in another (Nyakudya *et al.*, 2022).

That said, critics of circular entrepreneurship argue that it often fails to integrate principles of social justice, which diminishes its broader impact (Kirchherr *et al.*, 2017). Moreover, the full potential of circular entrepreneurship remains unattainable without fundamental reforms in governance, corporate practices, and consumer behavior, along with considerable investment and innovation. On the other hand, Lebanon offers a distinctive setting for circular entrepreneurship as a consequence of its numerous socio-economic and environmental hurdles, which ignited interest in circular economy principles through the adoption of circular and social entrepreneurship. The adoption of circular entrepreneurship in Lebanon is still in its infancy stages and requires greater attention from policymakers and supporting actors in the Lebanese entrepreneurial ecosystem, yet it holds great potential for sustainable development and environmental and economic improvements.

Lebanon's limited circular economy infrastructure and institutional support make it vital to analyze successful circular transitions. The upcoming section pinpoints several case studies, specifically in the Netherlands, Finland, Scotland, and South Africa, that will be later used as a benchmark for proposing a structured approach to implementing circular economy frameworks in Lebanon.

The Role of Digital Infrastructure in Circular Entrepreneurship

Digital infrastructure is a significant facilitator for circular entrepreneurship, especially in a country like Lebanon that deals with established socio-economic challenges. Digital tools (i.e., IoT, AI, blockchain, etc.) promote resource optimization, enhance data management, and ensure transparency, all of which are critical aspects of implementing circular economy practices. Digital tools generally simplify transitions of businesses toward circular business models through efficient processes that offer the opportunity for innovative solutions (Edeh, 2025).

In Lebanon, realities such as these can make such arrangements difficult and dissuade favorable transitions to circular economy principles due to aspects like limited ICT infrastructure and continued socio-economic political instability. However, Lebanon, as an example, has a long-standing educational system and strong entrepreneurial culture that can be developed to begin using digital tools to overcome these barriers. For example, digital platforms can be used to facilitate industrial symbiosis and resource-sharing networks, which are important constructs for circular entrepreneurship (Yunis, 2017).

A systematic study in South Asia and the Middle East emphasizes examples of how digitalization and infrastructure can be enablers of circular economy practices. For example, digital manufacturing and analytics have created regenerative economic models to illustrate how technology can transform how we evaluate sustainability (Patwa, 2025). If anything, this example serves to demonstrate the importance of integrating digital infrastructure to overcome systemic challenges for circular entrepreneurship in economic regions with similar socioeconomic challenges to Lebanon.

SECTION 4: INTERNATIONAL POLICY BENCHMARKS: WHAT CAN LEBANON LEARN?

It is now evident that the circular economy assures national advancement in several pillars: economic, environmental, and societal, underscoring the need for frameworks with clear, well-structured roadmaps to ensure a smooth and effective adaptation, implementation, and execution. Lebanon, being a country classified among the developing nations, is still far from any progress in this direction. To properly position the country on the right track, it is essential to highlight the experiences of other countries classified as pioneers in circular economy integration, which serve as the foundation of the roadmap proposed for Lebanon.

Finland's National Circular Economy Roadmap

The first country to publish a national circular economy roadmap was Finland; it was reported that applying it will contribute up to €3 billion to the economy by 2030 (Hinsa et al., 2025; Finnish Innovation Fund Sitra, 2019). The Finnish government has developed a structured Circular Economy (CE) roadmap consisting of eight sequential phases to ensure effective implementation (Hosseinian et al., 2021). The Groundwork and Preconditions phase seeks the implementation of a shared societal consciousness by engaging a wide range of government ministries and stakeholders, municipalities, NGOs, scientists, businesses, individuals, and politicians (Marjamaa et al., 2021). Such inclusivity ensures collective ownership and catalyzes lasting systemic transformation. In the second phase, Stakeholders and Participation, stakeholders are recognized as subject-matter experts tasked with identifying essentials to transition; to ensure effective coordination of the process, steering groups are formed, including representatives from private, public, and civil sectors (Pitkänen et al., 2020). Then, the situational picture should be identified with a comprehensive assessment of the current situation of the nation through two main methods: data analysis and stakeholder interviews (Hosseinian et al., 2021).

Building on the previous findings, the fourth phase is named Vision and Goals, where preliminary strategic objectives are formulated and the vision is refined to reflect collective goals with measurable indicators (Marjamaa et al., 2021). In the fifth phase, thematic priorities are recognized, forming what are called focus areas, supported by specific goals and indicators to enable continuous evaluation. The sixth phase, Planning the Actions, focuses on co-creating actions with stakeholders, evaluating their feasibility, addressing gaps, assigning responsibilities, and compiling them into a coherent, goal-aligned plan (Hinsa et al., 2025). At the seventh phase, Comply and Publish, a draft of the roadmap is created and then finalized after requesting stakeholders' feedback and ensuring its clarity and accessibility (Pitkänen et al., 2020). Last step, execution and implementation: a management model is established with clearly identified roles and timelines while securing funding (Hosseinian et al., 2021). Active collaboration, nonstop monitoring, and continuous coordination with public authorities are essential for the success of this roadmap (Järvinen and Sinervo, 2020).

Sitra's roadmap is a clear demonstration of Finland's serious commitment to circular economy transformation. The steps of stakeholder engagement, situational analysis, action planning, and execution ensure an inclusive and easily applicable framework. What makes it especially noteworthy is its ability to anticipate and address potential challenges through detailed planning and coordination. This roadmap is not only a strategic vision but also a highly applicable model, showing that Finland is not just aspiring to shift toward a circular economy but is doing so in a deliberate, structured, and replicable way.

As to the Lebanese case, despite the well-known, deeply identified, and discussed obstacles, one of the valuable examples to consider and reflect on in the future is Sitra's approach, a detail-oriented strategy that facilitates the identification of expected challenges; its particular importance is in enabling governments to take proactive steps to resolve anticipated issues.

The Netherlands Circular Economy Strategy

The Netherlands was globally recognized as an important pioneer in circular economy innovation due to its commitment to a full transition to a circular economy by 2050 (Block, 2019), with a semi-goal of reducing the consumption of primary raw materials by 50% by 2030. This goal has two purposes: it cuts material use and serves the broader transition toward a fully circular economy by 2050 (McCarville, 2019). A well-structured, phased strategy was established, highlighting the Netherlands' deliberate efforts to achieve its long-term circular economy objectives. As an action plan, a strategic roadmap was developed with three core dimensions (3Ps): people, policies, and places that work collaboratively to shape this transformation (Romano and Akhmouch, 2019).

People play an important role in the transition to a circular economy. Active participation of all sectors of society, including citizens, businesses, and public institutions, is needed (Tr n et al., 2022). Businesses are expected to adapt and promote circular business models, such as rental, repair, and reuse (Buren, 2016), while citizens are expected to be highly aware of their consumption choices, which will significantly influence demand patterns and contribute to systemic change (Bentkowska, 2024).

Policies are an essential component of the Netherlands' approach; the government displays a clear recognition of the significance of collaborative dynamics between several sectors in the attainment of a circular economy (Friant et al., 2021). This explains the establishment of cross-sectoral frameworks among several sectors, such as agriculture, industry, and waste management. This approach highlights the strategic vision of the Netherlands government with guiding principles targeting the implementation of circularity in the entire economy rather than being solely embedded in one of the sectors (Savini, 2019).

The last dimension to be considered, according to the Netherlands' government, was Places. The importance of this aspect to the transition was demonstrated in the adaptation of a space-efficient strategy that exceeded traditional geographical boundaries; the circular economy initiatives were applied across regions, promoting local production, resource efficiency, and innovation while nurturing cross-regional connections that flawlessly included all areas, even urban and rural ones (Akimova and Kovalenko, 2021). In this vision, boundaries are considered opportunities for deeper collaboration, integration, and shared value creation rather than constraints (OECD, 2020b). What makes the Netherlands the frontrunner is its true dedication to implementing the circular economy, demonstrated in issuing a report every two years as a proactive approach to identifying gaps and challenges in the transition and evaluating the progress (Hanemaaijer *et al.*, 2025).

The Netherlands case reveals its government's commitment to implementing the circular economy. Nevertheless, adapting the circular economy and developing circular enterprise principles do not depend only on the political will (Halog and Anieke, 2021). Availability of the needed resources and favorable national circumstances are a must. This is what explains why these transitions tend to be easier in developed countries, having both institutional capacities and infrastructure, while in developing countries like Lebanon, governments prioritize issues related to meeting the basic life needs like water and electricity, making the adoption of strategies like the circular economy a lower priority (Hilmi et al., 2024).

Both the Netherlands and Finland have demonstrated a true commitment to adapting and implementing the circular economy. However, the roadmap developed by Sitra was more detailed and systematically oriented, which reflected a more structured approach, at least at the implementation stage. This strategic planning enhanced Finland's ranking among countries seeking a circular economy transition.

Scotland's Transition to a Circular Economy: applying a legislative framework and the Role of Zero Waste Scotland.

The Circular Economy (Scotland) Act 2024, which came into effect on June 26, 2024, announced Scotland's shift toward a circular economy (Haris et al., 2024). This act entrusts ministers with responsibilities and authorities, such as empowering them to enforce limitations on the disposal of unsold consumer goods while expecting them to design a comprehensive national circular economy strategy that sets specific goals to be achieved, such as decreasing the emission of CO_2, recycling, and improving waste management (Hegde et al., 2024).

A not-for-profit group called Zero Waste Scotland works with the Scottish Government, communities, and businesses to promote the circular economy, helping to change from a traditional economic model to one that focuses on using resources wisely, keeping materials in use for as long as possible, and choosing to "repair, reuse, and recycle" instead of the old "make, use, dispose" method. Also among its responsibilities is to support small and medium-sized enterprises (SMEs) that have resource constraints limiting their capacity to adopt circular practices by fully funding training programs, enabling them to build internal capabilities, and encouraging them to align their operations with circular economy principles (Rizos *et al*., 2016). This will, in the long term, foster environmental sustainability, extend product life cycles, and promote economic resilience by reducing waste and promoting more efficient use of resources (Dada et al., 2024).

Both Scotland's Circular Economy (Scotland Act 2024) and Zero Waste Scotland played a vital role in classifying Scotland as a leader in advancing the circular economy, complementary to each other. While the first set the guidelines for implementing a circular economy, the importance of the latter is highlighted in transforming those guidelines and policies into action by providing SMEs with all they need, including funding, guidance, and training. However, there are still challenges to overcome. Scotland lacks a clear vision to evaluate its progress toward a circular economy. Transparent, data-driven monitoring systems should be established to ensure sustainability and accountability.

South Africa's Circular Economy Challenge: Addressing Policy Gaps

Implementing the circular economy is framed by two general guidelines: reducing waste generation and minimizing the consumption of raw materials and energy (Kadhila et al., 2023). The process of implementation varies according to the circumstances of each country, and it often faces greater challenges in developing nations (Tahulela and Ballard, 2019).

South Africa was among the targeted countries of JUST2CE, an initiative by the European Union's Horizon that has evaluated the prerequisites for establishing a circular economy in a critical trial to assess the frameworks needed for a responsible and inclusive transition to a circular economy (Käsner and Gihring, 2024). Although several policy frameworks and strategic initiatives, such as the Science, Technology, and Innovation (STI) framework, the National Waste Management Strategy (NWMS), the extended Producer Responsibility (EPR) regulations, and the Sustainable Development Goals (SDGs), have been introduced to support the transition to a circular economy, the obvious problem is the absence of a flawless regulatory framework that governs implementing the circular economy; and while these instruments support the transition indirectly, they are still not enough (Ceroni, 2024; Daramola et al., 2024).

Moreover, the transition to a circular economy in South Africa is hindered by multiple socio-economic and structural challenges. The high levels of unemployment, inequality, and educational deficiencies raise critical concerns regarding the nation's readiness for such a transformation (Tahulela and Ballard, 2019). There is a significant need for a skillful workforce with the ability to implement the "3Rs": reduce, reuse, and recycle through practices such as repairing and repurposing materials and products (Kadhila et al., 2023).

For a realistic approach to circular economy implementation in South Africa, there is an essential need for a clear vision and a roadmap tailored to South Africa's socio-economic context, associated with serious governmental efforts to set flawless and reliable frameworks while implementing strategies to bridge the gap between the current educational system and the skills required in a circular economy (Daramola et al., 2024).

Although international models from Finland and the Netherlands offer structured frameworks for the transition to a circular economy, governance strategies still need to consider the conditions of the MENA region. According to ESCWA (2021), Arab countries face specific institutional fragmentation, inadequate interministerial coordination, and limited enforcement capacity. To address this, ESCWA (2021) proposes a tailored governance framework based on three pillars:

- Decentralizing implementation by giving municipalities the financial and technical resources to spearhead community-based circular projects;
- Creating national cross-sectoral CE task forces to guarantee high-level coordination amongst the environment, industry, and finance ministries;
- Using inclusive platforms that unite government agencies, businesspeople, academic institutions, non-governmental organizations, and donor representatives to integrate stakeholder co-creation.

These suggestions highlight the viability of a circular economy and directly address the governance gaps that exist in Lebanon.

MENA Region: Emerging Practices

Countries in the MENA region have had unique experiences in recognizing the circular economy as one of their most important national projects. The Jordanian government implemented what is known as the "Solid Waste Strategy," targeting the improvement in service coverage and cost recovery along with expanding composting and recycling capacity in response to growing urban needs (Abu-Qdais et al., 2023). The Egyptian approach was to formalize informal waste collection by increasing recycling infrastructure and reducing dependency on uncontrolled dumping, especially in high-density areas like Greater Cairo (Hemidat et al., 2022).

The importance of the circular economy is recognized and identified globally, but the pace of adapting and implementing it varies according to the circumstances of the nations (Ruiz-Real et al., 2018). While advanced nations like Finland, the Netherlands, and Scotland have found their way to the circular economy, South Africa, MENA region countries, and Lebanon, which are classified as developing countries, are still away from it. However, even among the leading countries, the methods of adopting the circular economy have not achieved the same level of proficiency and efficiency (Mazur-Wierzbicka, 2021). After comparing several countries, we can confidently argue that Finland has excelled in terms of being the first country to publish a detailed, comprehensive, realistic national roadmap that can be applied precisely, leaving no room for ambiguity in the application while clarifying the importance of each stage from the adaptation till the implementation and evaluation.

The figure below synthesizes the key circular economy strategies adopted by several countries examined in this section. All of these experiences were discussed with the aim of identifying practical elements that Lebanon can build upon in developing its own roadmap toward a circular economy, which will be proposed and discussed in the chapter.

Figure 1. International Benchmarks in Circular Economy Policy

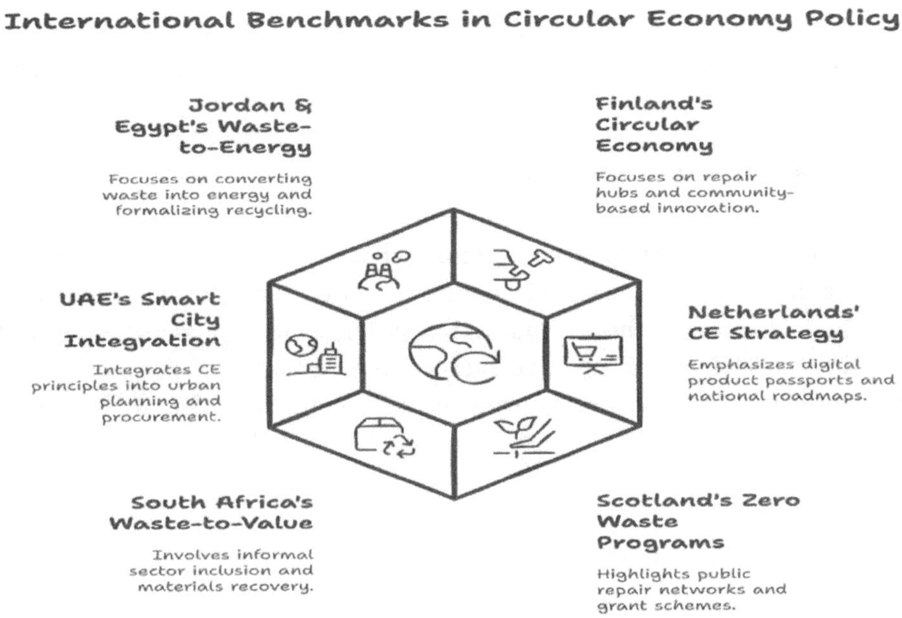

SECTION 5: STAKEHOLDER MAPPING AND IMPLEMENTATION STRATEGY

Transitioning to a circular economy cannot be achieved via new legislation alone because it is necessary for several stakeholders to coordinate in their approach to a range of systems and institutional complexities (Salvioni and Almici, 2020). The circular entrepreneurship pathway in Lebanon will need stakeholder roles defined and approaches for collective work because environmental crisis meets economic instability and governance is fragmented. Stakeholder engagement transforms circular policies into operations, a process of partnerships and operative models, and measurable results (OECD, 2020a).

The success of circular economy initiatives depends on integrated governance, which brings together public and private institutions, research organizations, and civil society to drive sustainable change (Ellen MacArthur Foundation, 2019). The institutional gaps in Lebanon create obstacles for coordinating efforts, which hinders grassroots innovation from flourishing (Chaarani and Raimi, 2021). The process of mapping the circular economy ecosystem transforms into a strategic instrument that defines roles and establishes logical intervention sequences and resource sharing between sectors (Kanda et al., 2021). This section defines the essential stakeholders involved in Lebanon's circular transition and presents a step-by-step implementation plan along with operational suggestions to enhance institutional coordination throughout the entire system.

Stakeholder Identification and Roles

Lebanon needs a comprehensive circular entrepreneurship policy framework, which requires thorough knowledge about the multiple elements that influence its socioeconomic environment and innovation system (Chaarani and Raimi, 2021). The design and delivery of circular interventions requires stakeholders to move past identification for meaningful engagement (Adenike et al., 2024). The circular economy transition in Lebanon depends on multiple stakeholder groups who perform distinct roles to achieve it.

1. Government Ministries and Public Agencies

Circular economy governance rests upon multiple ministries that direct environmental protection alongside industrial development and educational and economic strategic activities (Munonye and Ajonye, 2024).

- **The Ministry of Environment** (MoE) leads the national circularity agenda by overseeing waste management as part of resource efficiency and international environmental obligations (Elroi et al., 2023). The Ministry of Environment remains the best agency to support the institutionalization of the circular economy through mandated strategic roadmaps, parliamentary law reform, and ministerial coordination (ESCWA, 2021).
- **The Ministry of Economy and Trade** (MoET) has a key responsibility to integrate circular economy principles into SME policy and establish green market access and provide fiscal incentives through reduced tariffs on recycled inputs or eco-design tax exemptions (Ahmed and Julian, 2012; Wilts et al., 2016).
- **The Ministry of Industry** (MoI) controls industrial advancement while using its authority to establish shared-resource industrial zones and cleaner production standards for eco-industrial symbiosis development (UNIDO, 2020).
- **The Ministry of Education and Higher Education** (MEHE) supports circular economy education throughout all levels of education by promoting its skills. The educational institutions receive updated curricula for schools, uni-

versities, and technical institutes, while research and innovation in circular design and manufacturing receive support (Dabbous and Boustani, 2023).

2. **Local Authorities and Municipalities**

Given that municipalities in Lebanon are responsible for waste management, they are well positioned to serve as the primary institutions to execute circular economy strategies. With the appropriate technical and financial support, local authorities can serve as innovation centers that establish community composting programs along with repair cafés and reuse markets (UNDP, 2022).

3. **Entrepreneurs, Startups, and SMEs**

These actors serve as the drivers of circular innovation by developing business models through product-as-a-service approaches and remanufacturing and materials recovery practices (Bocken et al., 2016). The main obstacles facing these actors stem from financial constraints as well as unclear regulations and limited market adoption, according to OECD (2021). Circular economy ecosystem success depends on SMEs participating in policy dialogue and gaining access to infrastructure and incentives (Adenike et al., 2024).

To support local SMEs and startups in overcoming typical implementation obstacles, the following tactics are recommended:

- Start local and small: Lebanese business owners should start with small-scale, replicable projects like municipal composting programs, repair cafés, or upcycling workshops. These strategies can have a noticeable impact on local communities with little initial investment (UNDP, 2022; Rosenbaum & Kehdy, 2022).
- Make use of diaspora networks: Lebanon's international diaspora provides an essential network of support. By establishing connections with international communities that are interested in sustainable development, entrepreneurs can gain access to cross-border partnerships, seed funding, and mentorship (ESCWA, 2020).
- Work with NGOs and donor programs: Several international organizations and NGOs, such as the UNDP, GIZ, and Arcenciel, offer technical support, training, and incubation support to environmentally conscious startups in Lebanon (Chaarani & Raimi, 2022; Elmustapha & Hoppe, 2020).
- Create shared resource cooperatives, such as community-based cooperatives or shared fab labs, which can lower startup costs and boost operational effi-

ciency, particularly in the manufacturing, repair, or agro-processing industries (Rosenbaum & Kehdy, 2022).

- Make use of community funding and crowdfunding platforms: Alternative finance models, like Zoomaal, a MENA-based crowdfunding platform, and community-led funding events, have been useful in raising early-stage capital when formal VC or banking support is lacking (Katseli and Boufounou, 2020).
- Encourage awareness and advocacy: By participating in policy discussions and community outreach, promoting green incentives, and informing customers about the benefits of circular business models, entrepreneurs can increase market adoption (El Chaarani & Raimi, 2022).

4. Academia and Research Institutions

The intellectual core of circular economy efforts resides in universities and research centers, which produce locally applicable knowledge together with technological tools and impact evaluation frameworks (Nauffal and Nasser, 2007). The American University of Beirut (AUB) and the Lebanese University (LU) already conduct sustainability research, so they make excellent candidates to establish circular economy living labs and accelerators and experimental policy initiatives (Ahmadieh et al., 2016).

5. Civil Society Organizations and NGOs

Non-governmental organizations perform two essential duties by raising public understanding and promoting behavioral shifts and by implementing circular projects at community levels (Zhidebekkyzy et al., 2023). The critical role of civil society in promoting reuse and recycling and conscious consumption becomes evident through initiatives run by Arcenciel and Live Love Recycle (Chaarani and Raimi, 2021). The inclusion of civil society organizations in circular economy policy development remains essential for both legitimacy and grassroots momentum.

6. International Development Agencies and Donors

International partners, including the European Union, GIZ[1], UNDP, and the World Bank, maintain essential roles because Lebanon faces both financial limitations and institutional weaknesses. The organizations supply financial resources together with policy guidance and training programs. The World Bank (2021) reports that international organizations use their resources to develop pilot programs and exchange knowledge and create monitoring systems that match Lebanon's specific needs (World Bank, 2021b)[2].

7. **Private Sector Coalitions and Business Networks**

The Association of Lebanese Industrialists, together with established companies, maintain sufficient power and financial capabilities to expand circular practices throughout different industries (Supanut et al., 2024). The adoption of circular economy principles can progress more quickly when businesses commit to sustainability standards and when they reform their procurement processes to prioritize sustainable options (Bocken et al., 2017). Business networks play a key role in this process. They create opportunities for companies to share knowledge, experiences, and best practices, which helps them collaborate and adopt circular economy solutions more effectively and at a larger scale than they could alone (Perotti et al., 2024).

8. **The Lebanese Diaspora**

The Lebanese diaspora represents an underutilized resource that enormous great potential for circular entrepreneurship development (Gevorkyan and Issa, 2025). The diaspora professionals who have access to global capital, expertise, and networks can support CE startups through investment, mentorship, and cross-border collaboration (ESCWA, 2020). The establishment of structured diaspora engagement platforms will drive innovation by linking domestic solutions to worldwide business prospects (Benton, 2023).

Implementation Roadmap

To successfully implement circular entrepreneurship policies, Lebanon needs to take carefully planned steps, given the obstacles faced by the country, from economic instability to political conflicts, as well as its infrastructure gaps. The process should begin with basic and necessary reforms before strengthening institutions until circular economy principles become part of the entire economic framework. Below is a suggested implementation roadmap to be applied in the Lebanese context to assist in the proper implementation of circular economy initiatives in Lebanon.

- **Short-Term Actions (0–2 Years):** The first two years should focus on establishing awareness programs and launching pilot projects as part of short-term activities.
  - A National Circular Economy Task Force should be established first, as its primary mission is to bring together the Ministry of Environment

together with the Ministry of Economy and Trade alongside leading academic institutions and private sector representatives. The task force will define a national circular economy strategy while obtaining funding and engaging relevant stakeholders from the beginning.

- Higher education institutions, together with vocational training programs, need to start incorporating circular economy principles into their curricula. The introduction of circular economy concepts at an early stage helps develop modern skills that will prepare students for future challenges and establish circular economy principles within educational and technical institutions. To begin implementing circular economy ideas in Lebanon, it's helpful to start with small-scale pilot projects that can be tested in specific locations before being expanded, such as municipal composting schemes, reuse hubs, and repair cafés (UNDP, 2022). These types of projects can lead to quick results that may be beneficial in building public and political support for larger initiatives, provided they are supported by public awareness campaigns, especially those funded by international donors.

- **Medium-Term Actions (3–5 Years):** The next three to five years should focus on developing supporting ecosystems and regulatory changes. This period needs to expand the infrastructure while implementing circular economy principles into governing structures. The following priorities stand as essential for this phase.
  – The establishment of circular economy innovation hubs in universities and business incubators serves to promote experimentation and entrepreneurship (Bocken et al., 2016).
  – The development of public procurement guidelines should incorporate circular products together with services and life-cycle sustainability standards (Geng et al., 2019).
  – The waste legislation needs to undergo changes to support extended producer responsibility (EPR) while creating secondary material markets and enabling licenses for circular startups, according to the Ellen MacArthur Foundation (2019).
  – The development of blended finance instruments between development finance institutions and venture funds or green bonds will support high-impact circular economy ventures (OECD, 2020a; UNIDO, 2020).

- **Long-Term Actions (5+ Years)**: The long-term integration of circular economy principles into economic development strategies and industrial recovery plans represents the third stage of this process.
  – To ensure real progress, the National Circular Economy Strategy should become a law, which would serve to create formal circular economy goals

and performance targets for construction, agriculture, and manufacturing sectors to follow (Gagnon et al., 2022).
– A national circular economy observatory should be established to serve as a monitoring system to track the implementation while also measuring impact indicators to adjust any policies if needed based on what the data shows, according to OECD (2021) and ESCWA (2021).

By following this structured and realistic approach, Lebanon can overcome any structural challenges and create an inclusive environment that supports the growth of circular entrepreneurship.

Governance Mechanisms and Institutional Coordination

A powerful inclusive governance system must exist to translate circular entrepreneurship policies into real-world outcomes within Lebanon's challenging institutional framework (Chaarani and Raimi, 2021). A promising strategy involves creating a National Circular Economy Council that functions as a cross-sectoral body to direct, synchronize, and track nationwide circular economy policy execution. The Ministry of Environment should lead the National Circular Economy Council, which must consist of senior representatives from the economy, industry, and education ministries alongside members from private sector companies, academia, local government, civil society organizations, and international development partners.

The council is responsible for making sure that all regulatory frameworks align with circular economy policies while coordinating inter-ministerial efforts to develop circular economy infrastructure and educational reforms. The Council should also serve as a central hub for circular economy exchange of knowledge while assessing the performance of circular economy initiatives and engaging stakeholders to actively participate in circular economy implementation, all of which is inspired by successful international models such as Sitra Foundation (Sitra, 2019) in Finland and Scotland's Zero Waste Task Force (Zero Waste Scotland, 2014) and OECD's (2020a) circular economy governance framework. The Council needs more than design excellence to achieve success since political commitment together with sustainable funding and clear legal authority will drive systemic transformation of the circular economy.

Additionally, the region-specific frameworks created by ESCWA and other MENA-focused research projects can be advantageous to Lebanon. Formalizing coordination amongst ministries, municipalities, and private sector actors through the establishment of a National Circular Economy Council based on ESCWA's guidelines is one encouraging suggestion (ESCWA, 2021). A council like this would guide the development of national circular economy strategies, monitor important performance measures in different industries, coordinate pilot projects funded by donors that have measurable local benefits, and oversee the integration of circular practices into waste management laws, public purchasing, and industrial recovery efforts.

Furthermore, regional studies emphasize the significance of fiscal autonomy and local authority involvement in implementing circular initiatives. With the help of decentralized planning frameworks, municipalities in Tunisia, Jordan, and Egypt have shown that bottom-up implementation can succeed when technical assistance and community involvement are provided (SCP/RAC, 2020).

The figure below summarizes the proposed roadmap for implementing a circular economy, categorizing it into three interdependent phases—foundational, ecosystem and regulation, and governance—tailored to Lebanon's current context to guide its transition toward a circular economy.

The foundational phase seeks to reinforce the essential structural pillars for adapting the circular economy, such as national awareness, education, and initial pilot projects for introducing circular practices. The ecosystem and regulation phase is designed to reinforce and broaden foundational efforts by developing infrastructure, financial instruments, regulatory reforms, and innovation hubs that foster collaboration and scale. Finally, the governance phase assures sustainable outcomes by grounding circular economy principles into institutional frameworks by establishing a national council, enforcing legal frameworks, national strategies, coordination bodies, and monitoring systems.

Figure 2. Roadmap to Lebanese Circular Economy

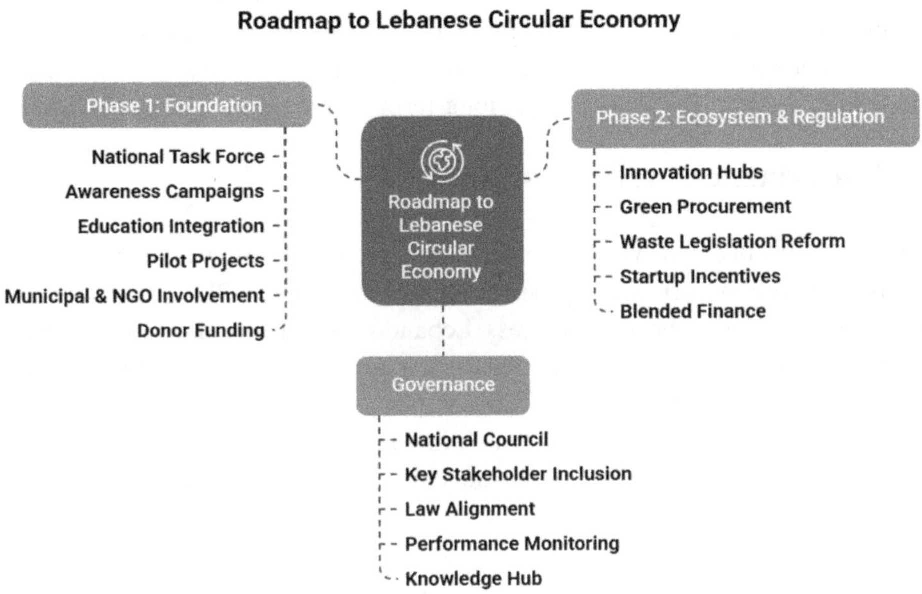

SECTION 6: MONITORING AND EVALUATION – METRICS FOR SUCCESS

Introduction to Circular Economy Monitoring

Circular entrepreneurship policies require robust monitoring and evaluation frameworks to quantify and report on effectiveness and credibility through well-described transparent measurements that inform policy change and include reporting on social and environmental outcomes (Ruohomaa and Ivanova, 2019). Given the fragmented data system in Lebanon and insignificant enforcement measures, the importance and urgency of having specific and measurable outcomes cannot be overstated (Chaarani and Raimi, 2021). In the context of the recent crisis, the monitoring and evaluation framework is a critical strategic asset allowing for evidence-based decision-making and a more intelligent and limited allocation of scarce resources, according to the UNEP (2021).

The framework should include linkages to both Lebanon's national sustainability targets and to international measures such as the UN Sustainable Development Goals (Bocken et al., 2017). The UN Sustainable Development Goals emphasize three specific targets: Goal 8 (Decent Work and Economic Growth), Goal 9 (Industry, Innovation, and Infrastructure), and Goal 12 (Responsible Consumption and Production) (Mariño and Banga, 2016). The integration of performance metrics into the circular economy strategy allows policymakers to track progress while correcting paths and establishing stakeholder trust through long-term accountability (OECD, 2020a).

Key Performance Indicators (KPIs)

The assessment of real-world circular entrepreneurship policy outcomes depends heavily on developing strong key performance indicators (KPIs) (Dolatabadet al., 2022). The indicators need to address Lebanon's specific policy and economic framework yet must follow international standards to guarantee both assessment consistency and framework unity. Circular transition progress requires evaluation through four main KPI categories, which include economic impact together with environmental outcomes and social value and systemic integration.

1. **Economic Impact Indicators**
    - Number of Circular Startups Supported: This indicator follows the annual numbers of newly registered circular economy startups which receive support from public programs and donor initiatives (Kanda et al., 2021).
    - Volume of Circular Economy Investments: This indicator measures all financial resources which include grants, equity investments, diaspora capital, and blended finance directed toward circular businesses (Geng et al., 2019).
    - Revenue Growth in Circular Economy Sectors: This indicator evaluates the yearly income increase from firms that operate in reuse and remanufacturing and eco-design sectors (Bocken et al., 2016).
2. **Environmental Performance Indicators**
    - The waste diversion statistics serve as a vital indicator to measure the amount of waste materials that are diverted from entering landfills. The indicator is particularly important for Lebanon because open dumping is still a common practice throughout the country (ESCWA, 2021).
    - Decreased Resource Consumption: This indicator measures the decrease in the use of raw material in key sectors, showing an improvement in resource management (Wiedenhofer et al., 2024).
    - Carbon Emissions Avoided: Calculates the decline in greenhouse gas emission through circular economy practices such as recycling, product reuse, or advanced production methods (Ellen MacArthur Foundation, 2019).

3. **Social and Employment Indicators**
   - Jobs Created: This indicator measures employment growth in circular economy sectors that include repair services together with reverse logistics and sustainable construction and recycling (Geng et al., 2019). The equity monitoring process requires complete gender and regional breakdowns of data.
   - Training and Certification Programs: This indicator follows the growth of training and certification programs for circular economy competencies, which people obtain through formal education or TVET systems and entrepreneurship programs (Dabbous and Boustani, 2023).
4. **Systemic Integration Indicators**
   - Public-Private Partnerships (PPPs): This indicator tracks formal partnerships that unite government agencies with NGOs and private businesses to deliver circular economy solutions (Kanda et al., 2021).
   - Integration of Circular Economy Principles into Institutional Procurement: This indicator assesses the percentage of public procurement that includes circularity criteria such as recycled content or life-cycle analysis (Geng et al., 2019).
   - Adoption of Social Economy Standards: This indicator assesses the extent to which firms and institutions apply circular economy certifications and assessment tools (Sehnem et al., 2021).

Such indicators should be traced using a single, circular economy monitoring system and would be under the oversight of a national data observatory or body coordinating the data, such as the proposed National Circular Economy Council. The assessment requires geo-referenced and sector-disaggregated enterprise-level data (e.g., SMEs and large enterprises) (OECD, 2021).

Building a sufficiently robust set of key performance indicators (KPIs) is critical for evaluating the real results of circular entrepreneurship policies (Dolatabad et al., 2022). KPIs should be representative of Lebanon's specific policy and economic context while still allowing for consistent international tracking and comparisons. KPIs can be grouped according to the four broad categories of (1) economic impacts, (2) environmental impacts, (3) social value, and (4) systemic integration to best assess the full scope for progress across all dimensions of circular transition (Bocken et al., 2016).

Tools and Evaluation Frameworks

To track Lebanon's circular entrepreneurship progress meaningfully, policymakers need to use both qualitative and quantitative evaluation tools (OECD, 2020a).

The assessment tools need to be responsive to Lebanese conditions but must follow international best practices for circular economy implementation. The evaluation framework needs to function beyond outcome recording because it needs to facilitate ongoing learning and maintain accountability to achieve sustained improvements between policies and practices (Wilts et al., 2016).

The Circular Economy Maturity Model is an important tool that helps identify how far organizations and systems have moved from traditional linear methods to circular systems. The Circular Economy Maturity Model serves Lebanese municipalities and public institutions and small to medium-sized enterprises by assessing waste reduction alongside product design innovation and circular business model adoption (Circle Economy, 2022).

Startup performance dashboards that specifically support circular entrepreneurship represent a promising implementation mechanism (Dabbous and Boustani, 2023). Digital platforms collect data from incubators and accelerators and financing programs, which provide instant access to essential performance indicators that track job creation alongside funding acquisition and environmental impact reduction (Kanda et al., 2021). The implementation of similar dashboards, which Amsterdam successfully uses, could be adapted for Lebanon through partnerships between universities and NGOs[3].

The Circularity Indicators Framework of the European Union offers a good way for Lebanon to measure how well it recycles materials, uses resources efficiently, and understands the effects of products over their entire life cycle using standard methods. The use of internationally recognized tools to compare outcomes between Lebanon and other countries will enhance Lebanon's green finance access and progress reporting capabilities for Sustainable Development Goals (European Commission, 2020).

The selection of tools must derive from practical realities. Given the limited digital infrastructure and certain institutional weaknesses faced in Lebanon, the best way to proceed would be by adopting a phased strategy with simple, low-cost data collection methods that can later evolve into more advanced and sophisticated platforms for evaluation (Chaarani and Raimi, 2021).

SECTION 7: CONCLUSION

This chapter investigated the current situation in Lebanon, underscoring the country's challenges in transitioning to a circular economy. Following that, international policies implemented by Finland, the Netherlands, Scotland, South Africa, and some MENA countries are benchmarked, illustrating successful cases of circular economy transition. These insights are analyzed to propose a Lebanese national roadmap tailored to the Lebanese context.

This chapter demonstrates that Lebanon is facing both structural and systemic challenges hindering the effective implementation of a circular economy. Among the systemic challenges, most notable is the lack of national regulations and recognition of the importance of adopting a circular economy, along with permanent political instability and persistent lack of public trust in governmental institutions; those factors are significant impediments for any progress toward formulating and enforcing long-term sustainable policies, eventually diminishing civic engagement (Issa, 2006), and weakening coordination across various sectors while limiting the impact of existing initiatives (Chaarani, 2021).

Due to the widespread corruption, Lebanon has been suffering since 2019 from a severe economic crisis, which led to currency devaluation, capital controls, and opaque financial practices. These factors have caused the collapse of the banking system—knowing that it was the cornerstone of the Lebanese economy—negatively impacting Lebanese society. Eventually, this led to a mass emigration of skilled professionals, draining the human capital essential for innovation and the efficient execution of circular economy strategies (Omar, 2025). Simultaneously, both public and private investments in sustainability have declined, undermining the feasibility of circular economy initiatives (Devi, 2020).

Bearing in mind that one of the most important aspects of the circular economy is waste management, garbage protests surged across Lebanon since 2015, highlighting the failure of waste management systems and insufficiency of centralized recycling infrastructure. Poorly managed landfills contributed to groundwater contamination and increased air pollution, as untreated sewage and industrial waste continue to pollute Lebanese rivers, worsening the ecological status and leading to more environmental degradation, eventually weakening the structural basis required for sustainable development (Castro, 2022).

The lack of financial help and support for startups, along with poor infrastructure, weak laws, and no formal support systems, has made it hard for new businesses to thrive. Rather than expecting a flourishing startup culture, these challenges led many Lebanese citizens, especially women, to adopt a necessity-driven entrepreneurship (Boustani, 2023). Additionally, extraordinary events such as the Beirut Port explosion in 2020 and the COVID-19 pandemic have intensified those challenges, significantly drawing back the progress toward building a resilient and sustainable economic model.

Despite the aforementioned challenges, the Lebanese entrepreneurial ecosystem is proving its strong resilience while Lebanon continues to rank among the highest in the MENA region for Total Early Stage Entrepreneurial Activity, as the local enterprises are refusing to give up, especially in sectors like agriculture and technology (Bouzakhem *et al.*, 2023), where significant growth is being recorded with optimism in creating some job opportunities. Furthermore, the unique Lebanese socio-economic and environmental conditions have laid the groundwork for the emergence of circular and social entrepreneurship. Lebanon is revealing an entrepreneurial culture responsive to emerging global trends and aligning with broader goals of sustainability and innovation. But chief among these considerations is that, even at its preliminary stage, the circular economy adaptation calls for and deserves full support from policymakers and ecosystem actors.

Recommendations

Policymakers directly influence the required institutional and regulatory infrastructure for circular economy adoption. Thus, the latter are directly responsible for incorporating circular economy principles into country-wide plans for industrialization, economic growth, and sustainability. This process enhances synergy and alignment across sectors and establishes a common framework for sustainable growth. Also vital is legal and regulatory action, which includes extended producer responsibility (EPR) and incentives for applying circular economy practices and circular procurement to transform business and consumer behaviors and patterns. Such initiatives stimulate both the supply and demand for environmentally responsible goods and services, promoting efficient use of materials and resources and reducing unnecessary waste.

Additionally, policymakers must consider launching a multi-stakeholder council that oversees the application of circular economy principles and increases integrated governance and strategic policy alignment. The council can be a cornerstone for collaborative initiatives among public and private bodies, including NGOs, warranting the proper implementation and evaluation of policies. By addressing local hurdles like political instability and governmental distrust, policymakers can create a supportive environment for a thriving circular economy.

Practitioners such as local governments and development agencies are vital in implementing principles of circular economy nationwide. Practical circular economy solutions can include project refurbishment centers, upcycling and creative reuse businesses, composting and organic waste management, *etc.*, which involve local communities in sustainable and responsible practices and encourage feelings of local ownership and civic engagement. Municipalities can implement various initiatives to foster local engagement. For instance, *municipalities can organize awareness sessions, implement circular procurement and green incentives, and provide support for local circular entrepreneurship.* It is also vital to explore means of decentralizing financing for such initiatives. Municipalities can monitor circular economy plans and programs through their own management and consistent financial support.

Additionally, practical implementation of circular economy practices should be portrayed in the establishment of circular entrepreneurship support mechanisms through circular incubators, accelerators, innovation hubs, and investment programs. On the other hand, current support structures—like the aforementioned—should be trained toward supporting more circular initiatives and encouraging circular thinking nationwide. Moreover, to improve data collection and transparency, practitioners must encourage the development of dashboards for increased visibility on the trajectory of the circular economy in the country.

Theoretically, this chapter has presented a roadmap and evaluation criteria for applying and monitoring circular economy principles in Lebanon, taking into account its constraining environment. Future studies should look more closely at the framework, stakeholders, and KPIs to ensure its applicability across the country, whether additional criteria should be considered for inclusion in the framework, and if a similar framework is applicable in other contexts and in different industries. Furthermore, when select municipalities apply the proposed framework, additional practical insights may highlight any necessary modifications, should they arise, to improve any potential wider application in the country.

REFERENCES

Ababio, J. O. M., Yiadom, E. B., Ofori-Sasu, D., & Sarpong–Kumankoma, E. (2024). Digital financial inclusion and inclusive development in lower-middle-income countries: The enabling role of institutional quality. *Journal of Chinese Economic and Foreign Trade Studies, 17*(2/3), 133–151.

Abbas, I. I., Chaaban, J. K., Al-Rabaa, A. R., & Shaar, A. A. (2017). Solid waste management in Lebanon: Challenges and recommendations. *Journal of Environment and Waste Management, 4*(2), 53–63.

Abbas, R. (2017). Solid waste management in Lebanon: Challenges and recommendations. *Waste Management & Research, 35*(2), 89–102.

Abu-Qdais, H. A., Shatnawi, N., & Al-Shahrabi, R. (2023). Modeling the impact of fees and circular economy options on the financial sustainability of the solid waste management system in Jordan. *Resources, 12*(3), 32. DOI: 10.3390/resources12030032

Adebayo, Y. A., Ikevuje, A. H., Kwakye, J. M., & Esiri, A. E. (2024). Driving circular economy in project management: Effective stakeholder management for sustainable outcomes. *GSC Advanced Research and Reviews, 20*(3), 235–245.

Ahmadieh, D., Nalbandian, S., & Noubani, K. (2016). A comparative citation analysis study of master's theses at the American University of Beirut, Lebanon. *Collection Building, 35*(4), 103–113.

Ahmed, Z. U., & Julian, C. C. (2012). International entrepreneurship in Lebanon. *Global Business Review, 13*(1), 25–38.

Aiguobarueghian, I., Adanma, U. M., Ogunbiyi, E. O., & Solomon, N. O. (2024). Waste management and circular economy: A review of sustainable practices and economic benefits. *World Journal of Advanced Research and Reviews, 22*(2), 1708–1719.

Akimova, Yu. A., & Kovalenko, E. G. (2021). The netherlands: Experience in the field of circular economy development. *Fundamental Research (Beijing), 12*, 17–21.

American University of Beirut (AUB) Nature Conservation Center. (2020). *Environmental initiatives and research reports*. Retrieved from https://www.aub.edu.lb/natureconservation/

Baz, S., Cathcart, L., & Michaelides, A. (2025). Lebanon: From dollars to lollars. *International Finance, 28*(1), 37–63.

Bentkowska, K. (2024). Informal institutions in the circular economy. *Ekonomia i Środowisko*, 2 (89).

Benton, W. (2023). Returnees, Institutions, and Networks: Making Space for Technology Entrepreneurship in Beirut. *Anthropology of the Middle East*, *18*(2), 69–84.

Block, T. (2019). The economy that runs on waste: Accumulation in the circular city. *Journal of Urban Technology*, *26*(1), 1–20.

Bocken, N. M., De Pauw, I., Bakker, C., & Van Der Grinten, B. (2016). Product design and business model strategies for a circular economy. *Journal of industrial and production engineering*, *33*(5), 308-320.

Boustani, N. M., & Hajj, S. (2023, June). The Lebanese Entrepreneurial Resilience In Times Of Crisis. In *ARPHA Conference Abstracts*. 6, e107045. Pensoft Publishers.

Bouzakhem, N., Farmanesh, P., Zargar, P., Ramadan, M., Baydoun, H., Daouk, A., & Mouazen, A. (2023). Rebuilding the workplace in the post-pandemic age through human capital development programs: A moderated mediation model. *Administrative Sciences*, *13*(7), 164.

Bozorg-Haddad, O., Zolghadr-Asli, B., Sarzaeim, P., Aboutalebi, M., Chu, X., & Loáiciga, H. A. (2020). Evaluation of water shortage crisis in the Middle East and possible remedies. *Journal of Water Supply: Research & Technology - Aqua*, *69*(1), 85–98.

Buren, N. (2016). Towards a circular economy: The role of Dutch logistics industries and governments. *Journal of Cleaner Production*, *134*, 1–10.

Calisto Friant, M., Lakerveld, D., Vermeulen, W. J., & Salomone, R. (2021). Transition to a sustainable circular plastics economy in the Netherlands: Discourse and policy analysis. *Sustainability*, *14*(1), 190.

Castro, R. (2022). Circular economy and its impact on environmental sustainability. *Journal of Environmental Studies (Northborough, Mass.)*, *15*(2), 45–67.

Ceroni, E. (2024). The role of extended producer responsibility (epr) in the transition to a circular economy. *SWS International Scientific Conference on Social Sciences*, 11, 293–300. https://doi.org/DOI: 10.35603/sws.iscss.2024/vs02/22

Chaarani, H. (2021). Determinant factors of successful social entrepreneurship in the emerging circular economy of Lebanon: Exploring the moderating role of NGOs. *Journal of Entrepreneurship and Circular Economy*, *10*(2), 123–145.

Chaarani, H., & Raimi, L. (2022). Determinant factors of successful social entrepreneurship in the emerging circular economy of Lebanon: Exploring the moderating role of NGOs. *Journal of Entrepreneurship in Emerging Economies*, *14*(5), 874–901.

Chahine, S. (2018). *Interconnectedness in entrepreneurial ecosystems: a social capital perspective* (Doctoral dissertation, University of Southampton).

Cieslik, K., Barford, A., & Vira, B. (2022). Young people not in employment, education or training (NEET) in Sub-Saharan Africa: Sustainable development target 8.6 missed and reset. *Journal of Youth Studies*, *25*(8), 1126–1147.

Cullen, U. A., & De Angelis, R. (2021). Circular entrepreneurship: A business model perspective. *Resources, Conservation and Recycling*, *168*, 105300.

Dabbous, A., & Boustani, N. M. (2023). Digital explosion and entrepreneurship education: Impact on promoting entrepreneurial intention for business students. *Journal of Risk and Financial Management*, *16*(1), 27.

Dada, M. A., Majemite, M. T., Obaigbena, A., Oliha, J. S., & Biu, P. W. (2024). Zero-waste initiatives and circular economy in the US: A review: Exploring strategies, outcomes, and challenges in moving towards a more sustainable consumption model. *International Journal of Science and Research Archive*, *11*(1), 204–221.

Dantas, R. M., Ilyas, A., Martins, J. M., & Rita, J. X. (2022). Circular entrepreneurship in emerging markets through the lens of sustainability. *Journal of Open Innovation*, *8*(4), 211.

Dapp, M. M. (2018). Toward a sustainable circular economy powered by community-based incentive systems. In *Business Transformation through Blockchain* (Vol. II, pp. 153–181). Springer International Publishing.

Daramola, O. M., Apeh, C. E., Basiru, J. O., Onukwulu, E. C., & Paul, P. O. (2024). Environmental law and corporate social responsibility: Assessing the impact of legal frameworks on circular economy practices. *International Journal of Social Science Exceptional Research*, *3*(1), 63–79.

De La Cuesta-González, M., & Morales-García, M. (2022). Does finance as usual work for circular economy transition? A financiers and SMEs qualitative approach. *Journal of Environmental Planning and Management*, *65*(13), 2468–2489.

Del Vecchio, P., Secundo, G., Mele, G., & Passiante, G. (2021). Sustainable entrepreneurship education for circular economy: Emerging perspectives in Europe. *International Journal of Entrepreneurial Behaviour & Research*, *27*(8), 2096–2124.

Devi, S. (2020). Economic crisis hits Lebanese health care. *Lancet, 395*(10224), 567–589.

Dolatabad, A. H., Mahdiraji, H. A., Babgohari, A. Z., Garza-Reyes, J. A., & Ai, A. (2022). Analyzing the key performance indicators of circular supply chains by hybrid fuzzy cognitive mapping and Fuzzy DEMATEL: Evidence from healthcare sector. *Environment, Development and Sustainability*, •••, 1–27.

Economy, C. (2022). *The circularity gap report*. Retrieved from https://www.circularity-gap.world/

Edeh, J. (2025). Bridging the Gap Living Standards in Africa: The role of entrepreneurship and digital infrastructure. *Sustainability Impacts Review, 1*(1).

El-Annan, S. H., & Haidoura, H. M. (2023). Entrepreneurship as a catalyst for employment: Navigating the unemployment challenge in Lebanon's private sector. *Management Research, 10*(11), 1–14.

El-Chaarani, H., Mawad, J. L., Mawad, N., & Khalife, D. (2023). Psychological and demographic predictors of investment in cryptocurrencies during a crisis in the MENA region: the case of Lebanon. *Journal of Economic and Administrative Sciences*.

El Chaarani, H., & Raimi, L. (2022). Determinant factors of successful social entrepreneurship in the emerging circular economy of Lebanon: Exploring the moderating role of NGOs. *Journal of Entrepreneurship in Emerging Economies, 14*(5), 874–901.

Ellen MacArthur Foundation. (2019). *Completing the picture: How the circular economy tackles climate change*. Retrieved from https://ellenmacarthurfoundation.org/

Elmustapha, H., & Hoppe, T. (2020). Challenges and opportunities of business models in sustainable transitions: Evidence from solar energy niche development in Lebanon. *Energies, 13*(3), 670.

Elroi, H., Zbigniew, G., Agnieszka, W., & Piotr, S. (2023). Enhancing waste resource efficiency: Circular economy for sustainability and energy conversion. *Frontiers in Environmental Science*, •••, 11.

ESCWA. (2020). *Harnessing the power of the diaspora for sustainable development in Lebanon*. United Nations Economic and Social Commission for Western Asia.

ESCWA. (2021). *The circular economy in the Arab region: Sustainable consumption and production policies*. United Nations.

European Commission. (2020). *Monitoring framework for the circular economy*. Retrieved from https://ec.europa.eu/environment/circular-economy/

Fayssal, N., Al Tawil, L., Danageuzian, H., Sabat, M., ElMerehbi, H., Darazi, D., & Romanos, J. (2024). Navigating the water–energy nexus amidst the Lebanese economic crisis. *AQUA—Water Infrastructure. Ecosystems and Society, 73*(5), 917–929.

Finnish Innovation Fund Sitra. (2019). *The critical move – Finland's road map to a circular economy 2.0*. Sitra. https://www.sitra.fi/en/publications/the-critical-move/

Gagnon, B., Tanguay, X., Amor, B., & Imbrogno, A. F. (2022). Forest products and circular economy strategies: A Canadian perspective. *Energies, 15*(3), 673.

Geissdoerfer, M., Savaget, P., Bocken, N. M. P., & Hultink, E. J. (2017). The Circular Economy – A new sustainability paradigm? *Journal of Cleaner Production, 143*, 757–768.

GEM. (2018). UAE Annual Report. UAEU & Global Entrepreneurship Research Association.

Geng, Y., Sarkis, J., & Bleischwitz, R. (2019). How to globalize the circular economy. *Nature, 565*(7738), 153–155.

Gevorkyan, A. V., & Issa, S. (2025). Diaspora and Sustainable Economic Development in Lebanon: New Survey-Informed Analysis. *Review of Development Economics.*

Halog, A., & Anieke, S. (2021). A review of circular economy studies in developed countries and its potential adoption in developing countries. *Circular Economy and Sustainability, 1*(1), 209–230.

Hamza, M. (2025). Empowering Startups through Accelerator Services in Lebanon: A Phenomenological Case Study. *Journal of Information Systems Engineering & Management, 10*(6).

Hanemaaijer, A., Muller, M., de Krom, M., Mangnus, A., Schotten, K., & in 't Veld, D. (2025). *Integral circular economy report: Assessment for the Netherlands 2025* (PBL publication no. 5849). PBL Netherlands Environmental Assessment Agency.

Haris, N. I. N., Al Edrus, S. S. O., Abdul Raof, N., Wondi, M. H., Khan, W. R., Sien, L. S., & Sawatdeenarunat, C. (2024). Toward low-carbon cities: A review of circular economy integration in urban waste management and its impact on carbon emissions. *Wiley Interdisciplinary Reviews. Energy and Environment, 13*(5), e535.

Hegde, S., Sumith, N., Pinto, T., Shukla, S., & Patidar, V. (2024). Optimizing Solid Waste Management: A Holistic Approach by Informed Carbon Emission Reduction. *IEEE Access : Practical Innovations, Open Solutions.*

Hemidat, S., Achouri, O., El Fels, L., Elagroudy, S., Hafidi, M., Chaouki, B., Ahmed, M., Hodgkinson, I., & Guo, J. (2022). Solid waste management in the context of a circular economy in the MENA region. *Sustainability, 14*(1), 480. DOI: 10.3390/su14010480

Hilmi, Y. S., Tóth, J., Gabnai, Z., Király, G., & Temesi, Á. (2024). Farmers' resilience to climate change through the circular economy and sustainable agriculture: A review from developed and developing countries. *Renewable Agriculture and Food Systems, 39*, e15.

Hinsa, D. P., Ezra, O., & Pardede, R. (2025). CIRCULAR ECONOMY IN INDONESIA: A COMPARATIVE STUDY OF EU COUNTRIES AND FINLAND. *Journal Research of Social Science, Economics & Management, 4*(10).

Hosseinian, A., Ylä-Mella, J., & Pongrácz, E. (2021). Current status of circular economy research in Finland. *Resources, 10*(5), 40.

Huđek, I., & Bradač Hojnik, B. (2020). Impact of entrepreneurship activity sustainable development. *Problemy Ekorozwoju, 15*(2), 175–183.

Islam, Z., Gangat, S. A., Mohanan, P., Rahmat, Z. S., El Chbib, D., Marfani, W. B., & Essar, M. Y. (2021). Mental health impacts of Lebanon's economic crisis on healthcare workers amidst COVID-19. *The International Journal of Health Planning and Management, 37*(2), 1160.

Issa, I. (2006). Impacts of political instability on tourism planning and development: The case of Lebanon. *Tourism Management Journal, 27*(3), 567–589.

Ivanović-Đukić, M., Rađenović, T., & Veselinović, N. (2022). Impact of entrepreneurship on sustainable development in emerging markets under the conditions of COVID-19. *Problemy Ekorozwoju, 17*(2).

Järvinen, L., & Sinervo, R. (2020). *How to create a national circular economy road map: A guide to making the change happen* (Sitra Studies 170). Sitra. https://www.sitra.fi/en/publications/how-to-create-a-national-circular-economy-road-map/

Kadhila, T., de Wit, M. P., & Schenck, R. (2023). A conceptual framework for sustainable waste management in small municipalities: The cases of Langebaan, South Africa and Swakopmund, Namibia. *Environmental Science and Pollution Research International, 30*(60), 125088–125103.

Kanda, W., Geissdoerfer, M., & Hjelm, O. (2021). From circular business models to circular business ecosystems. *Business Strategy and the Environment, 30*(6), 2814–2829.

Käsner, S.-A., & Gihring, K. (2024, September). *ACEN – South Africa's Policy Framework.* African Circular Economy Network. Retrieved from https://www.acen.africa

Kim, I., Park, D., Kyung, D., Kim, G., Kim, S., & Lee, J. (2015). Comparative influences of precipitation and river stage on groundwater levels in near-river areas. *Sustainability*, *8*(1), 1.

Kirchherr, J., Reike, D., & Hekkert, M. (2017). Conceptualizing the circular economy: An analysis of 114 definitions. *Resources, Conservation and Recycling*, *127*, 221–232.

Lit, F. C., Huijben, J. C., Cloodt, M. M., & Paredis, E. (2024). Business model innovation in circular start-ups: Overcoming barriers in the circular plastics economy. *International Small Business Journal*, *42*(4), 506–550.

Lüdeke-Freund, F., Gold, S., & Bocken, N. M. (2019). A review and typology of circular economy business model patterns. *Journal of Industrial Ecology*, *23*(1), 36–61.

Majed, R. (2021). In defense of intra-sectarian divide: Street mobilization, coalition formation, and rapid realignments of sectarian boundaries in Lebanon. *Social Forces*, *99*(4), 1772–1798.

Mangaroska, V. (2024). Circular built environment as international concept of sustainable innovation. In *Proceedings of the National Conference with International Participation* – (pp. 169–173). https://doi.org/DOI: 10.5937/greenb24022m

Mariño, R., & Banga, R. S. (2016). UN Sustainable Development Goals (SDGs): A time to act. *Journal of Oral Research*, *5*(1), 5–6.

Marjamaa, M., Salminen, H., Kujala, J., Tapaninaho, R., & Heikkinen, A. (2021). A sustainable circular economy: Exploring stakeholder interests in Finland. *South Asian journal of business and management cases, 10*(1), 50-62.

Mazur-Wierzbicka, E. (2021). Circular economy: Advancement of European Union countries. *Environmental Sciences Europe*, *33*(1), 111.

McCarville, M. (2019). Turning the Netherlands into a plastic circular hotspot. *Circular Economy Review*, *1*(2), 45–60.

Mohapatra, S., Roy, S., Upadhyay, A., & Kumar, A. (2024). Circular value creation through environmental entrepreneurship initiatives: A case-based exploration. *Business Strategy and the Environment*, *33*(5), 3811–3831.

Mouazen, A. M., & Hernández-Lara, A. B. (2023). Entrepreneurial ecosystem, gig economy practices and Women's entrepreneurship: The case of Lebanon. *International Journal of Gender and Entrepreneurship, 15*(3), 249–274.

Munonye, W. C., & Ajonye, G. O. Urban Policy and Governance for a Circular Economy: Opportunities and Challenges.

Muñoz, E., & Navia, R. (2021). Circular economy in urban systems: How to measure the impact? *Waste Management & Research, 39*(2), 197–198.

Nasreddine, L., Akl, C., Al-Shaar, L., Almedawar, M. M., & Isma'eel, H. (2014). Consumer knowledge, attitudes and salt-related behavior in the Middle East: The case of Lebanon. *Nutrients, 6*(11), 5079–5102.

Nauffal, D. I., & Nasser, R. N. (2007). The American higher educational model in Lebanon: organisational cultures and their impact on student outcomes and satisfaction.

Ncube, T., Dlodlo, N., & Terzoli, A. (2023). Blockchain-based Peer-to-Peer Energy Trading through a Community-based Virtual Power Plant. In *2023 2nd Zimbabwe Conference of Information and Communication Technologies (ZCICT)* (pp. 1-6). IEEE.

Netter, S., Pedersen, E. R. G., & Lüdeke-Freund, F. (2019). Sharing economy revisited: Towards a new framework for understanding sharing models. *Journal of Cleaner Production, 221*, 224–233.

Nyakudya, P., Madushele, N., & Madyira, D. M. (2022, May). A Review of Industrial Symbiosis in Influencing Green Manufacturing. In *2022 IEEE 13th International Conference on Mechanical and Intelligent Manufacturing Technologies (ICMIMT)* (pp. 80-84). IEEE.

OECD. (2020a). *The circular economy in cities and regions: Synthesis report.* Organisation for Economic Co-operation and Development.

OECD. (2020b). The circular economy in Groningen, Netherlands. *OECD Urban Studies*. OECD Publishing.

OECD. (2021). *Entrepreneurship policies through a circular economy lens*. Retrieved from https://www.oecd.org/cfe/smes/entrepreneurship-and-the-circular-economy.pdf

Omar, M. H., Nehme, M., & Al Mohtar, L. (2025). The Lebanese expatriation: Between return and connection. *Edelweiss Applied Science and Technology, 9*(2), 1636–1647.

Ozbay, B., & Koc, Y. (2022). Impact of Covid-19 lock-down period on variations of air pollutants around an industrialized city of Turkey, Izmit. *Environmental Forensics, 23*(1-2), 198–207.

Palalić, R., Ramadani, V., Welsh, D. H., Dizdarević, A., & Đilović, A. (2021). Impact of networking and business environment on student leadership styles. *The International Entrepreneurship and Management Journal, 17*, 447–475.

Patwa, N., Paul, R., Dsilva, J., & Chadha, K. K. (2025). Enhancing circular economy practices in Asia through digitalization and infrastructure. *Academia Environmental Sciences and Sustainability, 2*(1).

Perotti, F. A., Bargoni, A., De Bernardi, P., & Rozsa, Z. (2025). Fostering circular economy through open innovation: Insights from multiple case study. *Business Ethics, the Environment & Responsibility, 34*(2), 390–408.

Pitkänen, K., Karppinen, T. K. M., Kautto, P., Turunen, S., Judl, J., & Myllymaa, T. (2020). Sex, drugs and the circular economy: the social impacts of the circular economy and how to measure them. In *Handbook of the circular economy* (pp. 162–175). Edward Elgar Publishing.

Ramakrishna, S., & Jose, R. (2022). Addressing sustainability gaps. *The Science of the Total Environment, 806*, 151208.

Rizkallah, S. (2022). L'indépendance de la BDL Et Les Déterminants de la Crise Économique au Liban. *La Revue Internationale des Économistes de Langue Française, 7*(2), 9–31.

Romano, O., & Akhmouch, A. (2019). Water governance in cities: Current trends and future challenges. *Water (Basel), 11*(3), 500.

Rosenbaum, R. A., & Kehdy, J. F. (2022). Cultivating circular economies in the gaps of governance: Lessons from Lebanon's ecosystem of CE micro projects. *Local Environment, 27*(10-11), 1304–1320.

Ruiz-Real, J. L., Uribe-Toril, J., De Pablo Valenciano, J., & Gázquez-Abad, J. C. (2018). Worldwide research on circular economy and environment: A bibliometric analysis. *International Journal of Environmental Research and Public Health, 15*(12), 2699.

Ruohomaa, H., & Ivanova, N. (2019, November). From solid waste management towards the circular economy and digital driven symbiosis. [). IOP Publishing.]. *IOP Conference Series. Earth and Environmental Science, 337*(1), 012032.

Salvioni, D., & Almici, A. (2020). Circular economy and stakeholder engagement strategy. *Symphonya*, *1*, 26–44.

Savini, F. (2019). The economy that runs on waste: Accumulation in the circular city. *Environment and Planning A. Economy and Space*, *51*(3), 1–15.

Scottish Parliament. (2024). *Circular Economy (Scotland) Act 2024*. Retrieved from https://www.legislation.gov.uk/asp/2024/2/contents SCP/RAC. (2020). Success Stories on Circular Economy in the Mediterranean: Case Studies from Jordan, Tunisia, Egypt and Lebanon. Regional Activity Centre for Sustainable Consumption and Production.

Sehnem, S., Lopes de Sousa Jabbour, A. B., Conceição, D. A. D., Weber, D., & Julkovski, D. J. (2021). The role of ecological modernization principles in advancing circular economy practices: Lessons from the brewery sector. *Benchmarking*, *28*(9), 2786–2807.

Shibli, R. (2014). *Reconfiguring relief mechanisms: The Syrian refugee crisis in Lebanon*. Refugee Research and Policy in the Arab World.

Sitra. (2019). *Tackling root causes: Halving Finland's carbon footprint with circular economy*. Finnish Innovation Fund Sitra. Retrieved from https://www.sitra.fi/en/publications/tackling-root-causes/

Solomon, N. O., Simpa, P., Adenekan, O. A., & Obasi, S. C. (2024). Circular economy principles and their integration into global supply chain strategies. *Finance & Accounting Research Journal*, *6*(5), 747–762.

Stel, N. (2013). Diaspora versus refugee the political economy of Lebanese entrepreneurship regimes.

Supanut, A., Maisak, R., & Ratchatakulpat, T. (2024). Circular economy strategies in practice: A qualitative examination of industry adaptation and innovation. *Rev. Gestão Soc. Engenharia Ambiental*, *18*, e06723.

Tahulela, A. C., & Ballard, H. H. (2019). Developing the circular economy in South Africa: Challenges and opportunities. In Ghosh, S. K. (Ed.), *Sustainable waste management: Policies and case studies* (pp. 125–133). Springer., DOI: 10.1007/978-981-13-7071-7_11

Tr n, T. V., Phan, T. H., Lê, A. T. T., & Tr n, T. M. (2022). Evaluation of factors affecting the transition to a circular economy (CE) in Vietnam by structural equation modeling (SEM). *Sustainability*, *14*(2), 613.

UNDP. (2022). *Integrating the circular economy in Lebanon's local governance: Pilot initiatives and lessons learned.* United Nations Development Programme.

UNEP. (2021). *Measuring circularity: Indicators for a circular economy transition.* United Nations Environment Programme.

UNIDO. (2020). *Eco-industrial parks: Achieving the circular economy through industrial symbiosis.* United Nations Industrial Development Organization.

Velenturf, A. P., & Purnell, P. (2021). Principles for a sustainable circular economy. *Sustainable Production and Consumption, 27*, 1437–1457.

Wiedenhofer, D., Streeck, J., Wieland, H., Grammer, B., Baumgart, A., Plank, B., & Krausmann, F. (2024). From extraction to end-uses and waste management: Modeling economy-wide material cycles and stock dynamics around the world. *Journal of Industrial Ecology, 28*(6), 1464–1480.

Wiedenhofer, D., Streeck, J., Wieland, H., Grammer, B., Baumgart, A., Plank, B., & Krausmann, F. (2024). From extraction to end-uses and waste management: Modeling economy-wide material cycles and stock dynamics around the world. *Journal of Industrial Ecology, 28*(6), 1464–1480.

Wilts, H., Von Gries, N., & Bahn-Walkowiak, B. (2016). From waste management to resource efficiency—The need for policy mixes. *Sustainability, 8*(7), 622.

World Bank. (2021a). *Enabling the business of agriculture 2021: Lebanon profile.* World Bank Group.

World Bank. (2021b). *Lebanon Economic Monitor: The Deliberate Depression.* World Bank Group.

Yunis, M., El-Kassar, A. N., & Tarhini, A. (2017). Impact of ICT-based innovations on organizational performance: The role of corporate entrepreneurship. *Journal of Enterprise Information Management, 30*(1), 122–141.

Zero Waste Scotland. (2014). *The Role of Local Authorities in a Circular Economy: Scotland's Zero Waste Taskforce Report.* Retrieved from https://www.zerowastescotland.org.uk/resources/role-local-authorities-circular-economy

Zero Waste Scotland. (2023, October). *Building a circular ecosystem for Scottish businesses: Supporting businesses on their circular economy journey.* Zero Waste Scotland.

Zero Waste Scotland. (n.d.-a). *What is the Circular Economy?* Retrieved May 14, 2025, from https://www.zerowastescotland.org.uk/circular-economy

Zhidebekkyzy, A., Moldabekova, A., Amangeldiyeva, B., & Šanova, P. (2023). Transition to a circular economy: Exploring stakeholder perspectives in Kazakhstan. *Journal of International Students, 16*(3).

1 *GIZ (Deutsche Gesellschaft für Internationale Zusammenarbeit) is a German development agency that provides technical assistance, policy advice, and capacity-building support for sustainable development on behalf of the German Federal Government.*

2 *Donor contributions to circular economy initiatives in Lebanon have included grants for municipal pilot projects, technical assistance, and startup incubation programs.*

3 *These dashboards often include real-time analytics on funding, impact, and geographical distribution of circular enterprises.*

Chapter 3
Introduction to Circular Business Models (CBMs): Definition, Evolution, and Key Principles

Fatme El Zahraa Mahmoud Rahal
https://orcid.org/0000-0001-8666-0146
Islamic University of Lebanon, Lebanon

Aliaa Al Dirani
Islamic University of Lebanon, Lebanon

ABSTRACT

The circular economy has emerged as a compelling alternative to the traditional linear "take-make-dispose" economic model, gaining significant traction across academia, industry, and policymaking (Geissdoerfer et al., 2020). This shift is primarily driven by an increasing awareness of the environmental impacts associated with linear systems, especially the rapid depletion of resources and growing waste production (Henry et al., 2020). At the heart of this transformation, circular business models offer innovative solutions that decouple economic growth from resource depletion by prioritizing closed-loop systems and enhancing resource efficiency (Adam et al., 2017).In this section, the chapter will define circular economy business model (CEBM) in precise terms. The circular business model notion is based on two underlying concepts: the circular economy and business model innovation. This section will introduce the circular economy, business model innovation and circular business models topics. The researchers will conduct a literature review of the circular business models.

DOI: 10.4018/979-8-3373-7655-4.ch003

INTRODUCTION

The growing depletion of natural resources, intensified by the anticipated rise in global population to 9 billion by 2050, drove the demand for an economic model that prioritizes resource efficiency and effectiveness (Arruda et al., 2021; Ellen MacArthur Foundation, 2015). Environmental degradation, including ecological imbalance, biodiversity loss, and scarcity of raw materials, has destabilized the market dynamics and raised concerns about the long-term economic and environmental sustainability (Arruda et al., 2021). In this context, the Circular Economy has gained a global momentum as a paradigm to tackle these complex and intertwined economic, environmental, and social challenges (Montag, 2023; Korhonen et al., 2018).

The circular economy promotes a systemic shift from the conventional linear "take-make-dispose" model towards a regenerative model of closed-loop systems prioritizing resource efficiency, minimizing generated waste, and retaining value throughout a product's life cycle (Nußholz, 2017). In contrast to linear models that often discard the material value after one use, circular economy practices focus on preserving and extending the lifecycle of the resource through activities such as reuse, recycling, repair, and remanufacturing (Geissdoerfer et al., 2020; Ellen MacArthur Foundation, 2015). This shift holds significant advantages, with projections indicating that implementing CE principles could yield substantial economic savings amounting to hundreds of billions of dollars for the European Union, while also substantially reducing environmental degradation (WEF et al., 2014).

The transition to a circular economy relies on four key building blocks: sustainable product and material design, global reverse logistics networks, supportive regulatory frameworks, and new innovative business models (Ellen MacArthur Foundation, 2015). Among these, the design and implementation of Circular Business Models (CBMs) are particularly crucial. CBMs serve as the practical, micro-level operationalization of circularity and are instrumental in translating CE principles into practices across various sectors at the firm level (Nußholz, 2017; Montag, 2023). CBMs are designed to integrate economic value creation with environmental sustainability by enhancing resource efficiency and minimizing material waste across the product's lifecycle.

In recent years, CEBMs have gained growing interest from academics, policymakers, and industrial professionals (Nußholz, 2017). However, despite this increasing interest, there is still a lack of conceptual clarity and definitional consensus around CEBMs. The concept is relatively new and represents a fusion of two distinct fields: traditional business models, which describe value creation and delivery mechanisms; and circular economy strategies, which originate from the resource efficiency field (Montag, 2023; Nußholz, 2017). The integration of these two fields is still in its infancy stages, resulting in ambiguities in defining what makes a business model circular, which elements are fundamental, and how CEBMs can be systematically distinguished from a traditional linear business model.

The lack of a theoretical framework has adverse practical implications. This ambiguity creates obstacles for firms, including effective design, implementation, and scaling circular business models. Likewise, policy making and academic research struggle to formulate consistent typologies or frameworks that support practical implementation or guide future academic explorations (Montag, 2023). Bridging this gap is vital for enabling the transition toward a more circular and sustainable economic system.

To address this gap, this chapter seeks to systematize existing knowledge on Circular Business Models by exploring their historical evolution, definitions, key principles, and typologies. Drawing on a review of peer-reviewed literature, supplemented with snowballing and gray literature, this chapter consolidates fragmented knowledge and provides a cohesive overview of the CEBM field.

HISTORICAL AND CONCEPTUAL EVOLUTION OF CIRCULAR ECONOMY AND CIRCULAR BUSINESS MODELS

This section traces the evolution of Circular Economy as a conceptual and practical economic model, beginning with its roots in industrial ecology to its prominence in today's global policy and business practices. It highlights how Circular Business Models have emerged as a proactive strategic response to address the shortcomings of the traditional linear economic model.

History of the Circular Business Model (CBM) Concept

The concept of the Circular Economy Business Model (CEBM) emerged decades after the Circular Economy (CE). The first known use of the term "circular economy business model" appears in the work of Schwager & Moser (2006), who explored specific business model types aimed at enabling circular value creation. However, the term remained relatively obscure until almost seven years when the concept reemerge and gain attention, driven by the increased global interest in Circular Economy promoted by influential organizations such as the Ellen MacArthur Foundation (EMF) and the World Economic Forum (WEF) (Geissdoerfer et al., 2020).

In 2013, scholar researchers like Rashid et al. and Schulte began to explicitly link business models and the adoption of Circular Economy principles. Rashid et al. (2013) argued that business models could address incentive alignment issues, which were hindering the adoption of advanced technologies capable of enabling circular practices such as large-scale recycling. Meanwhile, Schulte (2013) asserted that businesses should view circularity not merely as a resilience strategy, but as a novel approach to create value and generate revenue.

Since 2015, the interest in circular business models has gained strong momentum. The number of related studies increased dramatically, from 13 in 2016 to 38 in 2017 and reached 88 in 2018 (See Figure 1), reflecting a fast-paced growth and expansion in this area of research (Geissdoerfer et al., 2020).

Figure 1. Development of Circular Business Model Journal Articles and Reviews Published over Time.

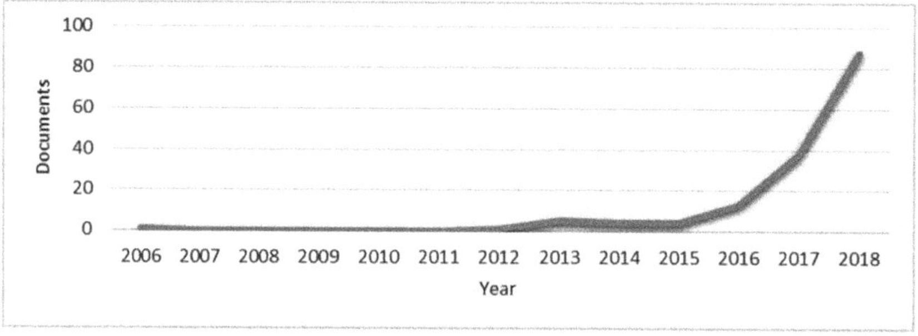

Source: Geissdoerfer et al., 2020

Despite being a relatively new and independent area of research, CEBM's core ideas have been found in several disciplines that existed before the formal CBMs conceptualization (Nußholz, 2017). Foundational concepts like *Cradle-to-Cradle* design (McDonough & Braungart, 2002) and *Performance Economy* (Stahel, 2010) embedded circular principles into economic and product design logics. In the 1990s, *Product-Service System* (PSS) was introduced as an environmentally driven approach to service-based value creation (Mont, 2002; Tukker, 2004), later evolving toward economic advantages through servitization (Baines et al., 2009). *Sustainable Business Model Innovation* (SBMI) a business model theory matured in the 2000s paved the way to develop a new concept, where CBMs were framed as models that transform waste into environmental and economic value (Lüdeke-Freund & Dembek, 2017; Wirtz et al., 2016; Bocken et al., 2014). Nußholz (2017) recognized CBMs as an emerging but independent field, while other reviews, such as (Annarelli et al., 2016; Tukker, 2015), reaffirmed PSS's environmental roots within circular economy discussions. In recent years, advancements in digitalization have become instrumental in enabling CBMs with technologies like Internet of Things (IoT), predictive maintenance, and data analytics, transforming business models to align with circular economy principles (Parida et al., 2019; Bressanelli et al., 2018).

Evolution Overview

Industrial transformations, such as the envisaged shift towards the Circular Economy (CE), are fundamentally about understanding the logic and mechanisms behind radical systemic change. As a transformative force, the CE necessitates a focus on its dynamic and evolving nature, an analysis that requires a systems perspective.

The term "evolutionary" is used to explain the characteristics of "the movement of something over time, or to explain why that something is what it is at a moment in time in terms of how it got there; that is, the analysis is expressly dynamic. Second, the explanation involves both random elements which generate or renew some variation in the variables in question, and mechanisms that systematically winnow on extant variation" (Dosi & Nelson, 1993, p. 154).

The Circular Economy (CE) marks a significant shift away from the traditional linear economic model, which is rooted in resource-intensive practices, continual extraction and consumption of resources, leading to environmental degradation and resource depletion. Originating during the Industrial Revolution in the 17th century, the linear model was driven by exploitative scientific and technological advancements that focused on maximizing production, often at the expense of the environment and without consideration for the long-term consequences for society (Prieto-Sandoval et al., 2018).

In response to these unsustainable practices, the CE offers a transformative shift from the linear "take-make-dispose" approach to a regenerative system focused on resource efficiency and waste minimization (See Figure 2). The CE is generally described as a continuous cycle involving the take (i.e., extraction), transformation, distribution, use, and recovery of goods and materials (Park et al., 2010; Stahel, 2010). Initially, firms extract resources from the environment to create products and services. These are then distributed to consumers or businesses and used within the market.

Nevertheless, unlike the linear model, the CE emphasizes closing the loop at the end of the product lifecycle (See Figure 2). Rather than discarding used goods, the CE advocates for their recovery and reintegration into the production cycle. At this stage, innovation plays a crucial role in recovering and enhancing materials through environmental or industrial processes, thereby avoiding the growing waste production and extending resource value rather than depleting them (Prieto-Sandoval et al., 2018; Stahel, 2010).

Figure 2. Linear and Circular Economies in Simple Representation

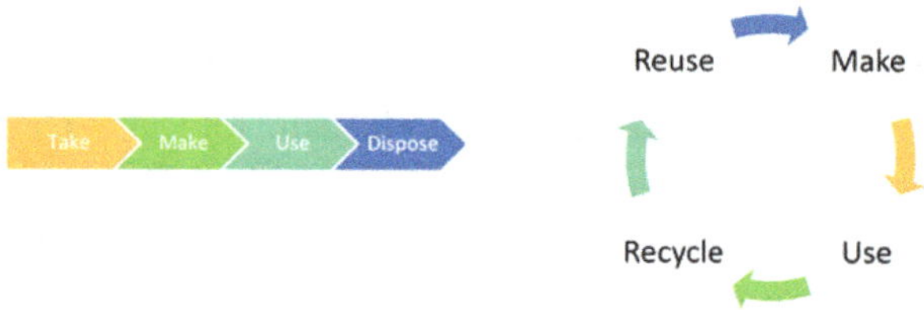

Linear Economy **Circular Economy**

The dichotomy between linear and circular economy models reflects a fundamental shift in approaches to sustainability and resource management (see Table 1). The linear economy follows a "take, make, dispose" model, characterized by a product-centric focus and a fundamental notion of disposability. In this model, resources such as materials and energy are extracted, transformed into products, and eventually discarded. Although the linear model incorporates elements of eco-efficiency, it inherently fails to achieve true circularity due to its structural reliance on disposability and product ownership. This orientation contributes to resource depletion, environmental degradation and raises questions about the model's long-term viability (Dabija & Năstase, 2024).

While sustainability within the linear paradigm is often framed as the ability to sustain economic growth and resource use without compromising the needs of future generations, its dependence on finite inputs and consistent waste generation undermines achieving this objective (Iagăru et al., 2023). The inherent limitations of the linear model demand a re-evaluation of its role in achieving sustainable development.

In contrast, the circular economy represents a regenerative framework that shifts the focus from one-time product consumption to recurring service-based systems. This model emphasizes continuous resource circulation and the regeneration of materials within a closed-loop system. By minimizing waste, optimizing resource efficiency, and promoting environmental restoration, the circular economy seeks to enhance the eco-efficiency of products and systems (Dabija & Năstase, 2024).

Through its emphasis on material circulation and regenerative practices, the circular model provides a more holistic and viable approach to sustainable development. It fosters long-term ecological balance and economic resilience by implementing cost-effective strategies aimed at restoring and regenerating natural capital (Calisto Friant et al., 2020; Morseletto, 2020). Thus, the circular economy emerges as a compelling alternative to the traditional linear model, aligning more closely with the principles of sustainability and environmental stewardship.

Table 1. Overview of Linear Versus Circular Economy Model Concepts

	Linear	Circular
Step plan	"Take- make – dispose"	3 Rs – 4 Rs – 9Rs – 10 Rs
System boundaries	Short term	Long-term
Focus	Eco-Efficiency	Eco-Effectivity
Business model	Emphasis on products	Emphasis on services
Reuse	Downcycling	Upcycling
Goal	Profitability	Sustainability
Value creation	Manufacturing products	Preserving products

Adapted from Dabija & Năstase (2024)

Circular Economy Levels

There is broad consensus in the literature that the Circular Economy (CE) is characterized by three distinct levels of research and implementation: micro, meso, and macro; each reflecting a different analytical scope. (See Figure 3)

Figure 3. Circular Economy Levels Representation

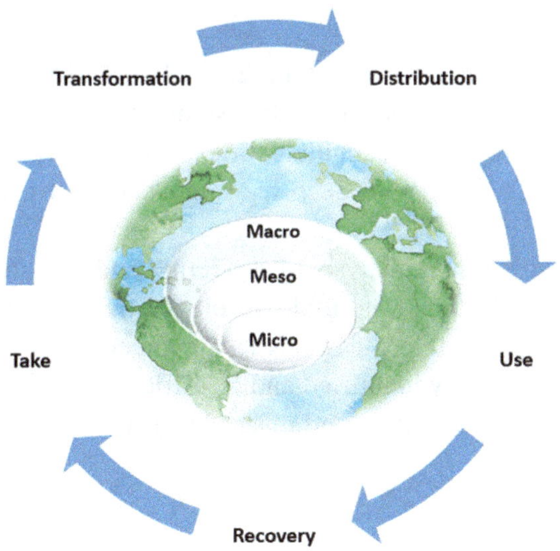

Adapted from (Prieto-Sandoval et al., 2018)

i. **Micro Level:** At this level, the focus is on the individual actors like enterprises, products/services, and consumers. Studies related to the micro level either examine how firms improve their internal processes and enhance their eco-innovation (e.g., Chen et al., 2020; Moreau et al., 2017; Park et al., 2010) or investigate consumer behavior and preferences in relation to circular practices (e.g., Kuokkanen & Sun, 2020; Bundgaard & Huulgaard, 2019; Sauvé et al., 2016; Ghisellini et al., 2016). As per Ormazabal et al. (2016), there is a positive correlation between a company's environmental management maturity level and its willingness to implement CE because of the positive impact it has on its reputation among consumers and the associated reductions in cost.
ii. **Meso Level:** This intermediate level focuses on collaborative efforts among companies engaged in industrial symbiosis, enabling resource sharing and waste reduction that benefit both the regional economy and the surrounding environment (Geng et al., 2012). At this scale, local policies and coordinated actions play a critical role in fostering collaboration and enhancing infrastructure sustainability (e.g., Frei et al., 2020; Baldassarre et al., 2019; Govindan & Hasanagic, 2018; Pan et al., 2015; Li, 2011).
iii. **Macro Level:** At this level, the circular economy is examined through a broader environmental policy and institutional lens, focusing on how national and global policies shape industrial structures and support long-term sustainability transitions

(McDowall et al., 2017; Winans et al., 2017; Jiao & Boons, 2014; Sakai et al., 2011; Yong, 2007). Research at this scale also emphasizes the implementation of circular principles across cities, municipalities, and even entire nations, with initiatives such as the development of eco-cities and eco-provinces (Prieto-Sandoval et al., 2018).

Drawing on an extensive analysis of academic and grey literature, Saidani et al. (2019) systematically reviewed tools developed by scholars, consulting firms, and governmental agencies to measure the implementation of circular economy (CE) principles. Their study identified and classified 55 distinct sets of circularity indicators across the micro, meso, and macro levels (See Table 2).

Table 2. Classification of 55 Circular Economy Indicators (C-Indicators) across Micro, Meso, and Macro Levels

Level	Circular Economy Indicators
Micro	Assessing Circular Trade-offs (ACT)
	Building Circularity Indicators (BCI)
	Material Reutilization Part (C2C)
	Circle Assessment (CA)
	Circularity Assessment Tool (CAT)
	Circular Benefits Tool (CBT)
	Circularity Calculator (CC)
	Circular Economy Company Assessment Criteria (CECAC)
	Circular Economy Indicator Prototype (CEIP)
	Circular Economy Performance Indicator (CEPI)
	Circular Economy Toolkit (CET)
	Circular Economy Toolbox US (CETUS)
	Circular Economic Value (CEV)
	Circularity Index (CI)
	Circular Pathfinder (CP)
	Circularity Potential Indicator (CPI)
	Super-efficiency DEA Model
	Eco-efficient Value Ratio (EVR)
	Hybrid LCA Model (HLCAM)
	Circularity Indicator Project (ICT)
	Indicators for Eco-design for CE in Europe (IECEE)
	Material Circularity Indicator (MCI)
	Product-Level Circularity Metric (PCM)
	Resource Duration Indicator (RDI)
	Recycling Indices (RIs) for the CE
	Reuse Potential Indicator (RPI)
	Sustainable Circular Index (SCI)
	Value-based Resource Efficiency (VRE)
Meso	Industrial Park Circular Economy
	Evaluation of Regional CE (ERCE)*
	Measuring Regional CE–Eco-Innovation (MRCEEI)*
	Regional CE Development Index (RCEDI)*

continued on following page

Table 2. Continued

Level	Circular Economy Indicators
Macro	Circular Economy Indicators for India (CEII)
	Circular Economy Monitoring Framework (CEMF)
	Circular Impacts Project EU (CIPEU)
	Evaluation of CE Development in Cities (ECEDC)
	Evaluation Indicator System of CE (EISCE)
	Indicators for Material Input for CE in Europe (IMCEE)
	End-of-Life Recycling Rates (EoL-RRs)
	Environmental Protection Indicators in CE Context (EPICE)
	Economy-Wide Material Flow Analysis (EWMFA)
	Five Category Index Method (FCIM)
	Indicators for Consumption for CE in Europe (ICCEE)
	Indicators of Economic Circularity in France (IECF)
	Integrative Evaluation on CE Development (IEDCE)
	Input-Output Balance Sheet (IOBS)
	Indicators for Production for CE in Europe (IPCEE)
	National Circular Economy Indicator System (NCEIS)
	Resource Efficiency Scoreboard (RES)
	Resource Productivity (RP)
	Recycling Rates (RRs)
	Zero Waste Index (ZWI)
	Evaluation of Regional CE (ERCE)*
	Measuring Regional CE–Eco-Innovation (MRCEEI)*
	Regional CE Development Index (RCEDI)*

* relevant at both meso and macro levels
Adapted from Saidani et al. (2019)

Circular Economy Stages

The concept of the Circular Economy has evolved through a multidisciplinary approach, drawing insights from ecology, engineering, design, economics, and business. Its development can be broadly categorized into three main historical stages, each of which has contributed to shaping the modern Circular Economy framework.

The first stage, known as the linear economy, emerged during the onset of the Industrial Revolution and was marked by the overexploitation of natural resources (Prieto-Sandoval et al., 2018). This era was characterized by a "take-make-dispose" model, involving intensive resource extraction, mass production, and the generation of vast amounts of waste, with little regard for environmental impacts. This model remained largely unchallenged until the 1960s, when growing concern for environmental issues sparked a wave of critical reflection, influenced by the work of prominent scholars. Notably, Rachel Carson's *Silent Spring* (Carson, 1962) highlighted the ecological damage resulting from industrial activity, catalyzing environmental awareness. Later on, the American economist Kenneth Boulding (1966) introduced the contrasting concepts of the "cowboy economy," whose success measure was production and consumption based on the assumption of unlimited resource use, and the "spaceman economy" which conceptualized the earth as a closed ecological system capable of recycling limited resources. In his works, "The economics of the coming spaceship earth", Boulding acknowledges the resource challenges society might face in the future: "Earth has become a single spaceship, without unlimited resources of anything [...], therefore, man must find his place in a cyclical ecological system" (Boulding, 2013, p. 7). These ideas laid the intellectual foundation for circular thinking by emphasizing the necessity of closed-loop systems and sustainable resource management.

The second stage, commonly referred to as the industrial ecology–metabolism metaphor, began in the late 1960s and extended through the 1980s (Chizaryfard et al., 2021; Prieto-Sandoval et al., 2018). This period represented a pivotal shift in both theoretical and practical approaches to industrial development, as scholars increasingly acknowledged the ecological and economic constraints inherent in traditional industrial systems. The field of industrial ecology was established during this era, with foundational contributions by Ayres & Kneese (1969), and later expanded by (Ayres, 1989), who introduced the concept of *industrial metabolism*. This framework posited that industrial systems could emulate the functioning of biological ecosystems by promoting the cyclical flow of materials and waste among interconnected actors, thereby enhancing resource efficiency and mitigating environmental impacts.

Several other influential contributions further shaped milestones in the development of the circular economy concept. Georgescu-Roegen (2011) introduced the entropy law, drawing attention to the irreversible degradation of materials and energy in economic processes. Similarly, Meadows et al. (1972), in *Limits to Growth*, underscored the unsustainability of unrestrained economic and population growth. Ward & Dubo (1983), in *Only One Earth*, also advocated for a fundamental reconsideration of conventional growth-oriented economic paradigms, thereby laying the conceptual foundation for the emergence of alternative, environmentally conscious economic models.

In line with these evolving perspectives, the United Nations Environment Programme (UNEP) later defined a green economy as one "that results in improved human well-being and social equity, while significantly reducing environmental risks and ecological scarcities" (UNEP, 2011, p. 5). Although the green economy has since become integral to the environmental strategies of various governments and international institutions, it has faced criticism for predominantly promoting *weak sustainability*. This approach is characterized by the assumption that economic capital can substitute for natural and human capital, thereby avoiding substantial structural changes to linear production and consumption systems. Consequently, weak sustainability often entails only marginal adjustments in societal behaviors and lifestyle patterns (Loiseau et al., 2016).

The third and final stage marks the formalization and subsequent expansion of the circular economy (CE) concept, beginning in the 1990s. Drawing upon Boulding's ecological insights, British environmental economists David Pearce and R. Kerry Turner (1990) introduced the term "circular economy" in their seminal work *Natural Resource and Environmental Economics* (Pearce & Turner, 1990). In this work, they conceptualized economic systems that incorporate environmental considerations by closing the loops of production and consumption (Xue et al., 2010). As noted by Chizaryfard et al. (2021), during the early 2000s, the circular economy framework began to integrate a range of complementary theories and concepts. These included regenerative design (Lyle, 1994), the performance economy (Stahel, 1982, 2010; Stahel & Reday, 1976), cradle-to-cradle design (McDonough & Braungart, 2002), and the laws of ecology (Commoner, 1971). Collectively, these approaches emphasized the need to maintain the value of resources for as long as possible, reinforcing the principles of resource efficiency and system resilience (Prieto-Sandoval et al., 2018).

In the past decade, the circular economy has evolved into a comprehensive, interdisciplinary framework, garnering increasing attention in academic, policy, and industrial domains. Scholars such as (Korhonen et al., 2018; Geissdoerfer et al., 2017; Murray et al., 2017; Bocken et al., 2016) have critically examined its theoretical foundations, contributing to the development of a more coherent and systematic understanding of CE. Their work has helped to position the circular economy as a transformative paradigm aimed at redefining value creation by decoupling economic activity from the consumption of finite resources.

DEFINITIONS OF CIRCULAR ECONOMY AND CIRCULAR BUSINESS MODEL

This section provides a comprehensive review of the definitions of Circular Economy and Business Models found in academic and gray literature. It pinpoints areas of consensus and divergence, examining how various definitions shape the understanding, scope, and objectives of circularity.

Defining Circular Business Models

Nowadays, businesses are attempting to operate in sustainable ways amidst environmental challenges and resource limitations. Circular Business Models (CBMs) are a well-known approach that supports sustainability. The primary aim of these initiatives is to transition from the traditional "take-make-dispose" economic system to a more sustainable and regenerative approach to business. This article incorporates the definition of Circular Business Models, the explanation of their principles, their functions, and their benefits for the environment, economy, and society.

Understanding the Circular Economy

It is noteworthy to mention the broader concept of the Circular Business Models in the Circular Economy (CE). By definition, the Circular Economy (CE) is an economic system that attempts to eliminate waste and the continual use of resources. Contrary to the linear model, which is based on extraction, production, consumption, and disposal, the circular economy works in loops. It reduces resource use, reuses materials, and recycles products at the end of their life cycle (Korhonen et al., 2018).

It can be said that the CE can be a dual-loop restorative system that sheds light on keeping both technical and biological materials in use for a long period. To elaborate more, food or organic materials are biological materials that can safely re-enter the eco-friendly environmental system. However, plastics, metals, and electronics are technical items that can be recovered, reused, or recycled without causing harm to the environment.

What is a Circular Business Model?

The Circular Business Model is a business strategy that incorporates the concept and principles of the sustainable economy. Korhonen et al. (2018) defined circular business models as a paradigm in which a business uses innovation and creation to produce, generate, distribute, and collect value by enhancing the efficiency of resources and extending the life of products and materials. The primary aim here is to provide the advantages for society, the environment, and the economy.

Lewandowski (2016) considers CBMs as business models that develop strategies such as reuse, repair, refurbishing, remanufacturing, recycling, and resource recovery into their core value proposition and operations. Their goal is to boost the efficiency of resources, extend product lifecycles, and minimize waste, thus enhancing both business resilience and sustainability (Tukker, 2015; Bocken et al., 2016).

Circular Business Models (CBMs) are a transformative approach that helps organizations create and offer value while reducing environmental impact by implementing circularity principles. They diverge from traditional linear business models that follow a "take-make-dispose" logic that leads to resource depletion and waste generation. On the other hand, CBMs keep products, components, and materials at their highest usage and value for a long time, which helps in decoupling the economic growth from resource consumption and environmental degradation (Geissdoerfer et al., 2017; Ellen MacArthur Foundation, 2013).

Circular Business Models (CBMs) are innovative frameworks that allow companies to create and offer high value by implementing the principles of the circular economy into their core operations. CBMs focus on closing, slowing, narrowing, intensifying, and dematerializing resource loops to reduce waste generation and dependence on virgin materials, whereas traditional linear business models follow a "take-make-dispose" logic characterized by resource extraction, production, consumption, and disposal (Geissdoerfer et al., 2020; Bocken et al., 2016). Fundamentally, CBMs are created to keep products, elements, and materials in use at their highest value by recovering and regenerating resources at the end of their lifecycle.

The core of CBMs lies in operationalizing the broader notion of the Circular Economy (CE), which is inspired by natural systems characterized by closed-loop cycles where waste is minimized and continually reintroduced as input into new production processes (Korhonen et al., 2018). Based on CBMS, it is a product that can be recovered and used again, rather than viewing waste as an endpoint. This encourages the restorative and regenerative economic activities (Bocken et al., 2016; Geissdoerfer et al., 2017).

The Shift from Linear to Circular Models

The dominant linear economic model was established since the Industrial Revolution. It relies heavily on the extraction of raw materials, manufacturing, consumption, and subsequent disposal of products. This approach depletes finite resources and leads to environmental degradation through waste, pollution, and greenhouse gas emissions (Sterev, 2019; Kirchherr et al., 2017). However, CBMs challenge this paradigm by reshaping the creation and sustainability of value.

Circular business models focus on closing, slowing, narrowing, intensifying, and dematerializing resource loops, which are the key mechanisms that help in achieving sustainability and resource efficiency. Closing loops include recycling materials to avoid waste. Indeed, slowing loops emphasize the extent of product life through maintenance and repair. Additionally, narrowing loops can reduce resource inputs per unit of value created. Intensifying loops promote maximizing the utility derived from products. Dematerializing includes shifting from physical products to services (Bocken et al., 2016; Geissdoerfer et al., 2020).

Unlike traditional business models, CBMs focus not just on profits, but also on reducing environmental impact, engaging stakeholders, and regenerating natural systems. They require businesses to rethink how they design products, manage resources, engage with customers, and create value.

CBMs are based on three key principles of the circular economy (Ellen MacArthur Foundation, 2013):

- **Design out waste and pollution**
- **Keep products and materials in use**
- **Restoring natural systems**

These principles guide businesses in developing innovative approaches to production, consumption, and end-of-life management.

1. **Key characteristics of Circular Business Models include**:
    - **Product Life Extension:** Products are created to last for a long time through maintenance, repair, recycling, and restoration. This prevents them from entering the waste systems and keeps them in use (Michelini et al., 2017).
    - **Resource Recovery:** Waste and end-of-life items can be collected and transformed into new products. As a result, fewer virgin resources are needed, effectively closing the material loop (Geissdoerfer et al., 2017; Bag et al., 2021).
    - **Product-as-a-Service (PaaS):** CBMs are moving away from traditional ownership of goods toward service-oriented models in which customers pay for the use of the product rather than its real cost. To maintain their value over time, companies are encouraged by this development to produce solid, durable, repairable, and adaptable goods (Michelini et al., 2017; Sterev, 2019).
    - **Collaboration Across Value Chains:** CBMs rely on networks of suppliers, consumers, recyclers, and producers who work together through value chains. Such cooperation promotes innovation by maximizing the utilization of resources and enabling closed-loop systems (Sterev, 2019; Susur & Engwall, 2022).
    - **Circular Supply Chains:** Management from manufacturing to final stages, efficiency is supported, and the effect on the environment is reduced by acquiring sustainable, recyclable, and eco-friendly materials from the beginning. (Bag et al., 2021).

The successful implementation of CBMs needs systemic change that goes beyond product redesign. Companies must innovate their value propositions, create new partnerships along the value chain, and cultivate deeper relationships with customers oriented toward sustainability and resource efficiency (Montag, 2023). Moreover, supportive regulatory frameworks, technological advancements, and shifts in consumer behavior are vital in overcoming obstacles like technological limitations, market acceptance, and policy misalignment.

Furthermore, CBMs offer a promising pathway to align business growth with sustainability goals. They reduce environmental impacts, such as waste generation and resource depletion, and open new economic opportunities. By optimizing resource use and innovating service models, companies can generate cost savings, diversify revenue streams, and strengthen brand reputation according to increasing stakeholder demands and regulatory pressures (Bocken et al., 2016; Montag, 2023).

At a conceptual level, CBMs change circular economy principles by promoting the progressive flow of materials within the economy to transform waste into valuable inputs for new production cycles (Nußholz, 2017). They represent a paradigm shift in how value is perceived and created. Thus, this helps in moving from linear consumption toward regenerative, restorative business practices that foster long-term resilience and environmental stewardship.

2. The Role of Innovation

Innovation is at the heart of Circular Business Models. Businesses have to reshape their products and services to be more sustainable. This includes using digital technologies, like the Internet of Things (IoT), data analytics, and blockchain to track products, manage resources, and optimize performance. For instance, sensors can detect how a machine is used and predict when it needs maintenance, which extends its life. Blockchain can help track materials through a supply chain, ensuring transparency and accountability in recycling and reuse.

Innovation also involves developing new business models, like subscription services, buy-back programs, or repair-and-refurbishment offerings that provide customers with more sustainable choices while maintaining or even increasing profitability.

CBMs can emerge through multiple routes, according to Susur and Engwall (2022):

1. **Transformation of Linear Models:** To engage circular strategies like extending the life of products and logistics reversal, current linear products are changed.
2. **Improvement of Existing CBMs:** Organizations with a circular mindset reinforce their circularity programs and initiatives further.

3. **Creation of New CBMs:** New business models are created from scratch, integrating the concepts and principles of the circular economy into their basis.

Implementing CBMs needs a holistic redesign of the whole business model that includes value creation, delivery, and capture mechanisms (Geissdoerfer et al., 2017). This redesign typically involves:

- Eco-design principles that promote durability, sustainability, and recyclability.
- Systems of reverse distribution that facilitate the recovery of materials, renovation of products, and take-back operations.
- Innovative customer interaction models such as sharing platforms, renting, emphasize access over ownership, and subscription services (Sterev, 2019; Bocken et al., 2016).

Organizational Planning and Stakeholder Engagement

Implementing a CBM is not just about changing products. It requires a complete shift in how a business operates, and this includes the following:

- o Strategic planning that incorporates the goals of sustainability.
- o Incorporating stakeholders such as customers, suppliers, employees, and the local community.
- o Encouraging the behavior of change by educating consumers about the importance of circular offerings.

According to the literature, businesses must align their value creation, delivery, and capture strategies with circular principles. This involves understanding flows of economic resources, such as how materials move through production and consumption systems, and identifying points where waste can be reduced or reused (Korhonen et al., 2018).

Benefits of Circular Business Models

a. Environmental Benefits

CBMs reduce pollution, waste, and emissions. These approaches help in addressing climate change, minimizing the demand for raw materials, and protecting the diversity by recycling resources and restoring natural systems.

b. Economic Benefits and Financial Gains

CBMs offer new opportunities for businesses and income sources. For example, companies can benefit from recycled resources, restored products, or service subscriptions. By using fewer components and spending less on eliminating waste, they can also save costs.

c. Social Benefits

Circular models promote social equity by creating jobs in recycling, refurbishment, and repair. They can also minimize the environmental harm to people by sharing models and increasing access to goods and services.

Challenges and Future Directions

Despite their potential, CBMs face several challenges and encounter several difficulties:

- **Consumer behavior**: A lot of people are used to buying products and then throwing them away. Motivation and education are important when shifting to use-based and service-based approaches.
- **Infrastructure**: Recycling and recovery systems may not be well developed in all areas.
- **Measurement and accountability**: It can be challenging to evaluate circular performance or make sure that procedures are sustainable.
- **Policy and regulation**: Circularity should be encouraged and supported by governments through certain rules, standards, and policies.

Research suggests that future studies should focus on how digital transformation can support CBMs and how to better manage performance across environmental, social, and economic dimensions (Korhonen et al., 2018).

Strategic Importance and Systemic Perspective

The transition to Circular Business Models is environmentally and strategically important for businesses. Increasing regulatory pressures, shifting consumer preferences towards sustainable products and services, and growing resource scarcity all lead companies to adopt CBMs (Dadiana & Năstase, 2024; Bocken et al., 2016).

To further illustrate, CBMs offer organizations a plethora of benefits beyond sustainability, including cost savings through improved resource efficiency, new revenue streams via innovative services or secondary markets, and enhanced brand reputation by aligning with societal values around sustainability (Preghenella & Battistella, 2021). This alignment can create competitive advantages and open access to emerging markets focused on sustainable consumption.

However, the success of CBMs depends on systemic innovation. They do not work alone but require supportive policies. This allows the improvement of technological infrastructure and collaborative networks spanning sectors and stakeholders (Susur & Engwall, 2022). The successful transition involves not only firm-level changes but also coordinated efforts at the supply chain, industry, and policy levels to overcome barriers and scale circular practices (Korhonen et al., 2018).

Theoretical Foundations

The notion of circularity builds upon ecological economics, specifically Kenneth Boulding's notion of a "closed economy," where material flows are contained and cyclical (Sterev, 2019). The circular economy has risen in the 2010s as environmental limits became clearer and the necessity for sustainable development has increased (Ghisellini et al., 2016). CBMs translate this broader theoretical foundation into practical business strategies that operationalize circular principles at the firm level.

Circular Business Models are a powerful way to transform how businesses operate in a world facing ecological limits. By closing resource loops, extending product lifespans, and rethinking value creation, CBMs help businesses become more sustainable and resilient. They provide a pathway for companies to reduce their environmental impact and create economic and social value.

Implementing CBMs requires innovation, strong planning, and stakeholder collaboration, but the long-term rewards are significant. As the circular economy continues to grow and evolve, CBMs will play a vital role in shaping a sustainable future for both businesses and society.

Circular Business Models is a fundamental paradigm shift in business strategy that is away from the traditional, resource-intensive, linear economy toward regenerative, resource-efficient, and sustainable economic systems. By embedding circular principles, such as product life extension, resource recovery, and service-based delivery into their core operations, businesses can directly achieve environmental sustainability and economic resilience.

CBMs are essential in the broader circular economy transition so that they help organizations respond effectively to ecological limits, resource scarcity, and evolving stakeholder expectations. Including the need for systemic collaboration and innovation, CBMs offer bright routes and ways for businesses to survive in a world with few resources while making beneficial improvements to the environment and society.

Circular Business Models can offer companies the practical strategies to enrich economic viability with environmental sustainability. Through product life extension, resource recovery, service-based models, and circular supply chains, CBMs contribute to closing resource loops, reducing ecological footprints, and supporting the transition toward a more sustainable and resilient economic system.

Principles and Typologies of Circular Business Models

The final section explores the fundamental principles that characterize CEBMs and presents an overview of the major typologies used to classify and analyze the different strategies within CEBMs.

Through systematically reviewing and critically evaluating the existing body of knowledge, this chapter contributes to the conceptual understanding of Circular Economy Business Models and provides a foundation for future studies and practical implementation to promote sustainable development.

The final section explores the fundamental principles that characterize CEBMs and presents an overview of the major typologies used to classify and analyze the different strategies within CEBMs.

Circular Economy Business Models (CEBMs) were created to transform economic systems from the traditional linear "take-make-dispose" model to a regenerative principle that sheds light on sustainability and the efficiency of resources. The core value of CEBMs is obvious in having various principles that guide the design, implementation, and operation of businesses intending to implement circularity into their values. These fundamentals are important in creating value and resources and in promoting innovation and collaboration to stakeholders. Therefore, this cultivates a sustainable and resilient economic ecosystem.

To begin with, CEBM's main principle is designing out waste and pollution. This includes recreating products and process design from the outset to reduce environmental harm and eliminate waste generation. Products are characterized by durability, reparability, disassembly, modularity, and recyclability in mind to enable better recovery for material reuse (Ellen MacArthur Foundation, 2013; Montag, 2023). Companies can decrease their dependence on virgin resources, achieve low consumption of energy, and minimize pollution in the ecosystem by involving circular design strategies. As a result, this promotes economic growth (Geissdoerfer et al., 2017; Nußholz, 2017).

Furthermore, the principle of using products and materials aligns with the above concept. It is worth mentioning that CEBM's main in is to focus on increasing the usage and lifespan of products, components, and materials through the reuse, repair, refurbishment, remanufacturing, and sharing platforms strategies (Bocken et al., 2016; Sterev, 2019). This highlights the extension of product lifecycles to preserve the value of materials, decrease waste, and the need for extracting and processing new raw materials. Indeed, it has a role in developing closed-loop systems so that products that have less lifespan are collected, disassembled, and implemented again into the production cycles. Hence, this helps in closing material loops and improving resource efficiency (Geissdoerfer et al., 2018; Reike et al., 2022). Companies can minimize environmental effects when generating new revenue models and sharing economies by retaining value across multiple use cycles; thus, this successfully helps in boosting the economic value from material consumption (Korhonen et al., 2018).

Moreover, the third principle includes regenerating natural systems. It is a notion that goes beyond decreasing negative environmental effects to restore and enhance ecological health. CEBMs develop regenerative practices like returning organic matter to soils to improve biodiversity and implement renewable resources into production and supply chains (Ellen MacArthur Foundation, 2013; Geissdoerfer et al., 2017). This principle considers the finite nature of natural capital and the necessity of building a resilient ecosystem to affirm the availability of long-term resources. Companies have a role in the renewal of natural systems by supporting regeneration. This improves carbon sequestration, soil fertility, and environmental quality, which goes hand in hand with economic activities with planetary boundaries, and sustainable development goals (Susur & Engwall, 2022).

To further illustrate, resource efficiency and waste minimization are fundamental principles of the circular economy. This includes enhancing the utilization of materials and energy throughout the product lifecycle to decrease virgin resource extraction and waste generation (Geissdoerfer et al., 2017). Resource efficiency is accomplished through accurate selection of material, lean manufacturing, and progressive enhancement in production processes. This emphasizes the narrowing of material and energy flows. Considering waste streams as precious resources for reintegration into production underscores the transformation from waste disposal to resource recovery and reuse. This supports closed-loop systems (Ellen MacArthur Foundation, 2013; Geissdoerfer et al., 2020).

Moreover, adopting systemic thinking and collaboration is significant. Circularity alone cannot be accomplished; instead, it needs a clear understanding of the connection within and across value chains, sectors, and societal systems (Korhonen et al., 2018). CEBMs support multi-stakeholder engagement, involving suppliers, customers, policymakers, waste management companies, and competitors to implement innovation and share valuable opportunities. This type of cooperation improves the scaling of circular initiatives and helps in overcoming obstacles that are related to infrastructure, regulations, and market dynamics (Sterev, 2019; Ellen MacArthur Foundation, 2013). Also, systemic collaboration facilitates the alignment of business incentives with environmental and social goals to foster a collaborative responsibility for resource stewardship and circularity.

In addition, CEBMs ensure value retention and creation beyond products. Contrary to linear value that highlights the extraction through product sales, circular models attempt to preserve and improve value included in materials and products through many cycles. Therefore, this reduces value destruction linked with waste or obsolescence (Susur & Engwall, 2022; Reike et al., 2022). This principle challenges the traditional business mindset by developing other revenue models like product leasing, service-based offerings, and platform economies that offer results rather than ownership. When decoupling revenue from material throughput, businesses can boost the lifespan, resource efficiency, and customer engagement in circular practices.

To sum up, business model innovation and progressive experimentation are important to the development of CEBMs. The transformation to circularity needs several approaches to product development, supply chains, and customer relationships (Susur & Engwall, 2022). Companies need to discover and test new models that go hand in hand with circular principles, like closed-loop manufacturing, reverse logistics, and product-as-a-service offerings. This creative mindset supports adaptation to modern technologies, market needs, and regulatory landscapes to ensure that circular economy principles are sustainable.

All in all, the main principles of Circular Economy Business Models shed light on designing out waste and pollution to keep the use of products and materials, regenerate natural systems, enhance resource efficiency, foster systemic collaboration, retain and create value away from traditional product sales, and innovate business models. Altogether, these principles offer a comprehensive framework for reimagining economic activity in restorative and resilient ways that align with the laws of the environment and society. Consequently, companies have a role in the great transformation towards sustainable development and circularity.

Key Typologies of Circular Economy Business Models (CEBMs)

Circular Economy Business Models (CEBMs) are well-planned frameworks that allow businesses to move from the traditional linear "take-make-dispose" approach to regenerative systems where resource efficiency, waste elimination, and product longevity are considered a priority. The important typologies of CEBMs are synthesized from academic literature, industry reports, and leading frameworks (notably Bocken et al., 2016; Kirchherr et al., 2017; Ellen MacArthur Foundation, 2013; and recent research) and include the following:

1. **Circular Supply Models**

These models highlight sourcing renewable, recycled, recyclable, or biodegradable materials as inputs, reducing dependency on finite virgin resources. Companies can build sustainable production systems by replacing linear resource flows with circular supply chains. For example, fashion brands use recycled textiles, and packaging firms utilize plant-based or post-consumer recycled materials. Circular supply chains are important for closing material loops from the outset to ensure products are created to safely re-enter natural or industrial cycles at end-of-life.

2. **Product Life Extension Models**

These models aim to focus on increasing the lifespan of products through strategies like maintenance, repair, refurbishment, remanufacturing, and upgrading. By prolonging product usability, businesses decrease waste generation and resource consumption. For example, electronics companies offer certified refurbished devices or trade-in programs to automotive firms remanufacturing engines. Indeed, brands like Patagonia suggest the utilization of repair and resale of used clothing, while Philips offers refurbished medical equipment. Additionally, extending product life opens accessible price points for consumers and supports circular value creation across product lifecycles.

3. **Resource Recovery Models**

This typology hinges on recovering valuable materials and energy from end-of-life products, waste streams, or by-products to reintroduce them into production cycles. It involves recycling, upcycling, composting, industrial symbiosis (where waste from one process becomes input for another), and take-back schemes. Additionally, resource recovery closes material loops by turning waste into assets, as shown in companies like Interface that recycles old carpets into new flooring, or apparel brands collecting garments for fiber recycling. Important collection, sorting, and preprocessing are significant components that enable high-value resource recovery.

4. **Sharing Platforms (Sharing Economy Models)**

Sharing platforms boost the implementation rates of products and assets by allowing shared access, collaborative consumption, or peer-to-peer use rather than individual ownership. This enhances efficiency and decreases the demand for new products. For instance, car-sharing services like Zipcar, accommodation-sharing platforms such as Airbnb, ride-sharing networks like BlaBlaCar, and tool libraries fit here. Sharing models promote dematerialization by minimizing the capacity. This encourages community engagement and fosters access over ownership.

5. **Product-as-a-Service (PaaS) Models**

These models transform the focus of business from selling products to providing the function or performance of products as services, with the company retaining ownership and responsibility for maintenance, upgrades, and end-of-life management. PaaS incentivizes manufacturers to design durable, maintainable products and cultivates accountability for the product lifecycle, such as Rolls-Royce's "Power by the Hour" jet engine leasing, office equipment leasing services, and industrial machinery pay-per-use models. PaaS aligns economic incentives with circularity by connecting revenue to product longevity and resource efficiency.

6. **Hybrid Models**

Hybrid models compile elements from the above typologies to increase circular value creation by recognizing that circularity benefits from integrated approaches. For example, a company can produce products for disassembly (circular supply), offer repair and refurbishment services (life extension), and integrate take-back and recycling programs (resource recovery). These combinations improve resilience, environmental benefits, and customer engagement.

7. **Dematerialized Services**

This developed typology can replace physical products with digital or virtual alternatives. This reduces material consumption and environmental impacts, such as streaming services that have replaced physical media like CDs and DVDs or digital documents that replaced printed materials. Dematerialization meets the circular economy principles by minimizing resource use through technology.

CONCLUSION

Circular Economy Business Models (CEBMs) change in several ways the traditional industries and economic systems to become more resilient and sustainable. By extending the life of the products and items, restoring natural systems, and minimizing waste and pollution, they seek to generate value. These models encourage and boost resource efficiency, circularity of materials, and sustainable consumption practices, which vary from the linear "take-make-dispose" patterns.

The typologies involve circular supply, product life extension, resource recovery, sharing platforms, product-as-a-service, hybrid models, and dematerialized services that represent different strategies so that companies can utilize them depending on their industry context, product types, and consumer needs. For instance, manufacturers of durable goods can focus on life extension and PaaS models, while consumer-facing companies can emphasize sharing platforms and circular supply chains.

The successful implementation of these business models depends on the number of enablers: technological innovation (such as advanced recycling technologies), supportive governmental and regulatory frameworks, shifts in consumer behaviors and acceptance, and collaborative ecosystem creation. Yet, challenges remain, including cultural resistance, regulatory complexity, infrastructure gaps, and the need for new metrics to assess circular value comprehensively.

In summary, CEBMs have various environmental benefits. First, they open new economic opportunities, foster innovation, and create competitive advantages in resource-constrained markets. As global awareness of sustainability grows, circular models present a compelling blueprint for resilient businesses and regenerative economies that balance economic, social, and environmental objectives. Businesses and policymakers should integrate and innovate upon these typologies to enhance a systemic shift toward a truly circular future.

REFERENCES

Annarelli, A., Battistella, C., & Nonino, F. (2016). Product service system: A conceptual framework from a systematic review. *Journal of Cleaner Production, 139*, 1011–1032. DOI: 10.1016/j.jclepro.2016.08.061

Arruda, E. H., Melatto, R. A. P. B., Levy, W., & Conti, D. D. M. (2021). Circular economy: A brief literature review (2015–2020). *Sustainable Operations and Computers, 2*, 79–86. DOI: 10.1016/j.susoc.2021.05.001

Ayres, R. U. (1989). Industrial metabolism and global change. *International Social Science, 41*, 363–373.

Ayres, R. U., & Kneese, A. V. (1969). Production, consumption, and externalities. *The American Economic Review*, •••, 282–296.

Bag, S.. (2021). Barriers to the transition towards circular economy: Evidence from the construction and demolition industry. *Business Strategy and the Environment, 30*(4), 1931–1945.

Bag, S.. (2021). Circular Supply Chains: A review and future research directions. *Journal of Cleaner Production*.

Baines, T. S., Lightfoot, H. W., Benedettini, O., & Kay, J. M. (2009). The servitization of manufacturing: A review of literature and reflection on future challenges. *Journal of Manufacturing Technology Management, 20*(5), 547–567. DOI: 10.1108/17410380910960984

Baldassarre, B., Schepers, M., Bocken, N., Cuppen, E., Korevaar, G., & Calabretta, G. (2019). Industrial Symbiosis: Towards a design process for eco-industrial clusters by integrating Circular Economy and Industrial Ecology perspectives. *Journal of Cleaner Production, 216*, 446–460. DOI: 10.1016/j.jclepro.2019.01.091

Bocken, N. M. P., De Pauw, I., Bakker, C., & Van Der Grinten, B. (2016). Product design and business model strategies for a circular economy. *Journal of Industrial and Production Engineering, 33*(5), 308–320. DOI: 10.1080/21681015.2016.1172124

Bocken, N. M. P., Short, S. W., Rana, P., & Evans, S. (2014). A literature and practice review to develop sustainable business model archetypes. *Journal of Cleaner Production, 65*, 42–56. DOI: 10.1016/j.jclepro.2013.11.039

Bocken, N. M. P., Short, S. W., Rana, P., & Evans, S. (2016). A literature and practice review to develop sustainable business model archetypes. *Journal of Cleaner Production, 65*, 42–56.

Boulding, B. K. E. (2013). *The economics of the coming spaceship Earth. Environ. Quality Issues a grow* (0 ed.). RFF Press., DOI: 10.4324/9781315064147

Bressanelli, G., Adrodegari, F., Perona, M., & Saccani, N. (2018). The role of digital technologies to overcome Circular Economy challenges in PSS Business Models: An exploratory case study. *Procedia CIRP*, *73*, 216–221. DOI: 10.1016/j.procir.2018.03.322

Bundgaard, A. M., & Huulgaard, R. D. (2019). Luxury products for the circular economy? A case study of Bang & Olufsen. *Business Strategy and the Environment*, *28*(5), 699–709. DOI: 10.1002/bse.2274

Calisto Friant, M., Vermeulen, W. J. V., & Salomone, R. (2020). A typology of circular economy discourses: Navigating the diverse visions of a contested paradigm. *Resources, Conservation and Recycling*, *161*, 104917. DOI: 10.1016/j.resconrec.2020.104917

Carson, R. (1962). *Silent Spring*. Houghton Mifflin.

Chen, L., Hung, P., & Ma, H. (2020). Integrating circular business models and development tools in the circular economy transition process: A firm-level framework. *Business Strategy and the Environment*, *29*(5), 1887–1898. DOI: 10.1002/bse.2477

Chizaryfard, A., Trucco, P., & Nuur, C. (2021). The transformation to a circular economy: Framing an evolutionary view. *Journal of Evolutionary Economics*, *31*(2), 475–504. DOI: 10.1007/s00191-020-00709-0

Commoner, B. (1971). *The closing circle: Nature, man, and technology*. Alfred A. Knopf.

Dabija, D., & Năstase, C. (2024). Exploring the Evolution of Sustainability Paradigms: From Linear to Circular Economy Models. *Proceedings of the International Conference on Business Excellence*, 18(1), 754–769. https://doi.org/DOI: 10.2478/picbe-2024-0066

Dadiana, D., & Năstase, C. (2024). Exploring the Evolution of Sustainability Paradigms: From Linear to Circular Economy Models. *Proceedings of the 18th International Conference on Business Excellence*, 754-769.

Dadiana, D., & Năstase, C. (2024). Exploring the Evolution of Sustainability Paradigms: From Linear to Circular Economy Models. *Proceedings of the 18th International Conference on Business Excellence*, 754-769.

Dosi, G., & Nelson, R. R. (1993). An introduction to evolutionary theories in economics. *Journal of Evolutionary Economics*, *4*(3), 153–172.

Ellen MacArthur Foundation. (2013). Towards the Circular Economy Vol. 1: Economic and business rationale for an accelerated transition. Ellen MacArthur Foundation Publishing.

Ellen MacArthur Foundation, E. (2015). Towards a Circular Economy: Business rationale for an accelerated transition.

Frei, R., Jack, L., & Krzyzaniak, S. (2020). Sustainable reverse supply chains and circular economy in multichannel retail returns. *Business Strategy and the Environment*, *29*(5), 1925–1940. DOI: 10.1002/bse.2479

Geissdoerfer, M., Pieroni, M. P. P., Pigosso, D. C. A., & Soufani, K. (2020). Circular business models: A review. *Journal of Cleaner Production*, *277*, 123741. DOI: 10.1016/j.jclepro.2020.123741

Geissdoerfer, M., Savaget, P., Bocken, N. M. P., & Hultink, E. J. (2017). The Circular Economy – A new sustainability paradigm? *Journal of Cleaner Production*, *143*, 757–768. DOI: 10.1016/j.jclepro.2016.12.048

Geng, Y., Fu, J., Sarkis, J., & Xue, B. (2012). Towards a national circular economy indicator system in China: An evaluation and critical analysis. *Journal of Cleaner Production*, *23*(1), 216–224. DOI: 10.1016/j.jclepro.2011.07.005

Georgescu-Roegen, N. (2011). From Bioeconomics to Degrowth (M. Bonaiuti, Ed.; 0 ed.). Routledge. https://doi.org/DOI: 10.4324/9780203830413

Ghisellini, P., Cialani, C., & Ulgiati, S. (2016). A review on circular economy: The expected transition to a balanced interplay of environmental and economic systems. *Journal of Cleaner Production*, *114*, 11–32. DOI: 10.1016/j.jclepro.2015.09.007

Govindan, K., & Hasanagic, M. (2018). A systematic review on drivers, barriers, and practices towards circular economy: A supply chain perspective. *International Journal of Production Research*, *56*(1–2), 278–311. DOI: 10.1080/00207543.2017.1402141

Iagăru, R., ipo , A., & Iagăru, P. (2023). Strategic Thinking and Its Role in Accelerating the Transition from the Linear to the Circular Economic Model—Case Study of the Agri-Food Sector in the Sibiu Depression Microregion, Romania. *Sustainability*, *15*(4), 3109. DOI: 10.3390/su15043109

Jiao, W., & Boons, F. (2014). Toward a research agenda for policy intervention and facilitation to enhance industrial symbiosis based on a comprehensive literature review. *Journal of Cleaner Production*, *67*, 14–25. DOI: 10.1016/j.jclepro.2013.12.050

Kirchherr, J., Reike, D., & Hekkert, M. (2017). Conceptualizing the circular economy: An analysis of 114 definitions. *Resources, Conservation and Recycling, 127*, 221–232. DOI: 10.1016/j.resconrec.2017.09.005

Korhonen, J., Honkasalo, A., & Seppälä, J. (2018). Circular Economy: The Concept and its Limitations. *Ecological Economics, 143*, 37–46. DOI: 10.1016/j.ecolecon.2017.06.041

Korhonen, J., Nuur, C., Feldmann, A., & Birkie, S. E. (2018). Circular economy as an essentially contested concept. *Journal of Cleaner Production, 175*, 544–552. DOI: 10.1016/j.jclepro.2017.12.111

Kuokkanen, H., & Sun, W. (2020). Companies, Meet Ethical Consumers: Strategic CSR Management to Impact Consumer Choice. *Journal of Business Ethics, 166*(2), 403–423. DOI: 10.1007/s10551-019-04145-4

Lewandowski, M. (2016). Designing the business models for circular economy—Towards the conceptual framework. *Sustainability, 8*(1), 43.

Li, W. (2011). Comprehensive evaluation research on circular economic performance of eco-industrial parks. *Energy Procedia, 5*, 1682–1688. DOI: 10.1016/j.egypro.2011.03.287

Loiseau, E., Saikku, L., Antikainen, R., Droste, N., Hansjürgens, B., Pitkänen, K., Leskinen, P., Kuikman, P., & Thomsen, M. (2016). Green economy and related concepts: An overview. *Journal of Cleaner Production, 139*, 361–371. DOI: 10.1016/j.jclepro.2016.08.024

Lüdeke-Freund, F., & Dembek, K. (2017). Sustainable business model research and practice: Emerging field or passing fancy? *Journal of Cleaner Production, 168*, 1668–1678. DOI: 10.1016/j.jclepro.2017.08.093

Lyle, J. T. (1994). *Regenerative design for sustainable development*. Wiley.

McDonough, W., & Braungart, M. (2002). *Cradle to cradle: Remaking the way we make things (first)*. North Point Press.

McDowall, W., Geng, Y., Huang, B., Barteková, E., Bleischwitz, R., Türkeli, S., Kemp, R., & Doménech, T. (2017). Circular Economy Policies in China and Europe. *Journal of Industrial Ecology, 21*(3), 651–661. DOI: 10.1111/jiec.12597

Meadows, D., Meadows, D., Randers, J., & Behrens, W. (1972). The limits to growth.

Michelini, G.. (2017). From linear to circular business models: The case of the mobile phone industry. *Sustainability, 9*(9), 1–17.

Mont, O. K. (2002). Clarifying the concept of product–service system. *Journal of Cleaner Production, 10*(3), 237–245. DOI: 10.1016/S0959-6526(01)00039-7

Montag, L. (2023). Roadmap to a Circular Economy by 2030: A Comparative Review of Circular Business Model Visions in Germany and Japan. *Sustainability, 15*(6), 5374. DOI: 10.3390/su15065374

Moreau, V., Sahakian, M., Van Griethuysen, P., & Vuille, F. (2017). Coming Full Circle: Why Social and Institutional Dimensions Matter for the Circular Economy. *Journal of Industrial Ecology, 21*(3), 497–506. DOI: 10.1111/jiec.12598

Morseletto, P. (2020). Restorative and regenerative: Exploring the concepts in the circular economy. *Journal of Industrial Ecology, 24*(4), 763–773. DOI: 10.1111/jiec.12987

Murray, A., Skene, K., & Haynes, K. (2017). The Circular Economy: An Interdisciplinary Exploration of the Concept and Application in a Global Context. *Journal of Business Ethics, 140*(3), 369–380. DOI: 10.1007/s10551-015-2693-2

Nußholz, J. L. K. (2017). Circular Business Models: Defining a Concept and Framing an Emerging Research Field. *Sustainability, 9*(10), 1810. DOI: 10.3390/su9101810

Ormazabal, M., Prieto-Sandoval, V., Jaca, C., & Santos, J. (2016). An overview of the circular economy among SMEs in the Basque country: A multiple case study. *Journal of Industrial Engineering and Management, 9*(5), 1047. DOI: 10.3926/jiem.2065

Pan, S.-Y., Du, M. A., Huang, I.-T., Liu, I.-H., Chang, E.-E., & Chiang, P.-C. (2015). Strategies on implementation of waste-to-energy (WTE) supply chain for circular economy system: A review. *Journal of Cleaner Production, 108*, 409–421. DOI: 10.1016/j.jclepro.2015.06.124

Parida, V., Sjödin, D., & Reim, W. (2019). Reviewing Literature on Digitalization, Business Model Innovation, and Sustainable Industry: Past Achievements and Future Promises. *Sustainability, 11*(2), 391. DOI: 10.3390/su11020391

Park, J., Sarkis, J., & Wu, Z. (2010). Creating integrated business and environmental value within the context of China's circular economy and ecological modernization. *Journal of Cleaner Production, 18*(15), 1494–1501. DOI: 10.1016/j.jclepro.2010.06.001

Pearce, D. W., & Turner, R. K. (1990). *Economics of Natural Resources and the Environment.* Harvester Wheats.

Preghenella, N., & Battistella, C. (2021). Circular business models for sustainable development: A "waste is food" restorative ecosystem. *Business Strategy and the Environment, 30*(4), 1931–1945.

Prieto-Sandoval, V., Jaca, C., & Ormazabal, M. (2018). Towards a consensus on the circular economy. *Journal of Cleaner Production, 179*, 605–615. DOI: 10.1016/j.jclepro.2017.12.224

Rashid, A., Asif, F. M. A., Krajnik, P., & Nicolescu, C. M. (2013). Resource Conservative Manufacturing: An essential change in business and technology paradigm for sustainable manufacturing. *Journal of Cleaner Production, 57*, 166–177. DOI: 10.1016/j.jclepro.2013.06.012

Saidani, M., Yannou, B., Leroy, Y., Cluzel, F., & Kendall, A. (2019). A taxonomy of circular economy indicators. https://doi.org/DOI: 10.48550/ARXIV.1901.02709

Sakai, S., Yoshida, H., Hirai, Y., Asari, M., Takigami, H., Takahashi, S., Tomoda, K., Peeler, M. V., Wejchert, J., Schmid-Unterseh, T., Douvan, A. R., Hathaway, R., Hylander, L. D., Fischer, C., Oh, G. J., Jinhui, L., & Chi, N. K. (2011). International comparative study of 3R and waste management policy developments. *Journal of Material Cycles and Waste Management, 13*(2), 86–102. DOI: 10.1007/s10163-011-0009-x

Sauvé, S., Bernard, S., & Sloan, P. (2016). Environmental sciences, sustainable development and circular economy: Alternative concepts for trans-disciplinary research. *Environmental Development, 17*, 48–56. DOI: 10.1016/j.envdev.2015.09.002

Schulte, U. G. (2013). New business models for a radical change in resource efficiency. *Environmental Innovation and Societal Transitions, 9*, 43–47. DOI: 10.1016/j.eist.2013.09.006

Schwager, P., & Moser, F. (2006). The Application of Chemical Leasing Business Models in Mexico. *Environmental Science and Pollution Research International, 13*(2), 131–137. DOI: 10.1065/espr2006.02.294

Stahel, W. R. (1982). The product life factor. In Orr, G. S. (Ed.), *An inquiry into the nature of sustainable societies. The Role of the Private Sector*. Houston Area Research Centre.

Stahel, W. R. (2010). *The Performance Economy.*, DOI: 10.1057/9780230274907

Stahel, W. R., & Reday, G. (1976). The potential for substituting manpower for energy, Report to the Commission of the European Communities.

Sterev, N. (2019). New Industrial Business Models: From Linear to Circular Economy Approach. *Trakia Journal of Sciences*, *17*(Suppl 1), 511–523.

Susur, E., & Engwall, M. (2022). A transitions framework for circular business models. *Journal of Industrial Ecology*, *27*(1), 19–32. DOI: 10.1111/jiec.13128

Tukker, A. (2004). Eight types of product–service system: Eight ways to sustainability? Experiences from SusProNet. *Business Strategy and the Environment*, *13*(4), 246–260. DOI: 10.1002/bse.414

Tukker, A. (2015). Product services for a resource-efficient and circular economy – a review. *Journal of Cleaner Production*, *97*, 76–91. DOI: 10.1016/j.jclepro.2013.11.049

UNEP,. (2011). Towards a Green Economy: Pathways to Sustainable Development and Poverty Eradication, Sustainable Development.

Ward, B., & Dubo, R. (1983). *Only one earth*. Norton.

Winans, K., Kendall, A., & Deng, H. (2017). The history and current applications of the circular economy concept. *Renewable & Sustainable Energy Reviews*, *68*, 825–833. DOI: 10.1016/j.rser.2016.09.123

Wirtz, B. W., Pistoia, A., Ullrich, S., & Göttel, V. (2016). Business Models: Origin, Development and Future Research Perspectives. *Long Range Planning*, *49*(1), 36–54. DOI: 10.1016/j.lrp.2015.04.001

World Economic Forum. Ellen MacArthur Foundation, & McKinsey Company. (2014). Towards the Circular Economy: Accelerating the scale-up across global supply chains. World Economic Forum.

Xue, B., Chen, X., Geng, Y., Guo, X., Lu, C., Zhang, Z., & Lu, C. (2010). Survey of officials' awareness on circular economy development in China: Based on municipal and county level. *Resources, Conservation and Recycling*, *54*(12), 1296–1302. DOI: 10.1016/j.resconrec.2010.05.010

Yong, R. (2007). The circular economy in China. *Journal of Material Cycles and Waste Management*, *9*(2), 121–129. DOI: 10.1007/s10163-007-0183-z

ADDITIONAL READING

De Keyser, E., & Mathijs, E. (2023). A typology of sustainable circular business models with applications in the bioeconomy. *Frontiers in Sustainable Food Systems Journal, 6*, 1028877. DOI: 10.3389/fsufs.2022.1028877

Korhonen, J., Honkasalo, A., & Seppälä, J. (2018). Circular Economy: The Concept and its Limitations. *Ecological Economics, 143*, 37–46. DOI: 10.1016/j.ecolecon.2017.06.041

Longo, S., Cellura, M., Luu, Q. L., & Nguyen, Q. T. (2023). Circular economy and life cycle thinking applied to the biomass supply chain: A review. *Renewable Energy, 220*, 119598. DOI: 10.1016/j.renene.2023.119598

Salvador, R., Barros, M. V., Da Luz, L. M., Piekarski, C. M., & De Francisco, A. C. (2020). Circular business models: Current aspects that influence implementation and unaddressed subjects. *Journal of Cleaner Production. Vol, 250*, 119555. DOI: 10.1016/j.jclepro.2019.119555

Stahel, W. R. (2016). The Circular Economy. *Nature, 531*(7595), 435–438. DOI: 10.1038/531435a

Vogiantzi, Ch., & Tserpes, K. (2023). On the definition, Assessment, and Enhancement of Circular Economy across Various Industrial Sectors: A Literature Review and Recent Findings. *Sustainability, 15*(23), 16532. DOI: 10.3390/su152316532

KEY TERMS AND DEFINITIONS

Sustainability: development that seeks Meeting current needs without affecting the future generations to satisfy their own needs, it's known as sustainable development; the ability to provide sustain conditions over time.

Circular Economy: involves a set of organization planning processes that aim no waste and pollution during delivering the products, components during the lifecycle of the material to assure the highest benefit for customers and society.

Linear Business Model: Traditional concept to "take-make-dispose" of the product. It aims to design the product, manufacture at the lowest price, sell at the highest price, and then simple to get rid of. Mpst products are made to be used just once.

Circular Business Models (CBMs): Business Models that include elements that slow, narrow, and close the resource loop with creating economic value are suitable for the circular economy. They boost productivity, enable recycling and remanufacturing, and extend the life time of the products.

Resource Loop: Allows products to be used for as long as possible by minimizing waste and maintaining circular resource flows. These loops follow strategies that can be closed through recycling, showing consumption phases and limiting the use of the resource.

Value Retention: Materials and Products may preserve their value by extending their lifetime through recycling, repairing, renovation, and remanufacturing.

Lifecycle Thinking: Lifecycle thinking aims to minimize negative impacts on the environment, economy, and society through assessing each step of the product's existence from raw materials to use and disposal. Using these resources prevent problems from occurring from one level to the another.

Chapter 4
Leadership Styles and Sustainability Practices:
Driving Forward Circular Economies

Ghada Khalil Kalakesh
https://orcid.org/0000-0002-0024-1926
Lebanese International University, Lebanon

Hala Muhieddine Koleilat Al Dilby
Lebanese International University, Lebanon

Bassam Mahmoud Tarhini
Lebanese International University, Lebanon

ABSTRACT

The concepts of circular economy is gaining momentum in addressing global issues in the areas of waste management, climate change, product life-cycle design and supply chain management. Leaders have significant impact on the strategic directions of their organizations and dedication to the circular economy goals. The chapter examines how the transformational, ethical, participative, and adaptive leadership influence sustainable resources use in circular economies (CE). The chapter used a descriptive analysis based on exploring an update of existing literature and articles and a peek on real world insights. The chapter aims at giving readers an insight at how leaders can effectively support the shift towards circular economies while maintaining their commitment to sustainability initiatives, and highlighting existing challenges in the field. It attempts to combine different perspectives from leadership theories, circular economy and sustainability principles, to address properly the research topic. It provides future recommendations in the field.

DOI: 10.4018/979-8-3373-7655-4.ch004

INTRODUCTION

The concept of circular economy (CE) was identified as a new sustainable development paradigm, specifically in its managerial context (Kisi, 2022). Organizations are living in an era where technologies are swiftly changing; consumers are demanding sophisticated products that cater to their needs, and climate changes are imposing global challenges. Circular economy and sustainability are gaining momentum to address significant global issues in the areas of, waste management, climate change, product life-cycle design and supply chain management. Sustainability initiatives themes in circular economies are highly relevant as organizations struggle to maintain their continuity in the business landscape. Assessing the effect of sustainable management on circular economy initiatives is crucial for organizations seeking business growth and competitiveness, as sustainable development aims at achieving the needs of society without consuming the future generations' ability to achieve their own requirements. The need to protect and conserve natural resources is paving the way to a surge in balancing environmental, social and economic development facets (Bashynska et al., 2024).

The circular economy strategies require organizations to re-evaluate their processes in terms of product re-design, to ensure the reduction in resource consumption, and to improve sustainability practices (Zhu et al. 2020). Walmart announced in early 2021 (Walmart, 2021) that they will reach a zero-waste production in the US market by end of 2025, and this achievement is the result of strategies focusing on enhanced recycling processes, reduced excess packaging, and the redistribution of unsold food to food banks. The circular economy strategies require in its implementation phase stakeholders' collaboration, transparency, engagement, knowledge sharing and increased efficiency (Schmidt & Donselaar, 2020). Circular strategies incorporate sustainable practices and cycles assessment throughout the product life-cycle span from the choice of material to the end of product life. Nike's strategic "Move To Zero" initiative is committed to zero carbon and zero waste throughout its product life cycle and supply chain management (Nike, 2022), and the company was able to introduce a line of products called" Nike Air" that illustrates the recycled materials achievement. Unilever has been committed to a long term strategy that will enable her by end of 2025 to make all of its plastic packaging recyclable, compostable or reusable (Unilever, 2021), in addition to its continuing initiatives towards sustainable sourcing and waste reduction.

The world is witnessing a need for sustainable practices driven by environmental concerns, economic instability and social inequalities. Multinational organizations, with their consumption of resources and global footprint, are under increased monitoring to demonstrate their commitment to sustainable practices. Sustainability in its simplest form refers to meeting the needs of the current generation without compromising the resources for future use. This requires incorporating sustainability practices into core business operations across a complex geographically dispersed supply chain, in the areas of environmental sustainability practices, social sustainability, product and services sustainability. Apple' s long term strategy to use recycled materials in its production, enabled her back in 2022 to decrease its aluminum use to 20% which came from recycled materials (Apple, 2022). Apple also encouraged their customers to return their old devices to be reused or recycled, as a part of their "Apple Trade-In program", thereby aligning their strategies with circular economy principles.

The need for effective leadership and management knowhow is surfacing as a profound driver to market dominance, as it embodies ethical conduct, environmental stewardship and societal impact. Using the right leadership styles enables organizations to support sustainable resource usage, and unites the multifaceted sustainability and circular economy initiatives. The effect of various leadership styles namely the transformational style, the ethical style, the participative and adaptive leadership styles is instrumental due to their significant impact on the strategic directions of their organizations. Leadership dedication to the circular economy goals and sustainable resources use, may facilitate the shift towards sustainable practices.

Leadership is a dominant internal organizational factor that serially affects circular economies, in the ability of organizations to manage and exploit efficiently its own resources and needs, and in adapting to future needs to ensure their future success (Katou et al., 2023). Leadership styles may foster a dynamic environment, adaptive to change that affects the circular strategies efficacy (Garcia-Morales et al., 2020; Kirkpatrick & Lock, 2020). Inspiring transformational leaders project a shared vision for sustainable practices. Participative leaders facilitate the adoption of sustainable initiatives through employee engagement at all department levels. Adaptive leaders make sure that their organizations are ready to overcome all the challenges of circular strategies implementation in a dynamic marketplace. Ethical leaders prioritize corporate social responsibility practices, thus ensuring organizational commitment to environmental practices.

Amid these challenges, we intend in this book chapter to address the below areas:

- Circular Economy: inception, principles and initiatives, in line with the implementation of the sustainable practices.
- The sustainability practices incorporated into core business operations across a complex geographically dispersed supply chain namely: environmental sustainability practices, social sustainability, product and services sustainability. In addition to the main challenges that organizations are facing in sustainability implementation.

- Overview of the Leadership styles namely: literature review and analysis of the transformational, ethical, participative, and adaptive leadership
- The effect that the different leadership on sustainable practices integration within organizations, in terms of the role that leadership plays an effective role in maintaining sustainable practices in circular economies; in the context of employee commitment and involvement in sustainability, and their impact on product redesign and supply chain collaboration

1. LITERATURE REVIEW

1.1 Circular Economy Initiatives

Circular economy refers to the concept of changing the traditional way of thinking about products, based on a traditional linear model to a totally new product system (table 1) based on the perpetual circulation of resources (Lowe & Genovese, 2022). As a result of the various manufacturing processes, many types of waste were generated in big quantities throughout the supply chain models across various industries (Shi et al., 2024). This paved the way to a revolutionary thinking of reversing the supply chain and referring it to the circular economy (Hazen et al., 2021).

Circular economies require the re-engineering of numerous facets of production and consumption, including the adoption of methods that facilitate repair, recycling, reuse and remanufacturing, as well as investments in long-term product design (Geissdoefer et al., 2018). The large presence of plastic waste, and specifically micro-plastic, in the global environment created global challenges for businesses who are seeking creative solutions for their management and cycling systems (Shi et al., 2024). Coca-Cola launched its "World-Without-Waste "campaign that involves collecting and recycling a bottle or a can for everyone sold by 2023 (Coca-Cola, 2021). This shift to circular economy processes requires organizations to transition from the current production pattern and overcoming technological, financial and organizational barriers (Russo et al., 2019). Many supply chain leaders are facing daily challenges in an unsystematic way in the fields of supply-chain management closed-loop, green supply chain management and sustainable supply chain (Govidan & Soleimani, 2017).

Table 1. Linear Economy to Circular Economy.

Resource flow Take/Make /Dispose Reduce/Reuse/Recycle	
Focus Short Term Profit Long-term Sustainability	
Generation of Waste High Waste Generation Minimal Waste due to Reuse and Recycle	
Product Design Recyclability Disposable Product Durability, Reparability, Recyclability	
Impact on Environment Degradation in Environment Decreased Environmental Footprint	

Source: Lowe and Genovese, (2022)

Circular economy in its resources efficiency and product redesign dimensions offers an innovative framework to extend the product life-cycle, thus preemptively catering for waste generation (Bocken, 2021). To foster recyclability and longer product life-span, organizations need to adopt strategies such as: design for disassembly, incorporating sustainable materials and modularity (Lyndon et al., 2021). Moreover, to facilitate the extending the longevity of resources and maximize their efficiency, organizations are focusing on integrating technologies such as predictive maintenance (Koutroumanidis & Tsironis, 2020).

Circular economy initiatives emphasize three main areas:

- The importance of re-designing business processes to enhance the long-term use or resources
- The necessity to upgrade the product life-cycle design
- The importance of encouraging collaboration in supply-chain management (Ellen MacArthur Foundation, 2013).

1.1.1 Redesigning Processes for Long-Term Resource Use

The worldwide shift towards sustainability initiatives is highlighting the importance of reevaluating the current business process which aim at short term profitability (Wang et al., 2020). Businesses are realizing that products should be designed in a way to facilitate their repair, their refurbishment and their recyclability (Bocken, 2021). The adoption of technologies that facilitate predictive maintenance enables organizations to make efficient use of their resources and to optimize their use (Koutroumanidis & Tsironis, 2020). Through timely interventions that reduce the need of replacement, firms may prolong their machines and equipment life-span.

1.1.2 Upgrading the Design of Product Life-Cycle

In designing circular strategies, the product life-cycle design appears to play a critical role in controlling the product life from inception to disposal. The product manufacturers are reviewing the environmental effect at every stage of the product life: beginning with the phase of extraction of raw material, to the production phase, then to the actual use of the product and lastly the decline phase (Tukker & Tischner, 2006). To identify opportunities in resource consumption and sustainability enhancement, some businesses went all the way to conduct life-cycle assessments (LCAs) (Zhu at al., 2020).

Businesses are using recycled and bio-gradable materials in the product design to protect resources and to reduce the carbon footprint in the production operations (Mok et al., 2020). Some products are designed to serve multiple uses and dual purposes to enhance resource efficiency and waste reduction (Lyndon et al., 2021).

1.1.3 Collaboration in Supply Chain Management

Circular strategy successful implementation requires collaboration in managing supply chain activities. Leaders are realizing the importance of fostering transparency, shared knowledge and resources management among stakeholders, through improved collaboration and efficiency (Schmidt & Doneslaar, 2020). The main residues of management collaboration may be seen in increased partnership with sustainability-driven suppliers, shift towards shared logistics to decrease the transportation-related emissions and joint recycling programs.

The collaboration among various stakeholders may boost diversity and expertise in creative practices, thereby accelerating innovation in supply chain management (D'Amato et al., 2021). For example, firms may cooperate on developing new products or new substance that enhance circularity, such as bio-plastics or recycling methods. Firms may support their collaborative efforts through increasing customer engagement take-back programs, thereby enhancing their customer loyalty and encouraging responsible consumption behaviors (Prendeville et al., 2021).

1.2 Sustainable Activities

Global leaders can standardize their frameworks of circular economy reporting to align with their commitment to sustainability practices, thereby guaranteeing accountability, transparency and the adoption of long term sustainable initiatives.

1.2.1 The Key drivers to Sustainability Initiatives

- **Product and Service Sustainability**: in addition to realizing circularity and sustainability, understanding that products and equipment service can, and should re-used and repurposed is of vital importance (Psarommatis & May, 2024). Designing products for recyclability and durability is gaining momentums, which includes recycled material, decreasing the negative impact of product life-cycle and adopting eco-friendly alternatives.
- **Social Sustainability**: The increased commitment to ethical and responsible conduct in global businesses is helping organization to be more accountable and transparent when they are faced with ESG issues (Ray & Hardi, 2024). Leaders are recognizing the importance of human rights and fair labor practices in their path towards community development. This involves applying safe working conditions, equitable wages and salaries, and promoting diversity in supply chain operations. The importance of transparency in supply chain surfaces as an ethical dimension in sustainability practices.
- . **Environmental Sustainability**: Responding to the growing need of environmental sustainability, global industries are continuously adopting innovative mechanisms to control their ecological footprints (Ejibe et al., 2024). The entire supply chain management must ensure optimization of resource uses, reduction in carbon emissions and promotion of circular economy models. The current practices in the field include investment in renewable energy sources, implementation programs on waste reduction and adoption of sustainable packaging.
- **Accountability and Governance**: Businesses' must realize that effective corporate governance enhances their performance by shaping their sustainability outcomes (Agyemang et al., 2025). The reporting mechanisms must be employed to ensure transparency and accountability especially in the following areas: clarity in sustainable targets, progress feedback, engagement of stakeholders and an accurate governance structure that oversees the performance sustainability.

1.2.2 Challenges to Sustainable Activities

Amid all these awareness activities, several challenges are still blocking the way towards sustainable practices namely:

- **Supply chain Complexity**: Multinationals have geographically dispersed supply-chains that make it difficult for leaders to efficiently manage them. Businesses may suffer from lack of traceability and transparency in communication systems, which affects negatively the ethical sourcing and environmental responsibility. Apple is witnessing some difficulties in implementing its uniform sustainability and accountability practices across all suppliers in a global and complex supply-chain. In its attempt to achieve global carbon-neutrality by 2030 (Apple, 2023), Apple is facing challenges in tracking and managing the emissions of third party suppliers. Amazon is also adapting its logistics and sourcing strategies to face the resources constraints and risks of global disruptions such as COVID-19 ad geopolitical tensions (Gartner, 2023), and is continuously adapting its logistics.

- **Constraints and Costs in Resources**: The investments in technologies needed to cover the costs of sustainable practices may increase the managerial financial constraints for multinationals, specifically for smaller MNCs, and affect their progress. Coca-Cola has been suffering from water and packaging rising costs, in addition to disruptions in supply-chain. The company received immense criticism over its water-usage policy in drought-prone regions (Coca-Cola, 2023), and is now working intensively on improving its water usage efficiency while balancing sustainability initiatives.
- **Resistance to Change**: the implementation of many sustainability initiatives were interrupted by internal employee resistance, and a lack of buy-in from senior management officials. General Motors GM is currently witnessing internal and external resistance (General Motors, 2023) from both employees and customers alike in its transition path to electric vehicles (EVs) and sustainability initiatives. Although GM is heavily investing in EV technology, however it is facing difficulties in its cultural shift internally among workforce adaption, and externally from consumers' uncertainty of new technology. Marathon Oil, in its commitment to a 50% reduction in scope 1 and 2 greenhouse emissions by 2030, is witnessing organizational inertia (Purpose Brand, 2023). Marathon Oil, in implementing new technologies and practices aimed at decreasing emissions and increasing commitment to sustainability since 2019, has been encountering increased resistance to change from its operational teams and various stakeholders.
- **Lack of Standardized Reporting Metrics:** The process of benchmarking and comparison among MNCs' sustainability performance is becoming more difficult to the lack of universal measurement metrics for tracking and reporting supplier progress. Walmart is facing extensive difficulties in its commitment to sustainability goals, due to the lack of sustainability metrics across its vast supply-chain (Walmart, 2023). The company project called Project Gigaton aims at reducing its emissions by 1 billion metrics by 2030, but is facing progress tracking flaws across its large supply chain. Although Live Nation adopted greenhouse gas emission targets and created

an Environmental Sustainability Charter, however the absence of regular sustainability metrics progress reports is still hampering its accountability and transparency (Purpose Brand, 2023).

1.3 Leadership Styles

One of the most critical element influencing the success of sustainability initiatives of business organizations is leadership (Bass & Avolio, 1994). The leader' vision, ability to influence others, behavior and approach to decision-making greatly affects and shapes organizational outcomes. Leadership is a process of influencing others to achieve common goals. Effective leadership not only guides organizational goal achievement, but also fosters employee engagement, innovation and adaptability to change (Bass & Avolio, 1974). Businesses are in constant need for adequate leadership that helps them adapt to both internal and external problems, in addition to adjusting to changing market conditions, consumer expectations, and technological breakthrough.

The concept of leadership is centered on how leaders motivate and inspire people to act in a particular manner. Because of this, leaders can use a variety of leadership styles, each with distinct characteristics and dimensions that are appropriate for particular individuals and circumstances (Meyer & Meijers, 2017). It becomes clear how important is leadership styles to businesses, especially those that compete in a fast-paced, international marketplaces (Akkaya & Tabak, 2020).

The effect of various leadership styles on the strategic management of organizations process differs as some styles concentrate on structure, control, and performance incentives, others encourage and enable their staff to embrace change, innovation, and risk taking. It is essential for organizations looking to achieve successful transformation to comprehend leadership styles, minimize resistance, and enhance productivity during transitions. Leadership is not only about managing change; it is about inspiring commitment, building trust, and creating an environment where innovation thrives.

In the below section, four main key leadership styles namely, transformational, ethical, adaptive and participative leadership are examined, along with their unique contributions to organizational change. Every one of these leadership styles has distinct traits that impact how change is viewed, welcomed, and implemented in a dynamic corporate environment.

1.3.1 The Transformational Leadership Style

In an effort to transform the organization into a behavioral one, the transformational leadership emphasizes the significance of implementing new enhancements and updating the behaviors of others. Through the effective use of resources and personal beliefs, transformational leaders attempt to modify the behavior of their employees so that they identify with the mission, goal and standards of the organizations (Kuhnert & Lewis, 1987).

The following are the five main primary elements of transformational leadership (Avolio & Bass, 2001):

-Idealized attitude (influence): transformational leaders are highly regarded and maintain their optimism in the face of all challenging circumstances.
-Idealized influence (behavior): transformational leaders establish corporate cultures that are marked by moral principles and high ethical standards (table 2).
-Inspirational motivation: Transformational leaders show concern for their followers' needs and desires and inspire them. By empowering and supporting them, they raise their followers' understanding of current issues and motivate them to take part in decision-making.
-Intellectual simulation: transformational leaders encourage their followers to think and act creatively and innovatively by virtues of their vision and personality. In order to match their attitudes and core values with the objectives of the firm, the followers of transformational leaders are motivated to make these changes.
-Individualized consideration: transformational leaders try to build their followers' capacities as well as their potential for success and professional progression, by serving as both a coach and a mentor

Table 2. The Transformational Leadership Style.

Transformational Style	Dimensions	Organizational Influence
	Idealized Influence (Attributes and Behaviors)	Leaders make followers feel proud
	Inspirational Motivation	Leaders inspire and encourage followers to be innovative and accomplish their objectives
	Individualized Motivation	Leaders interact with followers and show concern for their needs
	Intellectual Simulation	Leaders encourage new concepts and inspires others to be innovative

Source: Avolio and Bass (2001)

Because if their capacity to cultivate and dedicate themselves to a culture of change, organizations all over the world require transformational leaders. Since transformational leaders try to strengthen followers' commitment within a framework of trust, shared value and vision, this style of leadership has a good impact on employees' emotional health and well-being (Saad Alessa, 2021).

Some transformational leadership styles may share characteristics with emotional agility, and others may have intrinsic aspects that may be appropriate for switching and adapting to complicated situations and tumultuous environment (Meyer & Meijers, 2017). The following succinctly describes the primary EI traits of transformational leadership:

- Because they are dedicated to a strong sense of purpose, have faith in themselves and others, and are able to build trust, transformational leaders possess idealized influence (behaviors and attributes). The agility and resilience traits of having a clear vision, being persuasive, mentoring others, working collaboratively, and improving effectiveness, self-awareness, and social skills are all correlated with these dimensions.
- Transformational leaders demonstrate inspirational motivation by using their personalities to motivate others to accomplish effective organizational goals. This is comparable to the emotional agility feature of consistently aiming for quality improvement, as well as the resilience factor of emotional intelligence and social skills.
- Because they are able to interact with their followers and show concern for their Transformational leaders demonstrate individualized consideration. These qualities intersect with the resilience attributes, such as empathy and ability to communicate and listen effectively.
- Because they can generate fresh ideas think outside the box, transformational leaders exhibit intellectual simulation. They encourage their followers to use new and innovative methods to perform their tasks more efficiently. To the emotional intelligence motivation dimension, this involves boosting their followers' motivation through their charisma and personality. They are nimble leaders that appreciate good teamwork and have an imaginative and creative way of thinking.

The following characteristics of transformational leaders align with emotional intelligence, resilience and agility, namely:

- Change agent role which aligns with agile leaders' vision and quality improvements well as emotional intelligence's social skills and self-regulation traits.
- The risk-taking role aligns with agile leadership's entrepreneurial trait.
- The conflict handler role aligns with the resilience traits of tolerance, patience and conflict resolution.

- The role of learning from experience aligns with the emotional agility trait of learning from mistakes and the resilience trait of problem-solving and overcoming failures. Additionally, it supports the self-regulation aspect of emotional intelligence.

Leaders who create a vision and encourage staff to embrace sustainable practices and make changes are essential to the circular economy and sustainability projects. Therefore, transformational leaders who are visionary, emotionally intelligent, resilient, believe in cultural change, and can guide their followers to through-it with tenacity and sincerity are essential for organizations all over the world. They must also be able to respond quickly to the changing environment.

1.3.2 The Ethical Leadership Style

The social learning theory (Bandura, 1986) sets the base for ethical leadership by highlighting the importance of the motivational role of leaders in the context of influencing the overall organizational performance. A social learning perspective on ethical leadership proposes that leaders influence the ethical conduct of followers via modeling, which covers a broad range of psychological matching processes, including observational learning, imitation, and identification.

The Ethical Impact (EIT) Theory identified that ethical leadership may work well through its justice focus by reducing stress level in the work environment and enhancing the quality of job performance, and further proposes that unethical attitude in the firm can unfavorably influence employees' job stress and consequently their overall well-being (Giacalone, Promislo & Jurkeiwicz, 2016). Subsequently, individuals may be able to reduce job stress and improve employee well-being.

Ethical leadership is referred to as the parade of appropriate norms conducted throughout the leader's personal and interpersonal actions and relationships, it is by when the leader promotes such conduct to followers and encourages them to encounter two-way communication, reinforcement, and decision-making (Hsieh et al.,2023). Ethical leadership encompasses two major leaders' dimensions, namely the leader as:

- *A moral person* where the leader retains characteristics such as, honesty, credibility, integrity, openness, fairness, care for others, and trustworthiness:
- *And as a moral manager* where the leader is accountable for his own actions. He is considered as an idol or a role model to the followers and possesses values and ethics via words and actions, as well as rewards and disciplines followers for their conduct according to ethical standards (Treviño et al., 2000).

The influence of ethical leadership can be detected from diverse facets. Ethical leadership improves positive behaviors and attitudes of followers, such as job performance, involvement level, and long term commitment (Khuntia & Suar, 2004); organizational commitment; and trust in leaders (Zhu et al., 2004) and organizational citizenship behavior (OCB) (Mayer et al., 2009). Furthermore, organizational environment with respect to ethics is also prejudiced by leader's norms and actions; Ethical leader promotes ethical conduct in followers and encourages them to encounter two-way communication, reinforcement, and decision-making know-how (table 3).

Table 3. The Ethical Leadership Style.

Ethical Style	Focus	Organizational Influence
	Justice	Reduces stress level in the work environment and enhances the quality of job performance
	Norms	Promotes ethical conduct to followers and encourages them to encounter two-way communication, reinforcement, and decision-making
	Integrity	Moral leaders retain characteristics such as, honesty, credibility, integrity, openness, fairness, care for others, and trustworthiness
	Accountability	Ethical leader is an idol and role model to the followers and possesses values and ethics via words and actions, as well as rewards and disciplines followers for their ethical conduct.

Source (the authors)

Firms have the capacity to both positively and negatively influence individual's well-being via their effect on job stress. The aim is to acknowledge the ways for maximizing the overall and individualistic efficiency, while diminishing the impact of stress in the work environment. The leadership style contributes vastly in the overall firm's outcomes and may play a crucial role in setting and achieving its goals. Ethical leadership emphasizes on endorsing moral behavior among employees and stakeholders, and it has been recognized as an adequate style for reinforcing the ethical conduct of individuals within organizations (Brown et al., 2005).

Numerous organizational outcomes such as, job performance, employee ethical behavior, job happiness, and the commitment to the firm, are positively related to ethical leadership. Contrariwise, ethical leadership is negatively correlated to turnover intention, stress level at work, and abusive supervision (Bedi et al., 2016). Likewise, ethical leadership can spread beyond promoting an ethical environment to influencing the firm's members' approaches toward fairness, their job, commitment level to the organization (Brown & Treviño, 2006), and subordinates' green work behavior (Ahmad et al., 2021).

Transparency in supply chain surfaces as an ethical dimension in sustainability practices, and effective CSR implementation requires the presence of ethical leaders who foster environmental wellbeing, encourage fairness, transparency and accountability, open communication especially in achieving clarity in sustainable targets. Ethical leadership emerges as an important driver in sustainable circular strategies.

1.3.3 The Participative Leadership Style

Looking back into historical inception, the participative leadership style was related to Kurt Lewin's 1930s and 1940s concept of democratic leadership that encouraged the involvement of team members in decision-making. The participative style was formally introduced in 1961 by the social scientist Renis Likert, who encouraged leaders to seek the employees' opinions and to delegate them before making decisions. Likert was also responsible for the introduction of the famous Likert Scale that was a method adopted for measuring employee attitudes.

The participative leadership style was later identified by multiple theories from the social sciences as a style that influences the behavior of employees via different mechanisms (Wang et al., 2022). The social exchange theory defined participative leadership as a style that influences employees by promoting their mutual help behavior and job prosperity (Usman et. al., 2021). The social sciences theory identified participative leadership as a style that increased the employee self-esteem and their workload (Peng et al., 2021).

The social cognitive theory confirmed that this style increased the psychological security of employees and boosts their self-efficacy (table 4), thereby enhancing their innovation and performance (Zou et al., 2011). The social information processing theory and the implicit leadership theory both highlighting the growing positive impact of the participative leadership style on employee performance (Zhang et al., 2011; lam et al., 2015).

Table 4. The Participative Leadership Style.

Participative Style	Focus	Organizational Influence
	Self-esteem and Self-efficacy	increases the employees' sense of ownership so that they feel responsible for decision-making
	Collaboration and Communication	employees are equipped with the appropriate information and support from other resources and encouraged to facilitate their participation in problem solving
	Trust and Respect	Team empowerment and engagement in innovative solutions
	Employee Development	fostering a collaborative atmosphere, that increased employee accountability and involved them in all decision-making levels, in addition to developing employee behavior on the approach and motive levels

Source: (the authors)

Needless to say that the participative leadership style fostered a collaborative atmosphere, that increased employee accountability and involved them in all decision-making levels, in addition to affecting employee behavior on the approach and motive levels (Wang et al., 2022). The key variables of the participative leadership style included: decision-making, communicating, trust and respect, employee development and team morale (Wang, 2022). In terms of the effect of participative leadership style on the behavioral approach level: employees are equipped with the appropriate information and support from other resources and encouraged to facilitate their participation. In terms of the effect of the participative leadership style on the behavioral motive level: this style increases the employees' sense of ownership so that they feel responsible for decision-making and keener on solving collaboratively work problems,

In the current evolving circular economies, organizations are using advanced digital technologies to promote their competitiveness in the global market (Su a et al., 2021), through the engagement of teams in the development, implementation and refinement of circular strategies. The participative leadership style surfaces as am important driver towards team empowerment, innovative solutions and commitment to sustainability initiatives (Kirkpartick & Locke, 2020).

The literature identified that the circular economy initiatives advocates the need for a change in the corporate culture towards sustainability. Participative leaders embrace an open culture that ensures the active involvement of various stakeholders in the in the circular economy strategies, and promotes the creation of cross-functional teams who are aware and committed to the ecosystem protection issues such as: health related safeguards, waste reduction and effective use of resources (Salvioni & Almici, 2020).

1.3.4 The Adaptive Leadership Style

Adaptive leadership revolves around the ability of the leader to inspire others and assist in resolving challenges, think ahead and plan amid the potential changes in the future. This could be best accomplished by reviewing goals and priorities, identifying expectations and managing plans to achieve future progress (Nelson & Squires, 2017). Adaptive leaders need to distinguish between technical resolutions and adaptive encounters. While there may be direct and forward tactics for some problems (like hiring more staff), adaptive problems (like tackling low satisfaction levels) may need to investigate the provider's decisions and actions, behaviors and norms by producing a safe space to express uncertainties and thoughts for development (Nelson & Squires, 2017).

A technical problem can be handled via referring to technological solutions or programmatic fixes. However, an adaptive problem is different in the number of inputs that require various changes in terms of cognitive and conative actions. These changes must begin with examining existing priorities, expectations, conducts and devotions. Technical solutions can be complex, but adaptive problems are more challenging since they are infrequently connected to vibrant instantaneous resolutions. Instead, the methods to adaptive encounters depend on thoughtful considerations on what to reserve from past performs, what to abandon, and how to produce new methods for the future (Heifetz et al., 2009).

The Adaption-Innovation theory (A-I), identified that individuals have different styles in handling and solving encountered problems (Kirton, 1976), either by being more adaptive or more innovative in generating concepts, utilizing structure to endorse certain modifications, and responding to guidelines and group rules. In Adaption-Innovation theory, adaptive characters favor deep-rooted and organized situations, permitting them to cultivate innovative thoughts within the structure for the aim of making it better (Kirton, 2013). Adaptive personalities are observed by the more innovative then detail oriented, systematic, organized and traditional. On the other hand more innovative persons, tend to less favor planned situations where they may build innovative thoughts as a mode of changing or altering structural elements (Kirton, 2013). More innovative personalities are usually viewed by the more adaptive as liberal, rule-breaking, and unconventional.

An individual's favored problem-solving style cannot be changed or developed, it is relatively constant throughout one's life (Kirton, 2013); This contradicts an individual's understanding and approach to leadership, which may change depending on the pertinent attitudes and opinions regarding leadership (Priest & Middleton, 2016). Knowing the solution of the problem, individuals can select to function according to more adaptive or more innovative style (Kirton, 2011).

The Adaptive Leadership Theory (AL) assists leaders to engage with followers and motivate them to develop their firms in a changing environment (Heifetz et al., 2009). Although the concept of adaptive leadership have been established by numerous theorists, it progressed from situational, transformational, and complexity leadership theories (Cojocar, 2009), to later syndicate practical directions for the collectivistic-minded leader with a firm's view informed by complex adaptive systems theory (Northouse, 2022).

Both A-I theory and AL share parallel terms regarding the notion of adaption. They both focus on ways by which leaders and individuals sort out various types of challenges and manifest needed change, but one highlights the difference in the style of how individuals solve problems and the other describes a series of leader/group processes (Cletzer et al., 2021). Even though the expressions may be hard to separate, the outlines can be complementary. If AL provides the prescription for a problem-solving process, A-I theory helps explain why the process may be effective—and why the same process with a different group of people may be ineffective.

Various organizations nowadays are facing challenges in keeping the sustainability of the firm and its employees that might include matters, such as determining the adequate way to ensure mutual benefit of all stakeholders, or to resolve deep rooted systemic issues that restrain the fruitful setup of the firms. the framework of adaptive leadership identified highlighted a flexibility in dealing with adaptive problems in a different way from dealing with technical problems (Heifetz et al., 2009).

While most leadership theories emphasize enthusiasm, encouragement, and greater productivity, adaptive leadership emphasizes the leaders and followers' contribution to social learning (table 5) that enables firms to be flexible and to adapt in fast changing environments (Heifetz et al., 2009). Adaptive problems are ambiguous and need the ability to recognize the issue at all. Learning is required for solutions, and stakeholders must change their standards, motivations, advancements, or cultural practices in order to restructure their company's identity. The leader's role also changes with adaptive problems. The adaptive leader streamlines social learning by emphasizing questions for stakeholders to respond to since the answer is unknown. Adaptive leaders alert the organization to the impending hazard in the absence of a clear remedy.

Table 5. The Adaptive Leadership Style.

Adaptive Style	Focus	Organizational Influence
	Employee Engagement	Adaptive leaders foster an environment of employee engagement and continuous learning and experimentation within an organization. while responding to challenges, address various risks in a timely manner (Heifetz et al., 2009).
	Social Learning	Firms are more flexible and adapt in fast changing environments (Heifetz et al., 2009). Leaders alter stakeholders' standards, drives, progressions, or cultural customs to reorganize their firm's identity.
	Innovative Solutions	Adaptive leaders provide continuous feedback. and knowing the solution of the problem, individuals can select to function according to more adaptive or more innovative style (Kirton, 2011).
	Emotional Intelligence and Social Awareness	Adaptive leaders alert the organization to the impending danger by: (a) acknowledging their part as a leaders; (b) recognizing what works and what does not; (c) frequently pushing against the status quo; and (d) discovering the balance in the unbalanced (Cancialosi, 2014).

Source: (the authors)

Since stakeholders' current roles and standards are likely unsupportive in tackling the adaptive challenge, the adaptive leader resists stakeholders' desires to revert to their existing roles and norms. Lastly, because stakeholders must observe a necessity for alteration before any adaptation happens, the adaptive leader lets conflict emerge and, in many situations, actively pursues to resolve in an attempt to nurture adaptation (Heifetz et al., 2009). Adaptive leaders may have four main concerns within disequilibrium: (a) acknowledge their part as a leaders; (b) recognize what works and what does not; (c) frequently push against the status quo; and (d) discover the balance in the unbalanced (Cancialosi, 2014).

Adaptive leaders are able to foster an environment of continuous learning and experimentation within an organization while addressing challenges, and at the same time address various risks in a timely manner (Heifetz et al., 2009). Sustainability initiatives require supply chain collaboration through constant pivoting and fast responses to the changing market conditions. Leaders who can adapt to the dynamic environment may be able to engage their teams and supply chain partners quickly partner, through the identification of innovative solutions

1.4 Leadership and Circular Strategies

Successful circular strategies depend on the alignment of certain leadership styles with the organization strategic vision and its appropriate culture. The literature identified that the transformational, the ethical, the participative and adaptive styles are specifically most suitable to support the transitioning towards circular strategies and relevant to drive forward sustainability initiatives.

1.4.1 Transformational Leadership and Redesigning Processes

In redefining processes for circular economies, the transformational leadership surface as an important style that embraces innovative practices. Through its inspirational motivation and continuous communication dimensions, transformational leadership fosters an environment of cultural change, where employees feel empowered to creative sustainable practices (Garcia-Morales et al., 2020). Transformational leadership is a powerful tool (Ahsan, 2024) that inspires and motivates employees to achieve shared goals, thereby creating an effective culture that drives forward sustainability and corporate responsibility activities. Ray Anderson, founder of Interface, Inc. used a transformational style to encourage innovation in product design to align with circular economy and sustainability principles, which resulted in the "mission Zero" initiatives that reduced environmental footprint to Zero level in 2020 (Interface, Inc., 2021).

1.4.2 Ethical Leadership and Product Life-Cycle Design

Investment in sustainable products appears to be crucial to enable a successful circular strategy implementation. Leaders must be able to incorporate sustainability in their core business values, thereby increasing their stakeholders' buy-in and facilitating innovation. The ethical leadership style surface as an important driver and must, in view of the leadership ability to develop a voluntary environmental behavior among employees to achieve long term sustainable performance (Dey et al., 2022). Unilever incorporated ethical leadership in its product design, by increasing its commitment to sustainability practices throughout its product life cycle from raw material to product disposal (Unilever, 2023). This ethical conduct enabled Unilever to adopt a "Sustainable Living Plan" that aims at reducing its negative environmental impact, enhancing its social impact, thereby reducing their carbon emissions and improving their overall product health and wellbeing. Unilever partnered with farmers and was able to: source 100% of its agricultural products sustainability; it was also able to design recyclable products with minimum harmful ingredients and to reduce CO2 emissions by 50% in their factories (Gunduz, 2023). Unilever also optimized its distribution using transportation logistics solutions to reduce carbon emissions, and ensured to engage in initiatives that do not lead to ocean plastic.

1.4.3 Participative Leadership and Supply Chain Collaboration

Leaders with participative styles are characterized by open communication and inclusivity, which in turn may boost effective collaborative efforts (Kirkpatrick& Lock, 2020). Participative leadership positively correlates with knowledge sharing intentions among various stakeholders (Toufighi, 2024), and encourages employees' willingness to collaborate across cultural groups. Leaders who adopt participative style grow trust among the supply chain partners, and encourage a culture of trust and cooperation relationship, deemed a requirement for circular strategies implementation. Patagonia was able to integrate environmental responsibility to its image and identity through the participative leadership style of its founder, Yvon Chouinard (Pantagonia, 2022; Chouinard, 2016)., who adopted innovative practices that support circular economy and customer participation and engagement, such as the Worn Wear program that encouraged customer to repair their gears and recycle them.

1.4.4 Adaptive Leadership and Supply Chain Collaboration

Supply chain collaboration requires constant pivoting and fast responses to the changing market conditions. Leaders who can adapt to the dynamic environment may be able to engage their teams and supply chain partners quickly partner, through the identification of innovative solutions. Adaptive leaders may increase their employee self-efficacy (Chughtai, 2024), and use adaptive strategies that boosts circularity within the supply chain (Heifetz et al., 2009). The CEO of Coca-Cola, James Quincey, implemented the "World Without Waste Initiative" using a more collaborative and adaptive style (Coca-Cola, 2022; Quincey, 2019). Quincey emphasized collaboration among various stakeholders to align them with sustainability goals, and was able to pivot Coca-Cola's strategic direction towards circular packaging and recycling initiatives (Coca-Cola, 2022; Quincey, 2019).

Table 6. Circular Economy, Sustainability, Leadership Styles.

Codes		**Themes**	**Description**	**Implementation**
Circular Economy Initiatives	Redesign Business Processes	Long term Resources Use	Process Re-evaluation to extend the product life and minimize waste	Investment in design for disassembly and predictive maintenance
	Product life Cycle	Sustainable Product Design	Incorporate sustainability practices throughout the product life cycle	Use recyclable materials and conduct life-cycle assessments
	Collaboration in Supply Chain	Inter-Organizational Cooperation	Partnership with suppliers on sustainable practices and joint recycling efforts	Engage stakeholders in eco-practices and encourage transparency.
Sustainability Initiatives	Product and Service Sustainability	Recyclability and Durability	Re-used and re-purposed products and eco-friendly alternatives	Designing recyclable and durable products and decreasing the negative impact of product life-cycle.
	Social Sustainability	Transparency and Responsible Conduct	Fair labor practices and promoting diversity in supply chain	Applying safe working conditions and offering equitable wages.
	Environmental Sustainability	Renewable Energy Optimization	Reduction in carbon emissions and ecological footprint	Implementation programs on waste reduction and adoption of sustainable packaging
	Accountability and Governance	Targets clarity and Accurate Governance Structures	Progress feedback and engagement of stakeholders	Using an effective corporate governance structure that oversees sustainability outcomes

continued on following page

Table 6. Continued

Codes		Themes	Description	Implementation
Leadership Styles	Transformational Leadership	Inspiring Motivation	Leaders who inspires a vision and motivate employees to adopt sustainable practices and implement change	Investment in employee training and encouraging a culture of innovation and creativity
	Ethical Leadership	Sustainable Practices	Leaders who prioritize fairness, integrity and socially responsible activities	Implement Corporate responsibility strategies that fosters environmental well-being
	Participative Leadership	Employee Engagement	Leaders who involve employees in decision-making and increase their accountability and foster collaboration and ownership	Encouraging employee feedback and creating cross-functional teams for initiatives
	Adaptive Leadership	Driving Change	Leaders who are flexible and able to manage uncertainties in Circular Strategies	Empowering employees, responding to challenges and changes, and encouraging continuous learning while fostering resilience

Source: (the authors)

1.5 Leadership and Sustainability Initiatives

1.5.1 Transformational Leadership and Sustainability Practices

Transformational leaders are able to inspire employees and ignite a vision for the future, thereby driving forward organizational objectives (table 6). They are able to develop an emotional bond with followers, and instill a sense of purpose with their team members to go beyond themselves towards new innovations and sustainable businesses (Garcia-Morales, 2020). They are able to motivate their employees to adopt actions that support the long term use of resources thereby contributing to Sustainable economies. Environmental sustainability requires organizations to exhibit dynamic capabilities (Abbas, 2024) which encompass their ability to change and enhance their skills and resources to be able to respond to environmental changes (Dayioglu et al., 2024). Firms are in constant need for transformational leaders who are resilient, adaptive, flexible and quick to exploit green business opportunities and integrate environmental sustainable activities, such as environmentally friendly innovations, into their core business operations (Baia & Ferreire, 2024). Philips integrated product design for reuse and disassembly in the medical equipment and consumer electronics divisions, thereby ensuring that they are easily repaired, enhanced, recycled and reducing waste to extend lifecycles

1.5.2 Ethical Leadership and Sustainability Practices

Ethical Leaders prioritize social responsibility and environmental well-being, and encourage inter-departmental collaboration to achieve sustainable goals (Brown & Trevino, 2014). This type of leadership style grows socially responsible corporate citizens who are able to rise above their own interests to serve the societal well-being. Leaders with ethical inclination are able to merge the principles of integrity and accountability into their business practices to ensure the sustainability of their circular economies (table 6). Ethical leaders who are able to cultivate social capital characterized by high support to pro-environmental behavior, and committed to socially responsible growth objectives, succeed in integrating value-based practices and ethical competencies into their strategic system thinking (Suriyanketkaew et al., 2022). Important sustainable practices include empowering human capital with care for stakeholders and encouraging ethical values and altruism and cultivating social capital through social innovation (Suriyanketkaew et al., 2022). Ethical leaders support the involvement of communities in activities, such as Walmart (Walmart, Inc., 2025) who worked with municipalities to enhance its recycling process, whereby they ensured that their most valuable materials do not end up in landfills. This process helped Walmart to strengthen local economies by creating jobs in the waste and recycling management process.

1.5.3 Participative Leadership and Sustainability practices

Highly committed employees are empowered to participate in decision-making and execution strategies. The participative leadership style encourages employee engagement in the development, execution and restructuring of circular strategies and increases accountability (table 6). Whenever employees are more empowered, they are more likely to create solutions and opportunities for changes and improvement deemed necessary for commitment to sustainability initiatives (Kirkpatrick & Locke, 2020). The current business practices reveal that the new generation of employees is receptive to information and active, and the process of empowerment and participation in management and decision-making produces creative and innovative results deemed necessary to competitive sustainable practices (Wang et al., 2022). Participative leadership encourages the formation of cross-functional teams to enhance sustainable circular strategies. Nike (Nike, Inc., 2025) developed its Nike's Space Hippie collection through a cross-functional team that used insights from different perspectives such as engineering, material science, and sustainability experts.

Nike was able to create footwear made of factory waste and recycled materials, a process that enabled her to navigate the uncertainties imposed by resources scarcity and environmental regulations, while ensuring its commitment to sustainability.

1.5.4 Adaptive Leadership and Sustainability Initiatives

Adaptive Leaders foster an environment of continuous learning and experimentation within an organization while addressing challenges (Heifetz et al., 2009). They are able to respond swiftly to the risks and uncertainties related to the circular sustainable economies, including forming partnerships to overcome these uncertainties. Proctor & Gamble (Ellen MacArthur Foundation, n.d.) partnered with Ellen MacArthur Foundation to enhance its product design packaging and circularity practices, which enabled her to reduce waste and upgrade its recycling efforts. P& G also partnered with Terracycle in 2021 (Procter & Gamble, 2021) to create solutions for personal care and beauty products, in the areas of landfill waste and product life cycle (table 6). This adaptability makes organizations more responsive to sudden changes and enables them to develop and pivot their strategies to achieve sustainable goals efficiently. Adaptive leaders are crucial to increase the employee self-efficacy and pave the way to organizational innovation with the phenomenon of the learning organization (Chughtai, 2024).

2. RECOMMENDATIONS AND FUTURE PERSPECTIVES

The importance of leadership in driving forward circular economies is gaining momentum, in view of its alignment with sustainability practices imposed by government, legal and environmental entities. Transformational, ethical, participative and adaptive leaders enable firms, in implementing circular strategies, to adopt revolutionary approaches that boost efficient supply-chain, employee engagement, product and process life-cycle re-design for long-term resources utilization.

Organizations are recommended to use the below leadership strategies associated with circular strategies initiatives:

-Transformational leadership strategies include: growing a culture of innovation and creativity; encouraging product design processes for reuse and disassembly; promoting the sustainability initiatives and related values across the organization.

-Ethical leadership strategies include: promoting stakeholders' collaboration and increasing engagement and transparent communication; adopting responsible sourcing and sustainable practices; supporting the involvement of community in activities.

-Participative leadership strategies include: encouraging employee feedback to enhance sustainable practices; crowdsourcing ideas for circular products and services design; developing cross-functional teams to enhance their circular strategies.

-Adaptive leadership strategies include: boosting experimentation in circular processes; adjusting strategies according to market and resources availability; forming partnerships to overcome uncertainties in circular transitions.

Despite continuous advancement in this field, multi-national firms are facing obstacles in their way. The long-term efficiency and profitability of multi-nationals in the coming years will depend heavily on the integration of sustainability practices into circular strategies, technological breakthroughs, and active stakeholder involvement.

The future of sustainability in multinational firms is likely to include:

- Embedding sustainability into primary business strategies, and acknowledging its capacity for fostering innovation and achieving cost efficiencies.
- Enhancing collaborations with various stakeholders such as government bodies, non-profits organizations, and other enterprises to promote knowledge exchange and sharing of effective sustainability practices.
- Utilizing advanced technologies such as artificial intelligence and block chains

  to improve transparency in supply-chain, optimize resource management, and stimulate innovation in sustainable offerings.
- Engage all relevant parties to work proactively such as customers, employees, investors and local communities to grasp their needs and expectations concerning sustainability initiatives.

CONCLUSION

Adopting circular strategies necessitates transformative approaches that involves re-designing processes for the long-term resources use, an innovative product life-cycle design and an active supply-chain cooperation. Organizations may contribute to building a more resilient, socially responsible, and sustainable economy that reduces waste, saves resources, and encourages innovation. In doing so, firms may not only establish themselves as sustainability leaders, but also help create a healthier planet for coming generations.

REFERENCES

Abbas, J. (2024). Does the nexus of corporate social responsibility and green dynamic capabilities drive firms toward green technological innovation? the moderating role of green transformational leadership. *Technological Forecasting and Social Change*, *208*, 123698.

Agyemang, A. O., Yusheng, K., & Asei, A. (2025). Addressing Sustainability Footprint Disclosure for High Pollutant Firms in China and the US: The Roles of Firms Governance Structure, Financing Decisions, and Eco-Technology. *Corporate Social Responsibility and Environmental Management*.

Ahmad, S., Islam, T., Sadiq, M., & Kaleem, A. (2021). Promoting green behavior through ethical leadership: A model of green human resource management and environmental knowledge. *Leadership and Organization Development Journal*, *42*, 531–547.

Ahsan, M. J. (2024). Unlocking sustainable success: Exploring the impact of transformational leadership, organizational culture, and CSR performance on financial performance in the Italian manufacturing sector. *Social Responsibility Journal*, *20*(4), 783–803.

Apple. (2023). Environmental Progress Report. Retrieved from https://www.apple.com/environment/

Apple: Apple. (2022). Environment Progress Report. Retrieved from https://www.apple.com/environment/pdf/Apple_Environmental_Progress_Report_2022.pdf

Avolio, B. J., & Bass, B. M. (2001). *Developing potential across a full range of Leadership Tm: Cases on transactional and transformational Leadership*. Psychology Press. Baia, E. P., & Ferreira, J. J. (20240. Dynamic capabilities and performance: how has the relationship been assessed? *Journal of Management & Organization*, *30*(1), 188–217.

Bandura, A. (1986). *Social foundations of thought and action: A social-cognitive view*. Prentice-Hall.

Bashynska, I., Malynovska, Y., Kolinko, N. T., Jarvis, M., Kovalska, K., & Saiensus, M. (2024). Performance Assessment of sustainable leadership of enterprise's circular economy-driven innovative activities. *Sustainability*, *16*(2), 558.

Bedi, A., Alpaslan, C. M., & Green, S. (2016). A meta-analytic review of ethical leadership outcomes and moderators. *Journal of Business Ethics*, *139*, 517–536.

Bocken, N. M. P., Bakker, C., & Pauw, I. D. (2021). Product design and business model strategies for a circular economy. *Journal of industrial and production. Engineering*, *33*(5), 308–320. DOI: 10.1080/21681015.20116.1175126

Brown, M. E., & Treviño, L. K. (2006). Ethical leadership: A review and future directions. *The Leadership Quarterly*, *17*(6), 595–616.

Brown, M. E., & Trevino, L. K. (2024). Do role models matter? An investigation of ethical leadership and follower behavior. *Business Ethics Quarterly*, *24*(2), 227–252. https://doi.org/10.5840/beq201424219

Brown, M. E., Treviño, L. K., & Harrison, D. A. (2005). Ethical leadership: A social learning perspective for construct development and testing. *Organizational Behavior and Human Decision Processes*, *97*(2), 117–134.

Chouinard, Y. (2016). *Let my people go surfing: The education of a reluctant businessman—Including 10 more years of business unusual*. Penguin.

Chughtai, M. S., Syed, F., Nasser, S., & Chinchilla, N. (2024). Role of adaptive leadership in learning organizations to boost organizational innovations with change self-efficacy. *Current Psychology (New Brunswick, N.J.)*, *43*(33), 27262–27281.

Cletzer, D. A., Seibel, M. M., Kaufman, E. K., Friedel, C. R., & Elliott-Engel, J. (2021). When leadership terminology collides: A spirited comparison of adaption-innovation theory and adaptive leadership. In *Association of Leadership Educators 2021 virtual annual conference proceedings* (pp. 10–15). Association of Leadership Educators., https://www.leadershipeducators.org/resources/Documents/ALE%20 2021%20Proceedings%20Final.pdf

Coca-Cola. (2021). World Without Waste: Progress update. Retrieved from htpps:// www.cokecce.com/ou-strategic-priorities/sustainability/world-without-waste

Coca-Cola. (2022). World Without Waste: Progress update. Retrieved from htpps:// www.cokecce.com/ou-strategic-priorities/sustainability/world-without-waste

Cojocar, B. (2009). Adaptive leadership: Leadership theory or theoretical derivative? *Academic Leadership: The Online Journal*, *7*(1), 5.

D'Amato, A., Droste, N., & Piran, M. (2021). Circular economy and digital transformation: Opportunities for business model innovation. *Sustainability*, *10*(8), 2913. DOI: 10.3390/su10082913

Dey, M., Bhattacharjee, S., Mahmoud, M., Uddin, M. A., & Biswas, S. R. (2022). Ethical leadership for better sustainable performance: Role of employee values, behavior and ethical climate. *Journal of Cleaner Production*, *337*, 130527.

Ejibe, I., Nwankwo, T.C., Nwankwo, E.E., Okoye, C.C., & Scholastica, U.C. (2024). Advancing environmental sustainability in the creative sectors: A strategic HR framework based on data analytics and eco-innovation. *World Journal of Advanced Research and Reviews, 21*(3), 050-060.

Ellen MacArthur Foundation (N.D.). The Circular economy: A wealth of opportunities. Retrieved from https://www.ellenmacarthurfoundation.org

Garcia-Morales, V.j., & Martin-Rojas, R., & LIorens-Montes, F.J. (2020). The role of transformational leadership in the development of green innovation: Evidence from managers in the hotel industry. *Journal of Hospitality & Tourism Research (Washington, D.C.), 44*(8), 1200–1220. DOI: 10.1177/1096348018804604

Gartner. (2023). How Supply-Chain Thrive in a resource Constrained World. Retrieved from https://www.gartner.com/en/supply-chain/insights/beyond-supply-chain-blog/how-supply-chains-can-thrive-in-a-resource-constrainted-world

Geissdoefer, M., Morioka, S. N., DeCarvalho, M. M., & Evans, S. (2018). Business models and supply chains for the circular economy. *Journal of Cleaner Production, 190*, 712–721.

General Motors. (2023). Sustainability Report. Retrieved from https://www.gm.com/content/dam/company/docs/us/en/gmcom/company/GM_2023_SR.pdf

Giacalone, R. A., Promislo, M., & Jurkiewicz, C. (2016). Ethical impact theory: How unethical behavior at work affects individual well-being. *Global encyclopedia of public administration, public policy, and governance*, 1-5.

Govidan, K., & Soleimani, H. (2017). A review of reverse logistics and closed-loop supply chains: A journal of Cleaner Production focus. *Journal of Cleaner Production, 142*, 371–384.

Gunduz, C. P. B. (2023). Eco-Friendly and Cost-Effective Methods Applied to Sustainable Food Industries. In *Smart Food Industry: The Blockchain for Sustainable Engineering* (pp. 50-71). CRC Press.

Hazen, B. T., Russo, I., Confente, I., & Pellathy, D. (2021). Supply chain management for circular economy: Conceptual framework and research agenda. *International Journal of Logistics Management, 32*(2), 510–537.

Heifetz, R. A., Grashow, A., & Linsky, M. (2009). *The practice of adaptive leadership: Tools and tactics for changing your organization and the world.* Harvard business press.

Hsieh, C.-C., Tai, S.-E., & Li, H.-C. (2023). A Bibliometric Review of Ethical Leadership Research: Shifting Focuses and Theoretical Insights. *AERA Open, 9*. https://doi.org/ (Original work published 2023)DOI: 10.1177/23328584231209266

Interface. (2021). Mission Zero: 2020 sustainability goals. Retrieved form https;// www.interface/sustainability/emea/ecometrics-2020/SustainabilityHighlights_2020_EN.pdf

Katou, A. A., Kafetzopoulos, D., & Vayona, A. (2023). Investigating the serially mediating mechanisms of organizational ambidexterity and the circular economy in the relationship between ambidextrous leadership and sustainability performance. *Sustainability, 15*(10), 7937.

Khuntia, R., & Suar, D. (2004). A scale to assess ethical leadership of Indian private and public sector managers. *Journal of Business Ethics, 49*, 13–26.

Kirkpatrick, S. A., & Locke, E. A. (2020). Direct and indirect effects of three core charismatic leadership components on performance and attitudes. *The Leadership Quarterly, 12*(3), 459–483. https://doi.org/10.10`16/j.leaqua.2001.02.002

Kirton, M. J. (1976). Adaptors and innovators: A description and measure. *The Journal of Applied Psychology, 61*(5), 622–629.

Kirton, M. J. (2011). *Adaption-innovation: In the context of diversity and change.* Routledge. (Original work published 2003)

Kirton, M. J. (2013). *KAI theory workbook.* KAI Distribution Centre.

Kisi, N. (2022). The role of collaborative leadership in the circular economy. [Elsevier]. *Circular Economy and Sustainability*, •••, 535–544.

Koutroumanidis, T., & Tsironis, L. (2020). Predictive maintenance in circular economy: A systematic literature review. *Sustainability, 17*(19), 7830. DOI: 10.3390/su12197830

Kuhnert, K. W., & Lewis, P. (1987). Transactional and transformational leadership: A constructive developmental analysis. *Academy of Management Review, 12*(4), 648–657.

Lam, C. K., Huang, X., & Chan, S. C. (2015). The threshold effect of participative leadership and the role of leaders' information sharing. *Academy of Management Journal, 58*(3), 836–855.

Lowe, B. H., & Genovese, A. (2022). What Theories of value (could) underpin our circular future? *Ecological Economics*, •••, 195.

Lyndon, D., Gossling, R., & Kristensen, T. (2021). Designing for circularity in the fashion industry: A comparative analysis of circular design practices in SMEs and large companies. *Sustainability, 13*(4), 2054. DOI: 10.3390/su13042054

Mayer, D. M., Kuenzi, M., Greenbaum, R., Bardes, M., & Salvador, R. (2009). How low does ethical leadership flow? Test of a trickle-down model. *Organizational Behavior and Human Decision Processes, 108*, 1–13.

Meyer, R., & Meijers, R. (2017). *Leadership agility: Developing your repertoire of leadership styles*. Routledge.

Mok, Y. W., Arevalo, A., & Poon, C. S. (2020). Utilizing recycled materials in sustainable construction. *Sustainable Cities and Society, 19*, 35–45. DOI: 10.1016/j.scs.2015.06.002

Nelson, T., & Squires, V. (2017). Addressing complex challenges through adaptive leadership: A promising approach to collaborative problem solving. *Journal of Leadership Education, 16*(4), 111–123.

Nike. (2022). Move to Zero: A Journey toward zero carbon and zero waste. Retrieved from https;//www.nike.com/sustainability/move-to-zero

Nike, Inc. (2025). Sustainability and circular economy initiatives. Retrieved from https:// www.nike.com/sustainability/

Northouse, P. G. (2022). *Leadership: Theory and practice* (9th ed.). SAGE Publications.

Patagonia. (2022). Move to Zero: A Journey towards zero carbon and zero waste. Retrieved from https://www.patagonia.com/worn-wear/

Peng, J., Zou, Y.C., Kang, Y.J., and Zhang, X. (2021). Participative leadership and employee job well-being: perceived co-worker support as a boundary condition. *Journal of Psychological science*, 33, 873-880.

Prendeville, S., De Angelis, R., & Houghton, J. (2021). The Role of the consumer in the circular economy: Opportunities and challenges in understanding consumer behavior. *Journal of Consumer Behaviour, 17*(3), 201–210. https://dor.org/10.1002/cb.1693

Priest, K. L., & Middleton, E. (2016). Exploring leader identity and development. *New Directions for Student Leadership, 2016*(149), 37–47.

Procter & Gamble. (2021). P& G and TerraCycle partner to create circular solutions for personal care and beauty products. Retrieved from https://www.recyclingtoday.com/news/procter-and-gamble-joins-loop-reuse-recycle-platforms/

Psarommatis, F., & May, G. (2024). Digital product passport: A pathway to circularity and sustainability in modern manufacturing. *Sustainability*, *16*(1), 396.

Purpose Brand. (2023). Sustainability Reports Track Fortune 500 Corporate Climate Action. Retrieved from https://purposebrand.com/blog/sustainability-report-examples-fortune-2023/

Quincey, J. (2019). Sustainability at Coca-Cola: A focus on the future. Retrieved from https://www.coca-cola.com/content/dam/journey/us/en/private/fileassets/pdf/2019-annual-report.pdf

Ray, S., & Hardi, I. (2024). Refining ESG Disclosure's Role in Corporate Economic, Environmental., and Social Sustainability Performance. *Indatu Journal of Management and Accounting*, *2*(1), 1–8.

Russo, I., Confente, I., Scarpi, D., & Hazen, B. (2019). From trash to treasure: The impact of consumer perception of bio-waste products in closed-loop supply chains. *Journal of Cleaner Production*, *218*, 966–974.

Saad Alessa, G. (2021). The dimensions of transformational leadership and its organizational effects in public universities in Saudi Arabia: A systematic review. *Frontiers in Psychology*, *12*, 682092.

Salvioni, D.M., & Almici, A. (2020). Transitioning toward a circular economy: The impact of stakeholder engagement on sustainability culture. Sustainability, 12920), 8641.

Shi, X., Chen, Z., Wei, W., & Ni, B. J. (2024). Perspectives on sustainable plastic treatment: A shift form linear to circular economy. *Trends in Analytical Chemistry*, •••, 117631.

Su, Y., Li, Z., & Yang, C. (2021). Spatial interaction spillover effects betwen digital financial technology and urban ecological efficiency in China: And empirircal study based on spatial simutaneous equations. *International Journal of Environmental Research and Public Health*, *18*(16), 8535.

Toufighi, S. P., Sahebi, I. G., Govindan, K., Lin, M. Z. N., Van, J., & Brambini, A. (2024). Participative leadership, cultural factors, and speaking-up bahaviour: An examination of intra-organizational knowledge sharing. *Journal of Innovation & Knowledge*, *9*(3), 100548.

Treviño, L. K., Hartman, L. P., & Brown, M. (2000). Moral person and moral manager: How executives develop a reputation for ethical leadership. *California Management Review*, *42*(4), 128–142.

Tukker, A., & Tischner, U. (2006). *New business for old Europe: Product-service development, competitiveness, and sustainability*. Routledge.

Unilever. (2021). Unilever's plastic commitments: Our vision for a waste-free world. Retrieved from https://www.unilever.com/news/news-search/2021/unilever-announces-commitment-to-reduce-plastic-waste/

Usman, M., Ghani, U., Cheng, J., Farid, T., & Iqbal, S. (2021). Does participative leadership matters in employee' outcomes during COVID-19? Role of leader behavioral integrity. *Frontiers in Psychology*, *12*, 646442.

Walmart. (2023). Sustainability Report. Retrieved from https://corporate.walmart.com/purpose/esgreport/esg-approach/about-our-reporting

Walmart, Inc. (2025). Closed Loop Fund and community engagement in circular economy initiatives. Retrieved from https;//corporate.walmart.com/purpose/sustainability/planet/waste

Walmart: Walmart. (2021). Walmart's commitment to zero waste. Retrieved from https://corporate.walmart.com/newsroom/2021/10/06/walmart-announces-new-goals-to-reduce-packaging-waste-and-achieve-zero-waste-in-u-s-operations

Zhang, Z., Wang, M., & Fleenor, J. W. (2011, January). Effects of participative leadership: the moderating role of cultural values. *In Academy of management Proceedings* (Vol. 2011, No. 1. Pp 1-6). Briarcliff Manor, NY 10510: Academy of Management.

Zhu, Q., Geng, Y., & Yin, H. (2020). Circular economy practices: A comparative study of Chinese manufacturing enterprises. *Journal of Cleaner Production*, *196*, 1004–1015.

Zhu, W., May, D. R., & Avolio, B. (2004). The impact of ethical leadership behavior on employee outcomes: The roles of psychological empowerment and authenticity. *Journal of Leadership & Organizational Studies*, *11*, 16–26.

Zou, Y. C., Peng, J., & Hou, N. (2020). Participative leadership and creative performance: A moderated dual path model. *Journal of Management Science*, *33*, 39–51.

KEY TERMS AND DEFINITIONS

Adaption-Innovation theory (A-I): Individuals have different styles in handling and solving encountered problems

Adaptive Leadership Theory (AL): Assists leaders to engage with followers and motivate them to develop their firms in a changing environment

Adaptive leadership: Ability of the leader to inspire others and assist in resolving challenges, think ahead and plan amid the potential changes in the future

Circular Economy: Changing the traditional way of thinking about products, based on a traditional linear model to a totally new product system

Ethical Impact (EIT) Theory: Ethical leadership may work well through its justice focus by reducing stress level in the work environment and enhancing the quality of job performance

Ethical Leadership: Endorsing moral behavior among employees and stakeholders, and reinforcing the ethical conduct of individuals within organizations

Leadership: Process of influencing and guiding groups of people to achieve common goals

Participative Leadership: Involvement of team members in decision-making and delegation of authority

Social Cognitive Theory: Participative leadership style increased the psychological security of employees and boosts their self-efficacy

Social Information Processing Theory: Highlights the growing positive impact of the participative leadership style on employee performance

Sustainability: Meeting the needs of the current generation without compromising the resources for future use

Transformational Leadership: transforming the employees' behavior in order to make them identify with the organizational mission, goal, and standards

Chapter 5
Leading With Heart and Mind:
Neurobiological Dimensions of Decision-Making for Sustainable and Circular Economy Leadership

Selma Kalkavan
https://orcid.org/0000-0003-3252-0345
Independent Researcher, Turkey

Sonja Vlaar
Attune.nl, The Netherlands

ABSTRACT

Leadership decisions rarely follow a purely logical path. In our exploration of decision-making processes, we observed that cognitive reasoning, emotional signals, and physiological responses often intersect. Moments of increased heart rate, tightened muscles, or altered breathing are not just bodily reactions—they shape the way choices are made, especially under pressure. Drawing on both the literature and insights from a focused exploratory study, we argue that effective leadership emerges when these internal systems—mind, emotion, and body—are in balance. Yet, decision-making models tend to prioritize cognitive skills, often neglecting the embodied experiences that silently guide leaders' actions. This work invites a reconsideration of such frameworks, suggesting that greater physiological self-awareness may unlock a more adaptive, responsive, and authentic approach to leadership.

DOI: 10.4018/979-8-3373-7655-4.ch005

1. INTRODUCTION

For a long time, people believed that the best leadership decisions came from clear and rational thinking. But new findings from neuroscience suggest that this is only part of the story. Signals from the body such as changes in heart rate or muscle tension can give leaders important feedback. This is true especially when emotions of the leaders run high. Being aware of these signals does not weaken decision-making as it may make choices stronger and more responsive to the real situation.

There is also increasing evidence that the heart and brain are more connected than we once assumed (Villiger & Hammig, 2023). The way these two systems communicate affects the clarity of thought and the ability to stay calm under stress. Leaders who learn to listen their bodies are often better equipped to handle challenging situations with both flexibility and care (Qi et al., 2021). This skill has become even more important in today's era of sustainability and the circular economy. Effective leadership now demands a systems-level view. This means that effective leadership requires balancing economic success with environmental restoration and social well-being (Adedeji et al., 2014). From this perspective, the neurobiological integration of the heart and mind offers a strong framework for truly holistic thinking. It helps leaders connect logical analysis with empathy, ethical foresight and long-term environmental considerations. By building both physiological balance and emotional intelligence, leaders can approach complex sustainability challenges with greater clarity and resilience (Ezeudu et al., 2016). This approach ensures that decisions increase the organizational performance and support the renewal of natural and social systems (Almeida et al., 2024).

In this study, we set out to examine how leaders experience and apply these different types of awareness in their decision-making. We invited 60 participants to take part in a survey reflecting on these ideas. Twenty-seven responded giving us valuable insights into how the mind, emotions, body and intuition work together in leadership. In the following sections we share what we learned from their responses.

2. BALANCING COGNITIVE SYSTEMS: BRAIN AND BODY IN DECISION-MAKING

Theories in psychology and neuroscience describe decision-making often as the interaction between two distinct routes to making decisions. Daniel Kahneman popularized this idea in *Thinking, Fast and Slow* (2011), calling them System 1 and System 2.

System 1 operates fast, automatic, with little or no effort, relying on intuition, and is emotionally charged. It activates our innate and instinctive responses. According to

Kahneman "*intuition is recognition*", drawing his idea from expert performance—like a firefighter sensing danger before they can articulate why. System-2 runs slowly in an effortful manner, is more deliberate, and based on logical reasoning. System 2 is thought to be an evolutionary more recent system that can override the decisions from System 1 (Tversky & Kahneman, 1983).

In normal situations the intuitive System 1 may initiate the decision-making process in the brain and body, and the reasoning of System 2 checks whether the tendency is compatible. However, when under stress, the reasoning system may not check these response tendencies and instead allow leaders to rely on their default intuitive actions in response to challenges. Grounded on this "intuition proposes, reasoning decides" type of dual system, Yu (2016) proposes that when under stress, intuitive responses may bypass the examinations of reasoning and reach the threshold to become final decisions.

This would imply that stressed leaders may fall back on their intuition and less on their conscious reasoning. Hence intuition is a cognitive process that has multiple meanings and implications.

More recent neuroscience research reveals that decision-making is deeply embodied. Intuition is not just created by the brain's unconscious or automatic systems. Intuitive insights can also emerge as emotional responses that we feel physically, such as tension, relaxation, or a sudden shift in mood, or bodily reactions, like a gut feeling or a sense of unease.

Physical sensations like a racing heart or gut feeling can drive fast, intuitive System 1 responses, showing that intuition is shaped not just by the mind's rational thinking but by the entire body, not just the brain. For leaders, this connection is vital. Platt (2018) emphasizes that effective decisions arise from recognizing biological signals and balancing them with conscious analysis. In complex social contexts, relying solely on logic of System 2, or intuition of System 1 is risky; great leaders, as Platt notes, "*listen with their heart and verify with their mind.*" Integrating insights from both brain and body, especially the heart's neural network, supports more holistic, balanced leadership decisions.

3. BALANCING HEART AND BRAIN

The focus of this article is to explore the dynamic, bidirectional communication between the heart and the brain, emphasizing its relevance to cognitive and emotional decision-making.

3.1. Neural Communication Between Heart and Brain

The human heart has a more complex role in the body than simply maintaining circulation. Studies in neurocardiology reveal that the heart contains nearly 40,000 nerve cells—known as sensory neurons—that are arranged in structured ganglion networks within its walls (Armour, 1991; HeartMath Institute, 2023). This built-in neural system operates together with the autonomic nervous system and contributes to the body's ability to process internal signals (Jefferson Research, 2022). Interestingly, these neurons are not limited to managing cardiac rhythms alone; they are also involved in memory-related mechanisms, supporting both short-term and long-term information processing (AHA Journals, 2003).

The heart and the brain remain in constant communication through several biological routes. One of the key channels for this exchange is the autonomic nervous system, which includes the sympathetic branch, responsible for activating the body's responses, and the parasympathetic branch, which supports calm and recovery processes. Signals from the heart travel along these pathways to reach the brain. After this, these signals help brain to reach a balance between stress and relaxation. According to Breit et al. (2018), a key part of this system is the vagus nerve. This acts like a communication line between the heart and the brain. While signals travel in both directions it is striking that around 80 percent of this information actually flows from the heart to the brain. This means the heart is not just following orders. In fact, it is actively sending information about the body's internal state and influencing decisions. Other research supports this idea. That study has shown that messages from the heart reach brain regions that play a major role in emotional regulation and automatic functions. In this perspective specifically the amygdala, thalamus and hypothalamus play a significant role (Tendulkar et al., 2024). From there, these signals move on to the cerebral cortex. In here, tasks such as reasoning, controlling attention, and making decisions comes into life.

This constant conversation between the heart and brain shows that decision-making is not simply a mental process. It also draws on information from the body's physiological systems. How we process emotions, manage stress and focus our attention can all be shaped by signals from the heart. For leaders understanding this link offers an important advantage. Because it helps them to use internal awareness to make better choices in complex situations.

3.2. How the Heart communicates with the Brain through chemicals

In addition to electrical signals, the heart also communicates with the brain through certain chemicals, such as Atrial Natriuretic Factor (ANF) and oxytocin. The heart can also respond to chemicals like endorphins.

- ANF is a hormone produced by the heart. It helps regulate blood pressure and affects brain areas involved in stress regulation and emotional balance.
- Oxytocin, often called the "love hormone," is primarily made by the hypothalamus, and there is some research suggesting that oxytocin receptors are found in the heart and that the heart can produce small amounts of oxytocin locally, especially under stress. Oxytocin promotes trust, bonding, and emotional connection. While the main source of oxytocin is the hypothalamus, research has shown that oxytocin is also produced in the heart and other tissues, influencing brain regions linked to social and emotional processing.
- Endorphins are mainly produced by the central nervous system (brain and spinal cord) and the pituitary gland. They are the body's natural painkillers and can lower the heart rate. They contribute to feelings of well-being and impact brain circuits that regulate mood.

New neuroscience research shows that the brain constantly monitors internal body signals and integrates them into decision-making. In high-stress or anxiety-inducing situations, physical changes like a racing heart, high blood pressure, and rapid breathing can significantly alter how decisions are made (Kuvaas & Damasio, 2021). In a study with monkeys, researchers (Fujimoto, Murray & Rudebeck, 2021) found that about 15% of neurons in the brain's decision-making regions synchronized with heart rate fluctuations, acting as an "internal radar" that tracks the body's arousal levels, independent of the decision being made. This constant heart-brain communication shapes not only physiological responses but also emotional and cognitive processes. While leaders may not consciously recognize most physiological shifts of interoception in their bodies, they often can feel sensations in their heart.

Intuition can pick up on non-verbal cues from others, such as body language or tone of voice, which our bodies interpret before our logical mind catches on. What starts as an unspoken, embodied physiological experience in their heart can evolve into a narrative (Vlaar, 2024), a process that significantly influences conscious decision-making. These findings suggest that ancient sayings about the "*wisdom of the heart*" have a scientific basis. In modern terms, concepts like "heart intelligence" or "inner wisdom" describe this complex neural and biochemical connection.

3.3. Heart Rhythm Coherence

The key takeaway for leaders is clear: regulating HRV is essential for making sound decisions. When experiencing extreme stress or a reactive state, it is wise to pause and calm the biological system before making critical choices.

This approach aligns with the concept of "decision hygiene"—a systematic way to reduce random fluctuations (noise) in decision-making (Kahneman et al., 2021). In this context, emotional regulation serves as a key component of decision hygiene. Simple techniques like taking deep breaths, stepping away briefly, or reframing a situation can help lower emotional intensity, allowing the brain to regain clarity and balance.

By recognizing signs of high stress, such as an accelerated heart rate, and engaging in conscious breathing or mindfulness techniques, leaders need to first regulate this emotional "noise" to later be able to make more consistent, rational, and well-informed decisions.

Case Study 1:HeartMath Training in a High-Stress Call Center

A telecommunications company collaborated with the HeartMath Institute to reduce stress and enhance performance among call center employees. Over six weeks, employees practiced HRV-based breathing techniques to regulate emotional reactivity before engaging with customers.

Outcomes:

- 23% decrease in stress
- 17% increase in customer satisfaction
- 12% drop in absenteeism

This example illustrates how conscious physiological regulation improves performance under pressure and supports clearer, more empathetic decision-making. (McCraty et al., 2003)

4. THE IMPACT OF AROUSAL AND EMOTIONS

4.1. Arousal and Emotions Affect Decision-Making

Arousal refers to the body's physiological and psychological state of alertness, preparing an individual to respond to external and internal stimuli. It can manifest as increased heart rate, heightened sensory awareness, or emotional reactivity. While arousal is often associated with stress or excitement, it also plays a critical role in optimizing attention, motivation, and decision-making.

Moderate arousal—such as a slightly elevated heart rate or a sense of focused alertness—can enhance cognitive performance. This principle is illustrated by the Yerkes-Dodson law (Yerkes & Dodson, 1908), which proposes an inverted U-shaped relationship between arousal and performance: up to a certain point, increases in arousal improve performance, but beyond that threshold, further arousal leads to cognitive decline.

In a recent study involving non-human primates, moderate arousal (measured via increased heart rate) was linked to quicker and more accurate reward-based decisions, such as choosing a larger amount of fruit juice (Fujimoto et al., 2021). However, when arousal was artificially heightened—by suppressing amygdala activity and further accelerating heart rate—the monkeys' performance deteriorated. They made slower decisions and more frequent errors.

These findings suggest that mild physiological arousal facilitates efficient decision-making. However, excessive arousal disrupts cognitive functioning and leads to reduced judgment. This has critical implications for leaders and professionals operating under pressure. It is because it indicates that beyond a certain point, stress no longer sharpens decision-making. In fact, it sabotages the clear decision making.

4.2. High Arousal Alters Brain Function

When stress or strong emotions cause arousal to rise sharply it brings significant changes to the brain's decision-making systems. Under normal circumstances, specialized neural networks help us weigh options, consider outcomes and make choices. But during extreme arousal, these networks become less active. The brain redirects its energy to monitoring the body's internal state. In the same monkey study, researchers found that in moments of high arousal, fewer neurons were involved in decision analysis. Conversely, more neurons responded to physical signals like changes in heart rate. In other words, the brain shifts its focus from thinking about outside choices to dealing with the body's internal alarm signals.

This redirection of neural focus helps explain why decision-making deteriorates under panic, fear, or intense anger. When overwhelmed by internal distress, the brain's capacity for reasoning, foresight, and reflective thinking is compromised. Instead, it prioritizes survival signals, often at the cost of clarity and rationality.

For leaders and professionals, this insight underscores the importance of managing internal states before making critical decisions. Recognizing the influence of high arousal on brain function can foster more adaptive responses to stress and help prevent reactive, emotionally driven choices.

Case Study 2: Google's gPause – Mindfulness and Leadership Clarity

As part of its internal development programs, Google introduced "gPause," a mindfulness initiative to help leaders manage stress and improve presence in decision-making.

Through body scans and focused breathing, leaders learned to reduce mental overload and regulate physiological arousal.

Reported benefits:

- Greater clarity in emotionally tense meetings
- Less reactivity under time pressure
- Improved emotional tone in team conversations

This case highlights how brief, embodied interventions can shift physiological states and enhance cognitive control. (Hölzel et al., 2011)

5. PATHOS AND ETHOS: EMOTION AND INTEGRITY IN DECISION-MAKING

Effective leadership requires more than logic—it calls for the integration of pathos (emotion) and ethos (values and integrity) in decision-making. Especially under pressure, emotional and ethical dimensions shape the choices leaders make, often more than they consciously realize.

As discussed in earlier sections, high arousal states—marked by elevated heart rate, stress hormones, and limbic system activation—can impair rational thinking and trigger reactive behaviour. In such states, pathos dominates, as the amygdala and limbic structures prioritize emotional survival mechanisms over reflective cognition. This is particularly evident in crisis situations where leaders may default to instinctive responses or be swayed by emotional appeals.

A strong ethical compass (ethos) can act as an internal anchor during times of emotional turbulence. Leaders who have taken the time to reflect deeply on their values and develop inner balance through practices that enhance heart-brain communication and heart rate variability (HRV) are often able to regain mental clarity and emotional stability more quickly. This supports what is described in section 3.3 as decision hygiene where managing one's internal state is essential for making consistent and rational choices. According to Çağrı Kara (2025), persuasion and leadership are not purely logical activities. They are embodied and relational, shaped by emotional connection and ethical credibility. Therefore, in high-pressure situations, when emotions run high, ethos offers a stabilizing foundation. Leaders who are firmly grounded in their values and can regulate their internal physiology are less likely to act on impulse and more likely to make decisions that align with their long-term vision and purpose. The dynamic interaction between pathos (emotion) and ethos (values) requires leaders to develop strong self-awareness, especially of their internal bodily signals, and to communicate effectively with others.

As seen in section 4, when leaders become attuned to their physiological signals—like shifts in heart rhythm or bodily tension—they gain early insight into their emotional states. This awareness creates a pause, a moment in which they can reconnect with their ethical stance and regulate their response. In essence, pathos and ethos do not oppose each other—they work in tandem. Emotions provide vital information about what matters; values determine how that information is acted upon. By honouring both, leaders can make decisions that are emotionally intelligent, ethically sound, and biologically regulated hallmarks of truly embodied leadership.

6. DECISION-MAKING IN TEAMS: THE POWER OF PHYSIOLOGICAL SYNCHRONY

Effective decision-making in teams is not only about intelligence or strategy. It is also strongly connected to physiology. Recent research by Michael Platt (2024) shows that physiological synchrony, especially when team members' heart rhythms align, plays an important role in group performance and decision quality.

In one study, teams of three to six people worked together to choose the best candidate for a job while their heart rates were monitored in real time. Surprisingly, the level of heart rhythm synchrony between team members predicted the accuracy of their decision with more than 70% reliability. Teams with higher synchrony were more likely to select the best candidate. This indicates a clear link between biological alignment and mental performance. Even more interesting, heart rhythm synchrony was a better predictor of team success than traditional measures of cohesion, such as surveys or individual evaluations. This supports the broader insight from Section 3, where heart-brain communication and heart rate variability (HRV) were shown to influence emotional regulation, cognitive clarity, and decision hygiene. In a team setting, collective coherence—where individuals' physiological states align—enhances the group's ability to process information, coordinate behaviour, and make sound decisions. For leaders, this highlights the importance of creating conditions that promote trust, openness, and emotional connection. Teams that feel psychologically safe are more likely to experience physiological harmony, which in turn strengthens collective intelligence. This resonates with earlier discussions on arousal and interoception (section 4), where high-stress environments were shown to impair decision-making. By contrast, environments that foster calm, attuned states often through shared values, empathy, and a clear sense of purpose promote better group outcomes.

Case Study 3: Heart Synchrony and Group Intelligence

In a recent study, Michael Platt and his team measured heart rhythm synchrony among team members engaged in a hiring simulation.

Outcomes: Teams with higher heart synchrony were 70% more likely to select the optimal candidate.

Synchrony outperformed traditional predictors of team performance such as individual experience or verbal engagement.

This underscores the potential of physiological coherence as a tangible driver of group intelligence and collaborative decision quality.(Platt et al., 2024, PNAS)

Furthermore, physiological synchrony is not just a byproduct of good collaboration. It can be cultivated. Shared breathing exercises, rituals that build connection, or even moments of collective silence can help align team members' internal states. These practices activate the vagal pathways discussed in section 3, facilitating heart-brain regulation and enhancing emotional resonance within the group.

In short, the biology of decision-making extends beyond the individual to the collective. Leaders who understand and intentionally support physiological synchrony in their teams are better equipped to unlock deeper cohesion, clearer communication, and more effective decision-making all vital in today's complex, high-stakes environments.

7. NEUROECONOMIC INSIGHTS FOR LEADERSHIP

Advances in neuroeconomics which is the interdisciplinary study combining neuroscience, psychology, and economics offer valuable insights into how cognitive and emotional processes shape human decision-making (Glimcher & Fehr, 2013). For leaders, understanding these brain-based mechanisms provides a powerful framework for navigating complex, high-stakes decisions with greater awareness and effectiveness.

- The Interplay of Emotion and Reason in Decision-Making

In normal circumstances, logical thinking is often linked to the prefrontal cortex. On the contrary, our emotions are shaped by areas like the amygdala, insula and other parts of the limbic system. Contrary to earlier thinking, these parts also play a powerful role in how we see risks, rewards, and possible outcomes (Bechara & Damasio, 2005). Feelings such as fear, excitement, anger or anxiety trigger physical changes in the body that can sometimes sharpen our focus while sometimes make our thinking less clear. This connects with earlier sections (3 and 4))). In those sections we saw how the connection between the heart and brain can influence clarity and thinking. For leaders these emotional and physical reactions can either help them make better decisions or cause mistakes.

A well-known example is loss aversion (Kahneman & Tversky), which shows that the fear of losing something can push people toward overly cautious choices. On the other hand, too much optimism can lead to unrealistic expectations or decisions based on wishful thinking. The best leaders learn to stay balanced and find a way to balance courage and caution.

- **Neurochemicals and the Physiology of Choice**

Dopamine and cortisol are brain chemicals which are at the heart of Neurochemicals. Dopamine is linked to looking forward to rewards, staying motivated and learning new things. Cortisol, on the other hand is a stress hormone that influences attention, memory as well as how we judge risks. High levels of dopamine can encourage people to take bold actions or explore new opportunities, while high levels of cortisol can make someone focus too narrowly, react quickly without thinking and feel more stressed.

As discussed in earlier sections, leaders can manage the effects of these chemicals by regulating their physical and emotional state. Techniques such as mindfulness, keeping the heart and brain in sync and paying close attention to signals from the body can all help. These practices reduce emotional "noise" and make it easier to think clearly and make sound decisions, especially in stressful situations (Kahneman et al., 2021).

- **Leadership Implications**

Leaders who understand and apply neuroeconomic insights are better equipped to:

- Self-regulate in emotionally charged situations,
- Recognize when internal biases may be distorting judgment,
- Influence stakeholders more effectively by aligning logical arguments with emotional resonance,
- Create team environments that foster psychological and physiological safety.

As shown in section 6, physiological synchrony among team members enhances collective decision-making. Leaders who manage their own internal state—especially in terms of arousal and emotional tone—can help regulate group dynamics, setting the tone for trust, coherence, and shared purpose.

- Ultimately, effective leadership is not just a cognitive exercise—it is a neurobiological process shaped by the interplay of emotion, physiology, and environment. By cultivating emotional intelligence, self-awareness, and decision hygiene, leaders can navigate uncertainty with greater resilience and consistency, while modelling the kind of grounded presence that enables others to do the same.

Aligning heart and brain in leadership decision-making creates a ripple effect that can enable and accelerate the interconnectedness at the core of a human-centred circular economy. The rational capacities of the brain allow leaders to *see* the system - understanding complexity, identifying patterns, and strategizing effectively. At the same time, the biologically rooted system of the heart enables leaders to *feel* the system – attuning to the emotional, social and ecological consequences behind the data.

This integration enhances leadership by fostering decisions that are both intelligent and ethical, strategical and compassionate. When leaders align cognition with emotion, they move beyond linear thinking and short-term gains to support long-term, systemic value creation. In doing so, they help cultivate organizations—and economies—that are resilient, regenerative, and deeply human.

8. STUDY DESIGN AND PARTICIPANT PROFILE

Building on the theoretical framework and literature reviewed in the previous sections—particularly those exploring the interplay of heart, mind, and emotion in leadership decision-making—this section presents the design and findings of an exploratory empirical study. The purpose of this study was to investigate how leaders consciously or unconsciously engage the dimensions of cognition (mind), emotion, and physiological awareness (heart), and how the integration of these domains shapes their decision-making processes in real-life leadership contexts.

To examine these dynamics, a survey instrument was developed, consisting of 20 carefully formulated statements. These statements were designed to assess four interconnected dimensions:

- **Heart** (physiological awareness and coherence),
- **Mind** (cognitive clarity and reasoning),

- **Emotion** (emotional awareness and regulation),
- and their **Integrated Alignment**, which we have termed the **holistic dimension**.

8.1. Set up of the survey

A survey was distributed via email to a purposive sample of 60 individuals—selected for their current leadership roles or substantial experience in leadership settings. Participation was voluntary and anonymous, with 27 completed responses received, representing a 45% response rate. The collected data were analysed using descriptive statistics, as well as correlation and regression analyses, to explore potential relationships and patterns among the four dimensions.

This section outlines the structure of the survey, provides an overview of participant demographics, and presents key findings that highlight the significance of integrating emotional, cognitive, and physiological insight in leadership practice.

Table 1. Statements Listed by Dimension[1]

Dimension	Question	Statement
Heart	Q1	I notice an increase in my heart rate when making decisions.
Heart	Q2	My emotional state affects my heart rhythm during decision-making.
Heart	Q3	I feel physical tension in my chest when I'm indecisive.
Heart	Q4	I make decisions by listening to my heart.
Heart	Q5	I consciously regulate my breathing to manage my heartbeat in stressful decisions.
Mind	Q1	I focus on logical and systematic thinking when making decisions.
Mind	Q2	Mental fatigue reduces the quality of my decisions.
Mind	Q3	I visualize options in my mind before deciding.
Mind	Q4	I can't make sound decisions without mental clarity.
Mind	Q5	I mentally review past experiences while making decisions.
Emotion	Q1	My emotions guide my decisions.
Emotion	Q2	Negative emotions slow down my decision-making.
Emotion	Q3	Positive emotions help me take risks.
Emotion	Q4	Emotional awareness improves my decisions.
Emotion	Q5	Suppressing my emotions leads to less satisfying decisions.
Holistic	Q1	I consider my body, mind, and emotions as a whole when making decisions.
Holistic	Q2	Decision-making requires physical and mental balance for me.
Holistic	Q3	I make the best decisions when I feel internal alignment.

continued on following page

Table 1. Continued

Dimension	Question	Statement
Holistic	Q4	I recognize bodily signals during decision-making.
Holistic	Q5	Emotional intelligence plays a crucial role in my effective decision-making.

Participant Demographics

- **Age Distribution**: 33% of participants were aged 35–44, 30% were aged 45–54, and another 30% were aged 55 and above.
- **Gender**: 59% identified as female, 33% as male, and 4% did not disclose their gender.
- **Educational Attainment**: 56% held a master's degree, 22% a doctoral degree, and 22% a bachelor's degree.
- **Leadership Experience**: 44% were in active leadership positions at the time of the survey, 11% served in project-based leadership roles, and 15% had prior leadership experience but were not currently in a leadership role. In total, 70% of respondents reported having some form of leadership experience.
- **Geographic Distribution**: 63% of participants were based in Turkey, while 37% were working internationally.

This sample reflects diversity across age, gender, educational background, leadership experience, and geographical context, providing a broad foundation for understanding variations in leadership decision-making processes.

8.2. Hypotheses Considered in the Study and Data Analysis Results

We formulated several hypotheses for each dimension. For the statistical calculation we selected four hypotheses (one hypothesis for each dimension) that are most relevant to the research topic. In table 2 are presented the selected hypotheses and the related questions.

Table 2. Hypotheses Evaluation Results

Dimension	Hypothesis	Related Survey Items	R^2	Significant Variable	Result
Heart Hypothesis	H1: Leaders with high physiological awareness (heart rate, chest tension, breathing) are assumed to have a higher likelihood of making intuitive decisions.	Q1: "I notice an increase in my heart rate when making decisions." Q3: "I feel physical tension in my chest when I'm indecisive." Q4: "I make decisions by listening to my heart." Q5: "I consciously regulate my breathing to manage my heartbeat in stressful decisions."	0.03	None	Not supported
Mind Hypothesis	H2: Leaders' ability to mentally visualize past experiences and maintain mental clarity improves the quality of their decisions.	Q2: "Mental fatigue reduces the quality of my decisions." Q3: "I visualize options in my mind before deciding." Q4: "I can't make sound decisions without mental clarity." Q5: "I mentally review past experiences while making decisions."	0.37	Mental review of past experiences ($p = 0.022$)	Partially supported
Emotional Guidance Hypothesis	H3: Leaders who integrate emotions into their decision-making experience higher internal alignment, especially when positive emotions are present. However, over-reliance on emotions may negatively affect this alignment.	Q1: "My emotions guide my decisions." Q2: "Negative emotions slow down my decision-making." Q3: "Positive emotions help me take risks." Q5: "Suppressing my emotions leads to less satisfying decisions."	0.38	Q3 (+), Q1 (–), $p < 0.05$	Partially supported
Holistic Alignment Hypothesis	H4: Mentally reviewing past experiences contributes to internal coherence and satisfaction in decision-making under high pressure.	Q1: "I consider my body, mind, and emotions as a whole when making decisions." Q2: "Emotional awareness improves my decisions." Q3: "I mentally review past experiences while making decisions." Q4: "My emotional state affects my heart rhythm during decision-making." Q5: "I make the best decisions when I feel internal alignment."	0.38	Mental review of past experiences ($p = 0.022$)	Partially supported

8.3 Analysis of responses

H1: It was hypothesized that leaders with higher physiological awareness (expressed by heart rate, chest tension and breathing regulation) are more likely to make integrated (holistic) decisions.

However, regression analyses performed on the actual data revealed a very low explanatory power of the model ($R^2 = 0.035$, $p = 0.841$), and none of the independent variables heart rate, chest tension, and breathing were found to be statistically significant ($p = 0.841, 0.628, 0.947$, respectively). Physiological awareness (such as sensing increases in heartrate or chest tension or consciously regulating breathing) was not significantly associated with intuitive decision-making. These findings indicate that this hypothesis is not supported.

H2: The hypothesis assumes that leaders who possess mental clarity can mentally visualise past experiences and tend to make higher-quality decisions.

The regression model based on mental clarity explains 22% of the variance in decision quality ($R^2 = 0.222$, $p = 0.117$). The strongest contribution among the variables comes from mentally reviewing past experiences ($\beta = 0.4189$, $p = 0.123$), which, although not statistically significant, is close to the threshold. This suggests that with a larger sample size, this relationship might become more meaningful. Mental visualization (Q3) and cognitive fatigue (Q2) also contributed to the model, albeit without reaching significance. These results indicate that cognitive preparation plays a meaningful role in decision quality.

H3: Leaders who include emotions in their decision-making process experience higher internal alignment—particularly in the presence of positive emotions. However, over-reliance on emotions may reduce this alignment.

The model related to this hypothesis is statistically significant ($R^2 = 0.38$, $p = 0.027$). Positive emotions significantly and positively affect decision-making ($\beta = 0.441$, $p = 0.027$), suggesting that emotional motivation can enhance decision quality.

Conversely, relying too heavily on emotions (Q1) showed a significant but negative effect ($\beta = -0.392$, $p = 0.042$), indicating that overconfidence in emotional judgment may hinder internal alignment. Suppression and negative emotions did not yield significant results.

H4: The hypothesis posits that mentally recalling past experiences contributes to inner evaluation, leading to greater internal alignment and decision satisfaction under pressure.

This regression model was found to be statistically significant ($R^2 = 0.370$, $p = 0.0125$). The most meaningful contribution came from mental review of past experiences ($\beta = 0.5448$, $p = 0.012$). Other variables such as holistic reflection and emotional awareness were not statistically significant. These findings indicate that internal alignment is largely shaped through cognitive visualization and partially support the hypothesis.

In addition to the main hypothesis results, the following demographic observations offer further context:

- **By gender:** Female participants were more likely than males to agree with statements indicating that their emotions guide their decisions. This suggests that emotional awareness and the influence of positive emotions might be more prominent among female leaders. However, this difference was not tested statistically.
- **By age:** Participants aged 45 and over reported mentally reviewing past experiences during decision-making more frequently than younger participants. This finding indicates that the use of personal experience as a cognitive strategy may increase with age, supporting both the Mind and Holistic hypotheses.
- **By region:** Participants working outside of Turkey in Europe expressed higher agreement with the statement "I make my best decisions when I feel internally aligned." This suggests that cultural or organizational contexts may influence how internal awareness, holistic thinking, and decision satisfaction are connected.

These distinctions highlight that decision-making behaviours are influenced not just by individual traits but also by factors such as age, gender, leadership experience, and cultural background. Consequently, future studies should aim to diversify their samples and incorporate comparative group analyses to better understand these dynamics.

8.4. Conclusions and Interpretations of the Survey

This study reinforces the view that leadership decision-making extends beyond pure analytical reasoning, involving a complex interplay of cognitive processes, emotional responses, and physiological signals such as heart rate, chest tension, and breathing regulation. The findings support integrative decision-making models from the literature study, suggesting that effective leadership draws on alignment across mind, body, and emotion. However, the relative impact of these elements appears to differ by individual and context.

Heart-Based Awareness and H1: Interestingly, the first hypothesis (H1) was not supported: physiological awareness—while theoretically associated with intuitive processing—did not significantly predict holistic decision-making in this sample. However, interoceptive cues such as heart rate and breath regulation may still exert a subtle, background influence on decision awareness. We interpret this non-significant result as indicative of an enduring bias within prevailing leadership paradigms, which continue to prioritize cognitive over embodied forms of intelligence. These findings highlight that there may be a gap in leadership theory and practice, suggesting that physiological awareness may be undervalued or insufficiently developed in current models of decision-making. To address this, future leadership development initiatives should more deliberately integrate embodied awareness as a foundational, trainable dimension of effective leadership.

Cognitive Awareness and H2: Hypothesis 2 received the most consistent support among respondents, suggesting that leaders who maintain mental clarity and actively visualize past experiences tend to make higher-quality decisions. The ability to recall and engage with episodic memory strengthens both decision clarity and internal alignment. This cognitive process reflects a key executive function of the brain—logical analysis—which is closely linked to the depth and accessibility of one's experiential memory.

Neuroscientifically, this function is associated with activity in the prefrontal cortex, particularly the dorsolateral prefrontal region, which plays a central role in reflective thinking, planning, and decision-making.

Emotional Influence and H3: Hypothesis 3 proposed that leaders who integrate emotional awareness into their decision-making experience greater internal alignment—especially when guided by positive emotions—while over-reliance on emotions may diminish this coherence. The findings support this dual effect, reinforcing the idea that emotions can both enhance and disrupt decision quality depending on their regulation. This aligns with the studied literature emphasizing the importance of emotional intelligence in leadership, where positive affect can foster clarity and confidence, while emotional overload may impair judgment. These results underscore the need for leaders to develop emotional discernment, emotional regulation and not just emotional awareness.

Holistic alignment and H4: When these three systems—heart, mind, and emotions—function in alignment, leaders are more likely to make well-rounded and satisfying decisions.

Figure 1. Core Dimensions Supporting Holistic Decision Quality in Leadership

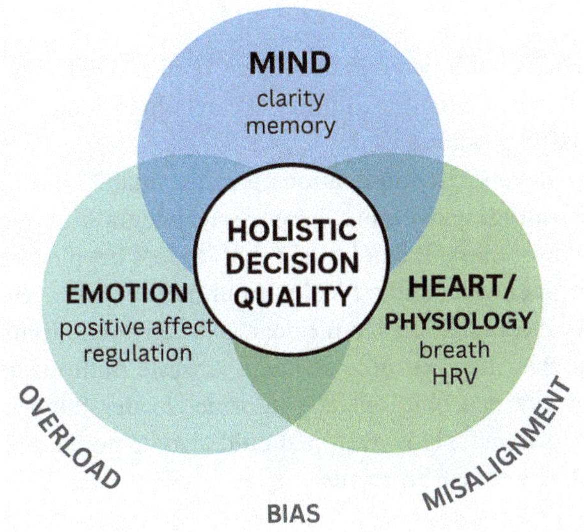

The model on the left demonstrates how cognitive clarity, emotional regulation, and physiological awareness overlaps each other's to support holistic decision quality in leadership.

To activate as well as to balance these decision-making dimensions leaders needs to follow the above practices:

- **Increase the level of heart awareness:** Leaders should practice conscious breathing exercises to develop awareness. They should use tools that monitor heart rates and observe body cues such as chest tension.
- **Cognitive Dimension:** Leaders should create post-decision reflection routines to enhance clarity about how their hearts effect their brains. They should practice mental simulations of similar scenarios before making decisions. They should engage in attention exercises and limit information overload to reduce mental fatigue and improve decision quality.
- **Emotional Dimension:** They should perform daily emotional awareness exercises and replace emotional destruction with emotion regulation strategies. Short pauses before making decisions and visualizing positive outcomes can strengthen the supportive role of emotions. This can help in increasing decision quality.
- **Holistic Integration:** Leaders can use mindfulness and meditation techniques to bring the body, mind and emotions into alignment. In addition, sharing decision-making reflections within leadership teams and integrating

these dimensions into coaching practices can additionally increase internal consistency.

These approaches enable leaders to engage both rational and intuitive intelligence in their decision-making. In addition, it can help in achieving more effective, balanced, and satisfying outcomes.

These findings have great implications for sustainable and circular economy leadership. By cultivating heart-brain coherence and integrating cognitive, emotional, and physiological awareness, it can be said that leaders become better equipped to make regenerative, inclusive, and ethically grounded decisions. Such an embodied approach supports the transition from linear, extractive economic models to circular systems that prioritize resource efficiency, waste minimization, and societal well-being. In this way, neurobiologically informed leadership becomes a driver of organizational performance. However, it should also be noted that it also helps for systemic sustainability transformations.

9. RECOMMENDATIONS FOR FUTURE RESEARCH

This study reinforces the understanding that leadership decision-making is not solely a cognitive process but rather emerges from an integrated interplay of mental clarity, emotional guidance, physiological signals, and a subjective sense of internal alignment.

As discussed in earlier sections—particularly in the interpretation of Hypotheses H1–H4—each of these dimensions contributes uniquely to decision outcomes. While cognitive reflection and emotional integration were shown to be significant, physiological awareness did not statistically emerge as a strong predictor in this sample.

We interpret this not as a lack of relevance, but as a reflection of prevailing leadership paradigms and mindsets that continue to prioritize cognitive reasoning over embodied intelligence. This suggests that body-based awareness remains under-recognized and underdeveloped in current leadership practices. To address this, future research should challenge traditional biases by embracing physiological awareness as a valid and trainable component of effective leadership. Broader, more diverse samples across cultures and sectors, along with qualitative methods and neuroscience-based technologies, can enrich our understanding of how leaders experience and express embodied decision-making. AI-supported tools that simulate real-world scenarios offer promising avenues for both research and development, fostering greater self-reflection and alignment between thought, emotion, and bodily awareness. Cross-cultural studies can further illuminate how leadership embodiment varies across contexts (Cameron & Quinn, 2011).

REFERENCES

Adedeji, O., Reuben, O., & Olatoye, O. (2014). Global Climate Change. *Journal of Geoscience and Environment Protection, 2*, 115. DOI: 10.4236/gep.2014.22016

Almeida, H., Kumi, S., & Fatima, L. (2024). Mapping organizational culture, work motivation and innovative behaviour, before and during the crisis: A bibliometric analysis. *SN Business & Economics, 4*(94), 1–29.

Armour, J. A. (1991). Intrinsic cardiac neurons. *Journal of Cardiovascular Electrophysiology, 2*(4), 331–338.

Baumeister, R. F., Vohs, K. D., & Tice, D. M. (2007). The strength model of self-control. *Current Directions in Psychological Science, 16*(6), 351–355.

Bechara, A., Damasio, H., & Damasio, A. R. (2000). Emotion, decision making and the orbitofrontal cortex. *Cerebral Cortex (New York, N.Y.), 10*(3), 295–307. PMID: 10731224

Breit, S., Kupferberg, A., Rogler, G., & Hasler, G. (2018). Vagus nerve as modulator of the brain–gut axis in psychiatric and inflammatory disorders. *Frontiers in Psychiatry, 9*, 44. DOI: 10.3389/fpsyt.2018.00044 PMID: 29593576

Cameron, K. S., & Quinn, R. E. (2011). *Diagnosing and changing organizational culture: Based on the competing values framework* (3rd ed.). Jossey-Bass.

Craig, A. D. (2002). How do you feel? Interoception: The sense of the physiological condition of the body. *Nature Reviews. Neuroscience, 3*, 655–666. PMID: 12154366

Critchley, H. D., Wiens, S., Rotshtein, P., Öhman, A., & Dolan, R. J. (2004). Neural systems supporting interoceptive awareness. *Nature Neuroscience, 7*(2), 189–195. PMID: 14730305

Damasio, A. (1994). *Descartes' Error: Emotion, Reason, and the Human Brain.* Putnam.

Decety, J., & Jackson, P. L. (2004). The functional architecture of human empathy. *Behavioral and Cognitive Neuroscience Reviews, 3*(2), 71–100. DOI: 10.1177/1534582304267187 PMID: 15537986

Ezeudu, S. A., Ezeudu, F. O., & Sampson, M. (2016). Climate Change Awareness and Attitude of Senior Secondary Students in Umuahia Education Zone of Abia State. *International Journal of Research in Humanities and Social Studies, 3*(3), 10.

Fujimoto, A., Murray, E. A., & Rudebeck, P. H. (2021). Interaction between decision-making and interoceptive representations of bodily arousal in frontal cortex. *Proceedings of the National Academy of Sciences of the United States of America, 118*(35), e2014781118. DOI: 10.1073/pnas.2014781118 PMID: 34452993

Glimcher, P. W., & Fehr, E. (2013). Findings in neuroeconomics provide critical insights for leadership, particularly in financial and strategic decision-making. *The Journal of Economic Perspectives, 27*(2), 105–120.

Goleman, D. (1995). *Emotional Intelligence: Why It Can Matter More than IQ*. Bantam Books.

HeartMath Institute. (2023). Mysteries of the Heart [Infographic]. https://www.heartmath.org/resources/infographic/mysteries-of-the-heart

Hölzel, B. K., Lazar, S. W., Gard, T., Schuman-Olivier, Z., Vago, D. R., & Ott, U. (2011). How does mindfulness meditation work? Proposing mechanisms of action from a conceptual and neural perspective. *Perspectives on Psychological Science, 6*(6), 537–559. PMID: 26168376

Jefferson Research. (2022). The Heart's Little Brain. https://research.jefferson.edu/2022-magazine/the-hearts-little-brain.html

Journals, A. H. A. (2003). Cardiac memory: Mechanisms and clinical implications. *Circulation, 108*(8), 950–955. DOI: 10.1161/01.cir.0000091402.34219.6c

Kahneman, D. (2011). *Thinking, Fast and Slow*. Farrar, Straus and Giroux.

Kahneman, D., Sibony, O., & Sunstein, C. R. (2021). *Noise: A Flaw in Human Judgment*. Little, Brown Spark.

Kara, Ç. (2025). From Neural Processing to Pathos: The Neuroscientific Foundations of Persuasive Messages. Available at: https://neuroscience.org.uk/blog/f/n%C3%B6ral-i%CC%87%C5%9Flemeden-pathos%E2%80%99ai%CC%87kna-edici-mesajlar%C4%B1n-n%C3%B6robilimseltemeli

Kuvaas, N. J., & Damasio, A. (2021). Interaction between decision-making and interoceptive representations of bodily arousal in frontal cortex. *Proceedings of the National Academy of Sciences of the United States of America, 118*(35), e2014781118. DOI: 10.1073/pnas.2014781118 PMID: 34452993

Magnon, V. (2022). The heart to make the right choice: Vagal (re)activity and recovery predict advantageous decision-making. *Physiology & Behavior, 249*, 113911. DOI: 10.1016/j.physbeh.2022.113911 PMID: 35820625

McCraty, R., Atkinson, M., & Tomasino, D. (2003). Impact of a workplace stress reduction program on blood pressure and emotional health in hypertensive employees. *Journal of Alternative and Complementary Medicine (New York, N.Y.)*, *9*(3), 355–369. PMID: 12816624

Nestor, J. (2020). *Breath: The New Science of a Lost Art*. Penguin Life.

Platt, M. L. (2018). *The Leader's Brain: Enhance Your Leadership, Build Stronger Teams, Make Better Decisions, and Inspire Greater Innovation with Neuroscience*. Wharton School Press.

Platt, M. L., ... (2024). Heart rate synchrony in teams: PNAS study linking physiological synchrony with group decision accuracy. Knowledge@Wharton. https://knowledge.wharton.upenn.edu

Qi, X., Liu, H., Li, X., & Liu, H. (2021). The influence of flexiblework arrangements on innovative employee behaviour in China: A perspective of person-job fit. *Asia Pacific Business Review*, *29*(1), 1–22. DOI: 10.1080/13602381.2021.2001181

Smith, R., Thayer, J. F., Khalsa, S. S., & Lane, R. D. (2017). The hierarchical basis of neurovisceral integration. *Neuroscience and Biobehavioral Reviews*, *75*, 274–296. PMID: 28188890

Tendulkar, M., Tendulkar, R., Dhanda, P. S., Yadav, A., Jain, M., & Kaushik, P. (2024). Clinical potential of sensory neurites in the heart and their role in decision-making. *Frontiers in Neuroscience*, *17*, 1308232. PMID: 38415053

Tversky, A., & Kahneman, D. (1983). Extensional versus intuitive reasoning: The conjunction fallacy in probability judgment. *Psychological Review*, *90*(4), 293–315.

Villiger, S., & Hämmig, O. (2023). Work Related Demands and Resources as Predictors of Well-being at Work Among Healthcare Workers in Switzerland. *Journal of Occupational and Environmental Medicine*, *65*(8), 689–693. DOI: 10.1097/JOM.0000000000002885 PMID: 37193642

Vlaar, S. (2024). Applied neuroscience in supervision. *ANSE Journal*, *8*(1), 27–32.

Yerkes, R. M., & Dodson, J. D. (1908). The relation of strength of stimulus to rapidity of habit-formation. *The Journal of Comparative Neurology and Psychology*, *18*(5), 459–482. DOI: 10.1002/cne.920180503

Yu, R. (2016). Stress potentiates decision biases: A stress-induced deliberation-to-intuition (SIDI) model. *Neurobiology of Stress*, *3*, 83–95. DOI: 10.1016/j.ynstr.2015.12.006 PMID: 27981181

ENDNOTE

1 ***For the Heart dimension***, *we formulated five statements or questions, drawing on literature from Craig (2002), and Critchley et al. (2004) for Q1; Smith et al. (2017) and Bechara et al. (2000) for Q2; Craig (2002), and Damasio (1994) for Q3; Damasio (1994) and Goleman (1995) for Q4; and Magnon (2022), Smith et al. (2017) and Nestor (2020) for Q5.* ***For the Mind dimension***, *we developed five statements or questions, informed by literature from Kahneman (2011) for Q1; Baumeister et al. (2007) and Kahneman (2011) for Q2 ; Goleman (1995) for Q3; Kahneman (2011) and Bechara et al. (2000) for Q4; and Damasio (1994) and Goleman (1995) for Q5.* ***For the Guided Emotion dimension***, *we formulated five statements or questions, drawing on literature from Damasio (1994) and Bechara et al. (2000) for Q1; Baumeister et al. (2007) for Q2; Baumeister et al. (2007) for Q3; Goleman (1995) and Decety & Jackson (2004) for Q4; and Baumeister et al. (2007) and Goleman (1995) for Q 5.* ***For the Integrated (holistic) dimension***, *we developed five statements or questions, informed by literature from Damasio (1994), Smith (2017) and Craig (2002) for Q1; Goleman (1995) and Smith (2017) for Q2; Decety & Jackson (2004), Damasio (1994) for Q3; Craig (2002) and Critchley et al. (2004) for Q4; and Goleman (1995) and Baumeister et al. (2007) for Q5.*

Chapter 6
Sustainable Hospitality: Reinventing Business Management Practices and the Overall Customer Experience

Raouf Fadlallah
https://orcid.org/0000-0003-0094-8953
Lebanese International University, Lebanon & European University Cyprus, Cyprus

Stelios Marneros
https://orcid.org/0009-0004-1814-9812
Cyprus University of Technology, Cyprus

George Papageorgiou
European University Cyprus, Cyprus

ABSTRACT

The hospitality industry is undergoing a transformative shift toward sustainability, driven by the urgent need to reduce environmental impact and adopt circular economy principles. This chapter explores how innovation and circular business models address environmental, economic, and social challenges in the sector. It highlights the industry's intensive use of natural resources and significant waste generation, noting a persistent gap between sustainability goals and actual practice. Key barriers include striking a balance between eco-friendly operations and service quality, as well as prioritizing long-term sustainability over short-term profits. The chapter calls for systemic change, positioning the hospitality industry as a model for sustainable development. By embracing circular innovation and aligning with the Sustainable Development Goals (SDGs), the sector can transition toward business models that conserve resources, strengthen ecosystem resilience, and generate lasting value.

DOI: 10.4018/979-8-3373-7655-4.ch006

1 INTRODUCTION: INNOVATION AND CIRCULAR ECONOMY IN THE HOSPITALITY SECTOR

This introduction highlights the increasing significance of innovation and circular economy principles in the hospitality industry, emphasizing how the transition from linear to circular business models addresses environmental and social challenges, and sets the stage for exploring the role of sustainable practices in enhancing the overall customer experience.

This chapter aims to explore how hospitality firms could apply sustainable business practices through innovation and CE practices to enhance customer experience and reduce environmental impacts. In the context of hospitality, sustainability refers to directing and managing all aspects of the hotel in a way that balances the triple bottom line: environmental, social, and economic performance, without compromising the needs of future generations. This chapter focuses on both large international hotel chains and small- to medium-sized hotels, drawing from global case studies to illustrate how circular business models can be implemented in real-world settings.

Innovation is now essential for achieving operational excellence in today's rapidly evolving hospitality sector. As noted by Avasiloaei (2022), process innovation is vital within the hospitality industry, not only to achieve operational excellence but also to empower firms to consider new business models based on the CE by introducing sustainable practices and reducing harm.

Transitioning to a circular economy from the traditional linear one is a significant milestone for hospitality firms. Currently, people are facing health, social, economic, and environmental problems primarily due to unsustainable business models. When implemented, the principles of the CE direct the courses of action and tactics taken by hotels, for example, to maximize long-term value creation and preserve resources. In this context, European countries consider transforming to CE from the traditional linear economy a priority, as it is regarded as a driver of innovation.

As a result of the COVID-19 pandemic and its effects, several technological developments have altered people's perspectives and led to the emergence of new business models that prioritize sustainability and the CE (Avasiloaei, 2022). In our era of advanced systems and practical marketing tools, the hospitality and tourism industry is becoming a significant contributor to each country's economic situation (Thommandru et al., 2023). In addition to raising awareness of health, social, financial, and environmental issues—many of which are caused by unsustainable business practices—the pandemic revealed weaknesses in international systems.

It is important to note that the hospitality and food service industries are among the highest consumers of energy, water, and other natural resources. To satisfy the needs of their customers, the hospitality industry consumes a vast amount of energy and natural resources (UNWTO, 2019). Due to the significant amounts of waste produced, energy consumed, and water utilized in the restaurant and food industry, the circular economy has garnered special attention in this sector (Rabbi & Bin Amin, 2024). There is increasing global attention to CE practices, including in the restaurant industry (Rabiu & Jaeger-Erben, 2022). The CE within the restaurant industry primarily focuses on addressing socio-economic issues, which also impact other sectors and society (Rabiu & Jaeger-Erben, 2022). These issues are mainly due to small business owners, both within and outside the hospitality industry, who prioritize short-term benefits and profits over long-term benefits, driven by their need for cash flow (Hoogendoorn et al., 2015).

Furthermore, multinational corporations have overused natural resources, such as plants, water, and other natural resources, to increase their profits (Sadiq et al., 2023). The environment is now polluted as a result of these activities, which have a detrimental effect on air quality and fuel climate change. It is now mandatory for firms to launch a new ecosystem that sustains natural resources, businesses, and life as well.

The critical challenge within the hospitality industry is to achieve environmentally friendly and sustainable practices. Firms are increasingly aware of the environmental impact of their operations and strive to provide customers with products and services that align with their green values. Hospitality providers are compelled by this shift in consumer behavior to innovate in the challenges it presents to the guest experience while reducing their environmental impact. The hotel industry faces difficulties in providing eco-friendly surroundings for its customers while upholding high standards of amenities and service (Prakash et al., 2023). This challenge requires innovative research to develop effective and lasting solutions in this industry. The hotel industry is considered one of the most energy-intensive and consuming sectors globally within the tourism industry (Mak & Chang, 2019).

Additionally, Yussof et al. (2020) found that for each night occupied in a hotel, the hospitality industry emits approximately 20.6 kilograms of CO_2. Moreover, this research showed that for each customer staying one night in a hotel, they produce approximately one kilogram of waste and consume 218 gallons of water per day for each room. Despite the availability of numerous environmental certifications, such as ISO14001 Certification, Green Globe 21, Leadership in Energy and Environmental Design (LEED) certification, the European Union Eco-Management and Audit Scheme (EMAS), TripAdvisor GreenLeaders, Green Seal, and others (Choi et al., 2019), there remains a significant gap between awareness and the application of effective environmental strategies (Leonidou et al., 2013).

Climate change, biodiversity loss, water scarcity, natural disasters, pandemics, and other factors have prompted businesses to adopt a new environmental business model (Ferrero-Ferrero et al., 2024). Regarding businesses, the hospitality industry is one of the largest industries concerned with the environmental and economic impacts of its operations (Manoj et al., 2020). Therefore, this industry, including the hotel sector, should lead by example to shift toward sustainable development. Initially introduced in the Brundtland Report (1987), sustainable development called for balancing the needs of the present generation without compromising the ability of future generations to meet their goals (World Commission on Environment and Development, 1987). The introduction of sustainable development at the United Nations in 1987 paved the way for a new approach to be adopted by individuals, firms, and governments to achieve sustainable performance and sustainable business models (Geissdoerfer et al., 2018). Thus, the circular economy and the Sustainable Development Goals are regarded as innovative strategies and tools for transitioning to a new business model and achieving sustainable growth, which will reduce risks and enhance ecosystem benefits.

2 REVIEW OF RELEVANT STUDIES

This section examines key research on the hospitality sector, highlighting its significance on a global scale, its environmental impact, and the increasing emphasis on sustainable practices. Additionally, it highlights essential patterns and obstacles that influence the industry's shift to sustainability.

2.1 Importance of the Hospitality Industry

The hospitality sector is a significant source of income and employment globally, accounting for approximately 10% of the world's GDP (WTTC Economic Impact Report, 2019). The hospitality sector is a trillion-dollar industry that makes a substantial contribution to global economic growth. It also accounts for 7% of global exports and a sizeable portion of the global domestic product (WTTC, 2017).

Within the hospitality sector, the hotel sector is its backbone, providing lodging options tailored to the needs of its customers. According to Prakash et al. (2023), the hotel industry is a vibrant and rapidly growing sector that is expanding globally due to high rates of urbanization and globalization. In Pakistan, the hotel industry contributed 2.9% of the nation's GDP in 2024 and is predicted to increase to more than 5.8% by 2028 (Tanveer et al., 2024). The significance of the hotel industry in both developed and developing countries is demonstrated by this expansion.

In addition to contributing to the national GDP, the hotel industry stimulates the local economy and creates a large number of jobs. According to research, the hotel sector significantly supports regional companies and sectors (Arshad et al., 2018). The World Travel & Tourism Council (WTTC, 2019) found in its research that the hospitality industry makes a significant contribution to each economy. Research by the WTTC (2019) indicates that the sector accounts for approximately 10% of the global GDP and contributes to poverty reduction by providing and creating 333 million jobs worldwide. Due to its high demand for both seasonal and permanent workers, the hotel industry consequently creates a large number of job opportunities, which benefits both the local and global economies.

It is noteworthy that the hospitality sector continues to expand, underscoring its global significance. Due to its considerable economic and employment potential, as well as its social and environmental implications, the hospitality sector is crucial to the European Union (de Grosbois, 2012). As a result, the industry is positioned as a key pillar in the global pursuit of inclusive and sustainable development.

On the other hand, the hospitality industry has a crucial responsibility—and an opportunity—to lead the transition to sustainable development given its significant economic and environmental effects.

Over the past five years, the hotel industry has made significant progress in achieving eco-friendly certifications, driven by environmental and consumer concerns. Below, you can find a summary of the evolving sustainability practices in the global hotel sector from 2020 to 2025, as hotels increase their eco-certifications.

Table 1. Growth of Eco-Certifications in the Global Hotel Industry (2020–2025)

Year	Hotels with Eco-Certification (%)	Year-on-Year Growth (%)
2020	25%	-
2021	30%	+5%
2022	36%	+6%
2023	42%	+6%
2024	48%	+6%
2025	53% (Projected)	+5%

Source: World Travel & Tourism Council (WTTC, 2022); WTTC (2023); Projections for 2025 based on current growth trends.

2.2 Environmental Concerns in the Hospitality Sector

The hospitality sector faces numerous challenges due to its significant environmental impact. The hotel industry still faces several obstacles to implementing eco-friendly practices, despite its desire to do so, including financial concerns (Khatter, 2023). The hospitality industry is influenced by larger global trends, even though it also contributes to environmental degradation. Environmental issues and the difficulty of accomplishing sustainability goals are two of the challenges facing the hospitality sector. This issue is not only a concern for hospitality firms but also matters to all stakeholders within this industry. Rather than the hospitality industry, the expansion of industrial activities, the increase in global population, global warming, environmental degradation, and climate change have collectively increased awareness of environmental concerns. Activities conducted by firms globally have had a positive impact on their economic systems. However, on the other side, many negative results have been reported, including climate change, global warming, and other environmental issues. These environmental consequences have underscored the need for global industries, including hospitality firms, to adopt a sustainable approach (Goudie, 2018).

Shifting toward sustainable business practices in the hospitality industry involves making difficult trade-offs between operational effectiveness, financial viability, and environmental benefits. Although 63% of travelers prioritize eco-friendly lodging, only 30% are willing to pay more for hotels that have received green certification, according to recent reports (World Travel & Tourism Council, 2022).

Earlier empirical research, such as that done by Ahmed et al. (2021), has demonstrated and emphasized these trade-offs. Although green HRM improves hotel performance, this study found that it necessitates a large investment in staff training and resource allocation. The most significant obstacles to sustainable strategies in the hotel industry, according to research by Mak and Chang (2019), who used a force field analysis approach, were operational and financial issues.

The findings above underscore the importance of addressing industry-specific concerns, such as the cost-benefit asymmetry of eco-innovation, irregular guest conduct, and the need for more assertive leadership in incorporating circular economy principles into hotel operations.

It is essential to acknowledge that the hospitality sector has a substantial environmental impact. Negative environmental issues are caused by poor hotel building design, inadequate service design, and inadequate maintenance, claim Prakash et al. (2023). Furthermore, Rodriguez-Anton et al. (2012) observed that the hospitality industry has long been criticized and blamed for its activities, as its operations utilize a considerable amount of water and materials, which can disrespect the environment. Those materials include disposable plastic containers, non-recyclable packaging, and containers and cleaning detergents. To mitigate the adverse effects of resource-intensive operations and maximize their potential benefits, many companies in the hospitality industry have made significant efforts to adopt environmentally friendly practices. In addition to the indirect financial benefits, companies, including those in the hospitality sector, can benefit from eco-friendly practices in a variety of ways (Khatter et al., 2021), including improvement of the firm's image and branding, reduction of costs, a boost of productivity, alignment with legal requirements, reduction of waste, and optimization of using available resources. This could be beneficial not only to the firm but also to other stakeholders, including investors, shareholders, employees, customers, the government, policymakers, and others. However, many of those activities are still limited and inconsistently implemented, reducing their effectiveness.

However, most hospitality firms are not fully aligned with the practical application of green strategies in the real world despite their growing awareness and adoption of sustainability initiatives and their positive environmental attitudes. Several global critical factors related to implementing sustainable practices in the hotel industry increase the pressure on these firms to enhance their green motivation in management policies (Ahmed et al., 2021). This disconnect highlights the need for effective leadership in the hospitality industry, stricter guidelines, and a genuine commitment to sustainability in all aspects of management.

Table 2. Summary of Empirical Trade-offs

Trade-off Category	Empirical Finding	Implication for Hotels
Consumer WTP vs Green Cost	Gen Z willing to pay up to $36 more (Fei et al., 2024)	Strategic pricing strategies needed
Certification Cost vs RevPAR	Certified first movers saw performance gains (2022)	Early adoption yields market advantage
Basic vs Advanced Investments	Malaysian hotels favor low-cost practices (2020)	SMEs may need incremental approach
GHRM Investment vs Retention	GHRM supports retention, requires resource input	HR strategy needed to balance cost and benefit

In Table 2, the various trade-off categories were discussed within the hospitality findings, along with the implications for the hotel managers for effective implementation.

2.3 Stakeholder Perspective on Sustainability in the Hospitality Sector

There is a complicated interplay of priorities among different stakeholders in the shift to sustainable hospitality practices. Due to their interests and limitations, managers, staff, visitors, legislators, and suppliers all view sustainability initiatives differently.

Hotel managers prioritize the operational effectiveness and financial viability of sustainability initiatives. For them, return on investment (ROI) times and competitive market positioning are frequently taken into consideration when making investments in eco-friendly technologies (Mak & Chang, 2019). Integrating sustainable solutions while preserving service quality and profitability is a challenge for managers.

For green initiatives to be implemented successfully, employees are essential. However, the degree of organizational support and training they receive frequently shapes their viewpoint. Research indicates that when sustainability is integrated into the company culture through Green Human Resource Management (GHRM) practices, employees are more likely to behave in environmentally beneficial ways (Muisyo et al., 2022).

Conversely, customers place a higher value on experiential, visible aspects of sustainability, such as waste minimization and eco-friendly facilities. Empirical data indicates a "green gap," wherein many customers express eco-friendly preferences but are hesitant to pay a premium, despite the growing demand for sustainable hotels (Fei et al., 2024).

Compliance, standardization, and the broader environmental impacts of the hospitality industry are the main concerns of policymakers and regulators. They promote greener practices in hotels through certifications and incentives, but they must balance industry flexibility with enforcement (WTTC, 2022).

Suppliers are essential to a hotel's ability to source sustainable products. Frequently, cost, scalability, and logistics are their top concerns. Access to reasonably priced, sustainable supply chains continues to be a significant obstacle for many hotels, particularly SMEs, in achieving the objectives of the circular economy (Prakash et al., 2023).

It is essential to understand these various viewpoints to develop inclusive and practical sustainability strategies. In addition to aligning sustainability initiatives with operational realities, a stakeholder-centric approach enhances organizational commitment and guest satisfaction.

2.4 Specific Environmental Challenges and Impacts

Based on previous research and statistical analysis, the hospitality industry is one of the largest industries in terms of energy and water consumption. Within the hospitality industry, there is an extensive use of natural resources (Scholz, 2019). A significant amount of electricity is needed by their equipment to light and cool the hotel. Water is required for laundry as well as for food preparation and cleaning. Additionally, the hotel generates a lot of waste from the use of batteries, furniture, and equipment. Furthermore, Fleming et al. (2015) found that the food and beverage industry's top concern was water, leading to a shift toward more environmentally friendly practices. This substantial usage highlights the need for the hotel sector to implement innovative strategies that reduce energy and water consumption.

In addition to consuming a significant amount of energy and water, the hotel industry generates substantial waste, including chemicals and paper, that pollute the environment. According to Calisto et al. (2021), small hospitality firms still lack knowledge of implementing environmentally friendly products and services and need to be aware of the long-term implications of effective waste management practices, using non-toxic cleaning chemicals, and the benefits of investing in energy-efficient equipment. Al-Aomar and Hussain (2017) found in their research that waste management techniques should be implemented by food and beverage operations to achieve sustainable growth in this industry. Therefore, hotel operations should undergo tactical and strategic environmental moves to achieve sustainable development. Based on that research, it is evident that failing to address waste management and pollution effectively not only leads to environmental consequences but also affects the long-term value of the hotel.

Beyond the intensive use of water and energy and the substantial generation of waste, hotel operations have a significant impact on climate change, a global concern. According to Mak and Chang (2019), the hospitality and tourism industry is facing critical environmental challenges, which have led to environmental degradation. The hospitality sector is highly spotted for its carbon footprint (Lenzen et al., 2018). The carbon footprint of the hospitality industry accounts for 8% of global greenhouse gas emissions. Additionally, the hotel industry should prioritize lowering carbon emissions (Calabrese et al., 2019). Hotels emit a significant amount of greenhouse gases and are considered one of the most energy-intensive sectors globally. For optimal use, energy resources in the hotel sector should be managed well. All this information sheds light on the importance of creating and implementing innovative methods to achieve effective management of energy resources, thereby reducing their negative environmental impact.

Although considerable effort has been made to encourage organizations to adopt and create a circular economy that reduces environmental negative impacts, several challenges and barriers are hindering its implementation. Despite the increase in environmental awareness, hospitality industry firms continue to face challenges in accurately implementing eco-friendly practices (Khatter, 2019). Research conducted by Al-Aomar and Hussain (2017) identified several obstacles that limit effective supply chain management, including environmental regulations and legislation. In return, those challenges compelled service supply chains to minimize waste and enhance the efficiency of their resources to meet environmental requirements. Chan (2008) found that a significant number of managers within the hotel industry still consider implementing environmentally friendly practices within the hotel as an obstacle to their success. The research by Chan considered this implementation a barrier, as the managers viewed it as costly. Additionally, this research revealed that several contextual factors hinder the adequate implementation of environmental practices by hotels, including a lack of education about these practices, a lack of expertise and knowledge, and the absence of strict policies for their implementation.

Another obstacle to implementing sustainable practices is the need for hotels to provide high-quality service to customers, as well as the question of how customers perceive this service quality. Mak et al. (2012) found in their research that adopting environmentally friendly practices may make many customers feel that they are not receiving good service in hotels. As a result, many managers in the hotel industry do not consider implementing environmentally friendly strategies, as they perceive this as leading to a degradation of service quality. According to Han et al. (2010), hotel firms need to adopt a new and innovative approach to provide customers with a unique experience, focusing on green practices that involve water conservation, reduction of carbon emissions, and reduction of food waste. Those studies highlight the importance of enhancing and providing a better guest experience while also developing innovative, sustainable practices.

2.5 Green Consumer Behavior and Guest Participation Strategies

“Green consumer behavior” refers to hotel guests' willingness to participate in sustainable practices, such as recycling waste, conserving water, and using energy efficiently (Demir et al., 2021). In addition to contributing to the issue, this consumer behavior supports hotels' environmentally friendly operations. Several factors, including perceived value and environmental awareness, influence customers' involvement in green practices. Those factors, in fact, according to Demir et al., impact the customer's choice of the hotel they need to stay in. Furthermore, a study in star-rated lodgings found that guests’ awareness of pro-environmental measures influences their green behavior (Matiza & Slabbert, 2025). Furthermore, according to a survey by Fei et al. (2024), guests from Generation Z are prepared to spend an extra USD 36 per night to take advantage of green features.

Discussing consumers' current level of green behavior and awareness reveals that several barriers prevent them from engaging in green practices. According to Ferreira et al. (2023), the shift from intention to behavior is influenced by particular contextual and psychological factors. To boost engagement, hotels are employing a range of strategies to encourage eco-friendly behavior among their guests. For example, IHG hotels reward their guests with 500 loyalty points when they implement various eco-friendly practices.

2.6 Sustainability Challenges and Solutions for Small and Medium Hotels (SMEs)

SMEs are hotels that operate with fewer than 50 employees, have a budget of less than € 10 million (Sobaih et al., 2025), and play a vital role in the tourism sector. However, several challenges compel SMEs to adopt sustainable practices. One of the challenges involves their limited financial capability to implement effective green and sustainable practices, the owner's attitude, as well as the seasonality and inconsistency. On the other hand, several advantages can help SMEs overcome these challenges, including their flexibility and the opportunity for closer guest interactions.

To overcome the challenges of implementing effective and sustainable green practices, SMEs could focus on low-budget activities, including energy and water efficiency practices, waste reduction, and local sourcing.

A selection of case studies highlighting how hotels of different sizes have incorporated sustainable practices in key operational focus areas, including energy, water, waste, and biodiversity management, is presented in the table below. These examples demonstrate the viability of both structured corporate programs and grassroots, low-tech initiatives.

Table 3. Matrix Table Summarizing Case Studies by Focus Areas (Energy, Water, Waste, Biodiversity)

Hotel/Case Study	Energy Efficiency	Water Management	Waste Reduction	Biodiversity Initiatives
Marriott's "Green Choice" Program	Smart HVAC systems, Energy Management Systems (EMS) to track usage	Towel and linen reuse programs to reduce water consumption	Digital check-in systems, reduced disposable amenities (plastics)	Habitat restoration partnerships
Small Eco-Lodge (Boutique Example)	Manual energy-saving (staff ensures lights, appliances are turned off when not in use)	Rainwater harvesting for garden irrigation and facility use	Composting kitchen waste, upcycling old furniture into decor items	Local tree planting initiatives, community eco-projects
IHG "Greener Stay" Program	Energy Management Systems (EMS) for optimizing energy use	Water reuse loops in housekeeping operations	Complete elimination of single-use plastic amenities	Collaborations with wildlife and biodiversity NGOs

2.7 Balancing High-Tech and Low-Tech Sustainability Innovations

This section compares high-tech and low-tech sustainability solutions in the hotel industry. It explains how combining innovative technologies with simple, cost-effective measures can improve environmental performance and guest satisfaction.

Sustainability within the hotel industry encompasses a range of innovations, from high-tech to low-tech solutions. From high-tech innovations involving IoT to low-tech innovations such as towel reuse, paperless check-in, and local sourcing, all have a particular impact on the circular economy within the hotel sector.

Many hotels have implemented high-tech sustainability innovations, which primarily focus on AI-driven dashboards that control energy and food waste (Eskerod et al., 2019). Although high-tech innovations improve environmental branding, their practical implementation by SMEs is limited by their high costs and complexity.

Switching to low-tech sustainability innovations, which have demonstrated success and are more feasible and economical to adopt. Low-tech innovations include towel reuse programs, LED lighting, locally sourced food and materials, occupancy light sensors, recycling bins, and others.

To effectively implement sustainability innovation, whether high-tech or low-tech, hotel management should first assess their budget and then implement the innovation that is most suitable for their abilities. After that, hotels should train their staff effectively, incentivize customers, and engage them in a meaningful way.

The following table outlines the concrete changes required for a circular and environmentally conscious hospitality model, comparing traditional hotel operations with sustainable practices in several key operational areas.

Table 4. Traditional vs Sustainable Hotel Operations

Operational Area	Traditional Approach	Sustainable Approach
Energy Usage	Continuous HVAC use, incandescent lighting	Smart energy systems, LED lighting, occupancy sensors
Water Consumption	Standard fixtures, daily linen/towel changes	Low-flow taps and showerheads, towels, and linen reuse programs
Waste Management	Single-bin disposal, plastic amenities, excessive packaging	Waste segregation (recycling bins), refillable dispensers, composting
Supply Chain	Global sourcing, high transportation footprint, non-sustainable vendors	Local sourcing, partnerships with eco-certified suppliers, seasonal products
Guest Engagement	Passive guest role, limited involvement in eco-initiatives	Active guest participation through incentive programs, education, and visible impact metrics

2.8 Low-Tech Sustainability Solutions: Quick Wins for Resource-Constrained Hotels

SMEs still encounter several obstacles in successfully implementing advanced technology, including concerns about cost and training, even though it provides an efficient tool for shifting operations toward sustainability. SMEs should therefore focus on low-cost solutions that deliver immediate results, known as "quick wins."

One of the quick-win tools is the optimal linen and towel reuse programs, which is implemented through encouraging customers to use the linen and towels provided in their rooms for multiple days. Another tool for effective, sustainable implementation with low cost and leading to quick wins is the paperless check-in process, by which hotels encourage the implementation of QR code technology for check-in or mobile check-in. Additionally, hotels should train their employees to switch off the electricity, including lighting and HVAC, in vacant rooms. Moreover, hotels should encourage the local sourcing of their food and beverage products to help reduce their emissions.

All the mentioned practices are low-cost and lead to immediate results, and also help in sustainable innovation within the CE.

2.9 The United Nations Sustainable Development Goals (SDGs)

The 17 Sustainable Development Goals (SDGs), first proposed in 2015 as part of the UN's 2030 Agenda, aim to promote social progress, environmental protection, and economic growth. These goals address global priorities like reducing poverty, combating climate change, promoting sustainable consumption, and ensuring equitable access to healthcare and education (Bexell & Jönsson, 2017; Ferrero-Ferrero et al., 2024). To accomplish the SDGs, governments, businesses, educational institutions, and civil society must all take an active role (UNESCO, 2017; OECD, 2020). The SDGs offer a framework for incorporating sustainability into operations and strategy for the hospitality sector. Hotels can have a positive impact through responsible resource management, community engagement, and transparent sustainability reporting. Research, however, indicates a sizable discrepancy between reporting and actual implementation. Many firms publicly mention SDG alignment, yet only a small fraction embed these goals into core operations or track performance with key indicators (Schramade, 2017; Izzo et al., 2020).

Moreover, studies reveal that much of corporate engagement with the SDGs is symbolic rather than substantive. Hotels and other firms often adopt SDG language for legitimacy or reputation management, a form of greenwashing, instead of driving measurable environmental and social impact (Van der Waal & Thijssens, 2020; Nicolao et al., 2022; Lashitew, 2021).

The main challenges hindering progress toward the SDGs include slow implementation, a lack of accountability, unrealistic timelines, and incomplete integration into management practices (Saxena et al., 2021; Fukuda-Parr, 2019; Silva, 2021). Overcoming these barriers requires hotels to establish clear KPIs, link SDGs to operational strategy, and ensure transparent reporting to achieve genuine, measurable sustainability outcomes.

2.10 Hotel Industry and SDG Adoption

In particular, the hotel sector is crucial to achieving and advancing the Sustainable Development Goals of the UN. The hotel sector is a key collaborator in achieving the Sustainable Development Goals, as highlighted by de Grosbois (2012). Similarly, Raub and Martin-Rios stated in 2019 that the reason for this alignment with the UN SDGs is that hotels have a direct and indirect impact on the context where they operate, encourage interaction through a broad range of activities, and create partnerships with the government and civil society. Despite this potential, Ferrero-Ferrero et al. (2024) demonstrate that the majority of sustainable hotels did not adopt a consistent and strategic approach to achieving sustainable development goals. This finding highlights the disparity between the hotels' professed commitments and their actual implementation of the SDGs.

Numerous studies have examined the relationship between hotels and the UN Sustainable Development Goals (SDGs), as seen in the work by Ferrero-Ferrero et al. (2024). Although they only view it as an external factor, one hotel stated that implementing the SDGs is their primary objective. While acknowledging that they support the UN Sustainable Development Goals, another hotel acknowledged that this does not align with their approach to sustainability strategic management. Only 11 of the 17 Sustainable Development Goals (SDGs) could be applied, according to a third case in this study. These instances show how hotels' interpretations and commitments to attaining the SDGs are inconsistent and how their current implementation methods necessitate a more thorough strategic integration. Furthermore, the findings concluded that the major sustainable hotel companies worldwide have not yet adopted a consistent strategic approach to align their strategies, targets, and measures with the Sustainable Development Goals (SDGs), and there is a notable lack of transparency in this matter. Although hotels stated that they were strategically aligned with the Sustainable Development Goals, the alignment discussion revealed a gap in how these goals are incorporated into the hotels' daily operations.

Additionally, because hotels are not integrating the SDGs into their core business plans, Lashitew (2021) cautions against adopting them merely as a token gesture. This superficial behavior is hazardous since those companies often use the SDGs for greenwashing, which impacts stakeholders' decision-making. Greenwashing by hotels undermines accountability and leads to negative long-term impacts on those hotels' reputations.

2.11 Visual Framework: Sustainable Business Dimensions in Hospitality

To provide a more straightforward overview of how sustainability is operationalized in the hospitality industry, this diagram maps out the key dimensions and their interconnections. Environmental sustainability, economic performance, social responsibility, operational innovations, and consumer engagement are the five main components that the model identifies as being crucial to advancing circular economy practices in the hospitality sector. These dimensions interact dynamically to create feedback loops that impact strategic decisions and operational outcomes rather than existing independently.

Environmental sustainability and economic performance can be directly improved through operational innovations such as intelligent enhanced systems and green human resource management (HRM) practices, which reduce operating costs and resource consumption. Simultaneously, Consumer Engagement through green loyalty programs and transparent sustainability communication enhances Social Responsibility and strengthens brand equity.

With the help of this integrative model, managers and stakeholders in the hospitality industry can ensure business viability and guest satisfaction while coordinating their strategic initiatives with the Sustainable Development Goals (SDGs).

Figure 1. Sustainable Business Dimensions in Hospitality

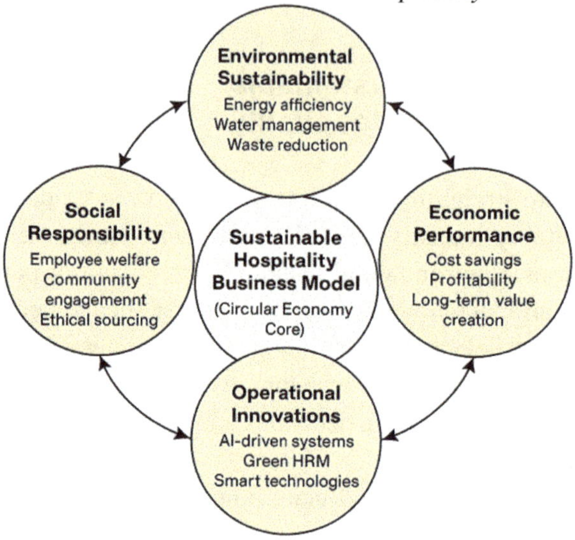

Framework of Sustainable Business Dimensions in Hospitality

2.12 Circular Economy: Concepts and Principles

The concept of circular economy was introduced by David Pearce in 1990, as mentioned by Andersen (2007) and Su et al. (2013). The main objective of the CE is to transform private businesses into a more sustainable system. The transformation from a linear to a CE primarily involves changing the way we think about resource usage and waste generation throughout the product life cycle.

The CE's fundamental tenet is to eliminate the conventional "take-make-dispose" paradigm. New systems that prioritize recycling, reusing, and maintaining materials and products are necessary to replace the traditional linear usage of materials and products in the hospitality industry, which involves using them only once (Bocken & Ritala, 2022). Scholarly interest in the idea of a "circular business model" has grown recently.

According to Linder and Williander (2017), the circular business model is a concept that emphasizes producing goods from previously used products to create value for customers, the company, and the economy. Additionally, Zucchella and Previtali (2019) defined a circular economy as designing business activities to develop a cost and revenue structure that is both beneficial and compatible with sustainability and profitability levels simultaneously. Compared to traditional models, circular business models account for both societal and environmental impacts in their operations (Boons & Ludeke-Freund, 2013).

Note that the circular economy can financially and environmentally improve resource usage (Bocken & Ritala, 2022). By reducing resources and minimizing waste output and emissions, the firm's financial and sustainability performance will be enhanced (Kanda et al., 2021). As Pieroni et al. (2019) noted, there is an increasing adoption of the CE to transition from a linear to a circular approach, especially in the European Union (EU) and other governments, such as Japan, China, Finland, France, the United Kingdom, and Sweden (Korhonen et al., 2018).

Additionally, companies need to integrate the circular economy at the operational level for it to be effective at the strategic level. Later researchers, such as Geissdoerfer et al. (2016), emphasized the integration of the CE within frameworks for stakeholder management and sustainable value creation, even though Pearce (1990) first proposed the idea as a response to environmental constraints.

2.13 Circular Economy in the Hospitality Industry

One of the world's most significant economic sectors, the hospitality industry has a substantial impact on the environment. Due to the high levels of contaminated food, the hospitality sector—and especially the restaurant industry—has a significant adverse environmental impact, contributing to greenhouse gas emissions and environmental degradation (Kaminska et al., 2021). Despite this, the national GDP and foreign exchange reserves benefit from the hospitality industry's operations.

Adopting circular economic principles could mitigate those negative impacts. Chen et al. (2019) found that hospitality firms that adopt environmentally friendly initiatives will have a better image, improved branding, and reduced waste.

When compared to other industries, the hospitality sector is among the quickest to adopt circular economy models (Avasiloaei, 2022). Circular tourism aims to provide travel and hospitality services with the least detrimental environmental impact possible, aligning with the principles of sustainable development.

A study by the University of Cambridge (2014) projects that emissions generated by the tourism and hospitality industry are expected to increase by 130% by 2035, posing a significant threat to the environment (Chen et al., 2019). Rather than focusing solely on carbon emissions, other key elements to consider include water usage, electricity consumption, and waste generation. Circular practices help reduce carbon emissions, limit water and electricity use, and minimize waste, all of which are essential to reversing this trend.

Because of the emerging trends and new business models which is characterized by the circular economy, and because the hospitality industry is a major player in most countries' economies, it is vital to proceed with adopting new business models, which are more circular than linear in their model (Avasiloaei, 2022). This new business model can help hospitality firms conserve natural resources while simultaneously preserving and protecting the environment.

Melo et al. (2025) specifically point out that the restaurant industry is adopting circular economy practices, such as waste reduction and improvements in resource efficiency, due to growing interest in sustainability applications. Furthermore, as a crucial element of environmental sustainability, the COVID-19 pandemic has highlighted the significance of embracing the CE concept (Muakami, 2025). According to this study, energy efficiency, domestic investment, and the preservation of natural and cultural resources are all components of the CE.

In particular, a key element of circular hospitality practices is water management. Water circularity is the most crucial component, as it leads to substantial energy savings and improved resource utilization (Samberger, 2022).

The management of food and beverages is also essential to achieving circularity. The AHRESP (2021) guide on sustainable catering states that the following are examples of best practices:

- Seasonal menus
- Reducing portion size
- Purchasing local food products
- Focusing on producing plant-based food.
- Reducing energy usage
- Selecting energy suppliers who are environmentally certified.
- Avoiding washing the dishes under running water.
- Purchasing durable machines and recyclable products.
- Using refillable products that carry the ECO label.
- Implementing recycling and minimizing negative environmental impacts.

Those practices align with the broader objectives of the circular economy and offer practical pathways for hospitality businesses to become more sustainable. Through locally sourced food, effective operations, and noticeable eco-certifications that guests increasingly value, these circular practices not only improve environmental outcomes but also create more genuine, sustainable guest experiences.

Applying the concepts of the Circular Economy to the hospitality industry entails a methodical process that continuously cycles resources through waste reduction, efficient use, sustainable sourcing, and guest co-creation. A conceptual framework model illustrating how these ideas are applied in hotel operations is presented in the table below.

Table 5. Circular Economy Model in Hospitality

Circular Economy Stage	Key Activities in Hospitality	Examples
Sustainable Resource Input	Sourcing eco-friendly, renewable materials; partnering with local suppliers to reduce transport emissions	Local sourcing of food and supplies (SMEs), eco-certified suppliers (Marriott, IHG)
Efficient Resource Use	Optimizing energy and water consumption through smart systems and low-tech interventions	EMS (IHG, Marriott), LED lighting, occupancy sensors, towel and linen reuse programs
Waste Minimization & Reuse	Implementing waste segregation, upcycling materials, composting organic waste, reducing single-use plastics	Compost stations (Eco-Lodge), elimination of plastics (IHG), upcycling furniture (SMEs)
Value Recovery & Circular Flow	Repurposing waste into usable materials; integrating circular design in operations to maximize resource lifespan	Furniture upcycling, digital systems reducing paper waste, partnerships for waste repurposing
Guest Participation & Co-Creation	Involving guests in sustainable practices through incentives, education, and visible impact tracking	Marriott's Green Choice program, IHG's guest participation schemes, personalized SME programs
Continuous Feedback & Innovation	Monitoring performance (energy, water, waste metrics) and continuously improving through innovation and stakeholder engagement	EMS dashboards (Marriott, IHG), staff eco-awareness training (SMEs), guest feedback mechanisms

3 GLOBAL AND REGIONAL APPLICATIONS OF THE CIRCULAR ECONOMY

3.1 Case Studies from Japan, China, and Other Countries

The hospitality industry in Japan is adopting several low-impact, high-efficiency technologies, such as electric vehicles as substitutes for conventional fuel-powered transportation and virtual reality (VR) for environmentally friendly transportation services. Another example of how integrating renewable energy sources with cultural preservation can result in sustainable tourism ecosystems is Miyama Town. Further examples of inventive uses of the circular economy can be found in Shanghai's creative integration of technology, which includes digital air quality monitoring and adaptive reuse of infrastructure. These examples illustrate how digital technology and environmental education can be integrated to promote sustainability in travel and hospitality planning.

Particularly in Japan, the circular economy is considered a decentralized approach to achieving sustainable tourism, focusing on the local circulation of tourist revenues, which aligns with the principles of a CE (Japan Tourism Agency, 2023). The Niseko region is a good example, as a direct bus service between Sapporo and

Niseko is planned to employ VR technology in 2023. This innovation improved customer satisfaction while reducing carbon emissions. Additionally, by substituting electric vehicles for conventional cars, Japan has embraced the electric vehicle concept, which lessens its environmental impact (Murakami, 2025). In addition, the thatched-roofed Japanese town of Miyama employs several CE strategies, including promoting local culture and reducing its carbon footprint by utilizing wood-burning stoves and hydroelectric power.

Through the use of beautiful virtual tours along the route, VR applications in Japan have enhanced the traveler experience while reducing carbon emissions, thereby combining convenience and engagement. Japan's decentralized approach prioritizes community integration, while China's centralized model highlights the potential of state-led innovative tourism frameworks. In China, the country adopts a centralized approach to sustainable tourism, characterized by a CE, by prioritizing the adoption of the digital economy for smart tourism and extensive tourist infrastructure to support environmental conservation while efficiently managing tourism resources (Murakami, 2025). Shanghai City integrates a CE with the development of urban tourism in the town through the innovative reuse of industrial heritage, by integrating PM2.5 air quality monitoring to merge environmental education with digital technology, and by utilizing spaces for multiple functions that cater to both tourists and residents (Murakami, 2025).

3.2 Circular Economy Initiatives in Hotels and Resorts

According to Avasiloaei (2022), several global hotels have adopted new business models based on the circular economy approach.

3.2.1 *Hilton Hotels*

The famous Hilton Hotels have adopted a renowned approach in their brand hotels. Hilton Garden Inn, for this reason, covered its roof with grass to shield the hotel from ultraviolet rays, which reduces its temperature. Moreover, this hotel chain utilized ultra-efficient heating systems and used LED lighting to prevent energy waste. Additionally, Hilton Garden Inn uses local renewable energy from a regional power plant. At Rome Cavalieri, A Waldorf Astoria Hotel, their new business model included training their housekeeping, food, and kitchen staff to reduce waste and installing low-flow dispensers on all taps and showerheads to reduce water usage as well. Hilton Bali is also using vegetable paper menus to reduce paper waste. Hilton Bali is also committed to working with responsible suppliers and local vendors.

Critical Evaluation: Green roofs, LED lighting, energy-efficient heating, and renewable energy sourcing are some of Hilton's initiatives that make a substantial contribution to sustainability and energy conservation. Localized staff training and behavioral changes at the Rome Cavalieri demonstrate a strong internal capacity-building approach. Hilton Bali promotes sustainable sourcing and waste reduction through its vegetable-based menus and partnerships with local vendors. These processes are scalable across Hilton's global business. Green roofs and renewable energy infrastructure are highly dependent on the local climate, available space, and policy support, whereas LED lighting and training programs are reasonably inexpensive and easily replicable. In areas where sustainable agricultural supply chains are scarce, local supplier networks and vegetable paper menus may encounter difficulties.

3.2.2 *Wyndham Hotels & Resorts*

Another international hotel chain that has adopted circular economy practices is Wyndham Hotels & Resorts, operating in several countries globally. Wyndham Deerfield Beach Resort has reduced energy and water consumption at its hotel, improved air quality, and increased its community engagement. As for Wyndham Grand Manama, the hotel has installed low-flow aerators throughout the property, which have resulted in a 37% reduction in water usage. Additionally, Wyndham Grand Manama installed a water usage system that collected the air conditioning condensate for landscaping irrigation. Wyndham Chongqing Yuelai has utilized its rooftop to install a solar farm and motorized curtains, improving thermal insulation and reducing energy consumption by minimizing waste. In addition to its extensive recycling program, which has achieved a 90% waste diversion rate, the Ramada by Wyndham Ajman has completed a zero-landfill project.

Critical Evaluation: Wyndham hotels showcase a robust combination of waste management (zero-landfill projects), energy efficiency (solar farms and motorized curtains), and water conservation (low-flow aerators and condensate collection). Particularly in urban or arid settings where energy and water resources are scarce, these methods significantly reduce operating costs and their negative environmental impacts. Despite their reliance on regional infrastructure and environmental factors, many of these initiatives are scalable and adaptable. Both financial resources and a conducive environment are needed for rooftop solar and condensate reuse. Although it depends on efficient municipal recycling and waste processing systems, which are less practical in developing nations without sophisticated waste infrastructure, the zero-landfill initiative is a prime example.

3.2.3 *InterContinental Hotels Group*

Various InterContinental hotels worldwide have also adopted circular economy practices, which have had a positive impact on the economy, society, and the environment. At InterContinental New York Barclay, the hotel has utilized its rooftop and converted it into a rooftop kitchen garden, producing fruits, vegetables, and herbs for use within the hotel's restaurant. Additionally, the InterContinental New York Barclay Hotel installed a system called EnviroPure Digestor, which uses zero enzymes to separate food waste into compost, resulting in a reduction of food waste. In the Caribbean Islands, Kimpton Seafire Resort + Spa has installed LED lights, solar power panels, and recyclable building materials. Additionally, the InterContinental Maldives Maamunagau Resort in the Maldives has installed a solar power system, which has resulted in a reduction of 365 tons of CO2 equivalent every year.

Additionally, the InterContinental Maldives Maamunagau Resort has installed an ultrafiltration and reticulation plant system with a total daily capacity of 155,000 liters of water. In Vietnam, the InterContinental Danang Sun Peninsula Resort also conducted several circular economy models. InterContinental Maldives Maamunagau Resort has created a forest around the resort, planting 2,500 hectares of trees. Now, the InterContinental Maldives Maamunagau Resort is encircled by 1,000 plants, more than 100 types of birds and butterflies, and dozens of mammals and reptiles. In partnership with regional farmers, Six Senses Bhutan has prioritized agriculture by cultivating a diverse range of organic fruits, vegetables, flowers, and herbs. Since relocating to Oman, Six Senses Zighy Bay has planted trees with the help of its locals and visitors. Additionally, Six Senses Zighy Bay has a waste recycling program in place, enabling the on-site recycling of approximately 80% of its waste. Crowne Plaza Copenhagen Towers, which relocated to Denmark, has solar panels installed to generate energy within the hotel.

In addition, Crowne Plaza Copenhagen Towers has implemented a system to maintain the hotel's high standards throughout the year, ensuring a warm atmosphere in the winter. To achieve this, Crowne Plaza Copenhagen Towers employed water- and waste-saving methods, automated intelligent lighting, and a groundwater-based system. Additionally, the Crowne Plaza Copenhagen Towers uses locally sourced organic food in its restaurants.

> *Critical Evaluation:* Water (ultrafiltration systems), food (rooftop gardens and composting), energy (solar and LED lighting), and biodiversity (local agriculture and forest restoration) are all integral components of IHG's comprehensive and diverse approach. The biodiversity initiatives in Bhutan and the Maldives provide a template for ecotourism and environmental restoration. The use of the EnviroPure Digester also demonstrates leadership in waste-to-

resource innovation. Solar panels and rooftop gardens are widely applicable. Still, models that focus on biodiversity (such as planting trees and creating forests) are more specialized and linked to the resort model in environmentally sensitive areas. Due to their high capital costs, sophisticated composting and ultrafiltration systems could be prohibitive for smaller hotels. However, selective scalability based on local context is made possible by IHG's modular approach.

3.2.4 *Accor Hotel Chain*

Regarding Accor, the hotel chain has also implemented several circular economy activities. In Austria, the Ibis Wien Mariahilf has introduced a rooftop garden to preserve the bees and combat their decline while also benefiting from their honey production. Additionally, the Ibis Wien Mariahilf has ignored the use of single-use plates in their catering services, focusing instead on local producers for every product while taking into consideration that it could be recycled. Moving to Spain, Ibis Barcelona Montmelo Granollers introduced green energy and was rewarded the Biosphere certification by the Responsible Tourism Institute. Mercure Porto Centro Aliados in Portugal has implemented several measures to reduce expenses and energy consumption. These include using solar panels to generate heat for the hotel, water, and pool; turning off heaters and air conditioners when rooms are empty; lowering the intensity of light during the day; and closing floors when occupancy is low. Moreover, in London, the Pullman London St Pancras also introduced an intelligent building management system to control the hotel's energy usage efficiently. The Pullman London St Pancras also partners with food banks to reduce food waste. In Brazil, Sofitel Guaruja Jequitimar has adopted several circular economy activities and systems. One of the systems at the Sofitel Guaruja Jequitimar was designed to reuse treated wastewater, converting it into drinkable water. Additionally, the Sofitel Guaruja Jequitimar Hotel features a private garden where they cultivate vegetables and herbs, which are used in their food production.

Critical Evaluation: Accor's circular economy initiatives are sensible and economical. There are immediate environmental and financial advantages to using rooftop gardens for biodiversity, energy conservation with solar panels, and intelligent building management systems. Reusing wastewater and collaborating with food banks are examples of a full-circle strategy that considers both social impact and sustainability. The majority of Accor's procedures can be readily replicated in various hotel types. Both urban and rural settings can benefit from the scalability of rooftop gardens and solar systems. Even mid-scale hotels can quickly implement low-cost interventions, such as dimming the lighting and shutting off the air conditioning when there are no guests. The Ibis model of avoiding single-use plates is highly transferable and aligns with shifting consumer expectations.

3.2.5 *Choice Hotels International*

Building on the five-star international hotels that have adopted and implemented several circular economy initiatives, Choice Hotels International has also invested in this economic model to benefit society, the environment, and the economy while enhancing its profits. To do so, the Comfort Suites Manheim – Lancaster has invested in energy management systems to control energy usage and purchased recycled soap and amenities for guest use. In San Francisco, the Comfort Inn by the Bay is recognized as the city's first net-zero carbon hotel, as it generates its energy using an on-site wind turbine and features 270 solar panels.

Critical Evaluation: With establishments like Comfort Suites Manheim and Comfort Inn by the Bay, Choice Hotels demonstrates a strong commitment to operational control (e.g., EMS and recycled amenities) and sustainable energy (e.g., wind turbines and solar panels). San Francisco's achievement of net-zero carbon emissions serves as a notable example of climate leadership in the urban hospitality sector. Although wind turbines and net-zero models are technically impressive, infrastructure, regulatory, and financial barriers make it more difficult to scale them across all Choice Hotels locations. However, the use of recycled materials and energy management systems is both cost-effective and scalable, providing other mid-tier hotels in the group with a strong platform on which to build circular practices.

The above case studies demonstrate how regional and local hotels, as well as global hotel chains such as Hilton, Wyndham, InterContinental, Accor, and Choice Hotels, are implementing the principles of the circular economy at various scales. The projects cover energy efficiency, waste reduction, local sourcing, and community engagement. They range from eco-resorts that grow local gardens and forests to urban high-rise hotels that use solar rooftops. Each example demonstrates how hotels can embody the spirit of sustainable hospitality by striking a balance between profitability and social and environmental responsibility.

4 IMPLEMENTING CIRCULAR ECONOMY PRACTICES IN HOSPITALITY

This section examines the primary barriers to implementing circular practices, including a lack of awareness and financial constraints. It also emphasizes the importance of employee training, green HRM, and strategic alignment in achieving successful adoption.

Hospitality firms face several challenges when implementing circular economy practices. The hotels' lack of orientation, knowledge, and awareness regarding the CE and green practices is one of the main problems, claim Tanveer et al. (2023). Incorporating corporate social responsibility into business plans is another challenge that many companies face. Furthermore, it can be not easy to implement the dual strategy that environmental initiatives frequently call for, which combines top-down and bottom-up approaches. Financial limitations further complicate the adoption of a CE, as investments in sustainable technologies may not yield immediate returns.

The successful adoption of the CE in the hospitality sector depends on raising employee awareness of environmental issues and providing training. According to Hu et al. (2010), hotels are becoming increasingly aware of environmental issues and recognizing that they can contribute to environmental sustainability by reducing their energy, water, and waste consumption. However, many hotels still lack structured training programs to raise employee awareness. Promoting awareness is vital to reach an organizational culture that involves sustainability as a core value.

Green HRM is one of the most important methods for obtaining a CE designation. Even more important than employee training is the strategic integration of sustainability into HR operations. According to Haddock-Millar et al. (2015), green HRM is essential for reducing the adverse effects of businesses' operations and encouraging environmentally friendly behavior. Furthermore, green human resource management has been shown to improve environmental performance and drastically lower environmental degradation (Yong et al., 2022). According to Muisyo et al. (2022), green HRM also fosters green creativity at both individual and group levels.

The successful implementation of green HRM is made possible by the various leadership initiatives and organized training programs that hotels are adopting to encourage sustainability within the hotel. To educate and engage its employees in the company's energy-saving practices and environmental goals, Ascott Kuningan Jakarta, for example, launched the "Sustainability 101" program. Furthermore, Accor hotels have instituted "Green Action Days," during which their staff members participate in workshops focused on waste minimization, water conservation, and environmentally friendly service. IHG's "Sustainable Leadership Academy" for managers is another illustration of how Green HRM is being implemented. Its objective is to help managers match the goals of their departments with those of the CE.

However, effective implementation of sustainability within hotels faces several managerial challenges. According to Epstein and Buhovac (2010), top-level managers would eliminate sustainable activities if they did not see them as core activities. Another challenge is the lack of knowledge among owners and managers of small and medium-sized hotels about the negative impact of chemicals and ineffective waste management practices (Khatter, 2023). Those business owners still prefer short-term and daily goals and achievements over long-term goals, as they consider the immediate cash flow to be highly influential in their operations and survival. Moreover, business owners still perceive environmental activities as costly.

4.1 Previous Results and Evolving Trends

Practices to improve food efficiency and reduce waste are strongly correlated, according to Melo et al. (2025). Additionally, this study found a link between sustainable practices related to food waste and resource consciousness. To mitigate their environmental impact and enhance operational sustainability, many hotels have implemented strategies to reduce their use of energy, water, and other resources.

4.1.1 Focus Areas in Circular Initiatives

Avasiloaei (2022) conducted a comprehensive investigation into five major international hotel chains: Wyndham Hotels & Resorts, Hilton Worldwide, InterContinental Hotels Group, Accor, and Choice Hotels International. Based on this research, Avasiloaei identified the following crucial areas of focus for the circular economy initiatives:

- **Energy Use and CO2 Emissions:** Modern heating and cooling systems, solar panels, and energy-efficient systems are installed in most hotels.
- **Water Usage:** The projects incorporated low-flow dispensers, greywater recycling, and water-efficient landscaping practices.
- **Reusable or biodegradable materials** are used to replace single-use plastics, which have been reduced or eliminated.
- **Food Systems:** By growing their produce, composting, and sourcing locally, hotels tried to reduce food waste.
- **Mobility and Health**: Topics covered included sustainable transportation and health-related measures, such as green spaces and clean air systems.

By providing eco-friendly facilities, locally and sustainably produced food, and healthier indoor spaces, these programs can not only improve environmental outcomes but also directly enhance the customer experience. Additionally, this study stated that the central hotels focused on the traditional 3Rs (reducing, reusing, and recycling), with less emphasis on the transformative aspects of circularity, the new 3Rs (redesigning, replacing, and rethinking). The outcomes of these circular practices can be observed both in internal performance and external brand perception.

Implementing CE practices leads to more effective operations and stakeholder perception within the hospitality industry. Pereira-Moliner et al. (2015) state that implementing green practices and strategies in the hospitality industry helps businesses meet customer demand for green products and services, improve their competitive advantage, and mitigate external environmental challenges faced by stakeholders. These initiatives not only help reduce negative environmental impacts but also support brand loyalty and attract a new segment of environmentally conscious travelers.

5 RESEARCH GAPS, FUTURE DIRECTIONS AND MANAGERIAL RECOMMENDATIONS

5.1 Research Gaps and Future Research Agenda

The analysis above has revealed several critical gaps that require further research. Examining and filling the following gaps is crucial to achieving successful circular economy practices:

- **Gap 1: Advanced Integration of the Modern 3Rs:** Traditional hospitality sustainability initiatives prioritize reducing, reusing, and recycling; however, the new idea of rethink, redesign, and replace is still not widely used. These concepts necessitate a more substantial overhaul of the hospitality sector's operational and service models.
- **Gap 2: Integration of Industry 4.0 into Circular Economy:** There is still a significant impact of technology on the transformation of the CE that needs to be addressed, especially in the hospitality industry, where it influences consumer interaction.
- **Gap 3: The Customer's Evolving Role:** Customers remain essential to the shift to a CE, despite the literature continuing to highlight the roles that hotels play in this regard.
- **Gap 4: The Social Dimension of the Circular Economy:** The significance of tackling the social facets of the CE while simultaneously concentrating on its economic and environmental consequences is highlighted by this disparity.

5.2 Need for Further Exploration of Circular Economy Practices

To address the above gaps, future research should focus on:

1. **Measuring Quantitatively:** Rather than addressing theories and recommendations for practice, further research should set measurable frameworks that assess the effectiveness of the hotels' CE practices and their return on investment.
2. **Investigate Circular Economy Practices at Small and Independent Hotels:** Rather than focusing on international five-star hotels, further research should examine the CE practices in small, family-owned, and independent hotels to motivate their application.
3. **Examine Customer Engagement in Circular Operations:** Further research should focus solely on the impacts of the CE and sustainability practices on hotels, with active participation and engagement within those practices being assessed.
4. **Cooperation between Hospitality and Other Sectors:** Further research should conduct case studies to explore the impact of collaboration between hospitality firms and other sectors, including waste recycling firms, energy-saving firms, and others.

5.3 Managerial Recommendations for Hospitality Firms

Moving beyond gaps and future research recommendations, this chapter offers several suggestions for hotel firms to improve customer satisfaction and engagement levels through green initiatives.

- <u>**Recommendation 1**</u>**: Customer Membership Green Program:** Hotels should implement not only loyalty programs based on frequent visits to the hotel, but also develop a green membership program that encourages customers to enroll. The core of this program is to motivate customers to adopt green practices while simultaneously enhancing their satisfaction and engagement levels. The following outlines how this strategy can be implemented: Customers will earn loyalty points in their membership when they opt for low-carbon transportation, properly recycle, use water efficiently, and clean their rooms frequently. When customers accumulate a specific number of points, they will be eligible for discounts and complimentary nights at the hotel.
- <u>**Recommendation 2**</u>**: Enhance Green Awareness:** Hotels should have continuous digital displays in public areas that play short videos showcasing their achievements in CE. Additionally, those videos should encourage view-

ers to visit their accommodations in an environmentally responsible manner. Beyond this, true customer stories about green initiatives and achievements should be included in those videos. Incorporating green awareness into the hotel's operations should enhance patrons' interest in green practices and the CE, while also improving their overall satisfaction.

- **Recommendation 3: Integrating AI into Operations:** To strengthen their green initiatives, hotel management should incorporate artificial intelligence (AI) into various aspects of their operations. This all-inclusive package includes front desk operations, maintenance duties, housekeeping services, and food and beverage services. This integration will enhance their operational efficiency, which in turn reduces their resource consumption.
- **Recommendation 4: Industry 4.0 Application:** Hotels should invest in advanced technology, which should be considered a crucial part of the CE. Machine learning and automated systems in input/output control, guest interaction, employee awareness and training, and sustainability dashboards would, in turn, reduce resource usage, enhance employee understanding of the CE, improve customer engagement and satisfaction levels, and boost the hotel's operational efficiency.

The above managerial recommendations and research gaps highlight the need for a comprehensive, interdisciplinary approach to the CE in the hospitality industry. In addition to supporting global sustainability goals, embracing cutting-edge technologies, customer co-creation, and socially conscious practices significantly redefines the customer experience in quantifiable ways. To promote genuine innovation, transformation, and long-term value for all stakeholders, future initiatives must go beyond compliance.

6 CONCLUSION

The key conclusions of the chapter regarding the shift from linear to circular hospitality models are outlined in the conclusion. It highlights how implementing circular practices can enhance customer satisfaction, provide companies with a competitive advantage, and promote environmental sustainability.

The transition from a linear to a circular economy is now required rather than optional due to social, environmental, and economic factors. The importance of innovation, CE ideas, and sustainable practices in revolutionizing the visitor experience in the hospitality industry is covered in this chapter. The literature primarily focuses on reducing resource consumption (e.g., water, waste, and energy) while enhancing the brand's perception and supporting alignment with the UN Sustainable Development Goals.

In this chapter, various research-based challenges are explored that impact the practical application of the CE in achieving the UN Sustainable Development Goals. Additionally, several gaps were highlighted, such as a lack of strategic integration, transparency, accountability, and greenwashing, among others. Beyond this, hotels are still focusing on the traditional 3Rs (reduce, reuse, and recycle) rather than focusing on the modern 3Rs (redesign, rethink, and replace).

Furthermore, international five-star hotels have introduced several practices to facilitate the effective implementation of green practices; however, smaller, independent hotels have not yet received particular attention from academics. Similarly, the role of customers and technology in CE transformation has been underexplored.

Summing up, the following suggestions are derived from the analysis carried out in this chapter:

- **Focus on Measurement and Impact**: Future research should be conducted on various aspects of CE practices through the implementation of key performance indicators KPIs and benchmarking tools.
- **Promote further customer Co-Creation:** Customers should be more involved and engaged in CE green practices through loyalty-based green programs and immersive educational experiences.
- **Leverage Technology and Industry 4.0:** Integrating technology, including environmental dashboards, AI, and machine learning, reduces time, increases efficiency, and enhances customer engagement and satisfaction levels about green initiatives. Technology should also be linked to data-driven decision-making and predictive analytics.
- **Strengthen Collaboration with Other Industries:** Hotels should strengthen their partnerships with other industries, including water, energy, and waste service providers.
- **Embrace Transformative Circular Strategies:** Traditional sustainability practices should be replaced with the newest approach. This approach mainly focuses on customer involvement and technology.

In particular, managers view the implementation of CE principles as a strategic step toward enhancing resilience and long-term competitiveness in the hospitality industry. To achieve a CE, however, the hotel industry must undergo a cultural shift; merely implementing green practices will not be enough. Managers should lead by example and foster transformation to a circular economy by integrating sustainable actions into their key performance indicators (KPIs) while also increasing accountability.

Furthermore, for policymakers, transitioning to a CE requires government support. Governments should lower taxes and provide financial incentives to firms, including hotels, that prove they are applying circular economy practices. Additionally, the private and public sector institutions should provide certificates to firms with the best sustainability performance. Furthermore, policymakers should encourage the inclusion of advanced CE and sustainability applications, not only through theory, but also in educational institutions.

Note that small and medium-sized hotels also require specialized assistance, including free training courses, access to sustainability experts, and user-friendly digital tools for monitoring waste and resource usage.

CE practices and sustainability are not only a matter of cost reduction and natural preservation; they enhance the competitive advantage of hospitality enterprises. CE and sustainability applications, for example, at hotels attract customers, improve the hotel's image and reputation, and create positive word-of-mouth. Additionally, sustainable activities enhance employee and customer satisfaction and engagement levels.

To meet stakeholder and customer expectations, hospitality managers should implement sustainability and CE strategies. In its transition to sustainability, the hospitality sector is at a turning point. Adopting the tenets of the CE redefines what it means to provide a genuinely sustainable visitor experience, while also improving operational effectiveness and competitive advantage.

7 REFERENCES

Ahmed, M., Guo, Q., Qureshi, M., Raza, S., Khan, K., & Salam, J. (2021). Do green HR practices enhance green motivation and proactive environmental management maturity in hotel industry? *International Journal of Hospitality Management, 94*, 102852. DOI: 10.1016/j.ijhm.2020.102852

AHRESP & Turismo de Portugal. (2021). Guia de boas práticas para uma restauração circular e sustentável. *Turismo de Portugal*. https://business.turismodeportugal.pt/SiteCollectionDocuments/sustentabilidade/guia-boas-praticas-para-restauracao-circular-e-sustentavel.pdf

Al-Aomar, R., & Hussain, M. (2017). An assessment of green practices in a hotel supply chain: A study of UAE hotels. *Journal of Hospitality and Tourism Management, 32*, 71–81. DOI: 10.1016/j.jhtm.2017.04.002

Andersen, M. (2007). An introductory note on the environmental economics of the circular economy. *Sustainability Science, 2*(1), 133–140. DOI: 10.1007/s11625-006-0013-6

Arshad, M., Iqbal, M., & Shahbaz, M. (2017). Pakistan tourism industry and challenges: A review. *Asia Pacific Journal of Tourism Research, 23*(2), 121–132. DOI: 10.1080/10941665.2017.1410192

Avasiloaei, D. (2022). Reinventing the business model in the tourism industry based on sustainable circular economy and innovation. *ENTRENOVA – ENTerprise Research InNOVAtion, 8*(1), 435–448. https://doi.org/DOI: 10.54820/entrenova-2022-0036

Baker, M., Davis, E., & Weaver, P. (2013). Eco-friendly attitudes, barriers to participation, and differences in behavior at green hotels. *Cornell Hospitality Quarterly, 55*(1), 89–99. DOI: 10.1177/1938965513504483

Bexell, M., & Jönsson, K. (2017). Responsibility and the United Nations' sustainable development goals. *Forum for Development Studies, 44*(1), 13–29.

Bocken, N., & Ritala, P. (2022). Six ways to build circular business models. *The Journal of Business Strategy, 43*(3), 184–192. DOI: 10.1108/JBS-11-2020-0258

Boons, F., & Lüdeke-Freund, F. (2013). Business models for sustainable innovation: State-of-the-art and steps towards a research agenda. *Journal of Cleaner Production, 45*, 9–19. DOI: 10.1016/j.jclepro.2012.07.007

Busco, C., Granà, F., & Izzo, M. (2018). *Sustainable development goals and integrated reporting*. Routledge.

Calabrese, A., Costa, R., Levialdi, N., & Menichini, T. (2019). Integrating sustainability into strategic decision-making: A fuzzy AHP method for the selection of relevant sustainability issues. *Technological Forecasting and Social Change, 139*, 155–168. DOI: 10.1016/j.techfore.2018.11.005

Chan, E. (2008). Barriers to EMS in the hotel industry. *International Journal of Hospitality Management, 27*(2), 187–196. DOI: 10.1016/j.ijhm.2007.07.011

Chen, H., Bernard, S., & Rahman, I. (2019). Greenwashing in hotels: A structural model of trust and behavioral intentions. *Journal of Cleaner Production, 206*, 326–335. DOI: 10.1016/j.jclepro.2018.09.168

De Grosbois, D. (2012). Corporate social responsibility reporting by the global hotel industry: Commitment, initiatives and performance. *International Journal of Hospitality Management, 31*(3), 896–905. DOI: 10.1016/j.ijhm.2011.10.008

Demir, M., Rjoub, H., & Yesiltas, M. (2021). Environmental awareness and guests' intention to visit green hotels: The mediation role of consumption values. *PLoS One, 16*(5). Advance online publication. DOI: 10.1371/journal.pone.0248815 PMID: 33956794

ElAlfy, A., Darwish, K., & Weber, O. (2020). Corporations and sustainable development goals communication on social media: Corporate social responsibility or just another buzzword? *Sustainable Development, 28*(5), 1418–1430. DOI: 10.1002/sd.2095

Epstein, M., & Buhovac, A. (2010). Solving the sustainability implementation challenge. *Organizational Dynamics, 39*(4), 306–315. DOI: 10.1016/j.orgdyn.2010.07.003

Eskerod, P., Hollensen, S., Morales-Contreras, M., & Arteaga-Ortiz, J. (2019). Drivers for pursuing sustainability through IoT technology within high-end hotels—An exploratory study. *Sustainability, 11*(19), 5372. DOI: 10.3390/su11195372

Fei, A., Kim, J., & Kim, S. (2024). Effects of environmental sustainability practice in the economy hotel to Gen Zer's purchase decision: Behavior economy approach using choice-based conjoint analysis. *International Journal of Hospitality Management, 118*, 103678. DOI: 10.1016/j.ijhm.2023.103678

Ferreira, S., Pereira, O., & Simões, C. (2023). Determinants of consumers' intention to visit green hotels: Combining psychological and contextual factors. *Journal of Vacation Marketing, 31*(3), 535–548. DOI: 10.1177/13567667231217755

Ferrero-Ferrero, I., León, R., & Muñoz-Torres, M. J. (2020). Sustainability materiality matrices in doubt: May prioritizations of aspects overestimate environmental performance? *Journal of Environmental Planning and Management*, *64*(3), 432–463. DOI: 10.1080/09640568.2020.1766427

Ferrero-Ferrero, I., Muñoz-Torres, M., Rivera-Lirio, J., Escrig-Olmedo, E., & Fernández-Izquierdo, M. (2024). Sustainable development goals in the hospitality industry: A dream or reality? *Journal of Accounting & Organizational Change*, *20*(5), 773–796. DOI: 10.1108/JAOC-09-2022-0146

Fleming, A., Rickards, L., & Dowd, A. (2015). Understanding convergence and divergence in the framing of climate change responses: An analysis of two wine companies. *Environmental Science & Policy*, *51*, 202–214. DOI: 10.1016/j.envsci.2015.04.003

Fukuda-Parr, S. (2019). Keeping out extreme inequality from the SDG Agenda: The politics of indicators. *Global Policy*, *10*, 61–69.

Geissdoerfer, M., Bocken, N., & Hultink, E. (2016). Design thinking to enhance the sustainable business modelling process – A workshop based on a value mapping process. *Journal of Cleaner Production*, *135*, 1218–1232. DOI: 10.1016/j.jclepro.2016.07.020

Geissdoerfer, M., Morioka, S., de Carvalho, M., & Evans, S. (2018). Business models and supply chains for the circular economy. *Journal of Cleaner Production*, *190*, 712–721. DOI: 10.1016/j.jclepro.2018.04.159

Goudie, A. (2018). *Human Impact on the Natural Environment* (8th ed.). John Wiley & Sons.

Haddock-Millar, J., Sanyal, C., & Müller-Camen, M. (2015). Green human resource management: A comparative qualitative case study of a United States multinational corporation. *International Journal of Human Resource Management*, *27*(2), 192–211. DOI: 10.1080/09585192.2015.1052087

Han, H., Chua, B., & Hyun, S. (2020). Eliciting customers' waste reduction and water saving behaviors at a hotel. *International Journal of Hospitality Management*, *87*, 102386. DOI: 10.1016/j.ijhm.2019.102386

Hoogendoorn, B., Guerra, D., & van der Zwan, P. (2015). What drives environmental practices of SMEs? *Small Business Economics*, *44*, 759–781.

Hu, H., Parsa, H., & Self, J. (2010). The dynamics of green restaurant patronage. *Cornell Hospitality Quarterly*, *51*(3), 344–362. DOI: 10.1177/1938965510370564

Humphrey, C., O'Dwyer, B., & Unerman, J. (2016). Re-theorizing the configuration of organizational fields: The IIRC and the pursuit of 'Enlightened' corporate reporting. *Accounting and Business Research, 47*(1), 30–63. DOI: 10.1080/00014788.2016.1198683

Izzo, M., Ciaburri, M., & Tiscini, R. (2020). The challenge of sustainable development goal reporting: The first evidence from Italian listed companies. *Sustainability, 12*(8), 3494. DOI: 10.3390/su12083494

Khatter, A. (2023). Challenges and solutions for environmental sustainability in the hospitality sector. *Sustainability, 15*(15), 11491. DOI: 10.3390/su151511491

Khatter, A., McGrath, M., Pyke, J., White, L., & Lockstone-Binney, L. (2019). Analysis of hotels' environmentally sustainable policies and practices. *International Journal of Contemporary Hospitality Management, 31*, 2394–2410.

Khatter, A., White, L., Pyke, J., & McGrath, M. (2021). Stakeholders' influence on environmental sustainability in the Australian hotel industry. *Sustainability, 13*(3), 1351. DOI: 10.3390/su13031351

Korhonen, J., Honkasalo, A., & Seppala, J. (2018). Circular economy: The concept and its limitations. *Ecological Economics, 143*, 37–46. DOI: 10.1016/j.ecolecon.2017.06.041

Lashitew, A. (2021). Corporate uptake of the Sustainable Development Goals: Mere greenwashing or an advent of institutional change? *Journal of International Business Policy, 4*, 184–200. DOI: 10.1057/s42214-020-00092-4

Lenzen, M., Sun, Y., Faturay, F., Ting, Y., Geschke, A., & Malik, A. (2018). The carbon footprint of global tourism. *Nature Climate Change, 8*(6), 522–528. DOI: 10.1038/s41558-018-0141-x

Lieberman, A. (2018). SDGs show slow progress, not on track to reach 2030 targets. *Devex*. https://www.devex.com/news/sdgs-show-slow-progress-not-on-track-to-reach-2030-targets-un-reports-92971

Linder, M., & Williander, M. (2015). Circular business model innovation: Inherent uncertainties. *Business Strategy and the Environment, 26*(2), 182–196. DOI: 10.1002/bse.1906

Mak, A., & Chang, R. (2019). The driving and restraining forces for environmental strategy adoption in the hotel industry: A force field analysis approach. *Tourism Management, 73*, 48–60. DOI: 10.1016/j.tourman.2019.01.012

Mak, A., Lumbers, M., Eves, A., & Chang, R. (2012). Factors influencing tourist food consumption. *International Journal of Hospitality Management, 31*(3), 928–936. DOI: 10.1016/j.ijhm.2011.10.012

Manoj, M., Ram Das, A., Chandran, A., & Mandal, S. (2020). Antecedents of environmental engagement and environmental learning behaviour. *Journal of Hospitality and Tourism Insights*, *3*(4), 431–450. DOI: 10.1108/JHTI-01-2020-0001

Matiza, T., & Slabbert, E. (2025). Towards green hospitality: Exploring the consumer perceived value of pro-environmental star-graded accommodation. *Journal of Humanities and Applied Social Sciences*, *7*(2), 163–188. DOI: 10.1108/JHASS-07-2024-0123

McLennan, M., Group, S., & Group, Z. (2022). *The Global Risks Report 2022* (17th ed.). World Economic Forum., https://www.weforum.org/reports/global-risks-report-2022

Melo, A., Azevedo, D., Silva, S., Silva, G., Figueiredo, A., & Melo, C. (2025). Circular economy in the restaurant sector: Do practices go hand in hand? In *Proceedings of the 8th International Conference on Tourism Research (ICTR 2025).* https://doi.org/DOI: 10.34190/ictr.8.1.3507

Ministry of Land. Infrastructure, Transport and Tourism, Japan Tourism Agency. (2022). Case studies on the implementation of sustainable tourism content: Based on the FY2022 sustainable tourism content enhancement model project. https://www.mlit.go.jp/kankocho/content/001595025.pdf

Molina-Azorin, J., Tari, J., Pereira-Moliner, J., Lopez-Gamero, M., & Pertusa-Ortega, E. (2015). The effects of quality and environmental management on competitive advantage: A mixed methods study in the hotel industry. *Tourism Management, 50*, 41–54. DOI: 10.1016/j.tourman.2015.01.008

Mrówczyńska-Kamińska, A., Bajan, B., Pawłowski, K., Genstwa, N., & Zmyślona, J. (2021). Greenhouse gas emissions intensity of food production systems and its determinants. *PLoS One*, *16*(4), e0250995. DOI: 10.1371/journal.pone.0250995 PMID: 33930083

Muisyo, P., Su, Q., Hashmi, H., Ho, T., & Julius, M. (2022). The role of green HRM in driving hotels' green creativity. *International Journal of Contemporary Hospitality Management*, *34*(4), 1331–1352. DOI: 10.1108/IJCHM-07-2021-0833

Murakami, K. (2025). Policy approaches to sustainable and circular economy tourism: Comparative case studies of Japan and China. In *Proceedings of the 8th International Conference on Tourism Research, 8*(1). https://doi.org/DOI: 10.34190/ictr.8.1.3405

Nicolò, G., Zanellato, G., Tiron-Tudor, A., & Tartaglia Polcini, P. (2023). Revealing the corporate contribution to sustainable development goals through integrated reporting: A worldwide perspective. *Social Responsibility Journal*, *19*(5), 829–857. DOI: 10.1108/SRJ-09-2021-0373

OECD. (2017). *Policy coherence for sustainable development 2017: Eradicating poverty and promoting prosperity*. https://www.oecd-ilibrary.org/development/policy-coherence-for-sustainable-development-2017_9789264272576-en

Pierroni, M., McAloone, T., & Pigosso, D. (2019). Business model innovation for circular economy and sustainability: A review of approaches. *Journal of Cleaner Production*, *215*, 198–216. DOI: 10.1016/j.jclepro.2019.01.036

Prakash, S., Sharma, V., Singh, R., Vijayvargy, L., & Nilaish, L. (2023). Adopting green and sustainable practices in the hotel industry operations: An analysis of critical performance indicators for improved environmental quality. *Management of Environmental Quality*, *34*(4), 1057–1076. DOI: 10.1108/MEQ-03-2022-0090

Rabbi, M., & Amin, M. (2024). Circular economy and sustainable practices in the food industry: A comprehensive bibliometric analysis. *Cleaner and Responsible Consumption*, *14*, 100206. DOI: 10.1016/j.clrc.2024.100206

Rabiu, M., & Jaeger-Erben, M. (2022). Appropriation and routinisation of circular consumer practices: A review of current knowledge in the circular economy literature. *Cleaner and Responsible Consumption*, *7*, 100081. DOI: 10.1016/j.clrc.2022.100081

Raub, S., & Martin-Rios, C. (2019). "Think sustainable, act local" – A stakeholder-filter-model for translating SDGs into sustainability initiatives with local impact. *International Journal of Contemporary Hospitality Management*, *31*(6), 2428–2447. DOI: 10.1108/IJCHM-06-2018-0453

Rodriguez-Anton, J., Alonso-Almeida, M., Celemin, M., & Rubio, K. (2012). Use of different sustainability management systems in the hospitality industry: The case of Spanish hotels. *Journal of Cleaner Production*, *22*(1), 76–84. DOI: 10.1016/j.jclepro.2011.09.024

Rosati, F., & Faria, L. (2019). Addressing the SDGs in sustainability reports: The relationship with institutional factors. *Journal of Cleaner Production*, *251*, 1312–1326. DOI: 10.1016/j.jclepro.2018.12.107

Sadiq, M., Kannaiah, D., Yahya Khan, G., Ullah, R., & Mahfooz, Y. (2023). Does sustainable environmental agenda matter? The role of globalization toward energy consumption, economic growth, and carbon dioxide emissions in South Asian countries. *Environment, Development and Sustainability*, *25*, 76–95. DOI: 10.1007/s10668-021-02043-2

Samgerger, C. (2022). The role of water circularity in the food-water-energy nexus and climate change mitigation. *Energy Nexus*, *6*, 100061. DOI: 10.1016/j.nexus.2022.100061

Saxena, A., Ramaswamy, M., Beale, J., Vázquez, C., & Shrivastava, P. (2021). Striving for the United Nations (UN) Sustainable Development Goals (SDGs): What will it take? *Discover Sustainability*, *2*, 20. DOI: 10.1007/s43621-021-00029-8

Scholz, P. (2019). Green management implementation in accommodation facilities in Bulgaria. *Economics and Environment, 68*(1), 16. https://ekonomiaisrodowisko.pl/journal/article/view/108

Schramade, W. (2017). Investing in the UN Sustainable Development Goals: Opportunities for companies and investors. *Journal of Applied Corporate Finance*, *29*(2), 87–99. DOI: 10.1111/jacf.12236

Silva, S. (2021). Corporate contributions to the Sustainable Development Goals: An empirical analysis informed by legitimacy theory. *Journal of Cleaner Production*, *292*, 125962. DOI: 10.1016/j.jclepro.2021.125962

Smith, J., & Gladstein, A. (2018). How the UN's Sustainable Development Goals undermine democracy. *Quartz*. https://qz.com/africa/1299149/how-the-uns-sustainable-development-goals-undermine-democracy/

Sobaih, A., Abdou, A., Alshamayleh, H., Alshebami, A., & Abu Elnasr, A. (2025). Greening minds before businesses: Navigating SDGs hurdles for micro and small hotels in Saudi Arabia. *Cogent Business & Management*, *12*(1). Advance online publication. DOI: 10.1080/23311975.2025.2459325

Su, B., Heshmati, A., Geng, Y., & Yu, X. (2013). A review of the circular economy in China: Moving from rhetoric to implementation. *Journal of Cleaner Production*, *42*, 215–227. DOI: 10.1016/j.jclepro.2012.11.020

Tanveer, M., Yusliza, M., & Fawehinmi, O. (2024). Green HRM and hospitality industry: Challenges and barriers in adopting environmentally friendly practices. *Journal of Hospitality and Tourism Insights*, *7*(1), 121–141. DOI: 10.1108/JHTI-08-2022-0389

UNESCO. (2020). *Education for Sustainable Development Goals: Learning Objectives*. United Nations Educational, Scientific and Cultural Organization. https://unesdoc.unesco.org/ark:/48223/pf0000247444

United Nations. (2019). *The Sustainable Development Goals Report 2019*. United Nations Department of Social and Economic Affairs. https://unstats.un.org/sdgs/report/2019/The-Sustainable-Development-Goals-Report-2019.pdf

United Nations World Tourism Organization. (2019). *Climate Change & Tourism*. https://sdt.unwto.org/en/content/climate-change-tourism

Van der Waal, J., & Thijssens, T. (2020). Corporate involvement in Sustainable Development Goals: Exploring the territory. *Journal of Cleaner Production*, *252*, 119625. DOI: 10.1016/j.jclepro.2019.119625

World Commission on Environment and Development. (1987). *Our Common Future*. Oxford University Press.

World Tourism Organization. (2016). *UNWTO Tourism Highlights 2016 Edition*. https://www.e-unwto.org/doi/pdf/10.18111/9789284418145

World Travel & Tourism Council. (2017). *Travel & Tourism: Economic Impact 2017*. https://www.wttc.org/-/media/files/reports/economic-impact-research/regions-2017/world2017.pdf

World Travel & Tourism Council. (2017). *Global talent trends and issues for the travel and tourism sector*. World Travel & Tourism Council.

World Travel & Tourism Council. (2019). *Travel & tourism economic impact 2019*. Proceedings of the 8th International Conference on Tourism Research (ICTR 2025). https://wttc.org204

World Travel & Tourism Council. (2022). *Travel & tourism economic impact 2022*. World Travel & Tourism Council.

Yong, J., Yusliza, M., Ramayah, T., Farooq, K., & Tanveer, M. (2023). Accentuating the interconnection between green intellectual capital, green human resource management and sustainability. *Benchmarking*, *30*(8), 2783–2808. DOI: 10.1108/BIJ-11-2021-0641

Yusliza, M., Norazmi, N., Jabbour, C., Fernando, Y., Fawehinmi, O., & Seles, B. (2019). Top management commitment, corporate social responsibility and green human resource management: A Malaysian study. *Benchmarking*, *26*(6), 2051–2078. DOI: 10.1108/BIJ-09-2018-0283

Yusoff, Y., Nejati, M., Kee, D., & Amran, A. (2018). Linking green human resource management practices to environmental performance in hotel industry. *Global Business Review*, *21*(3), 663–680. DOI: 10.1177/0972150918779294

Zhang, L., Godil, D., Bibi, M., Khan, M., Sarwat, S., & Anser, M. (2021). Caring for the environment: How human capital, natural resources, and economic growth interact with environmental degradation in Pakistan? A dynamic ARDL approach. *The Science of the Total Environment*, *774*, 145553. DOI: 10.1016/j.scitotenv.2021.145553 PMID: 33611006

Zucchella, A., & Previtali, P. (2018). Circular business models for sustainable development: A "waste is food" restorative ecosystem. *Business Strategy and the Environment*, *28*(2), 274–285. DOI: 10.1002/bse.2216

Chapter 7
Transforming Business Models for a Sustainable Future

Mohamad Saad El Dine Knio
https://orcid.org/0000-0001-9074-8618
Lebanese International University, Lebanon

Suha Ali Tahan
Lebanese International University, Lebanon

Hassan Riad Youness
Lebanese International University, Lebanon

Mabelle Maurice Haddad
https://orcid.org/0009-0001-3741-5010
Lebanese International University, Lebanon

Ali Eren Balikel
Istanbul Kent University, Turkey

ABSTRACT

This chapter explores how transforming traditional business models toward sustainability is essential for integrating social, economic, and environmental goals. Central to this shift is the circular economy, which replaces the linear "take, make, dispose" model with a regenerative one focused on reuse, recycling, and waste reduction. Circularity enables resource efficiency, extended product lifespans, and new revenue streams. Implementing circularity requires addressing planned obsolescence and engaging key stakeholders such as customers and employees. Effective change management—including clear goals, stakeholder involvement, and progress

DOI: 10.4018/979-8-3373-7655-4.ch007

metrics—is vital. Sustainable business models emphasize long-term value, ethical practices, and social responsibility. Organizational culture plays a crucial role in adopting these models, and shifting culture requires leadership, communication, and strategic planning. The AIDA model can guide cultural transformation by engaging and motivating stakeholders toward sustainable action.

1. DEVELOPMENT OF THE CIRCULAR ECONOMY MODEL

Whenever we think about a circular economy, there is quite a bit of seminal work that was done in different parts of the world by different academic institutions, foundations, and consultancy companies (Geissdoerfer et al., 2017; Ellen MacArthur Foundation, 2019). In this specific theme, we would like to emphasize the concepts related to the development of a circular economy model as seen in the eyes of different participants in this concept (Bocken et al., 2016). When we think about a circular economy model, we have to make a distinction between two folds:

One fold is what we consider as a linear model, related to extracting, producing, using, and disposing of resources towards a circular model that brings us to the second fold, where we have to think about the aspects of reusing, recycling, repairing, and remanufacturing of in-hand resources in the purpose of trying to minimize the usage and the extraction of new resources through utilizing what is already been used in probably some other activities in the economy (Braungart & McDonough, 2009; Kirchherr et al., 2018).

When we think about the circular economy model, a very simple question is raised and that is; why do we need a circular economy model to be introduced and implemented in companies? Firstly, around 90 billion tons of natural resources are extracted every year to support the global economy (UNEP, 2019). This number is very big and because there are finite resources on Earth, then we need to think about a circular economy as one solution to these issues (Ellen MacArthur Foundation, 2019). Secondly, and based on the current trends, the number of expected waste in the area of let's say plastics, cardboard or packaging is really expected to rise with more production and more consumption. Not to mention that currently only 90% of resources find their way back into products while the rest goes into landfills or the oceans (Ellen MacArthur Foundation, 2019). Last but not least, the degradation of our natural capital is an additional concern on why we can think about the circular economy model as a one to deal with these kind of issues (World Economic Forum, 2020).

Whenever we think about the circular economy model we can think about the circular economy principles. That is, thinking about these principles in terms of design, use and system. Also, thinking about circularity in the context of what we call circularity by design. In other words, companies wanting to produce a specific product, should be mindful early from the design stage to structure it in a way that can bring it back after production to reuses, repurposes, and remanufactures the components or the materials contained in that product (Bocken et al., 2016).

Another aspect about a circular economy is that the products and materials produced to be in use for as long as possible (Kirchherr et al., 2018). The third aspect is the system. All the systems in our economy are interconnected. A very important system that all companies think about is the supply chain with the need to be circular for the whole system in order to move in the right direction towards circularity and the ability to achieve the .circular economic principle (Ellen MacArthur Foundation, 2019).

In summary, when we think about design we need to design products that help us to reduce waste and pollution (Bocken et al., 2016). When we think about use we need to keep products and material in use for as long as possible and when we think about systems we regenerate some of our natural systems (Geissdoerfer et al., 2017). So the idea behind circular economy is to transmit towards a sustainable economy that generates green growth and provides new opportunities that will lead to new jobs and innovations that will contribute positively to the society and the environment (Ellen MacArthur Foundation, 2019).

So when we think about the circular economy framework, that deals with four major issues:

We need to think about circular economy in terms of being a new business model (Geissdoerfer et al., 2017).
We need to think about circular economy in terms of design.
We need to think about circular economy in terms of what we call reverse logistics,
We need to think about the circular economy in terms of what will enable circularity.

Therefore, we should ask: what are the enablers to circularity? (World Economic Forum, 2020). And in order to be sustainable, one must also ask about the enablers to sustainability? One of the enablers to sustainability is to implement a circular economy model (Bocken et al., 2016). This brings us to a simple question about the enablers to a circular economy model. As companies we need to think in a bigger scope about our indu0 =stry, our internal processes and infrastructure, our own value chain model and then rethink the way we produce and distribute our products and services so then ultimately it will be consumed in a sustainable way (Geissdoerfer et al., 2017).

We will introduce several examples and cases that shows that circular economy model is working for many industries and many companies.. We can think about companies such as “Tarkett” as one of the pioneers in the cradle-to-cradle approach; designing products that are perpetually beneficial in a sense of continuously reusing and recycling material in a closed-loop cycles that eventually eliminate wastes, and in developing the take-back programs (Tarkett, 2020); the concept of accepting back used products from customers, where the company will either reuse, recycle or properly dispose. Tarkett uses 100% renewable electricity hydropower in all of their locations (Tarkett, 2020). They identified the B-to-B market as a very important market where they can see that there's a lot of circularity in the business practices. We can think about companies such as “Splash” where they make some sustainable products that will be used or consumed by consumers (Splash, 2019). Another good example is “Braiform” which is a global leader company in garment hanger use, handling billions of hangers each year (Braiform, 2020). We can think about Charpak which is based in the UK that development new and innovative ways related to packaging (Charpak, 2019). All of these are great examples of circular economy model.

2. WHY CIRCULARITY MATTERS

Circular economy models contribute to higher efficiency and productivity in the supply chain of companies applying this concept. Circular economy model also contributes to the economic and financial viability of companies.

When companies apply the circular economy model what does that mean in relation to the supply chain? It means recovery and recycle building products with a sharing platforms and all the aspects related to extending the life of the assets, being more sustainable, and thinking about the economic growth through what we call “green growth”. All of these are keywords that can be extracted from the application of a circular economy model.

The success of a circular economy model depends mainly on circular supplies. .Circular supplies are based on supplying fully renewable, recyclable, or biodegradable resources or inputs that sustain the circular production and consumption system. The value proposition that adopts circular supplies focusses on the substitution of fossil fuel for example to a more critical and a very renewable type of material (Geissdoerfer et al., 2017; Ellen MacArthur Foundation, 2019).

Another aspects of circular supplies are access and performance. Access and performance are concerned with providing the capability or services to satisfy users' needs without owning the physical product. Companies following the circular economy model will be questioned every time they are demanding resources and that is do they really need to own assets or can they just buy the service of the asset? A number of questions will be raised such as: Do we really need to own our car? Do we really need as companies to own some of the machines or do we just buy the services of the machine? One example is about the Rolls-Royce model and that is the Rolls-Royce sell the engine so that the airliner does not own the engine but they have access to the service of the engine (Bocken et al., 2016). So accessing the service of a product as opposed to owning a product is part of a circular economy model. Another aspect is about extending the product value. Extending product value focuses on exploiting the residual value of the product and delivering high quality long lasting product services that are being enabled to be as such because its designed for durability, repairability, upgradability, and so on and so forth. So extending the product value is about extending the life of the product.

In addition to extending the life of the product to last long in use without malfunctioning, that if something goes wrong with the product can we repair it instead of buying a new one? Can we reuse it for other purposes and not have to buy something new for that other purpose? Can we upgrade it and make it more effective and more efficient without having to know that new product? So circular economy is about extending what we call as the product value.

Another thing about a circular economy is bridging. It is about structuring and developing platforms for collaborations amongst producers and consumers. That is, identifying the supply and demand for materials and components, thus creating a market for waste and for used products on a 8-to-8 level or a 8-to-C level or whatever level. We're beginning to see the concept of what we would call reverse logistics, whereby you bring back waste or used products into the supply chain. So it's not only forward delivering but also bringing back what was once produced, using these platforms to be able to bridge the supply demand that exists in there (Kirchherr et al., 2018). According to some research and articles when we think about a circular economy we need to identify the issue related to providing a platform where demanders and suppliers of waste or used material and components can identify themselves and create transactions. Thus, extending the product value and the life of the product, in addition to making sure that an asset is going to be used for its service not just for the sake of having the asset, thus encouraging the production of sufficient products.. To enhance the industrial. Effectiveness, it is very important to identify the key elements of producing the goods that will eventually be used and consumed by consumers. All of these are elements of a circular economy model and the key takeaway is about the distinction between a product and a service in a circular economy by emphasizing the purchase of the service and not necessarily the purchase of the product. Therefore, circular economy emphasizes extending the life of the product through platforms and sharing. And all of these aspects are very critical for company's decision makers and executives within these companies to think about in order to be able to deliver an effective circular economy model (Bocken et al., 2016; Ellen MacArthur Foundation, 2019).

3. CIRCULAR ECONOMY PRINCIPLES

We need to look at things that relate to circularity in the context of designing out waste building resilience by using energy thinking in systems and also think in cascade to reach zero waste. A circular economy is about building resilience through diversity. In other words considering alternative or whatever sources, material, or input that are part of a reuse and repurpose model (Geissdoerfer et al., 2017). A circular economy is about using energy from renewable sources. A circular economy is about thinking in a system by trying to understand the interdependencies of the systems. For instance, the supply chain production, distribution, and consumption. All of these are systems but they're interrelated and they need to be thought of as all being circular in order to have a full circular economy model (Kirchherr et al., 2018).

In addition to that a circular economy is about thinking in cascades. In other words a top-down approach or even a bottom-up approach. With the top-down we start thinking from the policy, the environment, and then trickle it down to the level of the individual company. While when thinking about circularity from the bottom up, we start thinking about company's innovation, start-ups, entrepreneurs, and things that are good for the environment, then that builds up into the system.

There's a lot of flexibility in terms of thinking about what the circular economy is and what are the kinds of principles that are there. When we think about a circular economy yes of course we're thinking about issues related to distribution, the use, the disposal, the recycling, the manufacturing, and so on and so forth. But whenever we think about each and every single aspect alone such as thinking about manufacturing and how can we make manufacturing circular, or when thinking about distribution and how can we make distribution circular, there will be little connectivity's that exists at each and every stage of the value chain of a business model but what we need is to be circular at each and every stage for the whole model to actually work (Bocken et al., 2016).

Circular economy can be applied to almost every industry such as construction, smart cities, garment industry, logistics, waste prevention and recycling, financial services, and a whole range of different sectors and different industries that can potentially be circular. So circular economy is not exclusive to one specific sector or one specific industry to circularity.

In order to achieve a sustainable economic system, we need to think about the circularity model. And that is where we can identify the type of industries that will have what is called the low hanging fruits. That is, the one that does not really have to reinvent the wheel. There are lots of low hanging fruits in every firm, sector, industry, and country where if identified for circularity then we would reduce our costs and achieve our objectives of a sustainable economic system. Every company needs to start with itself in identifying well what it can do to become circular. But without incurring too much costs and without having to redevelop and reinvent the wheel. Companies and industries should identify any low hanging fruits which will take few steps toward circularity? And that's where things could start.

It is very important to think about this model in the context of finance. When you think about finance or financial decisions, it is all about making decisions with regard to an investment in an asset, the raising of funding to pay for these investments, and then the creation of cash flow to make these investments worthwhile.

So the three elements to financial decisions are:

The starting point is to identify an asset. This asset could be any of the followings: a project, a machine, a company, or a concept that you decided to invest in. The second part is to raise the funding to pay for this investment/asset. Here we start looking for the funding and comes the big question, where can we get the money from? Is it through debt or equity? After you've identified the asset and raised the funding to pay for this asset, the third part is how to make sure that this asset will actually work and provide the needed cash flow.

The asset works best if you put it to work for as long as possible. For example:If a car is actually being parked 92% of the time then it is not working for you. If an airplane is sitting on the tarmac and is not flying then it is not actually working for you. If the machine is turned off most of the time then it is not working for you. If the office space is empty and is not being used then the asset is not working for you.

In finance the idea is to get these assets to create cash flow. However, from a circular economy perspective we need to identify how this cash flow that is going to be generated is going to be based on circular economy model. So one of the key elements that we need to ask ourselves when we are dealing with the introduction, the implementation, and the analysis of a circular economy model is to identify the impact of the introduction, implementation, and the analysis of a circular economy model on a cash flow in the financial statements.

It is a very important element in making decisions is to think about the impact from cash flow. And cash flow is usually impacted by three elements: the cost of sales or what we call the cost of goods sold (COGS), by the profit margins especially gross profit margin, and by what we call EBIT or EBITDA (the earnings before interest and tax). All of three elements will be affected and influenced by the introduction of circular economy model. So as part of our overall evaluation and assessment of the impact of a circular economy model is to see what will be the effect on cash flow margin, the bottom line operating profit ratios and so on and so forth (Geissdoerfer et al., 2017; Kirchherr et al., 2018).

4. ADVANTAGES AND DISADVANTAGES OF PLANNED OBSOLESCENCE

Here we are going to discuss the importance of planned obsolescence concept. Planned obsolescence is a term that is used when we identify products that are being used with the plan of getting rid of them after a certain period of usage that could be two years, three years, or four years (Katz, 2019). So there is a short-term life cycle for the product and the objective is to get rid of the current product in use after a certain period of time so that a new one replaces it and get purchased by customers (Bocken et al., 2016). So these products become obsolete after a certain period of usage. Many argue that the circular economy might be in direct conflict with the planned obsolescence model (Geissdoerfer et al., 2017). Before we talk about whether it is in direct conflict with the planned obsolescence model or not, let us start asking our self on what would be the advantages and disadvantages of a planned obsolescence model? A planned obsolescence model is a model that depends on building products and renewing these products with new versions ever so often (Packard, 1960). One advantage is when we think about planned obsolescence we are introducing probably the effect of new technology in the new product or the upgraded model that is being introduced to the market (Cohen & Klemperer, 2017). Another advantage is that planned obsolescence is also a model that will continue producing new products for consumers and thus creating jobs in the economy as we move forward (Sachs, 2015). Planned obsolescence give the advantage of making the company continuously innovating and thinking about how to position itself in the market (Irwin, 2020). So there are a lot of advantages to having a model which is based on planned obsolescence. However, this concept also carries with it some disadvantages that to a large extent concerned with the utilization of new resources, the utilization of new material, the utilization of new components that will need to be used in order to produce the final new product (Ghisellini et al., 2016). In this case, what we observe is that from a sustainability perspective a planned obsolescence could be a model that puts pressure on the demands the materials, components, as well as the natural resources that we have (Lieder & Rashid, 2016).

The question to ask: will the circular economy model be in direct conflict with the planned obsolescence model? Since if companies are thinking about building certain products that will last for two, three, or four years and then replacing it with a new product after that period, then the argument is, why don't companies start thinking about building the initial product with recycled, reused, repurposed material from the start (Mylan, 2018)? In such case when the product expires in terms of its useful life, then according to circularity by design, we bring the product back into the circulation of production and consumption, then a planned obsolescence model will not necessarily be in direct conflict with the circular economy (Kirchherr et al.,

2018). Therefore, it is very important to think that if we have circularity by design then it can be incorporated in a planned obsolescence type of model. Accordingly, we need to think about the kind of material, the kind of components, the kind of input that we use in a product in order to bring it back at the end of its usage by the consumers (Geissdoerfer et al., 2017). This model can be applicable to both B-to-B or B-to-C type of consumers..

5. STAKEHOLDERS AND THEIR IMPORTANCE

In this section, we're going to be talking about stakeholders. In order to achieve a change in the organization and to move away from a traditional business model to a circular business model or a business model that focuses on sustainability and its impact on the society and the environment, then it is very important for the organization to attract the attention and get the buy-ins from the stakeholders (Freeman, 1984). The stakeholders are decision-makers that impact the performance of the organizations (Mitchell et al., 1997). But who are the stakeholders? For any kind of organization, we can think about customers as stakeholders (Donaldson & Preston, 1995). We can think about suppliers as stakeholders, employees as stakeholders, financial analysts as stakeholders, bankers, and creditors as stakeholders (Brugmann & Prahalad, 2007). The government is a stakeholder (Sullivan & Mackenzie, 2017). We think about the management as a a stakeholder. Competitors could potentially be a stakeholder (Harrison & Freeman, 1999). All of these are very important decision-makers that impact the decisions made by the organization. Stakeholders have an interest in the performance of the company for their own different reasons. Customers as stakeholders would like to see the company actually delivers continuously good products, good services, and new versions of the products and services (Kotler & Keller, 2016). Suppliers as stakeholders like to see that the company is successful and that any kind of business model that the company adopts will create more demand for the kind of products or material they supply the company with (Lamming et al., 2000). That doesn't necessarily mean that they're going to be producing and offering new inputs that will put pressure on the national resources. But it could mean that the suppliers will come up with innovative ideas for themselves to be sustainable (Elkington, 1997). Of course, when you think about the employees, the employees are stakeholders. They're the ones who actually execute the strategy. They are the ones who implement the decisions of the management. So they have to have the buy-in, conviction and belief that when a new business model is introduced then they are part of the decision-making process (Barton et al., 2009). Creditors and bankers are stakeholders, especially if a company has borrowed money from financial institutions (Mishkin & Eakins, 2012). These financial institutions need to feel that the company is going to be able to pay back the credits and the loans that they have borrowed. And if they move from a traditional model to a sustainable model, will that have an impact on the cash flow and the company's ability to pay back the borrowed amount? Will that have an impact on the financial position? In addition to that, when we think about the government,as a stakeholder. The government needs to know that companies are complying with the rules, regulations and the policies (Aguilera et al., 2007). The community is a stakeholder. For instance, if a factory or a company is locating itself in a community where there is a river or a well and the company's operation is poluting the river then that's going to be affecting the community negatively. But when a company creates sustainable solutions to the pollution from their production, then this is going to leave a positive impact on the community and the society (Porter & Kramer, 2011). When you think about stakeholders, we can think about other kinds of stakeholders: competitors, and financial analysts. The later are the ones who are going to identify if the company is going to perform well financially. And if they are going to be identifying whether the company is going to perform well and accordingly they will make the recommendation to the investors in terms of buying the shares or selling the shareholding and the shares. That's what financial analysts do (Merton, 1995). In addition to that, investors are stakeholders. Investors are beginning to identify companies that are sustainable because being sustainable signals that the company is responsible and have stronger financial statements (Clark et al., 2015). And companies that are more responsible and have stronger financial statements effectively create good returns for the investors. So all of these are, in fact, stakeholders that will contribute to the final decision that is made by the management on their transitional journey from a traditional business model to a circular sustainable business model (Elkington, 1997).

6. SUSTAINABILITY IMPLEMENTATION AND CHANGE MANAGEMENT

In this section, we will be talking about sustainability implementation, which naturally is going to be requiring change management. What is change management? This is a general term that relates to organizations making changes at different levels as a result of either a new strategic direction, the introduction of a new technology, due to internal changes, as a result of a crisis management, or demographical shifts, changes in the market conditions, competitive pressures, or organizational restructurings; there's a whole range of different reasons that brings the need for change within the organization (Kotter, 1996).

Change management is a process, and that process has a number of aspects that need to be considered by the leadership or management of the company (Hiatt,

2006). Change management starts with changing the strategy, identifying probably the direction of the strategy, or maybe thinking about a new strategy. But of course, the new strategy must be thought of in relevance to the change intended by the management. Change is usually thought of as a result of some kind of disruption, or changes in the environment in which the company is operating (Kotter, 1996). Change management is about drawing up a plan towards achieving sustainability, a plan towards implementing a circular economy model (Geissdoerfer et al., 2017). Change management is about identifying the key elements that need to be included in that plan (Kotter, 1996). Change management requires the involvement and engagement of all the stakeholders at all levels and taking part in the change management for it to be successful (Freeman, 1984). Change management has to be a process that will generate and produce enhanced results and improved performance (Hiatt, 2006). Change management is about basically building teams that come together, understand each other, and work together in order to execute the strategy of the company for achieving a more sustainable cooperation and a more sustainable business that will impact the society as well as the environment (Senge, 2006).

There are other steps to consider for a change management. Companies need to acknowledge and understand the need to change due to social changes or demographical changes. An example on demographical changes is the consideration of the millennials generation compared to the baby boomers. The baby boomers are retiring while the millennials are making the decisions on consumption, production, and management. Companies need to address the needs and demands of the millennials (Howe & Strauss, 2000). For many years, the baby boomers were the ones that saved wealth, invested, and actually consumed products and services. Now we're beginning to see the millennials and their echo. Such demographic changes will put pressure on companies to change strategies in order to fulfill the needs and wants of the millennials and the new generation (Howe & Strauss, 2000). It is very important to mention that we are now dealing with a generation that is socially and environmentally aware, and that is why we need to think about circular economy (Elkington, 1997). Another step to consider for change management is a detailed analysis on the impact of the required change. How will this change impact the organization and the internal as well as external aspects of the organization? Change management requires that companies and management apply a very important step which is developing scenarios, that is: a best-case scenario, a base-case scenario, a worst-case scenario that is going to be associated with the change (Kotter, 1996). Change management requires that we develop teams that include people from different departments (Hiatt, 2006). Change management requires that we communicate to stakeholders the need to change and the outcome of the change (Kotter, 1996). Moreover, change management requires a good effective plan and on top of all of that, requires that companies implement and review each of the mentioned steps to monitor if heading in the right direction on the journey towards sustainability (Geissdoerfer et al., 2017).

7. METRICS FOR CHANGE MANAGEMENT

In this section, we will be talking about the metrics that can be used to assess change management. These metrics relate to financial, operational, and strategic metrics. As we mentioned before, change management can follow a number of steps. But one of the key elements that relate to change management is improvement. Any kind of a business model or any kind of change within the organization has to be designed with a vision of improving the results (Kotter, 1996). Improving the financial, operational, and the strategic results (Kaplan & Norton, 2004). Companies are there in the marketplace with an objective to generate profit and create value. So if there is a change management and if there are positive results from the change that has taken place within the organization, these results have to be seen in a financial sense, in an operational sense, and in a strategic sense (Kaplan & Norton, 2004). When we think about the financial aspect and the financial implication of change management, the improvement to the bottom line is very critical. When we improve the bottom line as companies our profits go up, or our cash flow improves, or the value of the company or the share price of the company improves. This is considered to be one of the elements or one of the aspects of what we would call a positive implication of a change management (Porter, 1985). So the financial results have to be consistent with that positive change. If there are positive changes here and there but with no financial results that corroborate these changes, then obviously the company is not consistent in terms of what it's trying to achieve (Kaplan & Norton, 2004). So when we think about the financial metrics, we are thinking about things relating to the performance of the balance sheet and the performance of the financial statements such as the income statement (Porter, 1985). Some of the financials could be to reduce the cost of goods sold or the cost of production of different alternatives to the kinds of goods and services the company is trying to offer. When you think about the financial, we're thinking about the OPEX, the operating expenses and how the operating expenses could be affected by implementing this change management (Kaplan & Norton, 2004). The idea of generating revenue, increasing cash flow, improving the financial ratios, the profitability ratios, liquidity ratios, or the asset-based ratios as a result of the change. But in addition to that, the financials could be the perception of the financial market. For instance, can we observe that the share price of a company has actually improved or has gone up as a result of a change management? Or the share price of a company on the stock market improves as a result of change management, then this is some kind of a financial metric that we can think about and we can look at (Porter, 1985). One thing to understand is that there is a need to do more research in the area of the relationship between the financial impact of change management resulting from introducing sustainability models (Geissdoerfer et al., 2017). There's the operational aspect or the operational metric. The operational metric resulting from change management that will specifically focus on efficiency and productivity. That is, what is going to happen to the operational process? Are we becoming more efficient? Is more technology being applied? Are we optimizing as a company? Are we reducing our costs? Are we becoming more productive? All of these elements are indications of a change management because ultimately when there's going to be a change, the company, the leadership, and the management have to do this change with a view of producing better results, improved results, and results that are going to last (Kotter, 1996). And then there's a strategic metric.

The strategic metric on the other hand is about the company showing that their strategic direction is consistent with what is happening in the market. The strategic direction is consistent with what the consumer wants or what the competitors are doing (Porter, 1985). So the company cannot ignore all of these factors. Therefore, when we think about change management, we need to be able to measure it. And in order to measure change management, we should look at the financials and what is happening to the financials (Kaplan & Norton, 2004). In order to measure change management, we look at the operational. What's happening to the operational and the processes that are taking place in there in terms of the cost, in terms of efficiency, and in terms of productivity? We look at the strategic direction, which is specifically about what is our competitive position and our comparative position in the industry, the sector, or the economy in which we are operating (Porter, 1985).

8. BUSINESS MODELS FOR SUSTAINABILITY

In this section, we will be talking about business models for sustainability and ask the questions what, how, and for whom, or we can say what, who, and how. Developing a sustainable business model requires that we think about a number of things. We need to make a distinction between a sustainable business model and a business model that incorporates socially and environmentally sustainable practices and objectives.

Sustainable business models are ones that take into account the economic viability by achieving profit, the financial viability by creating monetary value, efficiency by minimizing costs, and productivity that maximizes the output per unit of input. This kind of model is what every business owner, leader, and manager desires to achieve (Schaltegger & Wagner, 2017). A business model that incorporates socially and environmentally sustainable practices is one that practices corporate social and environmental responsibility. It is one that considers all stakeholders of the business and not just the shareholders or the investors. It is one that addresses social and environmental impact. The one that translates environment and social policies as well as targets into actions (Bocken et al., 2014). A business model that incorporates social and environmental sustainable practices is one that continuously reviews and measures the impact of their business on the society and the environment. Additionally, it is one that considers the impact on investment. The focus here is on business models that prioritize social and environmental sustainability. Let us start by asking the following questions relating to these kinds of business models. What to produce in terms of the product or the service? Who to produce for, and how to produce it? The idea is to produce goods and services that meet the needs and wants of the consumers or the end users. Example: food, housing, infrastructure, transportation, health care, education, financial services, etc. These goods and services are produced given the analysis and understanding of the market forces of supply and demand that the company conducts. We need to understand the factors that influence demands such as prices, income, tastes and preferences, as well as demographics and market structure (Porter & Kramer, 2011). So, in order to identify what to produce, we need to be able to understand our target market. Who to produce for and that's a continuation. There is a continuous growing demand for products and services to be produced and offered taking sustainability factors into consideration. Much of the mindset of current consumers and end users focus on sustainability goals and targets. This is because of the increased awareness of climate change, the depletion of resources, degradation of the air, water, and soil. Businesses need to produce for all customers in the global marketplace but by considering the impact on society and the environment (Sullivan & Mackenzie, 2020). How to produce? Businesses need to plan the sale of goods and services by considering that the process should be done with the efficient allocation of the scarce resources in production. Production requires innovation and knowledge by combining the inputs efficiently and effectively. For example, should the business use more technology, fewer new materials, and instead focus on reuse, recycle, and repurpose materials? Should they use e-commerce as opposed to brick-and-mortar? And instead of brick and mortar, should they go for click and mortar? Should the business look at the aspects related to the usage of fossil fuel, and use alternative energy instead? What about real estate and location or consider the option of outsourcing? Should businesses reduce their acquisition of realestate because people can simply work digitally and remotely from home? This is how we should produce by combining the factors of production, where the production has to be done in such a way where businesses become more sustainable (Geissdoerfer et al., 2018).

What factors must be taken into account to reduce the pressure on the environment? And there are a number of things that can be used as examples for sustainable business models related to what, who, and how to produce. The textile industry is one important example. In the textile industry, cotton is used, water is used, and fossil fuel is used. How can the textile industry become more sustainable? And that is when they source things that are sustainable and when the supply chain is sustainable. But in addition to that, once they produce fabrics that can be reused and repurposed and remanufactured. And once the final consumer has used the final product and wants to get rid of that product, then that product should go back to the industry to repurpose it and reuse it and identify the kind of things that they can be recycled and be part of what we call a closed-loop system (Ellen MacArthur Foundation, 2013). So, in general, when we think about the concept of what and how to produce, we are really thinking about the company making decisions that will be friendly to the environment and contributing positively and impactfully to the society, and that will include production that meets the needs and wants of the shareholders as well as the investors in the company. This approach creats environmental values as well as social values in there. There are multiple values that we need to think about. There's economic values, environmental values, and social values, and the challenges for companies to combine all the three in one (Schaltegger et al., 2017).

9. WHAT IS ORGANIZATIONAL CULTURE

In this section, we will be introducing the organizational culture. What is an organizational culture and why it is important when we discuss sustainability issues? An organizational culture is a combination of a business philosophy, a combination of values, expectations, and management practices that guide the actions of all the employees in an organization (Schein, 2010). So, the organizational culture is about the characteristics that make an organization or a company what it is. There are different organizational cultures depending on the different industries, depending on the leaders, on the management structure, on the countries, and so on and so forth. But one of the important things that we would like to emphasize here is that an organizational culture is crucial to the introduction of sustainability in a business or in a company (Hart, 1995). An organizational culture affects all aspects of the business from decision-making processes, management style, behavior, attitude, contract terms, and employees' benefits. An organizational culture aligns the idea of a strategy with the employees and when we think about the employees, we're thinking about their expectations and the way that they're going to be managing and, introducing the different new ideas into a company. The employees have to feel good about the organizational culture. They have to feel comfortable. They have to feel supported and they have to value and consequently enhance their efficiency and productivity. So if the organizational culture produces such an outcome, then it'll be easy or easier for any new idea to be introduced into the organization. Simply because the stakeholders and the employees within the organization will buy into new ideas because of their confidence in the culture, their confidence in the management, and confidence in the leadership of the company. Companies that prioritize culture can be more resilient to business disruptions (Denison, 1990). What are the factors affecting organizational culture? Well, there are a number of factors: Leadership, management systems and practices, doing things right, dood decisions, Type of business and its industry, relationship with the clients and the stakeholders, HR policies, inclusion, diversity, stability, continuity, caring, and relationship with the society and the environment (Kotter, 1996).

10. STRATEGIES AND PITFALLS OF CHANGING ORGANIZATIONAL CULTURE

When it comes to changing the organizational culture one can argue that changing an organization's culture is one of the most difficult leadership challenges sometimes. That's because an organization's culture comprises of an interlocking set of: goals, roles, processes, values, communication practices, attitudes, and assumptions (Schein, 2010). So it is very important to understand that in order to initiate a change in general, the most productive and positive success strategy is to begin with leadership tools including a vision or a story of the future (Kotter, 1996). We need to be able as leaders as well as managers in organizations to cement the change in place with management tools such as the role that is given to the different teams, to the different departments, and to the different individual. These roles have to be defined, things have to be measured, and there need to be some kind of a control system (Beer & Nohria, 2000). It is also sometimes impossible to actually use pure power as a way to dictate change. Be as a last resort of course and that is when everything else fails. There are some mistakes made in an organizational change and some of these mistakes could apply to overuse of the power tools of trying to dictate the change on the organization and expect that everybody in the organization to respond to that positively. That is a mistake (Hiatt, 2006). We need to be able to invite the stakeholders to buy into the kind of change that the company wants to initiate. But it is very important that when there is an organizational change that management and the top leadership begin with a vision or a story by identifying the different aspects and the different strategies that the company wants to achieve and aspire to be (Kotter, 1996). All of these things are very important because the organizational culture in a way deals with some kind of a cultural transformation. So the word transformation here is critical and when we think about transformation the transformation applies to different levels: Transformation relating to the organizational aspect of the company and to the team as well as to the individuals (Schein, 2010). When you think about the organization we need to be able to define and communicate the vision and the strategy. We need to be able to build the different compartments that will carry the vision as well as the strategy. And we need to be able to ensure that all of these have to be measured and can be measured (Beer & Nohria, 2000). When you think about teams, the teams have to understand the goals and be able to react to these goals positively and to themselves following these goals (Hackman, 2002). We need to be able from a team's perspective to address the impact of the change not only on the company but on the individual teams, the individual units, and the individual departments within the organization (Hiatt, 2006). So it is very important that at that point the management and the leadership of the company build a high performing team in order to ensure that the transformational change that is taking place in the culture is going to be positive and it is going to be effective (Kotter, 1996). In addition to that there is the individual aspect and that is you addressing the me question as an individual within the organization. How is that going to affect me as an individual within the organization? Would it secure my job? Would it increase my income? And so on and so forth (Schein, 2010). Lots of job get lost as a result of the transformation that takes place. Definitely individuals and employees have to understand that the transitional changes could have a positive impact and the transformational changes will have a lasting impact (Hiatt, 2006). So when you think about the organization's structure, we think about the organization, the team, and in addition to that, we do think about the individual. But why do we need to understand the organizational structure and the organizational transformation in the context of sustainability? It is simply because sustainability can be a model that could disrupt the status quo of an organization (Bansal & Roth, 2000). And this sustainability objective can lead to changes in the operations, can lead to changes in the interactions, can lead to changes in the strategy, and can lead to the changes in the performances (Doppelt, 2017). So it is very important to understand the organizational structure as part of understanding sustainability issues.

11. USING AIDA TO TRANSFORM ORGANIZATIONAL CULTURE

What we will be talking about now is how to build a sustainable culture and we talked about cultural change within an organization. We talked about cultural transformation within an organization. We talked about how these changes impacting the organization itself, the teams within the organization, and the individuals that run the organization. Now we want to focus a little bit about and on the sustainable culture. We need to use a marketing approach within the organization if we as an organization are planning to achieve transformational change towards sustainability. An interesting marketing tool that in our opinion and we feel it is a very good to consider what we call the AIDA principle. It is about attention, interest, desire, and action (Kotler & Keller, 2016). So if there's going to be a need for a transformation in the culture of an organization and there's going to be a change in the culture of the organization, we need to be able as leadership and management to attract the attention of the organization and the stakeholders about the need for that change (Kotter, 1996). We need to stimulate their interests, arouse their desire, and get the action going with regard to that change. When we think about marketing, we learn from marketing that to change an organizational culture, we can start with attracting the attention of everybody within the organization. But it's not only within the organization; but also outside the organizations and to the different stakeholders. We need to increase and raise the awareness about the need for change and the same applies when talking about sustainability. We must increase the awareness with regards to the need for change within that organization (Porter & Kramer, 2006). We need to be able to stimulate the interest again of the stakeholders by highlighting the benefits to the organization, the benefits to the teams, the benefit to the individuals, the benefits to the society, and the benefits to the environment (Elkington, 1999). This is very important as a way by which we can get some buy-ins into the change. It is very important to engage the stakeholders so that they will all desire the change and become more engaged in order to achieve the results. Then it is very important to plan and implement the actions (Kotter, 1996). So all of these things relate to the AIDA principle that we apply on an internal level as opposed to just applying it to customers. So we want to treat the stakeholders as the customers as the clients when introducing the idea of sustainability.

When building a sustainable culture, and as mentioned earlier through: raising awareness, information, and education relating to the different things that need to be introduced (Murray, 2014). We should not expect that everybody knows about sustainability, its benefits, and the costs of not having sustainability on the society and the environment. This is why we need to inform, educate, and additionally consider the supply chain. As an organization we definitely have a supply chain whether we're in the manufacturing or in a service-based industry. So we need to also think about the supply chain. Members of the supply chain have to be sustainable because their sustainability is part of our sustainability as an organization (Bansal, 2005). We need to think about capacity building; there are teams, their departments, their units, and their projects that they may need training. We need to be able to facilitate training in order to achieve the objective, the change, and the transformation that we want to aspire to get to (Beer & Nohria, 2000). We need to inform all the stakeholders and learn from competitors. We need to know what's happening in the market and what are the competitors doing, and see if we can do things better and attract more attention in the market. We also need to learn from other industries as it's not enough to look at our own industry or our own company. It is very important to learn from other industries and different sectors then come up with an impact analysis that is going to measure whether that transformational change is going to deliver the kind of results that we want to deliver as an organization, bearing in mind that our objective is to introduce sustainability that will leave positive impact on the society and the environment (Doppelt, 2017). So introducing a sustainable culture requires following some of these steps that we have just mentioned.

REFERENCES

Aguilera, R. V., Williams, C. A., Conley, J. M., & Rupp, D. E. (2007). Corporate governance and social responsibility: A comparative analysis across the U.S., U.K., and Japan. *Corporate Governance, 15*(3), 300–315.

Bansal, P. (2005). Evolving sustainability: A longitudinal study of corporate sustainable development. *Strategic Management Journal*, *26*(3), 197–218.

Bansal, P., & Roth, K. (2000). Why businesses should take leadership in promoting sustainability. *The Academy of Management Perspectives*, *14*(3), 42–57.

Barton, D., Koller, G., & Morrow, J. (2009). *Mergers and acquisitions: Corporate strategy and the business cycle*. McKinsey & Company.

Beer, M., & Nohria, N. (2000). Cracking the code of change. *Harvard Business Review*, *78*(3), 133–141. PMID: 11183975

Bocken, N. M. P., de Pauw, I., Bakker, C., & van der Grinten, B. (2016). Product design and business model strategies for a circular economy. *Journal of Industrial and Production Engineering*, *33*(5), 308–320.

Bocken, N. M. P., Short, S. W., Rana, P., & Evans, S. (2014). A literature and practice review to develop sustainable business model archetypes. *Journal of Cleaner Production*, *65*, 42–56.

Braungart, M., & McDonough, W. (2009). *Cradle to Cradle: Remaking the Way We Make Things*. North Point Press.

Brugmann, J., & Prahalad, C. K. (2007). *Co-creating business value: New global business models for emerging markets*. Harvard Business Press.

Charpak. (2019). Sustainable Packaging Solutions. Retrieved from www.charpak.co.uk

Clark, G. L., Feiner, A., & Viehs, M. (2015). *From the stockholder to the stakeholder: How sustainability can drive financial outperformance*. Deutsche Asset & Wealth Management.

Cohen, A., & Klemperer, P. (2017). The economics of planned obsolescence. *The Journal of Economic Perspectives*, *31*(4), 51–68. PMID: 29465216

Denison, D. R. (1990). *Corporate culture and organizational effectiveness*. Wiley.

Donaldson, T., & Preston, L. E. (1995). The stakeholder theory of the corporation: Concepts, evidence, and implications. *Academy of Management Review*, *20*(1), 65–91.

Doppelt, B. (2017). *Leading change toward sustainability: A change-management guide for business, government, and society*. Greenleaf Publishing.

Elkington, J. (1999). *Cannibals with forks: The triple bottom line of 21st century business*. Capstone Publishing.

Ellen MacArthur Foundation. (2013). *Towards the circular economy: Economic and business rationale for an accelerated transition*. Ellen MacArthur Foundation.

Ellen MacArthur Foundation. (2019). The Circular Economy: A New Economic Model for the 21st Century. Retrieved from www.ellenmacarthurfoundation.org

Freeman, R. E. (1984). *Strategic management: A stakeholder approach*. Pitman.

Geissdoerfer, M., Savaget, P., Bocken, N. M. P., & Hultink, E. J. (2017). The Circular Economy – A new sustainability paradigm? *Journal of Cleaner Production, 143*, 757–768.

Ghisellini, P., Cialani, C., & Ulgiati, S. (2016). A review on circular economy: The expected transition to a balanced interplay of environmental and economic systems. *Journal of Cleaner Production, 114*, 11–32.

Hackman, J. R. (2002). *Leading teams: Setting the stage for great performances*. Harvard Business Press.

Harrison, J., & Freeman, R. E. (1999). Stakeholders, social responsibility, and performance: Empirical evidence and theoretical perspectives. *Academy of Management Journal, 42*(5), 479–485.

Hart, S. L. (1995). A natural-resource-based view of the firm. *Academy of Management Review, 20*(4), 986–1014.

Hiatt, J. M. (2006). *ADKAR: A model for change in business, government, and our community*. Prosci.

Howe, N., & Strauss, W. (2000). *Millennials rising: The next great generation*. Vintage Books.

Irwin, D. A. (2020). Innovation, obsolescence, and the environment: The unintended consequences of planned obsolescence. *Environmental Economics and Policy Studies, 22*(1), 55–73.

Kaplan, R. S., & Norton, D. P. (2004). *Strategy maps: Converting intangible assets into tangible outcomes*. Harvard Business School Press.

Katz, J. (2019). The paradox of obsolescence: A study of the environmental impact of planned product obsolescence. *Environmental Sociology, 5*(1), 35–45.

Kirchherr, J., Reike, D., & Hekkert, M. (2018). Conceptualizing the circular economy: An analysis of 114 definitions. *Resources, Conservation and Recycling, 127*, 221–232.

Kotler, P., & Keller, K. L. (2016). *Marketing management* (15th ed.). Pearson Education.

Kotter, J. P. (1996). *Leading change*. Harvard Business Press.

Lamming, R., Caldwell, N., & Harrison, D. (2000). An analysis of the sustainable supply chain. *The Journal of Supply Chain Management*, *36*(3), 54–65.

Lieder, M., & Rashid, A. (2016). Towards circular economy implementation: A comprehensive review in context of manufacturing industry. *Journal of Cleaner Production*, *115*, 36–51.

Merton, R. C. (1995). A functional perspective of the role of financial analysts. *The Journal of Finance*, *50*(4), 1413–1424.

Mitchell, R. K., Agle, B. R., & Wood, D. J. (1997). Toward a theory of stakeholder identification and salience: Defining the principle of who and what really counts. *Academy of Management Review*, *22*(4), 853–886.

Murray, A. (2014). The importance of sustainability in business. *Journal of Business Ethics*, *125*(1), 3–12.

Mylan, J. (2018). The circular economy and consumer protection law: A case study of planned obsolescence. *Journal of Consumer Policy*, *41*(1), 105–123.

Packard, V. (1960). *The Waste Makers*. David McKay Company, Inc.

Porter, M. E. (1985). *Competitive advantage: Creating and sustaining superior performance*. Free Press.

Porter, M. E., & Kramer, M. R. (2006). Strategy and society: The link between competitive advantage and corporate social responsibility. *Harvard Business Review*, *84*(12), 78–92. PMID: 17183795

Porter, M. E., & Kramer, M. R. (2011). Creating shared value. *Harvard Business Review*, *89*(1-2), 62–77.

Sachs, J. D. (2015). *The age of sustainable development*. Columbia University Press.

Schaltegger, S., Hansen, E. G., & Lüdeke-Freund, F. (2017). Business models for sustainability: A co-evolutionary analysis of sustainable entrepreneurship. *Business Strategy and the Environment*, *26*(4), 456–474.

Schaltegger, S., & Wagner, M. (2017). Sustainable entrepreneurship and sustainable business models. In *Handbook of sustainable innovation* (pp. 229–255). Edward Elgar Publishing.

Schein, E. H. (2010). *Organizational culture and leadership* (4th ed.). Jossey-Bass.

Senge, P. M. (2006). *The fifth discipline: The art and practice of the learning organization*. Doubleday.

Splash. (2019). Sustainable Products for a Better Tomorrow. Retrieved from www.splash.com

Sullivan, R., & Mackenzie, C. (2017). *Responsible investment: Guide to ESG data providers and relevant trends*. Springer.

Sullivan, R., & Mackenzie, C. (2020). *Sustainable business: Concepts, methodologies, tools, and applications*. IGI Global.

Tarkett. (2020). Sustainable Innovation and Circular Economy. Retrieved from www.tarkett.com

UNEP. (2019). *Global Resources Outlook: Natural Resources for the Future We Want*. United Nations Environment Programme.

World Economic Forum. (2020). Circular Economy in the Global Economy. Retrieved from www.weforum.org

Chapter 8
Utilizing the Lebanese Diaspora to Promote Circular Economy Entrepreneurship: A Strategic Policy Proposal for Post-Crisis Recovery

Sarah Hassan Chahine
https://orcid.org/0000-0001-5109-130X
Lebanese International University, Lebanon

Amira Ahmad Daouk
https://orcid.org/0000-0002-4955-1685
Lebanese International University, Lebanon

Najib Boulos Bou Zakhem
https://orcid.org/0000-0002-5260-6851
Lebanese International University, Lebanon

ABSTRACT

Lebanon is undergoing an unprecedented convergence of crises—economic collapse, institutional failure, and environmental degradation—undermining public confidence, reducing economic productivity, and exacerbating social fragmentation. This chapter argues that circular economy (CE) innovation, supported by targeted diaspora engagement, is an effective and contextually plausible pathway toward national recovery and resilience. CE is defined as a regenerative model that reduces waste, reuses materials, and focuses on localized production and repair. CE can

DOI: 10.4018/979-8-3373-7655-4.ch008

meet urgent socio-economic demands and enable long-term sustainability in fragile contexts like Lebanon. The chapter highlights Lebanon's socio-economic context and critiques structural weaknesses in entrepreneurship. It emphasizes the diaspora's untapped potential in expertise, networks, and capital. International case studies (India, Rwanda, Philippines, Ireland, Tunisia) support this. A three-pillar policy framework and mitigation strategies are proposed. The crisis becomes a catalyst for inclusive, sustainable innovation.

1. INTRODUCTION

1.1 What is the Circular Economy?

The circular economy (CE) is an economic system that is focused on maximizing the use of resources via closed-loop (circular) systems to reduce waste and optimize the benefits from the rethinking, reuse, repair, refurbishment, and recycling of products and materials. CE can be differentiated from a linear economy (take-make-dispose) because CE attempts to break the link between economic growth and consumption of resources and contribute to sustainability and resilience (Geissdoerfer et al., 2017). Examples of CE may include: product design with maximum intended longevity, ease of repair and maintenance, facilitated sharing economy, take-back recovery systems of materials. Increased intention to maximize longevity and minimize environmental harm, while still contributing to new business models, innovation, new jobs, and economic diversification (Kirchherr et al., 2017).

1.2 Lebanon's Crisis and the Socio-Economic Relevance of CE Innovation

Lebanon is facing a complex crisis that incorporates the elements of economic collapse, dysfunctional administration and social unrest, and environmental degradation. Since 2019, Lebanon has been in a severe financial crisis, with the national currency losing over 90% of its value and inflation rates soaring to trigger chronically high levels of national poverty that approach 80% of the population (World Bank, 2023). Lebanon's financial instability, in combination with the deterioration of its infrastructure and administrative problems that weaken public services provided (e.g., electricity supply and garbage collection), has not only resulted in the use of a greater number and more expensive private generators, but also increased reliance on private generators, and environmental pollution (International Monetary Fund, 2023). In precarious situations like the one that Lebanon is experiencing, it is possible to consider circular economy (CE) innovation as a realistic and beneficial middle space for an expanded approach to alleviating Lebanon's insecurities (socio-economic and environmental). CE projects - resource use efficiency, waste management, sustainable production, and consumption - may provide new business activity opportunities, employment opportunities, and environmental sustainability, from a wide range of consumer and producer perspectives (El Chaarani & Raimi, 2022).

1.3 Entrepreneurship as the Bridge Between Diaspora Support and CE Innovation

Entrepreneurship is one of the essential practices for enabling CE principles to be realized in contexts where economic development is creating challenges. As opportunities are constructed in the context of CE, entrepreneurs are afforded a viable solution and an opportunity for economic renewal and sustained sustainability through market access (Schaltegger et al., 2016). Despite the many challenges in establishing an entrepreneurial sector in Lebanon, the entrepreneurial ecosystem has shown perseverance and adaptability that is demonstrated by the rise of a number of startups and social enterprises that are focused on sustainable processes. However, the challenges of building out this sector still remain insurmountable - this often exists due to the inability to find funding sources, access mentorship opportunities, and find market traction (El Chaarani & Raimi, 2022). Additionally, the Lebanese diaspora also represents an opportunity to build out these challenges through networks, capital, capacity, and expertise. The diaspora can support local entrepreneurs with CE innovations and weave them into the traditional economy since diaspora members can also invest cash flow, exchange knowledge, and facilitate access to global markets (Nielsen & Riddle, 2010).

The application of Circular Economy (CE) principles in fragile states is sorely constrained by structural and institutional factors. In the first place, there are weak waste management systems and a minimal formal recycling system in place to enable recovery of materials. Second, the CE policy framework necessitates sound governance, regulation, and enforcement, all of which are tenuous at the best of times, and usually extremely fragile in post-conflict situations. Third, the incapacity to develop circular solutions means that financial, technological, and access to funding, as well as a lack of technical expertise and reliance on others for 'innovation' are hindered. Finally, the lack of public awareness and engagement, as well as informal economies, limit the wider stakeholder engagement and make meaningful participation and engagement all but impossible in this context (Gopalakrishnan & Miller, 2023).

1.4 Central Argument

This chapter contends that CE entrepreneurship in Lebanon could be strategically supported by the diaspora and their knowledge, networks, and capital. By leveraging their knowledge, networks, and capital, the diaspora can help to build a sustainable and resilient economy in Lebanon, alleviating socio-economic challenges as well as environmental problems. This collective problem-solving presents an opportunity for innovation, job creation, and sustainable development while helping the country recover and grow.

2. THE LEBANESE CONTEXT: CRISIS, OPPORTUNITY, AND THE CIRCULAR ECONOMY IMPERATIVE

2.1 Lebanon's Triple Crisis: Economic Collapse, Institutional Dysfunction, and Environmental Degradation

Lebanon has been caught up in a complicated crisis for a number of years, made up of an economic collapse, problems with institutions, and a deteriorating environment. Lebanon's economic crisis since 2019 has been considered one of the worst in the world, with the national currency devaluing by more than 90% and inflation over 150% in 2023 (World Bank, 2023). The results have forced more than half the population into poverty, increased social inequalities, and threaten basic livelihoods (World Bank, 2023; Guechati & Chami, 2022). Lebanon's economic collapse is coupled with institutional dysfunction. Decades of political gridlock, entrenched corruption, and weak governance have stalled efforts to reform essential services needed for recovery (Guechati & Chami, 2022). Political paralysis negatively affects basic services like electricity, water services, and waste management that have now become unreliable or non-existent in many places (Massoud et al., 2019). Although the electricity sector is already in a chronic state of shortage with a kind of blackout occurring for up to 20 hours a day, families and businesses turn to private energy generators to operate (World Bank, 2023). Private generators are expensive too, and the formal energy sector operates with minimal carbon threshold limitations for pollution. Another pressing dilemma that attaches itself to the crises in Lebanon is environmental degradation. Lebanon is experiencing deforestation, water pollution, and poor solid waste management; notably, Lebanon experienced a "waste crisis" in 2015 when the main landfill in Naameh closed down, and no alternative resulted in garbage left piled in the streets for months (Ellakkis et al., 2024). This environmental crisis poses public health risks and lowers life quality. The absence of coordinated environmental governance mechanisms only adds complication to mitigation efforts (Massoud et al., 2019).

2.2 Socioeconomic Fallout: Unemployment, Brain Drain, and Sectoral Stagnation

The economic collapse has caused escalated levels of unemployment, which are likely to continue to escalate, to a height that has not been experienced in Lebanon since the end of the civil war. The Lebanese Central Administration of Statistics estimates the current levels of unemployment rate to be roughly 36 percent (October 2022), and youth unemployment was over 47 percent (Central Administration of Statistics Lebanon, 2022). The poor state of the economy, in turn, is worsening the level of poverty, and the opportunity for social unrest is deteriorating, particularly for youth whose legitimate chance for viable employment continues to deteriorate (Guechati & Chami, 2022). The dismal economic state, combined with a lower level of hope, has led to an outflow of talented professionals (permanent migrants). Surveys indicate that out of Lebanese youth respondents aged 18-30 showed that 73% wish to exit permanently (UNDP Lebanon, 2020) to a stable and more prosperous life in other countries. The continued exodus of skilled labor (doctors, teachers, engineers) is limiting Lebanon's abilities to recover from the economic crisis and eroding Lebanon's base of human capital (Youssef et al., 2023). Furthermore, the brain drain aspect threatens future potential growth and innovation. Also, the existing traditional economy (agriculture, manufacturing, and a little bit of tourism) is already at a standstill and in some instances collapsing, due to the ongoing economic crisis. The agricultural sector, for example, is facing steep declines due to supply chain challenges, increased input costs, and land degradation, with a forecast output loss of US$ 1 billion for 2022 (Ushakov & Shatila, 2022). The manufacturing sector is also contracting due to energy shortages and reduced domestic demand. The tourism sector, which was once a critical contributor to GDP, has also suffered as a result of political instability and poor infrastructure conditions (World Bank, 2023).

2.3 Circular Economy: A Practical and Transformative Response

Under this lens, the framework of the circular economy (CE) can allow Lebanon to develop a way out of simultaneous socio-economic and environmental crises by moving from a linear "take-make-dispose" structure to one that promotes efficiency, cuts waste, and regenerates sustainably (Geissdoerfer et al., 2017). The CE operates by setting out a design process that eliminates waste, prolongs the lifecycle of products, and promotes reuse, repair, and recycling (Korhonen et al., 2018). The processes entailed under CE have the potential to provide sustainable job opportunities, bolster local economies, and lessen environmental stressors. Some CE models that are particularly applicable to Lebanon's socio-economic realities include:

Agri-waste reuse: Lebanon's significant organic waste generated by agriculture often ends up in landfills or is ultimately disposed of in open dumps, which not only contributes to pollution but also develops greenhouse gas emissions. There are significant gains to be made in composting agricultural residue and developing agricultural waste for improving soil quality, creating less reliance on chemical fertilizers, and generating income for rural municipalities (Kataya et al., 2023). As shown through pilot initiatives of converting olive tree pruning waste into biochar, improving soil quality, and increasing carbon sequestration, has a significant gain.

Second-hand economy: Due to difficult economic conditions, the reuse and resale of items is on the rise in Lebanon, offering access to more affordable options and diverting waste. Shops selling second-hand goods, digital resale platforms, and community exchange projects are available to leverage the durability of items and reduce resource depletion (Rizk & Matta, 2025).

Local repair hubs: Repair businesses that are focused on electronics, furniture, or appliances have emerged and have assisted homes and small businesses in extending the usable life of an item.

These hubs contribute to reducing electronic waste, which is a growing environmental issue in Lebanon, while creating some skilled employment opportunities (Massoud et al., 2019). Supporting governance, investment in infrastructure, capacity development, and public awareness campaigns can all contribute to successful CE implementation. Nonetheless, Lebanon still has institutional gaps that need to be addressed before CE practices can be scaled (Guechati & Chami, 2022).

2.4 Local Entrepreneurs and Civic Initiatives in the Circular Economy

Despite these barriers, several Lebanese entrepreneurs and civic initiatives exemplify CE values:

Nedaa Al-Ard: Has demonstrated community-based waste reduction and recycling efforts, including a composting initiative of organic waste, to prove the effectiveness of local community-based engagement in environmental management.

Souk el Tayeb: A farm-to-consumer farmer's market operating in Beirut promotes organic and locally produced food to reduce food miles and promote sustainability.

Engineers Without Borders - Lebanon (EWB-Lebanon): This NGO emphasizes sustainable rural development projects like beekeeping and energy efficiency in projects, which correspond with degrees of CE.

Beirut Madinati: Originating from civic activism, this volunteer-led political movement offers an alternative vision of urban policies, focusing on sustainable policies related to waste management and green infrastructure around the concept of CE.

3. LEBANON'S ENTREPRENEURIAL ECOSYSTEM AND THE MISSING MIDDLE

3.1 Overview of Lebanon's Entrepreneurial Landscape

Lebanon is well known for its great entrepreneurial drive, especially among its youth demographic, despite the persistent social, economic, and political instability in the region. Entrepreneurship here is supported by a prevailing culture of creativity, resilience, and adaptability - all key elements for innovating during turbulent times (Guechati & Chami, 2022). The entrepreneurial ecosystem in Lebanon continues to grow, with a growing number of startups, incubators, accelerators, and universities acting as centers for learning and capacity development. Youth make up a large share of Lebanon's population, and over 28% of the population is aged 15 to 29 (World Bank, 2023). This demographic environment presents considerable entrepreneurial energy, as many Lebanese youth are turning towards entrepreneurship to create their own employment opportunities amid high levels of joblessness (ILO, 2022). Lebanese universities and universities that offer courses in entrepreneurship, such as the American University of Beirut (AUB), Lebanese American University (LAU), and University of Balamand, have developed "entrepreneurship centers" where they offer courses, workshops, and mentorship programs to assist startup creation. Various incubators and accelerators, including Berytech, AltCity, and the Lebanese Business Angels Network (LebBAN), have been pivotal to supporting the leverage of startup ventures by providing technical support, networking, and services for business development (Guechati & Chami, 2022). Each of the aforementioned contributes to this entrepreneurial ecosystem's vibrancy, and youth entrepreneurs navigate an overly complex socio-economic environment in Lebanon.

3.2 Strengths of the Entrepreneurial Ecosystem

Lebanon's entrepreneurs exhibit a number of notable strengths in the entrepreneurial ecosystem:

· **Creativity and Innovation:** Lebanese entrepreneurs have a reputation for being innovative under constraints and are known for developing frugal solutions to local challenges such as energy shortages and waste management issues (Kataya et al., 2023). Their innate creativity has facilitated the development of tech startups, social enterprises, and green businesses that combine social value with economic value (Toufaily & Bou Zakhem, 2024).

· **Youth Energy and Aspirations:** Lebanon has a large population of youth who have high educational attainment rates. This allows for the talented youth population of Lebanon to pursue entrepreneurship, provided they have access to funding (ILO, 2022).

· **Academia:** Universities contribute significantly to entrepreneurship education and research at the education level, promote an innovation culture, and link academic programs with industry (Toufaily & Bou Zakhem, 2024).

· **Incubators and Accelerators:** Specialized enterprises like Berytech give startups access to seed funding and office spaces, and often mentorship, resulting in successful early-stage business development (Guechati & Chami, 2022).

3.3 Gaps and Challenges: The Missing Middle

Recognizing these strengths, it is important to note, Lebanon's entrepreneurial ecosystem also suffers from numerous challenges which limit the ability for startups to be capitalized upon, scale independently, and be sustainable. These significant challenges for startups are commonly referred to as the "missing middle" of entrepreneurial support and finance (World Bank, 2023).

· Limited Early-Stage Funding: Startups in Lebanon struggle to attain sufficient early-stage funding. Although seed funding can be found via accelerators or angel investors, early-stage funding in Lebanon can be limited, and/or not enough to help commercialize a business intended to go beyond ideation or prototype (Guechati & Chami, 2022). The venture capital space is not well-developed in Lebanon, due in part to financial instability in the country and also due to the risk aversion from potential investors in regard to the unknowns of operating as a venture capitalist in Lebanon (Toufaily & Bou Zakhem, 2024).

· Unpredictable Mentorship & Support: Incubators can also offer mentorship for entrepreneurs; however, their ability to provide access to this mentorship can vary, and also the quality of what is offered. Many entrepreneurs report little to no continuity and supporting guidance on their business strategic direction, growth trajectory, and regulatory framing (Kataya et al., 2023).

· Beirut-Centered Ecosystem: The vast majority of the entrepreneurial activity in Lebanon occurs in Beirut. Similarly, the entrepreneurial support services that exist are predominantly located in Beirut. Rural and peripheral regions of Lebanon provide start-up opportunities for local innovation and significantly to undertake circular economy ventures, but lack the entrepreneurial and support infrastructure (World Bank, 2023). The focus of Beirut's entrepreneurial ecosystem provides limited inclusivity and limits regional economic diversification.

· Flimsy Policy and Regulatory Environment: Due to Lebanon's political and economic instability, there are weak policy frameworks in place to support entrepreneurship. There is no clear national strategy for entrepreneurship development, and regulatory bottlenecks deter business registration, taxation, and access to finance (Guechati & Chami, 2022). Furthermore, there is little intellectual property protection and weak government incentives for startups, which are limiting innovation (Toufaily & Bou Zakhem, 2024).

These gaps prohibit Lebanon's ability to convert promising startups into enterprises that are sustainable, particularly those in the circular economy space.

3.4 Underdevelopment of Circular Economy Entrepreneurship

The circular economy and entrepreneurship in Lebanon are underutilized and largely unsupported despite the potential to solve urgent environmental and socio-economic issues. The challenges of conducting business in a circular way are multifold, including:

· **Limited Awareness and Understanding:** Circular economy ideas and concepts are still very early within Lebanon's business community. Many entrepreneurs lack satisfactory levels of awareness of CE principles and how to leverage these principles for profit (Massoud et al., 2019).

· **Insufficient Concessional Support:** There are no dedicated financial instruments and little focus on impact investing in CE opportunities. CE startups often have long time horizons before achieving profitability and employ unique business models that make it difficult to attract traditional investment (Kataya et al., 2023).

· **No Supporting Policy Measures:** The Lebanese government does not have a policy framework that integrates CE solutions into its national development strategy or environmental strategy. There is no supportive plan to promote policy measures that encourage the private sector to invest in CE ideas (Massoud et al., 2019).

· **Fragmented Ecosystem:** Circular economy entrepreneurship relies on more than one stakeholder, including waste management companies, local governments, universities, and financiers. However, Lebanon has a fragmented institutional environment that prohibits the establishment of collaborative bureaucratic relationships that could better allow for the sharing of knowledge and scaling of CE models (Ellakkis et als., 2024).

3.5 Diaspora Engagement as a Strategic Enabler

Diaspora communities are not homogeneous; they exhibit a variety of distinctive internal segments that are shaped by factors such as migration history, socio-economic status, and location. One frequent segmentation contrasts recent professional migrants (such as skilled workers and knowledge professionals in the Gulf) with legacy diaspora communities that have been established in western countries for generations. The former are often still very closely tied economically and culturally to their home country, often through remittances, investments, and temporary migration cycles. Legacy diaspora communities often have very engaged political engagement and/or identity-based activism through long-term integration.. It is important that all these segments be understood for the purposes of diaspora engagement and diaspora entrepreneurship support.

Lebanon has a large and established diaspora estimated to be around 14 million people transnationally, which is substantially higher than resident citizens and is an important yet rarely leveraged asset to support the entrepreneurial ecosystem, particularly in the circular economy/CE space (Hage, 2021). Leveraging diaspora engagement in Lebanon can directly address the structural gaps in various ways:

· Knowledge Transfer: Members of the diaspora are often highly skilled professionals and entrepreneurs who can exchange the operational expertise of the diaspora through environmentally and socially sustainable concepts, innovation, business models, and access to international markets. The knowledge transfer can be facilitated through mentorship programs, workshops, and organizational partnerships that support the development of Lebanese entrepreneurs operating through their CE ventures (Hage, 2021; Youssef et al., 2023).

· Access to Networks: the diaspora can provide critical access to networks and connections for Lebanese startups, internationally, with investors, technology clusters, and research institutions infrastructure. These essential networks will inform Lebanese entrepreneurs about local constraints and shortcomings in Beirut's ecosystem and provide pathways for the connection of Lebanon's startups to international value chains (World Bank, 2023).

· Capital Investment: the diaspora's remittance flows into the country represent a significant portion of GDP, and offer stability in times of crisis, representative of a continuous stream of capital investments. Finding ways to mobilize the diaspora wealth into impact investing, venture capital, or crowdfunding platforms directed toward CE startups could fill early-stage funding gaps (Hage, 2021).

· Advocacy and Policy Support: Diaspora communities can leverage their power as speakers, influencers, and citizen-advocates in the host country and in international circles to advocate for better policies and reforms that facilitate foreign aid, technology transfer, and partnerships to advance Lebanon's entrepreneurial ecosystem (Youssef et al., 2023).

There have been initial strides made through initiatives like the Lebanese Diaspora Energy Network that look at tapping the expertise of diaspora communities for renewable energy and environmental projects. This reflects the potential for scalable support for CE entrepreneurship initiatives.

4. THE LEBANESE DIASPORA: A TRANSNATIONAL ENGINE FOR INNOVATION

Realigning our understanding of the Lebanese diaspora as a transnational strategic partner in innovation, entrepreneurship, and sustainable development, rather than solely as a traditional remittances-heavy source of funding, is crucial. This diaspora is far larger in terms of global reach than Lebanon's resident population and represents a diverse and largely uninvestigated pool of human, financial, and intellectual capital traveling across borders (Benton, 2023).

4.1 Size and Global Distribution

The estimates of the Lebanese diaspora majority around the world range between 4 to 14 million, while there are approximately 4.6 million people residing in Lebanon (Gevorkyan & Issa, 2024). This new demographic fact is that Lebanon is a scarce country around the world in which the diaspora population is substantially higher than the domestic population. There are many Lebanon-hosting communities in Latin America (especially Brazil and Argentina), North America, Europe, Africa, and Australia. Brazil is estimated to have as many as 5 to 7 million people of Lebanese descent—the largest such community in the world (Gevorkyan & Issa, 2024).

This population is indicative of Lebanon's history of transnationalism, shaped through several waves of migration as an economic opportunity, war and conflict, and increasingly through globalization. These communities can serve as cultural and opportunity linkages that could contribute to innovation-driven collaboration between Lebanon and the world marketplace Arbash, 2023).

4.2 Economic Power and Contributions

Remittances from the Lebanese diaspora are still fundamental to the national economy. In 2023, Lebanon received about $6.7 billion in remittances, which represents 30.7% of its GDP and is the third highest ratio in the world (Note, 2022). While remittances have always provided support for education and health care previously, they are now being redirected towards basic needs such as food, rent, and energy due to the economic crisis (L'Orient Today, 2023).

By focusing on financial remittances, we run the risk of ignoring other possibilities of diaspora engagement across transnational spaces. The diaspora can offer more than remittances; they are seizable sources of potentially strategic contributions to Lebanon's innovation and entrepreneurship ecosystems needed to develop a sustainable recovery and resilience (Boiardi & Stout, 2021).

4.3 Professional Profile: A Knowledge-Rich Transnational Network

Not only is the Lebanese diaspora exceptional in terms of size, but they are also extraordinarily educated, successful, and engaged in global leadership. Lebanese expatriates are prominent in academia, policy, green technology, and business across North America, Europe, and the Gulf (Omar, 2025). For example, many diaspora professionals have taken leading roles in the evolution of renewable energy and environmental engineering and sustainable entrepreneurship. In addition, many Lebanese expats have initiated or supported clean energy innovations in Lebanon, spanning areas from solar power initiatives to waste management programs, providing technical expertise, financing, and support to local actors (Boiardi & Stout, 2021). This mobilization and transfer of knowledge and ideas enable Lebanese expats to contribute uniquely to advancing Lebanon's circular economy and green innovation sectors.

4.4 A Shift in Global Thinking: From Philanthropy to Transnational Co-Development

Engagement of diasporas has a historical tradition of philanthropy, based on charitable donations and emergency relief. However, a gradual transition to structured co-development has begun to take place, positioning diasporas as partners in the national transformation rather than as passive beneficiaries (Benton, 2023).

Investment in diasporas has been formalized in some countries like India, Ireland, and Rwanda, which all have formal programs that leverage diasporas' skills, networks, and innovative investments in education and infrastructure. These examples show that transnational partnerships can be sustainable and scalable if strategically positioned (Gelb et al., 2021)

Lebanon has fallen short of adopting these models because of political uncertainty, ineffective governance of fragile states, and a disjointed self-determined strategic vision. Despite these problems, this current economic and governance crisis creates the inflection point for change, allowing Lebanon to reposition the diaspora as a long-term co-developer of developmental progress, rather than a long-term safety net (Hazbun, 2016).

4.5 Collaborative Models for Transnational Innovation

Diaspora engagement in innovation and entrepreneurship can take many forms, including cofounding startups, impact investing, mentoring, advocacy, and acting as innovation ambassadors in the country where they are living. Successful examples of structured approaches to diaspora engagement include the LIFE (Lebanese International Finance Executives) network and the Lebanon Opportunities diaspora platform. Both exemplify the potential of structured mechanisms of collaboration that have institutional support (Gevorkyan & Issa, 2024).

What is needed now is a systematic and transnational way of approaching diaspora engagement that goes beyond one-off projects. Lebanon needs to reframe its diaspora, not simply as a source of financial assistance to Lebanon, but as partners in co-creating a knowledge economy, rooted in green innovation, sustainable entrepreneurship, and inclusive growth.

5. GLOBAL MODELS: DIASPORA-DRIVEN CIRCULAR AND GREEN INNOVATION

Diaspora communities around the globe are increasingly important actors when it comes to circular economy (CE) and green innovation in their home countries. Through their transnational mobility, financial capital, technical skills, and extensive global networks, these communities have created bridges connecting local needs and international opportunities to achieve sustainable development (Gelb et al., 2021; Plaza & Ratha, 2011). This section presents five case studies: India, Rwanda, the Philippines, Ireland, followed by Tunisia, which provide strategies that Lebanon can leverage to mobilize its diaspora for CE and green innovation (Pouessel, 2017).

5.1 India: Diaspora-Led Clean Energy Investments and Rural Entrepreneurship

The Indian transnational diaspora has been at the forefront of renewable energy and grassroots entrepreneurship. For example, organizations like SELCO India and co-founder, Harish Hande, have increased the number of energy-poor rural households with decentralized solar energy systems, changing their access to energy and their living conditions. Up to now, SELCO has put solar lighting systems in over two million homes (Rosvall, 2020).

Because of the strong Indian diaspora based in the U.S., some social entrepreneurs have continued the work of providing sustainable solutions, such as Dr. BP Agrawal's initiative of "River from the Sky," which is a rainwater harvesting initiative he has since expanded to "Clinics for Mass Care", that provides rural access to healthcare using a model that is technology forward and scalable (Agrawal, 2020). These programs are examples of how diasporic partnerships can generate social and environmental impacts. India's experience suggests that transnational partnerships with diasporic ties hold promise for catalyzing clean energy initiatives and socio-economically embedded entrepreneurship. Lebanon may want to consider similar constructs by Council providing diaspora green technical expertise to create further rural development and energy transitions.

5.2 Rwanda: Government-Facilitated Diaspora Engagement for Youth Innovation

The Rwandan government, in collaboration with the International Organization for Migration (IOM), has mechanized ways to connect its diaspora to national development. The Rwandan Diaspora Engagement Project has provided mentorship, technical assistance, and funding for grassroots environmental and recycling projects, particularly those led by youth entrepreneurs Munana, 2025). Rwanda illustrates how a state-led mechanism can channel transnational diaspora expertise into scaled youth-driven innovation. Lebanon can use Rwanda's example to meet the challenges of youth unemployment and environmental sustainability.

5.3 Philippines: Social Enterprises Enabled by Diaspora-Cooperative Finance

The Filipino diaspora remains one of the world's largest and has been instrumental in using remittances and cooperative funds to promote social enterprises based on sustainable agriculture, organic farming, and ecotourism (Opiniano, 2020). The formalized investment process, created through diaspora support for cooperatives, opened longer-term, locally rooted economic opportunities. This case illustrates the need for transnational financial instruments, cooperatives, or social investment funds that will allow Lebanon to engage the diaspora in contributing to green innovation and local resilience building.

5.4 Ireland: Structured Returnee Entrepreneurship Schemes

Ireland's "Back for Business" initiative is an exemplary practice in return migration policy. The "Back for Business" initiative provides returning Irish emigrants with business establishment support and resources such as peer-learning, mentoring, and government support, thereby facilitating the chances of success, as well as the reintegration of the diaspora community back into the domestic innovation ecosystem (McDonagh, 2023). Structured returnee programs may also help Lebanon to leverage the skills and resources of returning diaspora communities with incentives and support for reintegration. Furthermore, structured returnee support programs can help increase the capacity of transnational innovation across green sectors in Lebanon.

5.5 Tunisia: Diaspora Engagement within a MENA Context

Tunisia has seriously explored opportunities for institutionalizing diaspora engagement since the post-revolutionary period in the arena of diaspora policy. Both the creation of the Office of Tunisians Abroad (OTE) and accompanying legal reform have provided an opportunity for the diaspora to be engaged in national development initiatives. In particular, Tunisian expatriates have taken a particular interest in areas such as clean tech, civic governance, and ICT (Plaza & Ratha, 2011; Diaspora for Development, 2020). Tunisia is a regionally relevant example of how nation-states are integrating transnational diaspora communities into national policies. To engage in this policy process, Lebanon could use Tunisia as a model to institutionalize processes for diaspora engagement, as it relates to CE and green innovation initiatives, in the context of the MENA region.

6. POLICY PROPOSAL: STRATEGIES TO LEVERAGE THE DIASPORA FOR CIRCULAR ECONOMY (CE) ENTREPRENEURSHIP

6.1 Knowledge Transfer & Technical Mentorship

The Lebanese diaspora can be a transnational partner in innovation, but designing pathways for knowledge transfer and mentorship will be instrumental to this opportunity. The diaspora have experience and felt responsibility globally in green technologies, entrepreneurship, or sustainable development, and are motivated by their participation in local green and sustainable development initiatives. It is critical to establish systems for technical mentorship, as well as secure tacit knowledge transfer. The following strategies propose various practical approaches to structuring and codifying this engagement (Doukali, 2023).

6.1.1 Establish a Digital Diaspora Mentorship Network for CE Entrepreneurs

Develop an online platform for Lebanese circular economy (CE) entrepreneurs to connect with professionals living in the diaspora for peer mentoring, technical assistance, or collaboration.

Executing this strategy will necessitate a number of coordinated and professional-level processes to realize an online support platform for Lebanese circular economy (CE) entrepreneurs. First, platform development entails the creation of a matching digital platform where entrepreneurs can satisfy their specific project needs. The project profiles would have to be matched with qualified diaspora mentors using an algorithm based on the sector or theme the project is focused on, such as clean energy, waste management, sustainable food systems, or green finance. Second, mentor recruitment is fundamental and should take place via partnerships with Lebanese embassies, diaspora-based organizations, and professional associations around the world, where they can help identify Lebanese professionals without also encouraging them to volunteer as CE mentors. Third, high-quality mentorship programs must be integrated into the platform, with clearly defined goals, timelines, accountability, and an opportunity for a successful mentorship to inform the feedback process and help with effectiveness and sustainability. A pertinent example of such a model is the E-Mentor Corps of the U.S. State Department, which connects entrepreneurs with globally experienced mentors (George and De Sousa, 2022) through a structured and digital platform that facilitates communication using email, video call, and webinars to allow for effective cross-distance knowledge exchange (De Sousa, 2021). In the Lebanese context, this platform holds strategic importance because it would allow

CE startups to leverage the transnational knowledge, knowledge that is encapsulated within the experiences of the Lebanese diaspora. Such knowledge exchange would address an important innovation gap and would allow local entrepreneurs to infuse international best practices into their local ecosystem.

6.1.2 Partner with Universities or NGOs to Host "Visiting Innovators" Programs

To establish short-term residencies for diaspora experts to engage in partnership with local organizations, undertake workshops, and jointly develop CE solutions.

The implementation strategy is more comprehensive than digital engagement alone; it also includes an opportunity for in-person, intensive collaboration, facilitated by a process of "Visiting Innovators." This starts with the program design where the diaspora experts are invited to engage in short-term residencies (2-4 week periods) at Lebanese universities, innovation hubs, and/or NGOs. Residencies are organized around a structured training program that develops preparation for the visiting experts to participate as teachers, mentors, and co-developers of circular economy (CE) projects with local actors, in addition to experiential learning. A critical element to achieving sustainability is securing funding for the implementation of the residencies; therefore, multi-year funding from national and international grant-making bodies, development agency support, and private sector support should be sought to support costs related to the logistics of the visits and to operationalize the residencies. Important to this model is to create joint projects so each visit produces a visible output (eg, co-published research article; joint incubation of a start-up; or co-developed academic curriculum), which might contribute towards achieving the circular economy objectives. A positive model that illustrates this approach is the Meltwater Entrepreneurial School of Technology (MEST) in Ghana, which brings international experts to Ghana to help and mentor local entrepreneurs in the software and business development areas of the business. Since its launch, MEST has incubated over 80 start-ups across Africa (Boost, 2021). For Lebanon, embarking on a similar Visiting Innovators model would simultaneously galvanize transnational co-creation while also building lasting and innovation-led partnerships between local and diaspora CE practitioners, thereby ensuring Lebanon's increased capabilities for sustainable development led by circular economy approaches.

6.1.3 Facilitate Regular Virtual Workshops Led by Diaspora Professionals

The objective is to participate in monthly online workshops with diaspora leaders presenting Community-Economy (CE) trends/solutions and relevant global case studies with Lebanese place-based stakeholders. The strategy's complementary component is to enable virtual engagement with curated knowledge exchange sessions. The first stage is identifying topics of interest and the priority areas within the circular economy and waste plastics, renewable energy systems integration, circular food systems, and sustainable finance. These topics will be chosen in regard to the national CE goals and the expertise in the diaspora. The second stage is identifying speakers, which will involve diaspora professionals with domain expertise and regional market experience who are willing to host interactive sessions. From there, the organizers should engage available interface tools (Zoom, Webex, general regional webinar hub) to afford broad accessibility and long-term usage (all sessions will be recorded and usable afterwards). The best model for this is to work closely with the iDiaspora Platform developed by the International Organisation for Migration (IOM), which has developed a global framework for diaspora and homeland stakeholders to regularly engage virtually and exchange knowledge. This model was particularly useful during the pandemic as it helped facilitate ongoing transnational collaboration, even with restrictions on mobility (Lara-Guerrero, 2020). For Lebanon, having live virtual sessions of this type would allow CE entrepreneurs to quickly access relevant expertise that is globally available while also overcoming limited local knowledge in real time with an international context. Additionally, it would help develop appropriate tools to allow for ambiguity in dealing with continuous sustainability change.

6.1.4. Promote Success Stories and Hypothetical Use Cases

The purpose here is to showcase practical, real and believable fiction collaborations to demonstrate to diaspora and local innovators what is possible. In Kosovo, diaspora technologists supported a rural school with the implementation of digital learning solutions, which allowed for educational innovation and greater engagement and interaction with the students (King & Gëdeshi, 2024).

Hypothetical cases can also be of importance. For instance, a Lebanese engineer working in Germany is providing a mentorship relationship with a startup in the Beqaa Valley that takes agricultural waste and converts it into bioenergy. The engineer is providing virtual technical mentorship, links to appropriate partners in Europe, and assisting the startup with setting up a circular business model.

These stories can contextualize and highlight the real and palpable impact that is achievable when diaspora and local communities collaborate, and inspire the participants, which could lead to a broader commitment to Lebanon's circular transition. As Lebanon moves into procedures for knowledge transfer, it can maximize its transnational diaspora. Digital mentoring networks, "visiting innovator" residencies, virtual workshops, and compelling storytelling can create an exciting ecosystem of innovation, learning, and sustainable entrepreneurship. The action strategies described above will provide ongoing support to CE startups, while at the same time providing support to Lebanese cities within their own transnational position within global green innovation systems.

6.2 Diaspora Investment & Financing Mechanisms

Using the financial power of the Lebanese diaspora is paramount in enhancing circular economy (CE) innovation. The diaspora constitutes a transnational community with both economic and emotional ties to Lebanon, and is a unique source of impact capital. Lebanon can unlock this dormant potential into an activated connection with sustainable ventures in Lebanon by enabling and supporting dedicated investment vehicles and policy instruments that simultaneously aid in long-term economic recovery, green transition, and environmental resilience (Rosenbaum & Kehdy, 2022).

6.2.1 Design a Diaspora Circular Innovation Fund

The purpose of this project is to create a dedicated investment fund that allows members of the Lebanese diaspora to invest in circular economy (CE) startups through a range of financial instruments (e.g., matching grants, concessional loans, equity investments). The structure of the fund will follow a public-private partnership (PPP) model, combining diaspora funds with co-financing from the government or developing partners, such as through the World Bank, UNDP, or EU programs, to share the risk, increase market confidence, provide acceptable financial returns, and provide institutional credibility to the fund. The investment instruments will use a blended finance approach based on the stage of startup: grants for early-stage and scalable supply-side ventures; equity for viable CE businesses; and concessional loans for companies where only some financing is required. Fund operations and oversight would be managed by a reputable and qualified impact fund manager with demonstrated experience in Lebanese entrepreneurship and international green finance, ensuring oversight of finances, due diligence, and alignment with CE objectives. An example of a relevant benchmark would be the India Development Foundation of Overseas Indians (IDF-OI) - a government-endorsed trust overseeing diaspora donations into development initiatives like sanitation, education, and green infrastructure. IDF-OI further distinguishes itself from other support programs by designating transparency, structured due diligence, and allowing diaspora contributions to specify an investment by sector or region, which builds trust and creates a good impact (Hercog & Siegel, 2013). In a Lebanese context, a similar diaspora-led development fund could become a significant contribution toward mobilizing financial capital dedicated to CE ventures. With target sector focus (i.e., green startups, waste-to-energy) and robust mechanisms for risk mitigation, the trust structure would deliver a transparent and credible vehicle for diaspora participation, driving sustainable innovation and reinvesting in Lebanon's long-range development goals.

6.2.2 Create Diaspora-Focused Crowdfunding and Crowd-Equity Platforms

A primary objective, to increase participatory options for Lebanon's circular economy (CE) ecosystem, would be to create dedicated online platforms, allowing Lebanese diaspora members to actively contribute, whether through donations or equity investments, to properly assessed Lebanese CE projects. Platform development would begin with having a transparent, user-friendly digital interface with thoroughly vetted CE and startup ventures that collect seed or scale-up funding. It would provide accessible information, track record, and due diligence documents to build investor confidence in their funding decisions. A regulatory framework would also need to be developed in parallel with platform technical infrastructure, which would require working with the Central Bank of Lebanon and international regulatory authorities to create policies to protect investors while complying with local and international anti-money laundering (AML) laws and regulating regulatory accountability for hosting platforms based on compliance and reporting requirements. Outreach campaigns should recruit diaspora networks through Lebanese embassies, alumni, professional associations, chambers of commerce, and social media platforms since these types of networks or similar established examples of platforms like LaunchGood, a crowdfunding platform that has received more than $688 million worldwide for thousands of impact- projects, demonstrates just how massive diaspora funding can be with digital access and trust (Karakulah & Muneeza, 2024). In the Lebanese context, creating a similar platform with local and community roots would democratize access to CE investment opportunities for diaspora constituents with low financial capacity and expand the contributor base and amount of funding available for sustainable innovation in Lebanon.

6.2.3 Offer Tax Relief and Legal Recognition for Diaspora Green Investments

To incentivize diaspora engagement in Lebanon’s green and circular economy (CE) activities, a comprehensive set of financial and legal incentives must be implemented that mitigate risks and promote maximum return. Taxes are an important tool for furthering diaspora involvement, which can occur in numerous ways, such as through the creation of tax deductions or tax credits for diaspora funders who invest in certified and qualified CE businesses, directly impacting return on investment (ROI) and making the ventures more attractive financially. In addition to tax incentives, strong legal mechanisms should be put in place to protect foreign direct investments (FDI) by diaspora. This would allow for a unique set of laws, expectations, procedures, ownership protections, and dispute resolution processes to create an environment that would instill confidence in FDI. Mechanisms for green certifications should also be built into a national CE framework. The green certification system should work like this: startups can be certified by demonstrating they met sustainability and innovation goals/milestones. These firms can get certified and display the certificate to investors as a sign of credibility and long-term sustainability. A good example is the UK Enterprise Investment Scheme (EIS), where investors can receive up to 30% tax relief on funds invested in early-stage businesses, many of which are green, effectively mobilizing private capital into innovation and sustainability (Okeke & Asekomeh, 2024). Adapting a similar policy ecosystem in Lebanon would bring the diaspora investors' financial needs into alignment with the national environmental goals and support the development of trust on a community scale in the emerging CE enterprises of Lebanon.

6.2.4 Enable Micro-Investments Through Banks and Fintech Partnerships

One way to expand broad-based diaspora engagement in financing Lebanon's circular economy (CE) is to create pathways for small-scale contributions via trusted financial intermediaries. This can be accomplished by developing micro-investment platforms partnering with local banks and fintech companies for diaspora members to invest small amounts - say from 10- 50$ CAD into vetted CE ventures. Micro-investment platforms should integrate automated features like "round-up investments" or monthly debits to lessen the burden on users and increase participation. At the same time, it is imperative to provide diaspora investors with literacy skillsets on topics such as, risk valuation, impact investing, or startup performance metrics, to help build their confidence and facilitate well-informed decisions. For example, Eureeca is a UK equity crowdfunding platform that facilitates small and medium-sized enterprises (SMEs) to raise funding from a global investors network, inclusive of members of the Middle Eastern diaspora, while also allowing for a seamless equity finance-based experience to participate in high-impact ventures (Efraij, 2022; Abdeldayem & Aldulaimi, 2022). For Lebanon, such fintech-enabled micro-investment models can democratize diaspora participation, allowing it to be more inclusive and accessible across multiple income levels, making diaspora engagement in CE financing more diverse and inclusive.

Diaspora investment is more than simply a funding vehicle - it is a means of transnational economic citizenship. Lebanon can turn its global diaspora community into the catalyst for CE entrepreneurship by creating inclusive, regulated, and accessible mechanisms, like innovation funds, equity platforms, tax incentives, and micro-investment mechanisms. These mechanisms are necessary steps for Lebanon to leverage passive remittance flows into productive, sustainable investment and unleash green growth, social resilience, and national recovery.

6.3 Ecosystem Enablement and Institutional Coordination

Several constraints challenge Lebanon's adoption of circular economy practices, mainly the struggling banking system, volatile political landscape, economic fragility, and corrupted institutional entities *etc.* (Shallal, 2021; Salloukh, 2025). Nonetheless, few potential pathways serve as a beacon of hope, which include the utilization of diaspora networks, capabilities, and resources as well as multi-stakeholder collaboration involving governmental and non-governmental organizations. The aforementioned opportunities are highlighted in this section while advocating the significance of facilitating entrepreneurial ecosystems and enhancing institutional coordination as crucial foundations for circular economy implementation. The following recommendations are vital for overcoming constraints and establishing an enabling environment for circular economy enterprises.

6.3.1 Government-NGO-Diaspora Task Force

The creation of a purpose-driven task force consisting of the government, NGOs and diaspora and directed toward filling institutional and socio-economic gaps is a potential solution for the current local challenges facing Lebanon's circular economy (Soni, 2023). Acting as a governing authority, this task force would establish and evaluate circular economy initiatives in line with national goals and agenda leveraging diaspora's connections and resources. The diaspora can leverage its expertise and investments to fulfill the gaps in the resource-constrained Lebanese context (Rosenbaum, 2022). Given their unique focus on community engagement and project management, NGOs can mediate the connection between the diaspora and the local community while fostering partnerships and enforcing transparency and responsibility (Veleva, 2018).

Practically, inefficient regulatory frameworks, political instability, and limited trust towards the task force stakeholders can act as barriers that can obstruct the establishment and operation of the task force in Lebanon including. Furthermore, inadequate institutional capabilities can further hinder such collaboration, thus impeding its smooth execution (Plotnic, 2024). In light of that, clear definition of responsibilities and scope of work of each participant is key to minimize redundancy and enforce accountability. The use of online platforms and tools would also increase collaboration, evaluation and transparency (Djampou, 2023). Additionally, training, workshops and capacity buildings can bridge gaps and enhance comprehension of the standards and practices of circular economy (Ahda, 2025; Ho, 2024). By overcoming these obstacles and utilizing opportunities, the government-NGO-diaspora task force can function as a trigger of change for circular economy entrepreneurship and innovation in the country (Munir, 2025; Fernandes, 2023).

Lebanon can benefit from numerous task force examples from countries around the world. For instance, and following the 2010 earthquake, a task force was established in Haiti between diaspora, NGOs and governmental institutions to aid the post-crisis initiatives (Esnard, 2016). The collaboration fostered reconstruction, transmission of social capital, humanitarian relief and disaster recovery. The task force was able to influence policymakers in countries that have hosted Haitian immigrants to support and enhance their living conditions. In Mexico, the three-stakeholder task force was devoted to local growth and development projects. This collaboration has enabled diaspora organizations to influence public policy (Malone, 2020). In Afghanistan, the task force was digitally-enabled revolving around reconstruction, communication and development (Brinkerhoff, 2004). The significance of digital platforms in enabling such task forces is apparent particularly in collaboration with overseas experts and change makers (Djampou, 2023). Economic development was the main force in the UK as task forces were directed towards emphasizing public-private partnerships (Fernandes, 2023). As for the Netherlands, the government has focused on training and capacity building for knowledge transfer (Akimova, 2021). These cases underscore the significance of establishing clear vision and objectives, diversification, supportive policies and digitally-enabled collaboration. Lebanon can adopt similar approaches tailoring them to fit its context.

6.3.2 Public Registry of Circular Economy Entrepreneurs and Diaspora Partners

The second approach to ecosystem enablement and institutional coordination is through the establishment of a public registry with the purpose of registering, monitoring and disseminating information related to circular economy entrepreneurs and diaspora partners (Suzanne, 2020; Djampou, 2023). The registry is intended to achieve multiple objectives including boosting transparency and accountability, assisting institutions and governments in measuring progress, supporting required data collection about sectors, types of circular businesses, and sizes, promoting circular businesses to investors and other potential stakeholders, as well as benchmarking (Kusters, 2017). It is best to have a digital registry from day 1 for easier access for all stakeholders. In several settings like China and the Netherlands, digital registries have enabled inclusivity and dynamic registration and collaboration (Suzanne, 2020).

In Lebanon, several challenges arise for establishing such public registries. For instance, the corrupt nature of the government would resist the visibility and accountability features of the registry probably under the excuse of large financial requirements (Chaarani, 2021). Additionally, and considering the underdevelopment of the digital infrastructure along with weak internet access and aging technological infrastructure in the country (Suzanne, 2020), data collection is a hassle. Information is decentralized and somewhat fragmented making it problematic to find. Stakeholders may also resist participation due to limited awareness and lack of trust in governmental bodies (Plotnic, 2024). Rosenbaum (2022) argues that inclusivity cannot be guaranteed without great amounts of effort and resources.

Several strategies can be employed to overcome local challenges. To start with, awareness campaigns are a must (Ho, 2024). Officials must span universities, NGOs, diaspora institutions, research institutions, incubators, accelerators, and other support organizations in the Lebanese entrepreneurial ecosystem to promote the vital role that can be played by the public registry. Additionally, by employing user-friendly digital tools and proper communication on the importance of participation, resistance should be minimized (Suzanne, 2020). On the other hand, partners in the ecosystem can guarantee inclusivity by sharing necessary information on circular economy entrepreneurs whenever a new business idea is established (Ahda, 2025).

6.3.3 Policy Reform to Support Circular Economy Startups

An enabling entrepreneurial environment cannot be created without significant policy reform in Lebanon. Restructuring policy and regulations around waste-to-profit laws, startup-friendly procurement laws, tax incentives, extended producer responsibility (EPR) and innovation and collaboration support can directly influence innovation and decrease market barriers (Gorokhova, 2024). Regulations can act as an incentive for businesses in a circular economy especially through waste-to-profit laws that encourage them to transform waste into resources. In China, such policies forced businesses to reuse waste by-products and materials in return for financial incentives as well as reduce waste in the country and increased recycling (Li, 2016). Similar laws can be adopted in Lebanon to reduce the waste crisis in the country and encourage circular economy principles.

Startup-friendly procurement rules help emphasize circular products and services. By employing such rules, startups guarantee a market for their products. In the EU, for example, countries are obliged to prioritize circular products in governmental contracts. In order to ensure proper implementation in Lebanon, officials must be trained on circular economy principles to build well-defined metrics for assessing circularity in submitted bids. Tax incentives, on the other hand, highly stimulate investments in circular economy startups. Incentives comprise exemptions and deductions for companies embracing circular economy businesses, as well as credits. Tax incentives in Germany helped in cutting down on the use of natural resources by 35% (Gorokhova, 2024), while in Africa, higher innovation and sustainability were recorded.

Extended producer responsibility (EPR) policies make manufacturers responsible for all stages in the product life cycle, from design to disposal and recycling, emphasizing the need to implement the stages with responsible thinking, thus increasing the efficient use of resources (Li, 2016). Additionally, other policies can ensure subsidies, grants, collaboration, and knowledge exchange platforms, all of which fall under the innovation and collaboration support policies. For instance, in the UAE, such support allows sustainability and scalability for startups (Alqassimi, 2025).

In Lebanon, policy formulation is frequently hindered by structural and contextual hurdles. Unstable political infrastructure, economic challenges, as well as limited awareness and resistance from well-established industries, can add up to limit or delay the formulation of proper policies. Despite these challenges, strategic planning, capacity building, diaspora networks, and NGOs are the key, especially through implementing the aforementioned task force, to support policy reform.

Table 1. all policy recommendations to leverage the diaspora for a smooth implementation of circular economy in Lebanon.

Policy Area	Recommendation	Key Actions
Knowledge Transfer & Technical Mentorship	Establish a Digital Diaspora Mentorship Network for CE Entrepreneurs	* Create online platform for mentor matching * Recruit mentors via embassies/NGOs * Structure high-quality mentorship programs
	Partner with Universities or NGOs to Host 'Visiting Innovators' Programs	* Design short-term residency programs * Secure funding for the implementation of the residencies * Create joint outputs to achieve circular economy objectives * Use innovation hubs/universities for diaspora-local collaboration
	Facilitate Regular Virtual Workshops Led by Diaspora Professionals	* Identify topics/speakers * Host monthly webinars * Adopt iDiaspora model for curated knowledge sharing
	Promote Success Stories and Hypothetical Use Cases	* Document real and fictional case studies * Showcase diaspora-local collaborations * Inspire broader engagement and participation
Diaspora Investment & Financing	Design a Diaspora Circular Innovation Fund	* Structure a public-private partnetrship model * Adopt a blended finance approach with stage-based instruments * Appoint credible fund manager
	Create Diaspora-Focused Crowdfunding and Crowd-Equity Platforms	* Develop dedicated digital platforms * Ensure transparency and AML compliance * Launch outreach campaigns via diaspora networks
	Offer Tax Relief and Legal Recognition for Diaspora Green Investments	* Introduce tax credits/deductions * Establish legal protections for FDI * Launch national green certification for CE ventures
	Enable Micro-Investments Through Banks and Fintech Partnerships	* Partner with banks/fintechs to develop micro-investment platforms * Allow small contributions into vetted CE ventures * Offer diaspora investor literacy programs

continued on following page

Table 1. Continued

Policy Area	Recommendation	Key Actions
Ecosystem Enablement & Institutional Coordination	Establish Government-NGO-Diaspora Task Force	* Establish and evaluate circular economy initiatives * Define responsibilities and scope of work for each participant * Adopt digital collaboration tools * Enhance coordination via training and workshops
	Create Public Registry of CE Entrepreneurs and Diaspora Partners	* Launch digital registry for easier participant access * Promote transparency and benchmarking * Run awareness campaigns to ensure participation
	Reform Policies to Support CE Startups	* Introduce waste-to-profit laws, procurement policies, tax incentives, EPR * Train officials on CE principles to properly assess circularity in submitted bids * Implement tex incentives, subsidies, grants, collaboration, and knowledge exchange

7. RISKS, BARRIERS, AND MITIGATION STRATEGIES

As discussed earlier, although great potential for diaspora initiatives and strategies for the circular economy exists in Lebanon, numerous challenges remain that might hinder the implementation of these strategies. This chapter focuses in particular on political volatility, institutional weakness, and distrust in the government and its institutions, all of which require tackling through the assistance of the Lebanese diaspora (El Assaad, 2022).

7.1 Volatile Political Landscape

Lebanon is one of those countries with constant governmental changes, sectarian fragmentations, and underdeveloped institutional structures (Chaarani, 2021). Such an environment increases distrust, inconsistencies in policies, sectarian divisions, and weak institutional capacity (Stel, 2013; Platonic, 2024). To begin with, trust in the government and its institutions is diminished due to the aforementioned factors, along with the ongoing systemic corruption and political patronage. Additionally, frequent changes in the governmental bodies impact regulations and policies; for instance, tax incentives that were legislated as part of a previous government are repealed upon the transition of power, reflecting shifts in the new administration's fiscal strategy (Suzanne, 2020). More than that, the sectarian nature of the government unfortunately agrees to benefit a minority group over national development, which hinders the development of inclusive circular economy solutions (Stel, 2013).

To properly overcome these challenges, proper reforms should be introduced. First of all, transparency and inclusivity should be the main targets in all governmental institutions (Suzanne, 2020). Well-defined governance frameworks and accountability mechanisms should be implemented. Moreover, circular economy policies must be designed to focus on the development of all parts of the country (Fernandes, 2023). Diaspora networks, when leveraged properly, assist in managing circular economy initiatives without local political support. Another significant measure is probably isolating such policies from local political turnover to ensure the stability and longevity of these policies.

7.2 Institutional Weakness

Institutional fragmentation, corruption, and limited governmental capabilities increase institutional weaknesses (Majdalani, 2024). Corruption has led to the creation of unnecessary roles in governmental institutions, along with people in positions with limited experience and educational backgrounds (Nassar, 2021). Authorities have overlapping responsibilities for the sake of benefiting the minority, thus increasing inefficiencies in governance and policy implementation. Additionally, even if policies were established, weak policy enforcement threatens the proper implementation of these policies (Maolani, 2024). What if the diaspora fears interfering in the Lebanese institutions, considering its constrained functionality and corrupt nature?

To overcome such an outcome, several mitigation strategies should be considered, focusing on strengthening governance structures, capacity building, promoting stakeholder engagement, and enhancing policy enforcement. Similar to the unstable political landscape, institutional weakness cannot be overcome without clear, transparent mechanisms that guarantee the implementation and accountability, while setting up independent monitoring bodies to oversee the implementation of policies and policy reforms. Such reforms also underscore the importance of only hiring experts and those with relevant educational backgrounds in roles that are necessary for the government (Kumar, 2022). More than that, existing staff who have good experience and skills must sit for several capacity-building and training programs to enhance and formulate new skills to strengthen institutions and the formulation and implementation of circular economy initiatives (Rosenbaum, 2022). The government can also make use of the aforementioned government-NGO-diaspora workforce to design efficient institutional structures that can empower the circular economy and overcome current institutional weaknesses. Finally, better structures, mechanisms, and legal frameworks must be in place to enforce all the above.

7.3 Government Distrust

Lebanon has had a history of government distrust, considering the corruption, weak institutional entities, limited governmental capabilities, lack of law enforcement, and longevity, along with several other factors (Harb, 2024). This has actually caused an enormous increase in brain drain over the years from people who lost hope in a better government (Zreik, 2025). These issues can also cause distrust from the diaspora in regards to the misuse of resources, misallocation of funds, and embezzlement (Chaarani, 2021). Failure to properly communicate with the diaspora, along with limited stakeholder engagement, further increases these issues. For that, and similar to the aforementioned barriers, government distrust can only be mitigated through increasing transparency, promoting stakeholder engagement, communication channels, and implementing government reforms (Omar, 2025). Digitization is key to making the reforms visible, enabling two-way communication, as well as empowering the government-NGO-diaspora task force.

8. CONCLUSION

The road to overcoming Lebanon's socio-economic and environmental crises should be through the application of circular economy practices. Considering its transformative potential, the circular economy can be utilized to achieve sustainability, waste reduction, as well as economic resilience. Issues such as the economic collapse, brain drain, unemployment, sectoral stagnation, institutional dysfunction, volatile political landscape, corruption, environmental degradation, etc.

1. **Entrepreneurship and Diaspora Engagement**: Highlight the role of entrepreneurship as a bridge to CE innovation, supported by Lebanon's resilient entrepreneurial ecosystem and the strategic engagement of the diaspora. Stress the diaspora's contributions in knowledge transfer, capital investment, and advocacy.
2. **Barriers and Mitigation Strategies**: Address the institutional and political barriers, such as corruption, weak governance, and distrust, and propose solutions like transparency, stakeholder engagement, and the establishment of a government-NGO-diaspora task force.

3. **Global Models and Local Adaptation**: Reference successful diaspora-driven CE initiatives from other countries (e.g., India, Rwanda, Tunisia) and their relevance to Lebanon's context, advocating for structured transnational collaboration.
4. **Policy Reform and Ecosystem Enablement**: Stress the importance of policy reforms, such as waste-to-profit laws, tax incentives, and extended producer responsibility, to create an enabling environment for CE startups.
5. **Call to Action**: Conclude with a call to action for leveraging Lebanon's diaspora as a catalyst for CE entrepreneurship, emphasizing inclusive, regulated, and accessible mechanisms to fuel green growth, resilience, and recovery.

REFERENCES

Abdeldayem, M. M., & Aldulaimi, S. H. (2022). Predicting crowdfunding economic success in the gulf cooperation council. *International Journal of Engineering Business Management, 14*, 18479790221074477.

Ahda, M. (2025). Assistance and capacity building for entrepreneurship through optimization of field and sea products based on community circular economy. *Journal of Community Empowerment, 12*(4), 245–260.

Akimova, T. (2021). Netherlands: Experience in circular economy development. *Journal of Circular Economy Studies, 12*(3), 45–58.

Alqassimi, A. (2025). Sustainability and scalability in circular economy startups: The UAE experience. *Journal of Sustainable Development, 18*(2), 45–58.

Arbash, T. (2023). Migration Trajectories: Narratives in Lebanon (Master's thesis).

Benton, W. (2023). Returnees, Institutions, and Networks: Making Space for Technology Entrepreneurship in Beirut. *Anthropology of the Middle East, 18*(2), 69–84.

Boost, I. H. E. E. C. (2021). The Future of Africa.

Brinkerhoff, J. M. (2004). Digital diasporas and governance in fragile states: The case of reconstruction in Afghanistan. *Public Administration and Development, 24*(5), 397–413. DOI: 10.1002/pad.326

Central Administration of Statistics Lebanon. (2022). Labour Force and Unemployment Survey. Beirut: CAS. http://www.cas.gov.lb/index.php/latest-news-en/201-labour-force

Chaarani, B. (2021). Corruption and governance challenges in Lebanon: Implications for economic development. *Middle Eastern Studies, 57*(3), 345–362. DOI: 10.1080/00263206.2021.1874567

De Sousa, D. L. (2021). The use of interactive communication technologies for collaborative E-mentoring (Master's thesis, Universidade da Madeira (Portugal)).

Diaspora for Development. (2020). Tunisia's diaspora engagement strategy in the MENA region. https://diasporafordevelopment.eu

Djampou, J. (2023). Rethinking our food systems: A guide for multi-stakeholder collaboration. UNEP, FAO, and UNDP Joint Report, 1-45.

Doukali, I. (2023). Enhancing Circular Economy and Waste Management in Zanzibar: By leveraging young entrepreneurship and innovation.

Efraij, D. A. (2022). Crowdfunding Market in the UAE: Triangulation Study for the Success Factors in the Market (Master's thesis, The British University in Dubai). Freedom House. (2023). Nations in Transit: Lebanon._https://freedomhouse.org

El Assaad, N. (2022). Shaping public service delivery: a hybrid governance approach in the Lebanese public education sector (Master's thesis, University of Malta).

El Assaad, R. (2022). Political volatility and its impact on diaspora engagement in Lebanon. *Journal of Political Economy*, *34*(1), 78–92.

El Chaarani, H., & Raimi, L. (2022). Determinant factors of successful social entrepreneurship in the emerging circular economy of Lebanon: Exploring the moderating role of NGOs. *Journal of Entrepreneurship in Emerging Economies*, *14*(5), 874–901. DOI: 10.1108/JEEE-08-2021-0323

Ellakkis, M., Dehghan Nayeri, M., & Rajabzadeh Ghatari, A. (2024). From Conflict to Cooperation: A Multi-Methodological Approach to Managing the Solid Waste Crisis in Lebanon. *Journal of Systems Thinking in Practice*, *3*(1), 1–22.

Esnard, A. M. (2016). Diaspora engagement in post-disaster recovery: Lessons from Haiti. *Disaster Prevention and Management*, *25*(4), 512–526. DOI: 10.1108/DPM-03-2016-0052

Fernandes, P. (2023). Entrepreneurship as a transition to the circular economy. *Journal of Sustainable Business*, *18*(2), 34–56.

Geissdoerfer, M., Savaget, P., Bocken, N. M. P., & Hultink, E. J. (2017). The Circular Economy – A new sustainability paradigm? *Journal of Cleaner Production*, *143*, 757–768. DOI: 10.1016/j.jclepro.2016.12.048

Gelb, S., Kalantaryan, S., McMahon, S., & Perez-Fernandez, M. (2021). *Diaspora finance for development: From remittances to investment*. Publications Office of the European Union.

Gevorkyan, A. V., & Issa, S. (2024). Lebanese Diaspora and Sustainable Economic Development in Lebanon: new survey-informed analysis. Available at *SSRN* 5016805.

Gevorkyan, A. V., & Issa, S. (2024). Lebanese Diaspora and Sustainable Economic Development in Lebanon: new survey-informed analysis. Available at *SSRN* 5016805.

Gopalakrishnan, T., & Miller, J. (2023). Energy transition in fragile states: A critical primer. *World peace foundation*.

Gorokhova, N. (2024). Tax incentives for circular economy: Lessons from Germany. *Environmental Policy and Governance*, *34*(2), 123–135. DOI: 10.1002/eet.1956

Hage, G. (2021). *The diasporic condition: ethnographic explorations of the Lebanese in the world*. University of Chicago Press.

Harb, M. (2024). From protests to polls: A study on voting intentions in Lebanon. *Journal of Political Engagement*, *12*(3), 45–67.

Hazbun, W. (2016). Assembling security in a 'weak state:'the contentious politics of plural governance in Lebanon since 2005. *Third World Quarterly*, *37*(6), 1053–1070.

Hercog, M., & Siegel, M. (2013). Diaspora engagement in India: From non-required Indians to angels of development. In *Emigration nations: Policies and ideologies of emigrant engagement* (pp. 75–99). Palgrave Macmillan UK.

Ho, C. (2024). Circular economy education: Student feedback from five higher education institutions in the Asia Pacific. *Journal of Circular Economy Education*, *10*(3), 123–145.

International Labour Organization (ILO). (2022). Youth Employment in Lebanon: Challenges and Opportunities. Geneva: ILO._https://www.ilo.org/resource/article/ilo-skills-training-key-unlocking-decent-employment-lebanon#:~:text=According%20to%20the%20ILO%2C%20Lebanon's,is%20essential%20to%20support%20employment

International Monetary Fund. (2023). IMF Executive Board Concludes 2023 Article IV Consultation with Lebanon. Retrieved from_https://www.imf.org/en/News/Articles/2023/06/28/pr23245-lebanon-imf-executive-board-concludes-2023-article-iv-consultation-with-lebanon

International Monetary Fund. (2023). Lebanon: Article IV consultation report. IMF eLibrary._https://www.imf.org

Karakulah, M., & Muneeza, A. (2024). Exploring the Role of Donation-Based Crowdfunding in Islamic Social Finance. International Journal of Islamic Economics and Finance Research, 7(1 July), 42-58.

Kataya, G., Cornu, D., Bechelany, M., Hijazi, A., & Issa, M. (2023). Biomass waste conversion technologies and its application for sustainable environmental development—A review. *Agronomy (Basel)*, *13*(11), 2833.

King, R., & Gëdeshi, I. (2024). The Albanian Scientific Diaspora from Kosovo: Prospects for Cooperation and Return. Sussex Centre for Migration Research, 1-35.

Kirchherr, J., Reike, D., & Hekkert, M. (2017). Conceptualizing the circular economy: An analysis of 114 definitions. *Resources, Conservation and Recycling*, *127*, 221–232. DOI: 10.1016/j.resconrec.2017.09.005

Korhonen, J., Honkasalo, A., & Seppälä, J. (2018). Circular Economy: The Concept and its Limitations. *Ecological Economics*, *143*, 37–46. DOI: 10.1016/j.ecolecon.2017.06.041

Kumar, R. (2022). Leveraging blockchain and smart contract technologies to overcome circular economy implementation challenges. *Journal of Circular Economy Technology*, *15*(3), 89–102. DOI: 10.1016/j.jce.2022.03.004

Kusters, K. (2017). Participatory planning, monitoring, and evaluation of multistakeholder platforms in integrated landscape initiatives. *Landscape and Urban Planning*, *165*, 1–10. PMID: 28324144

L'Orient Today. (2023a). Diaspora fatigue and diminishing hope. https://today.lorientlejour.com

L'Orient Today. (2023b). Remittances now fueling basic needs amid crisis. https://today.lorientlejour.com/article/1337950/remittances-fueling-food-and-rent-in-lebanon.html

Lara-Guerrero, L. (2020). Diasporas engaging during the pandemic: International global exchanges in response to the Covid-19 crisis. *HAPSc Policy Briefs Series*, *1*(1), 177–182.

Li, X. (2016). Waste-to-profit policies in China: A pathway to circular economy. *Journal of Cleaner Production*, *112*, 1–10. DOI: 10.1016/j.jclepro.2015.07.123

Majdalani, R. (2024). Dancing at the foot of a volcano: Bad governance, corruption, and ecological disaster in Lebanon. *Journal of Political Ecology*, *31*(2), 245–260.

Malone, M. (2020). The Tres por Uno program: Diaspora engagement in Mexico's community development. *Migration Studies*, *8*(1), 56–74. DOI: 10.1093/migration/mnz045

Maolani, T. (2024). Governance and corruption: Evaluating anti-corruption policies and their effectiveness in strengthening institutional integrity. *Journal of Governance Studies*, *18*(4), 123–145.

Massoud, M. A., Mokbel, M., Alawieh, S., & Yassin, N. (2019). Towards improved governance for sustainable solid waste management in Lebanon: Centralised vs decentralised approaches. *Waste Management & Research*, *37*(7), 686–697. PMID: 30912714

McDonagh, K. (2023). Ireland's Foreign Relations in 2022. *Irish Studies in International Affairs*, *34*(1), 243–259.

Munana, F. A. (2025). Under What Conditions Does National Identity Contribute to National Stability in Rwanda and Burundi? (Doctoral dissertation, American Public University System).

Munir, A. (2025). The role of circular economy in green entrepreneurship: Sustainable business models. *Journal of Green Innovation*, *22*(1), 78–92.

Nassar, A. (2021). Corruption in Lebanon: An exploratory study about Lebanese managers' and employees' perceptions. *Journal of Business Ethics*, *34*(1), 78–92.

Nielsen, T. M., & Riddle, L. (2010). Investing in peace: The motivational dynamics of diaspora investment in post-conflict economies. *Journal of Business Ethics*, *89*(4), 435–448. DOI: 10.1007/s10551-010-0399-z

Note, C. (2022). Results and Performance of the World Bank Group 2022.

Okeke, O., & Asekomeh, A. (2024). A Systematic literature review on the UK's enterprise investment scheme and seed enterprise investment scheme and comparison with similar schemes in selected countries. *International Journal of Business & Economic Development*, *12*(02).
Okeke, O., & Asekomeh, A. (2024). A Systematic literature review on the UK's enterprise investment scheme and seed enterprise investment scheme and comparison with similar schemes in selected countries. *International Journal of Business & Economic Development*, *12*(02).
Omar, A. (2025). Engaging the Lebanese diaspora: Socioeconomic determinants, barriers, and opportunities for sustainable development. *Journal of Diaspora Studies*, *22*(4), 567–582.

Omar, M. H. (2025). Engaging the Lebanese diaspora: Socioeconomic determinants, barriers, and opportunities for sustainable development. *Edelweiss Applied Science and Technology*, *9*(2), 1784–1793.

Opiniano, J. M. (2020). The 'new'Philippine future "beside" the exodus. *Asian Education and Development Studies*, *10*(1), 53–68.

Plaza, S., & Ratha, D. (2011). Harnessing diaspora resources for Africa. Diaspora for development in Africa, 1-54.

Plotnic, M. (2024). Institutional barriers to circular economy in Lebanon: A governance perspective. *Journal of Environmental Policy*, *29*(3), 245–260.

Pouessel, S. (2017). Tunisia and its diaspora: Between protection and control. Emigration and diaspora policies in the age of mobility, 205-220.

Rizk, R., & Matta, J. (2025). The Impact of Green Finance and Green Consumption on Sustainable Economies: A Comparative Study of Lebanon and UAE. *Journal of Sustainable Economies*, *1*(1), 48–54.

Rosenbaum, E. (2022). Leveraging diaspora networks for circular economy: A global perspective. *Global Networks*, *22*(4), 567–582. DOI: 10.1111/glob.12345

Rosenbaum, R. A., & Kehdy, J. F. (2022). Cultivating circular economies in the gaps of governance: Lessons from Lebanon's ecosystem of CE micro projects. *Local Environment*, *27*(10-11), 1304–1320.

Rosvall, M. (2020). *Pursuit of Sustainability*. Decentralized Renewable Energy Services in India.

Salloukh, B. (2025). The dynamics between banking performance and economic stability in Lebanon. *Middle Eastern Finance Review*, *18*(1), 34–56.

Schaltegger, S., Lüdeke-Freund, F., & Hansen, E. G. (2016). Business models for sustainability: A co-evolutionary analysis of sustainable entrepreneurship, innovation, and transformation. *Organization & Environment*, *29*(3), 264–289. DOI: 10.1177/1086026616633272

Shallal, A. (2021). Lebanon's economic collapse: A systemic review. *Journal of Global Health*, *11*(3), 3052. DOI: 10.7189/jogh.11.03052 PMID: 33828836

Soni, S. (2023). Harnessing the power of collaboration to expand the coverage and equity of COVID-19 vaccinations in India: A community collaboration model. *Journal of Public Health Practice*, *18*(3), 245–260. DOI: 10.1016/j.jphp.2023.03.004 PMID: 37376411

Stel, N. (2013). Governance and corruption in Lebanon: The role of sectarianism. *Third World Quarterly*, *34*(5), 705–722. DOI: 10.1080/01436597.2013.800747

Suzanne, T. (2020). Digital registries for circular economy: Case studies from China and the Netherlands. *Journal of Digital Innovation*, *15*(2), 89–102. DOI: 10.1016/j.jdi.2020.03.004

Toufaily, B., & Bou Zakhem, N. (2024). Drivers of Student Social Entrepreneurial Intention Amid the Economic Crisis in Lebanon: A Mediation Model. *Sustainability*, *16*(7), 2807.

Ushakov, D., & Shatila, K. (2022). The impact of agricultural sector on boosting the Lebanese economy throughout the economic crisis. *International Journal of Agricultural Extension*, *10*(3), 377–385.

Veleva, V. (2018). The role of NGOs in fostering circular economy practices. *Sustainability*, *10*(6), 2145. DOI: 10.3390/su10062145

World Bank. (2023). Lebanon Economic Monitor, Fall 2023: In the Grip of a New Crisis. Washington, DC: World Bank. https://openknowledge.worldbank.org/entities/publication/1c302eca-bd1e-4751-9ebd-d425169ed161

World Bank. (2023, December 21). Lebanon's fragile economy pulled back into recession [Press release]. https://www.worldbank.org/en/news/press-release/2023/12/21/lebanon-s-fragile-economy-pulled-back-into-recession

Youssef, S., Ramadan, M., Baydoun, H., Zakhem, N. B., Tahan, S., Diab, M. B., & Yassine, D. (2023). Entrepreneurial Intentions in Crisis: Shaping Through the Triad of Influence-Government, Education, and Environment. *Journal of Law and Sustainable Development*, *11*(6), e890–e890.

Zreik, R. (2025). The factors driving Lebanon's medical brain drain. *Journal of Health Policy*, *34*(1), 78–92.

Compilation of References

Ababio, J. O. M., Yiadom, E. B., Ofori-Sasu, D., & Sarpong–Kumankoma, E. (2024). Digital financial inclusion and inclusive development in lower-middle-income countries: The enabling role of institutional quality. *Journal of Chinese Economic and Foreign Trade Studies*, *17*(2/3), 133–151.

Abbas, I. I., Chaaban, J. K., Al-Rabaa, A. R., & Shaar, A. A. (2017). Solid waste management in Lebanon: Challenges and recommendations. *Journal of Environment and Waste Management*, *4*(2), 53–63.

Abbas, J. (2024). Does the nexus of corporate social responsibility and green dynamic capabilities drive firms toward green technological innovation? the moderating role of green transformational leadership. *Technological Forecasting and Social Change*, *208*, 123698.

Abbas, R. (2017). Solid waste management in Lebanon: Challenges and recommendations. *Waste Management & Research*, *35*(2), 89–102.

Abdeldayem, M. M., & Aldulaimi, S. H. (2022). Predicting crowdfunding economic success in the gulf cooperation council. *International Journal of Engineering Business Management*, *14*, 18479790221074477.

Abu-Qdais, H. A., Shatnawi, N., & Al-Shahrabi, R. (2023). Modeling the impact of fees and circular economy options on the financial sustainability of the solid waste management system in Jordan. *Resources*, *12*(3), 32. DOI: 10.3390/resources12030032

Acemoglu, D., & Restrepo, P. (2018). Artificial intelligence, automation and work. *Working Paper Series (National Bureau of Economic Research)*, •••, 24196.

Adebayo, Y. A., Ikevuje, A. H., Kwakye, J. M., & Esiri, A. E. (2024). Driving circular economy in project management: Effective stakeholder management for sustainable outcomes. *GSC Advanced Research and Reviews*, *20*(3), 235–245.

Adedeji, O., Reuben, O., & Olatoye, O. (2014). Global Climate Change. *Journal of Geoscience and Environment Protection*, *2*, 115. DOI: 10.4236/gep.2014.22016

Aguilera, R. V., Williams, C. A., Conley, J. M., & Rupp, D. E. (2007). Corporate governance and social responsibility: A comparative analysis across the U.S., U.K., and Japan. *Corporate Governance*, *15*(3), 300–315.

Agyemang, A. O., Yusheng, K., & Asei, A. (2025). Addressing Sustainability Footprint Disclosure for High Pollutant Firms in China and the US: The Roles of Firms Governance Structure, Financing Decisions, and Eco-Technology. *Corporate Social Responsibility and Environmental Management*.

Ahda, M. (2025). Assistance and capacity building for entrepreneurship through optimization of field and sea products based on community circular economy. *Journal of Community Empowerment*, *12*(4), 245–260.

Ahmadieh, D., Nalbandian, S., & Noubani, K. (2016). A comparative citation analysis study of master's theses at the American University of Beirut, Lebanon. *Collection Building*, *35*(4), 103–113.

Ahmad, S., Islam, T., Sadiq, M., & Kaleem, A. (2021). Promoting green behavior through ethical leadership: A model of green human resource management and environmental knowledge. *Leadership and Organization Development Journal*, *42*, 531–547.

Ahmed, M., Guo, Q., Qureshi, M., Raza, S., Khan, K., & Salam, J. (2021). Do green HR practices enhance green motivation and proactive environmental management maturity in hotel industry? *International Journal of Hospitality Management*, *94*, 102852. DOI: 10.1016/j.ijhm.2020.102852

Ahmed, Z. U., & Julian, C. C. (2012). International entrepreneurship in Lebanon. *Global Business Review*, *13*(1), 25–38.

AHRESP & Turismo de Portugal. (2021). Guia de boas práticas para uma restauração circular e sustentável. *Turismo de Portugal*. https://business.turismodeportugal.pt/SiteCollectionDocuments/sustentabilidade/guia-boas-praticas-para-restauracao-circular-e-sustentavel.pdf

Ahsan, M. J. (2024). Unlocking sustainable success: Exploring the impact of transformational leadership, organizational culture, and CSR performance on financial performance in the Italian manufacturing sector. *Social Responsibility Journal*, *20*(4), 783–803.

Aiguobarueghian, I., Adanma, U. M., Ogunbiyi, E. O., & Solomon, N. O. (2024). Waste management and circular economy: A review of sustainable practices and economic benefits. *World Journal of Advanced Research and Reviews*, *22*(2), 1708–1719.

Akbaba, A. İ., & Gündoğdu, Ç. (2021). Bankacılık hizmetlerinde yapay zekâ kullanımı. *Journal of Academic Value Studies*, *7*(3), 298–315.

Akimova, T. (2021). Netherlands: Experience in circular economy development. *Journal of Circular Economy Studies*, *12*(3), 45–58.

Akimova, Yu. A., & Kovalenko, E. G. (2021). The netherlands: Experience in the field of circular economy development. *Fundamental Research (Beijing)*, *12*, 17–21.

Al-Aomar, R., & Hussain, M. (2017). An assessment of green practices in a hotel supply chain: A study of UAE hotels. *Journal of Hospitality and Tourism Management*, *32*, 71–81. DOI: 10.1016/j.jhtm.2017.04.002

Almeida, H., Kumi, S., & Fatima, L. (2024). Mapping organizational culture, work motivation and innovative behaviour, before and during the crisis: A bibliometric analysis. *SN Business & Economics*, *4*(94), 1–29.

Alqassimi, A. (2025). Sustainability and scalability in circular economy startups: The UAE experience. *Journal of Sustainable Development*, *18*(2), 45–58.

American University of Beirut (AUB) Nature Conservation Center. (2020). *Environmental initiatives and research reports*. Retrieved from https://www.aub.edu.lb/natureconservation/

Andersen, M. (2007). An introductory note on the environmental economics of the circular economy. *Sustainability Science*, *2*(1), 133–140. DOI: 10.1007/s11625-006-0013-6

Annarelli, A., Battistella, C., & Nonino, F. (2016). Product service system: A conceptual framework from a systematic review. *Journal of Cleaner Production*, *139*, 1011–1032. DOI: 10.1016/j.jclepro.2016.08.061

Annisa, S., Siahaan, E., & Lumbanraja, P. (2024). Impact of digital transformation on banking employee performance with self-efficacy as a mediator. *Problems and Perspectives in Management*, *22*(4), 523–531. DOI: 10.21511/ppm.22(4).2024.39

Apendi, D. A. O., Li, K., Pea-Assounga, J. B. B., & Bambi, P. D. R. (2025). Investigating the Impact of E-Banking, Employee Job Security, Innovativeness, and Productivity on Organizational Performance: Perspectives from South Africa. *Sustainable Futures : An Applied Journal of Technology, Environment and Society*, •••, 100605.

Apple. (2023). Environmental Progress Report. Retrieved from https://www.apple.com/environment/

Apple: Apple. (2022). Environment Progress Report. Retrieved from https://www.apple.com/environment/pdf/Apple_Environmental_Progress_Report_2022.pdf

Arbash, T. (2023). Migration Trajectories: Narratives in Lebanon (Master's thesis).

Armour, J. A. (1991). Intrinsic cardiac neurons. *Journal of Cardiovascular Electrophysiology*, *2*(4), 331–338.

Arruda, E. H., Melatto, R. A. P. B., Levy, W., & Conti, D. D. M. (2021). Circular economy: A brief literature review (2015–2020). *Sustainable Operations and Computers*, *2*, 79–86. DOI: 10.1016/j.susoc.2021.05.001

Arshad, M., Iqbal, M., & Shahbaz, M. (2017). Pakistan tourism industry and challenges: A review. *Asia Pacific Journal of Tourism Research*, *23*(2), 121–132. DOI: 10.1080/10941665.2017.1410192

Autor, D. (2015). Why are there still so many jobs? *The Journal of Economic Perspectives*, *29*(3), 3–30.

Avasiloaei, D. (2022). Reinventing the business model in the tourism industry based on sustainable circular economy and innovation. *ENTRENOVA – ENTerprise Research InNOVAtion, 8*(1), 435–448. https://doi.org/DOI: 10.54820/entrenova-2022-0036

Avolio, B. J., & Bass, B. M. (2001). *Developing potential across a full range of Leadership Tm: Cases on transactional and transformational Leadership*. Psychology Press. Baia, E. P., & Ferreira, J. J. (20240. Dynamic capabilities and performance: how has the relationship been assessed? *Journal of Management & Organization*, *30*(1), 188–217.

Ayres, R. U. (1989). Industrial metabolism and global change. *International Social Science*, *41*, 363–373.

Ayres, R. U., & Kneese, A. V. (1969). Production, consumption, and externalities. *The American Economic Review*, •••, 282–296.

Bag, S.. (2021). Barriers to the transition towards circular economy: Evidence from the construction and demolition industry. *Business Strategy and the Environment*, *30*(4), 1931–1945.

Bag, S.. (2021). Circular Supply Chains: A review and future research directions. *Journal of Cleaner Production*.

Baines, T. S., Lightfoot, H. W., Benedettini, O., & Kay, J. M. (2009). The servitization of manufacturing: A review of literature and reflection on future challenges. *Journal of Manufacturing Technology Management, 20*(5), 547–567. DOI: 10.1108/17410380910960984

Baker, M., Davis, E., & Weaver, P. (2013). Eco-friendly attitudes, barriers to participation, and differences in behavior at green hotels. *Cornell Hospitality Quarterly, 55*(1), 89–99. DOI: 10.1177/1938965513504483

Baldassarre, B., Schepers, M., Bocken, N., Cuppen, E., Korevaar, G., & Calabretta, G. (2019). Industrial Symbiosis: Towards a design process for eco-industrial clusters by integrating Circular Economy and Industrial Ecology perspectives. *Journal of Cleaner Production, 216*, 446–460. DOI: 10.1016/j.jclepro.2019.01.091

Bandura, A. (1986). *Social foundations of thought and action: A social-cognitive view*. Prentice-Hall.

Bansal, P. (2005). Evolving sustainability: A longitudinal study of corporate sustainable development. *Strategic Management Journal, 26*(3), 197–218.

Bansal, P., & Roth, K. (2000). Why businesses should take leadership in promoting sustainability. *The Academy of Management Perspectives, 14*(3), 42–57.

Barton, D., Koller, G., & Morrow, J. (2009). *Mergers and acquisitions: Corporate strategy and the business cycle*. McKinsey & Company.

Bashynska, I., Malynovska, Y., Kolinko, N. T., Jarvis, M., Kovalska, K., & Saiensus, M. (2024). Performance Assessment of sustainable leadership of enterprise's circular economy-driven innovative activities. *Sustainability, 16*(2), 558.

Baumeister, R. F., Vohs, K. D., & Tice, D. M. (2007). The strength model of self-control. *Current Directions in Psychological Science, 16*(6), 351–355.

Baz, S., Cathcart, L., & Michaelides, A. (2025). Lebanon: From dollars to lollars. *International Finance, 28*(1), 37–63.

Bechara, A., Damasio, H., & Damasio, A. R. (2000). Emotion, decision making and the orbitofrontal cortex. *Cerebral Cortex (New York, N.Y.), 10*(3), 295–307. PMID: 10731224

Bedi, A., Alpaslan, C. M., & Green, S. (2016). A meta-analytic review of ethical leadership outcomes and moderators. *Journal of Business Ethics, 139*, 517–536.

Beer, M., & Nohria, N. (2000). Cracking the code of change. *Harvard Business Review, 78*(3), 133–141. PMID: 11183975

Bentkowska, K. (2024). Informal institutions in the circular economy. *Ekonomia i Środowisko*, 2 (89).

Benton, W. (2023). Returnees, Institutions, and Networks: Making Space for Technology Entrepreneurship in Beirut. *Anthropology of the Middle East, 18*(2), 69–84.

Bexell, M., & Jönsson, K. (2017). Responsibility and the United Nations' sustainable development goals. *Forum for Development Studies, 44*(1), 13–29.

Bingöl, Ç. (2023). Yapay zeka destekli uygulamalı eğitim platformu-bankacılık simülasyonu. [PABD]. *Parion Akademik Bakış Dergisi, 2*(1), 1–22.

Block, T. (2019). The economy that runs on waste: Accumulation in the circular city. *Journal of Urban Technology, 26*(1), 1–20.

Bloomberg, H. T. (2024). AI is driving more layoffs than companies want to admit, 8 February 2024, https://www.bloomberg.com/news/articles/2024-02-08/ai-is-driving-more-layoffs-than-companies-want-to-admit (Access date: 24 September 2024).

Bocken, N. M., De Pauw, I., Bakker, C., & Van Der Grinten, B. (2016). Product design and business model strategies for a circular economy. *Journal of industrial and production engineering, 33*(5), 308-320.

Bocken, N. M. P., Bakker, C., & Pauw, I. D. (2021). Product design and business model strategies for a circular economy. *Journal of industrial and production. Engineering, 33*(5), 308–320. DOI: 10.1080/21681015.20116.1175126

Bocken, N. M. P., De Pauw, I., Bakker, C., & Van Der Grinten, B. (2016). Product design and business model strategies for a circular economy. *Journal of Industrial and Production Engineering, 33*(5), 308–320. DOI: 10.1080/21681015.2016.1172124

Bocken, N. M. P., Short, S. W., Rana, P., & Evans, S. (2014). A literature and practice review to develop sustainable business model archetypes. *Journal of Cleaner Production, 65*, 42–56. DOI: 10.1016/j.jclepro.2013.11.039

Bocken, N., & Ritala, P. (2022). Six ways to build circular business models. *The Journal of Business Strategy, 43*(3), 184–192. DOI: 10.1108/JBS-11-2020-0258

Boons, F., & Lüdeke-Freund, F. (2013). Business models for sustainable innovation: State-of-the-art and steps towards a research agenda. *Journal of Cleaner Production, 45*, 9–19. DOI: 10.1016/j.jclepro.2012.07.007

Boost, I. H. E. E. C. (2021). The Future of Africa.

Boulding, B. K. E. (2013). *The economics of the coming spaceship Earth. Environ. Quality Issues a grow* (0 ed.). RFF Press., DOI: 10.4324/9781315064147

Boustani, N. M., & Hajj, S. (2023, June). The Lebanese Entrepreneurial Resilience In Times Of Crisis. In *ARPHA Conference Abstracts*. 6, e107045. Pensoft Publishers.

Bouzakhem, N., Farmanesh, P., Zargar, P., Ramadan, M., Baydoun, H., Daouk, A., & Mouazen, A. (2023). Rebuilding the workplace in the post-pandemic age through human capital development programs: A moderated mediation model. *Administrative Sciences*, *13*(7), 164.

Bozorg-Haddad, O., Zolghadr-Asli, B., Sarzaeim, P., Aboutalebi, M., Chu, X., & Loáiciga, H. A. (2020). Evaluation of water shortage crisis in the Middle East and possible remedies. *Journal of Water Supply: Research & Technology - Aqua*, *69*(1), 85–98.

Bratişanu, V. (2017). Digital innovation the new paradigm for financial services industry, *Bucharest 'University of Economic Studies*, Speacial Issue, 84-93.

Braungart, M., & McDonough, W. (2009). *Cradle to Cradle: Remaking the Way We Make Things*. North Point Press.

Breit, S., Kupferberg, A., Rogler, G., & Hasler, G. (2018). Vagus nerve as modulator of the brain–gut axis in psychiatric and inflammatory disorders. *Frontiers in Psychiatry*, *9*, 44. DOI: 10.3389/fpsyt.2018.00044 PMID: 29593576

Bressanelli, G., Adrodegari, F., Perona, M., & Saccani, N. (2018). The role of digital technologies to overcome Circular Economy challenges in PSS Business Models: An exploratory case study. *Procedia CIRP*, *73*, 216–221. DOI: 10.1016/j.procir.2018.03.322

Brinkerhoff, J. M. (2004). Digital diasporas and governance in fragile states: The case of reconstruction in Afghanistan. *Public Administration and Development*, *24*(5), 397–413. DOI: 10.1002/pad.326

Brown, M. E., & Treviño, L. K. (2006). Ethical leadership: A review and future directions. *The Leadership Quarterly*, *17*(6), 595–616.

Brown, M. E., & Trevino, L. K. (2024). Do role models matter? An investigation of ethical leadership and follower behavior. *Business Ethics Quarterly*, *24*(2), 227–252. https://doi.org/10.5840/beq201424219

Brown, M. E., Treviño, L. K., & Harrison, D. A. (2005). Ethical leadership: A social learning perspective for construct development and testing. *Organizational Behavior and Human Decision Processes*, *97*(2), 117–134.

Brugmann, J., & Prahalad, C. K. (2007). *Co-creating business value: New global business models for emerging markets*. Harvard Business Press.

Bueno, L. A., Sigahi, T. F., Rampasso, I. S., Leal Filho, W., & Anholon, R. (2024). Impacts of digitization on operational efficiency in the banking sector: Thematic analysis and research agenda proposal. *International Journal of Information Management Data Insights*, *4*(1), 100230.

Bundgaard, A. M., & Huulgaard, R. D. (2019). Luxury products for the circular economy? A case study of Bang & Olufsen. *Business Strategy and the Environment*, *28*(5), 699–709. DOI: 10.1002/bse.2274

Buren, N. (2016). Towards a circular economy: The role of Dutch logistics industries and governments. *Journal of Cleaner Production*, *134*, 1–10.

Busco, C., Granà, F., & Izzo, M. (2018). *Sustainable development goals and integrated reporting*. Routledge.

Calabrese, A., Costa, R., Levialdi, N., & Menichini, T. (2019). Integrating sustainability into strategic decision-making: A fuzzy AHP method for the selection of relevant sustainability issues. *Technological Forecasting and Social Change*, *139*, 155–168. DOI: 10.1016/j.techfore.2018.11.005

Calisto Friant, M., Lakerveld, D., Vermeulen, W. J., & Salomone, R. (2021). Transition to a sustainable circular plastics economy in the Netherlands: Discourse and policy analysis. *Sustainability*, *14*(1), 190.

Calisto Friant, M., Vermeulen, W. J. V., & Salomone, R. (2020). A typology of circular economy discourses: Navigating the diverse visions of a contested paradigm. *Resources, Conservation and Recycling*, *161*, 104917. DOI: 10.1016/j.resconrec.2020.104917

Cameron, K. S., & Quinn, R. E. (2011). *Diagnosing and changing organizational culture: Based on the competing values framework* (3rd ed.). Jossey-Bass.

Carson, R. (1962). *Silent Spring*. Houghton Mifflin.

Castro, R. (2022). Circular economy and its impact on environmental sustainability. *Journal of Environmental Studies (Northborough, Mass.)*, *15*(2), 45–67.

Central Administration of Statistics Lebanon. (2022). Labour Force and Unemployment Survey. Beirut: CAS. http://www.cas.gov.lb/index.php/latest-news-en/201-labour-force

Ceroni, E. (2024). The role of extended producer responsibility (epr) in the transition to a circular economy. *SWS International Scientific Conference on Social Sciences*, 11, 293–300. https://doi.org/DOI: 10.35603/sws.iscss.2024/vs02/22

Chaarani, B. (2021). Corruption and governance challenges in Lebanon: Implications for economic development. *Middle Eastern Studies, 57*(3), 345–362. DOI: 10.1080/00263206.2021.1874567

Chaarani, H. (2021). Determinant factors of successful social entrepreneurship in the emerging circular economy of Lebanon: Exploring the moderating role of NGOs. *Journal of Entrepreneurship and Circular Economy, 10*(2), 123–145.

Chaarani, H., & Raimi, L. (2022). Determinant factors of successful social entrepreneurship in the emerging circular economy of Lebanon: Exploring the moderating role of NGOs. *Journal of Entrepreneurship in Emerging Economies, 14*(5), 874–901.

Chahine, S. (2018). *Interconnectedness in entrepreneurial ecosystems: a social capital perspective* (Doctoral dissertation, University of Southampton).

Chan, E. (2008). Barriers to EMS in the hotel industry. *International Journal of Hospitality Management, 27*(2), 187–196. DOI: 10.1016/j.ijhm.2007.07.011

Charpak. (2019). Sustainable Packaging Solutions. Retrieved from www.charpak.co.uk

Chen, H., Bernard, S., & Rahman, I. (2019). Greenwashing in hotels: A structural model of trust and behavioral intentions. *Journal of Cleaner Production, 206*, 326–335. DOI: 10.1016/j.jclepro.2018.09.168

Chen, L., Hung, P., & Ma, H. (2020). Integrating circular business models and development tools in the circular economy transition process: A firm-level framework. *Business Strategy and the Environment, 29*(5), 1887–1898. DOI: 10.1002/bse.2477

Chizaryfard, A., Trucco, P., & Nuur, C. (2021). The transformation to a circular economy: Framing an evolutionary view. *Journal of Evolutionary Economics, 31*(2), 475–504. DOI: 10.1007/s00191-020-00709-0

Chouinard, Y. (2016). *Let my people go surfing: The education of a reluctant businessman—Including 10 more years of business unusual*. Penguin.

Chughtai, M. S., Syed, F., Nasser, S., & Chinchilla, N. (2024). Role of adaptive leadership in learning organizations to boost organizational innovations with change self-efficacy. *Current Psychology (New Brunswick, N.J.), 43*(33), 27262–27281.

Cieslik, K., Barford, A., & Vira, B. (2022). Young people not in employment, education or training (NEET) in Sub-Saharan Africa: Sustainable development target 8.6 missed and reset. *Journal of Youth Studies, 25*(8), 1126–1147.

Clark, G. L., Feiner, A., & Viehs, M. (2015). *From the stockholder to the stakeholder: How sustainability can drive financial outperformance*. Deutsche Asset & Wealth Management.

Cletzer, D. A., Seibel, M. M., Kaufman, E. K., Friedel, C. R., & Elliott-Engel, J. (2021). When leadership terminology collides: A spirited comparison of adaption-innovation theory and adaptive leadership. In *Association of Leadership Educators 2021 virtual annual conference proceedings* (pp. 10–15). Association of Leadership Educators., https://www.leadershipeducators.org/resources/Documents/ALE%20 2021%20Proceedings%20Final.pdf

Coca-Cola. (2021). World Without Waste: Progress update. Retrieved from htpps:// www.cokecce.com/ou-strategic-priorities/sustainability/world-without-waste

Coca-Cola. (2022). World Without Waste: Progress update. Retrieved from htpps:// www.cokecce.com/ou-strategic-priorities/sustainability/world-without-waste

Cohen, A., & Klemperer, P. (2017). The economics of planned obsolescence. *The Journal of Economic Perspectives*, *31*(4), 51–68. PMID: 29465216

Cojocar, B. (2009). Adaptive leadership: Leadership theory or theoretical derivative? *Academic Leadership: The Online Journal*, *7*(1), 5.

Commoner, B. (1971). *The closing circle: Nature, man, and technology*. Alfred A. Knopf.

Craig, A. D. (2002). How do you feel? Interoception: The sense of the physiological condition of the body. *Nature Reviews. Neuroscience*, *3*, 655–666. PMID: 12154366

Critchley, H. D., Wiens, S., Rotshtein, P., Öhman, A., & Dolan, R. J. (2004). Neural systems supporting interoceptive awareness. *Nature Neuroscience*, *7*(2), 189–195. PMID: 14730305

Cullen, U. A., & De Angelis, R. (2021). Circular entrepreneurship: A business model perspective. *Resources, Conservation and Recycling*, *168*, 105300.

D'Amato, A., Droste, N., & Piran, M. (2021). Circular economy and digital transformation: Opportunities for business model innovation. *Sustainability*, *10*(8), 2913. DOI: 10.3390/su10082913

Dabbous, A., & Boustani, N. M. (2023). Digital explosion and entrepreneurship education: Impact on promoting entrepreneurial intention for business students. *Journal of Risk and Financial Management*, *16*(1), 27.

Dabija, D., & Năstase, C. (2024). Exploring the Evolution of Sustainability Paradigms: From Linear to Circular Economy Models. *Proceedings of the International Conference on Business Excellence*, 18(1), 754–769. https://doi.org/DOI: 10.2478/picbe-2024-0066

Dada, M. A., Majemite, M. T., Obaigbena, A., Oliha, J. S., & Biu, P. W. (2024). Zero-waste initiatives and circular economy in the US: A review: Exploring strategies, outcomes, and challenges in moving towards a more sustainable consumption model. *International Journal of Science and Research Archive*, *11*(1), 204–221.

Dadiana, D., & Năstase, C. (2024). Exploring the Evolution of Sustainability Paradigms: From Linear to Circular Economy Models. *Proceedings of the 18th International Conference on Business Excellence*, 754-769.

Damasio, A. (1994). *Descartes' Error: Emotion, Reason, and the Human Brain*. Putnam.

Dantas, R. M., Ilyas, A., Martins, J. M., & Rita, J. X. (2022). Circular entrepreneurship in emerging markets through the lens of sustainability. *Journal of Open Innovation*, *8*(4), 211.

Dapp, M. M. (2018). Toward a sustainable circular economy powered by community-based incentive systems. In *Business Transformation through Blockchain* (Vol. II, pp. 153–181). Springer International Publishing.

Daramola, O. M., Apeh, C. E., Basiru, J. O., Onukwulu, E. C., & Paul, P. O. (2024). Environmental law and corporate social responsibility: Assessing the impact of legal frameworks on circular economy practices. *International Journal of Social Science Exceptional Research*, *3*(1), 63–79.

De Grosbois, D. (2012). Corporate social responsibility reporting by the global hotel industry: Commitment, initiatives and performance. *International Journal of Hospitality Management*, *31*(3), 896–905. DOI: 10.1016/j.ijhm.2011.10.008

De La Cuesta-González, M., & Morales-García, M. (2022). Does finance as usual work for circular economy transition? A financiers and SMEs qualitative approach. *Journal of Environmental Planning and Management*, *65*(13), 2468–2489.

De Sousa, D. L. (2021). The use of interactive communication technologies for collaborative E-mentoring (Master's thesis, Universidade da Madeira (Portugal)).

Decety, J., & Jackson, P. L. (2004). The functional architecture of human empathy. *Behavioral and Cognitive Neuroscience Reviews*, *3*(2), 71–100. DOI: 10.1177/1534582304267187 PMID: 15537986

Del Vecchio, P., Secundo, G., Mele, G., & Passiante, G. (2021). Sustainable entrepreneurship education for circular economy: Emerging perspectives in Europe. *International Journal of Entrepreneurial Behaviour & Research, 27*(8), 2096–2124.

Demir, M., Rjoub, H., & Yesiltas, M. (2021). Environmental awareness and guests' intention to visit green hotels: The mediation role of consumption values. *PLoS One, 16*(5). Advance online publication. DOI: 10.1371/journal.pone.0248815 PMID: 33956794

Denison, D. R. (1990). *Corporate culture and organizational effectiveness*. Wiley.

Devi, S. (2020). Economic crisis hits Lebanese health care. *Lancet, 395*(10224), 567–589.

Dey, M., Bhattacharjee, S., Mahmoud, M., Uddin, M. A., & Biswas, S. R. (2022). Ethical leadership for better sustainable performance: Role of employee values, behavior and ethical climate. *Journal of Cleaner Production, 337*, 130527.

Diaspora for Development. (2020). Tunisia's diaspora engagement strategy in the MENA region. https://diasporafordevelopment.eu

Djampou, J. (2023). Rethinking our food systems: A guide for multi-stakeholder collaboration. UNEP, FAO, and UNDP Joint Report, 1-45.

Dolatabad, A. H., Mahdiraji, H. A., Babgohari, A. Z., Garza-Reyes, J. A., & Ai, A. (2022). Analyzing the key performance indicators of circular supply chains by hybrid fuzzy cognitive mapping and Fuzzy DEMATEL: Evidence from healthcare sector. *Environment, Development and Sustainability*, •••, 1–27.

Donaldson, T., & Preston, L. E. (1995). The stakeholder theory of the corporation: Concepts, evidence, and implications. *Academy of Management Review, 20*(1), 65–91.

Doppelt, B. (2017). *Leading change toward sustainability: A change-management guide for business, government, and society*. Greenleaf Publishing.

Dosi, G., & Nelson, R. R. (1993). An introduction to evolutionary theories in economics. *Journal of Evolutionary Economics, 4*(3), 153–172.

Doukali, I. (2023). Enhancing Circular Economy and Waste Management in Zanzibar: By leveraging young entrepreneurship and innovation.

Economy, C. (2022). *The circularity gap report*. Retrieved from https://www.circularity-gap.world/

Edeh, J. (2025). Bridging the Gap Living Standards in Africa: The role of entrepreneurship and digital infrastructure. *Sustainability Impacts Review, 1*(1).

Efraij, D. A. (2022). Crowdfunding Market in the UAE: Triangulation Study for the Success Factors in the Market (Master's thesis, The British University in Dubai). Freedom House. (2023). Nations in Transit: Lebanon. https://freedomhouse.org

Ejibe, I., Nwankwo, T.C., Nwankwo, E.E., Okoye, C.C., & Scholastica, U.C. (2024). Advancing environmental sustainability in the creative sectors: A strategic HR framework based on data analytics and eco-innovation. *World Journal of Advanced Research and Reviews, 21*(3), 050-060.

El Assaad, N. (2022). Shaping public service delivery: a hybrid governance approach in the Lebanese public education sector (Master's thesis, University of Malta).

El Assaad, R. (2022). Political volatility and its impact on diaspora engagement in Lebanon. *Journal of Political Economy*, *34*(1), 78–92.

ElAlfy, A., Darwish, K., & Weber, O. (2020). Corporations and sustainable development goals communication on social media: Corporate social responsibility or just another buzzword? *Sustainable Development*, *28*(5), 1418–1430. DOI: 10.1002/sd.2095

El-Annan, S. H., & Haidoura, H. M. (2023). Entrepreneurship as a catalyst for employment: Navigating the unemployment challenge in Lebanon's private sector. *Management Research*, *10*(11), 1–14.

El-Chaarani, H., Mawad, J. L., Mawad, N., & Khalife, D. (2023). Psychological and demographic predictors of investment in cryptocurrencies during a crisis in the MENA region: the case of Lebanon. *Journal of Economic and Administrative Sciences*.

Elkington, J. (1999). *Cannibals with forks: The triple bottom line of 21st century business*. Capstone Publishing.

Ellakkis, M., Dehghan Nayeri, M., & Rajabzadeh Ghatari, A. (2024). From Conflict to Cooperation: A Multi-Methodological Approach to Managing the Solid Waste Crisis in Lebanon. *Journal of Systems Thinking in Practice*, *3*(1), 1–22.

Ellen MacArthur Foundation (N.D.). The Circular economy: A wealth of opportunities. Retrieved from https://www.ellenmacarthurfoundation.org

Ellen MacArthur Foundation, E. (2015). Towards a Circular Economy: Business rationale for an accelerated transition.

Ellen MacArthur Foundation. (2013). Towards the Circular Economy Vol. 1: Economic and business rationale for an accelerated transition. Ellen MacArthur Foundation Publishing.

Ellen MacArthur Foundation. (2013). *Towards the circular economy: Economic and business rationale for an accelerated transition*. Ellen MacArthur Foundation.

Ellen MacArthur Foundation. (2019). *Completing the picture: How the circular economy tackles climate change*. Retrieved from https://ellenmacarthurfoundation.org/

Ellen MacArthur Foundation. (2019). The Circular Economy: A New Economic Model for the 21st Century. Retrieved from www.ellenmacarthurfoundation.org

Elmustapha, H., & Hoppe, T. (2020). Challenges and opportunities of business models in sustainable transitions: Evidence from solar energy niche development in Lebanon. *Energies*, *13*(3), 670.

Elroi, H., Zbigniew, G., Agnieszka, W., & Piotr, S. (2023). Enhancing waste resource efficiency: Circular economy for sustainability and energy conversion. *Frontiers in Environmental Science*, •••, 11.

Epstein, M., & Buhovac, A. (2010). Solving the sustainability implementation challenge. *Organizational Dynamics*, *39*(4), 306–315. DOI: 10.1016/j.orgdyn.2010.07.003

Ersoy, Ç. (2017). *Robotlar, Yapay Zeka ve Hukuk*, 2. Bs., İstanbul, On İki Levha Yayıncılık.

ESCWA. (2020). *Harnessing the power of the diaspora for sustainable development in Lebanon*. United Nations Economic and Social Commission for Western Asia.

ESCWA. (2021). *The circular economy in the Arab region: Sustainable consumption and production policies*. United Nations.

Eskerod, P., Hollensen, S., Morales-Contreras, M., & Arteaga-Ortiz, J. (2019). Drivers for pursuing sustainability through IoT technology within high-end hotels—An exploratory study. *Sustainability*, *11*(19), 5372. DOI: 10.3390/su11195372

Esnard, A. M. (2016). Diaspora engagement in post-disaster recovery: Lessons from Haiti. *Disaster Prevention and Management*, *25*(4), 512–526. DOI: 10.1108/DPM-03-2016-0052

European Commission. (2020). *Monitoring framework for the circular economy*. Retrieved from https://ec.europa.eu/environment/circular-economy/

Ezeudu, S. A., Ezeudu, F. O., & Sampson, M. (2016). Climate Change Awareness and Attitude of Senior Secondary Students in Umuahia Education Zone of Abia State. *International Journal of Research in Humanities and Social Studies*, *3*(3), 10.

FasterCapital. (2023). *Online Banking: The Role of Dematerialization in Modern Finance.* Available at: https://www.fastercapital.com/content/Online-Banking--Online-Banking--The-Role-of-Dematerialization-in-Modern-Finance.html#:~:text=Dematerialization%20in%20finance%20refers%20to,physical%20resources%20and%20%2013

Fayssal, N., Al Tawil, L., Danageuzian, H., Sabat, M., ElMerehbi, H., Darazi, D., & Romanos, J. (2024). Navigating the water–energy nexus amidst the Lebanese economic crisis. *AQUA—Water Infrastructure. Ecosystems and Society*, *73*(5), 917–929.

Fei, A., Kim, J., & Kim, S. (2024). Effects of environmental sustainability practice in the economy hotel to Gen Zer's purchase decision: Behavior economy approach using choice-based conjoint analysis. *International Journal of Hospitality Management*, *118*, 103678. DOI: 10.1016/j.ijhm.2023.103678

Fernandes, P. (2023). Entrepreneurship as a transition to the circular economy. *Journal of Sustainable Business*, *18*(2), 34–56.

Ferreira, S., Pereira, O., & Simões, C. (2023). Determinants of consumers' intention to visit green hotels: Combining psychological and contextual factors. *Journal of Vacation Marketing*, *31*(3), 535–548. DOI: 10.1177/13567667231217755

Ferrero-Ferrero, I., León, R., & Muñoz-Torres, M. J. (2020). Sustainability materiality matrices in doubt: May prioritizations of aspects overestimate environmental performance? *Journal of Environmental Planning and Management*, *64*(3), 432–463. DOI: 10.1080/09640568.2020.1766427

Ferrero-Ferrero, I., Muñoz-Torres, M., Rivera-Lirio, J., Escrig-Olmedo, E., & Fernández-Izquierdo, M. (2024). Sustainable development goals in the hospitality industry: A dream or reality? *Journal of Accounting & Organizational Change*, *20*(5), 773–796. DOI: 10.1108/JAOC-09-2022-0146

Finnish Innovation Fund Sitra. (2019). *The critical move – Finland's road map to a circular economy 2.0.* Sitra. https://www.sitra.fi/en/publications/the-critical-move/

Fleming, A., Rickards, L., & Dowd, A. (2015). Understanding convergence and divergence in the framing of climate change responses: An analysis of two wine companies. *Environmental Science & Policy*, *51*, 202–214. DOI: 10.1016/j.envsci.2015.04.003

Freeman, R. E. (1984). *Strategic management: A stakeholder approach.* Pitman.

Frei, R., Jack, L., & Krzyzaniak, S. (2020). Sustainable reverse supply chains and circular economy in multichannel retail returns. *Business Strategy and the Environment*, *29*(5), 1925–1940. DOI: 10.1002/bse.2479

Frey, C. B., & Osborne, M. A. (2013). *The Future of Employment: How Susceptible are Jobs to Computerisation?* University Martin School.

Fujimoto, A., Murray, E. A., & Rudebeck, P. H. (2021). Interaction between decision-making and interoceptive representations of bodily arousal in frontal cortex. *Proceedings of the National Academy of Sciences of the United States of America, 118*(35), e2014781118. DOI: 10.1073/pnas.2014781118 PMID: 34452993

Fukuda-Parr, S. (2019). Keeping out extreme inequality from the SDG Agenda: The politics of indicators. *Global Policy, 10*, 61–69.

Gacar, A. (2019). Yapay zekâ ve yapay zekânın muhasebe mesleğine olan etkileri: Türkiye'ye yönelik fırsat ve tehditler. *Balkan Sosyal Bilimler Dergisi, 8*, 389–394.

Gagnon, B., Tanguay, X., Amor, B., & Imbrogno, A. F. (2022). Forest products and circular economy strategies: A Canadian perspective. *Energies, 15*(3), 673.

Garcia-Morales, V.j., & Martin-Rojas, R., & LIorens-Montes, F.J. (2020). The role of transformational leadership in the development of green innovation: Evidence from managers in the hotel industry. *Journal of Hospitality & Tourism Research (Washington, D.C.), 44*(8), 1200–1220. DOI: 10.1177/1096348018804604

Gartner. (2020). *Top trends in banking and investment services for 2020*. https://www.gartner.com/en/documents/3984417

Gartner. (2023). How Supply-Chain Thrive in a resource Constrained World. Retrieved from https://www.gartner.com/en/supply-chain/insights/beyond-supply-chain-blog/how-supply-chains-can-thrive-in-a-resource-constrainted-world

Geissdoefer, M., Morioka, S. N., DeCarvalho, M. M., & Evans, S. (2018). Business models and supply chains for the circular economy. *Journal of Cleaner Production, 190*, 712–721.

Geissdoerfer, M., Bocken, N., & Hultink, E. (2016). Design thinking to enhance the sustainable business modelling process – A workshop based on a value mapping process. *Journal of Cleaner Production, 135*, 1218–1232. DOI: 10.1016/j.jclepro.2016.07.020

Geissdoerfer, M., Morioka, S., de Carvalho, M., & Evans, S. (2018). Business models and supply chains for the circular economy. *Journal of Cleaner Production, 190*, 712–721. DOI: 10.1016/j.jclepro.2018.04.159

Geissdoerfer, M., Pieroni, M. P. P., Pigosso, D. C. A., & Soufani, K. (2020). Circular business models: A review. *Journal of Cleaner Production, 277*, 123741. DOI: 10.1016/j.jclepro.2020.123741

Geissdoerfer, M., Savaget, P., Bocken, N. M. P., & Hultink, E. J. (2017). The Circular Economy – A new sustainability paradigm? *Journal of Cleaner Production, 143*, 757–768.

Gelb, S., Kalantaryan, S., McMahon, S., & Perez-Fernandez, M. (2021). *Diaspora finance for development: From remittances to investment*. Publications Office of the European Union.

GEM. (2018). UAE Annual Report. UAEU & Global Entrepreneurship Research Association.

General Motors. (2023). Sustainability Report. Retrieved from https://www.gm.com/content/dam/company/docs/us/en/gmcom/company/GM_2023_SR.pdf

Geng, Y., Fu, J., Sarkis, J., & Xue, B. (2012). Towards a national circular economy indicator system in China: An evaluation and critical analysis. *Journal of Cleaner Production, 23*(1), 216–224. DOI: 10.1016/j.jclepro.2011.07.005

Geng, Y., Sarkis, J., & Bleischwitz, R. (2019). How to globalize the circular economy. *Nature, 565*(7738), 153–155.

Georgescu-Roegen, N. (2011). From Bioeconomics to Degrowth (M. Bonaiuti, Ed.; 0 ed.). Routledge. https://doi.org/DOI: 10.4324/9780203830413

Gevorkyan, A. V., & Issa, S. (2024). Lebanese Diaspora and Sustainable Economic Development in Lebanon: new survey-informed analysis. Available at *SSRN* 5016805.

Gevorkyan, A. V., & Issa, S. (2025). Diaspora and Sustainable Economic Development in Lebanon: New Survey-Informed Analysis. *Review of Development Economics*.

Ghisellini, P., Cialani, C., & Ulgiati, S. (2016). A review on circular economy: The expected transition to a balanced interplay of environmental and economic systems. *Journal of Cleaner Production, 114*, 11–32. DOI: 10.1016/j.jclepro.2015.09.007

Giacalone, R. A., Promislo, M., & Jurkiewicz, C. (2016). Ethical impact theory: How unethical behavior at work affects individual well-being. *Global encyclopedia of public administration, public policy, and governance*, 1-5.

Glimcher, P. W., & Fehr, E. (2013). Findings in neuroeconomics provide critical insights for leadership, particularly in financial and strategic decision-making. *The Journal of Economic Perspectives, 27*(2), 105–120.

Goleman, D. (1995). *Emotional Intelligence: Why It Can Matter More than IQ*. Bantam Books.

Gopalakrishnan, T., & Miller, J. (2023). Energy transition in fragile states: A critical primer. *World peace foundation.*

Gorokhova, N. (2024). Tax incentives for circular economy: Lessons from Germany. *Environmental Policy and Governance*, *34*(2), 123–135. DOI: 10.1002/eet.1956

Gotthardt, M., Koivulaakso, D., Paksoy, O., Saramo, C., Martikainen, M., & Lehner, O. (2020). Current state and challenges in the implementation of smart robotic process automation in accounting and auditing. *ACRN Journal of Finance and Risk Perspectives*, *9*(1), 90–102.

Goudie, A. (2018). *Human Impact on the Natural Environment* (8th ed.). John Wiley & Sons.

Govidan, K., & Soleimani, H. (2017). A review of reverse logistics and closed-loop supply chains: A journal of Cleaner Production focus. *Journal of Cleaner Production*, *142*, 371–384.

Govindan, K., & Hasanagic, M. (2018). A systematic review on drivers, barriers, and practices towards circular economy: A supply chain perspective. *International Journal of Production Research*, *56*(1–2), 278–311. DOI: 10.1080/00207543.2017.1402141

Gültekin, A. (2021). *Spinoza Ontolojisi Bağlamında Yapay Zekânın İmkânı*. Doktora Tezi, İnönü Üniversitesi Sosyal Bilimler Enstitüsü.

Gümüş, E., Medetoğlu, B., & Tutar, S. (2020). Finans ve bankacılık sisteminde yapay zekâ kullanımı: Kullanıcılar üzerine bir uygulama. *Bucak İşletme Fakültesi Dergisi*, *3*(1), 28–53.

Gunduz, C. P. B. (2023). Eco-Friendly and Cost-Effective Methods Applied to Sustainable Food Industries. In *Smart Food Industry: The Blockchain for Sustainable Engineering* (pp. 50-71). CRC Press.

Hackman, J. R. (2002). *Leading teams: Setting the stage for great performances*. Harvard Business Press.

Haddock-Millar, J., Sanyal, C., & Müller-Camen, M. (2015). Green human resource management: A comparative qualitative case study of a United States multinational corporation. *International Journal of Human Resource Management*, *27*(2), 192–211. DOI: 10.1080/09585192.2015.1052087

Hage, G. (2021). *The diasporic condition: ethnographic explorations of the Lebanese in the world*. University of Chicago Press.

Halog, A., & Anieke, S. (2021). A review of circular economy studies in developed countries and its potential adoption in developing countries. *Circular Economy and Sustainability*, *1*(1), 209–230.

Hamza, M. (2025). Empowering Startups through Accelerator Services in Lebanon: A Phenomenological Case Study. *Journal of Information Systems Engineering & Management*, *10*(6).

Hanemaaijer, A., Muller, M., de Krom, M., Mangnus, A., Schotten, K., & in 't Veld, D. (2025). *Integral circular economy report: Assessment for the Netherlands 2025* (PBL publication no. 5849). PBL Netherlands Environmental Assessment Agency.

Han, H., Chua, B., & Hyun, S. (2020). Eliciting customers' waste reduction and water saving behaviors at a hotel. *International Journal of Hospitality Management*, *87*, 102386. DOI: 10.1016/j.ijhm.2019.102386

Harb, M. (2024). From protests to polls: A study on voting intentions in Lebanon. *Journal of Political Engagement*, *12*(3), 45–67.

Haris, N. I. N., Al Edrus, S. S. O., Abdul Raof, N., Wondi, M. H., Khan, W. R., Sien, L. S., & Sawatdeenarunat, C. (2024). Toward low-carbon cities: A review of circular economy integration in urban waste management and its impact on carbon emissions. *Wiley Interdisciplinary Reviews. Energy and Environment*, *13*(5), e535.

Harrison, J., & Freeman, R. E. (1999). Stakeholders, social responsibility, and performance: Empirical evidence and theoretical perspectives. *Academy of Management Journal*, *42*(5), 479–485.

Hart, S. L. (1995). A natural-resource-based view of the firm. *Academy of Management Review*, *20*(4), 986–1014.

Hazbun, W. (2016). Assembling security in a 'weak state:'the contentious politics of plural governance in Lebanon since 2005. *Third World Quarterly*, *37*(6), 1053–1070.

Hazen, B. T., Russo, I., Confente, I., & Pellathy, D. (2021). Supply chain management for circular economy: Conceptual framework and research agenda. *International Journal of Logistics Management*, *32*(2), 510–537.

HeartMath Institute. (2023). Mysteries of the Heart [Infographic]. https://www.heartmath.org/resources/infographic/mysteries-of-the-heart

Hegde, A. G. (2019). Artificial intelligence and law. *Pen Acclaims*, *7*, 1–10.

Hegde, S., Sumith, N., Pinto, T., Shukla, S., & Patidar, V. (2024). Optimizing Solid Waste Management: A Holistic Approach by Informed Carbon Emission Reduction. *IEEE Access : Practical Innovations, Open Solutions*.

Heifetz, R. A., Grashow, A., & Linsky, M. (2009). *The practice of adaptive leadership: Tools and tactics for changing your organization and the world.* Harvard business press.

Hemidat, S., Achouri, O., El Fels, L., Elagroudy, S., Hafidi, M., Chaouki, B., Ahmed, M., Hodgkinson, I., & Guo, J. (2022). Solid waste management in the context of a circular economy in the MENA region. *Sustainability, 14*(1), 480. DOI: 10.3390/su14010480

Hercog, M., & Siegel, M. (2013). Diaspora engagement in India: From non-required Indians to angels of development. In *Emigration nations: Policies and ideologies of emigrant engagement* (pp. 75–99). Palgrave Macmillan UK.

Hiatt, J. M. (2006). *ADKAR: A model for change in business, government, and our community*. Prosci.

Hilmi, Y. S., Tóth, J., Gabnai, Z., Király, G., & Temesi, Á. (2024). Farmers' resilience to climate change through the circular economy and sustainable agriculture: A review from developed and developing countries. *Renewable Agriculture and Food Systems*, *39*, e15.

Hinsa, D. P., Ezra, O., & Pardede, R. (2025). CIRCULAR ECONOMY IN INDONESIA: A COMPARATIVE STUDY OF EU COUNTRIES AND FINLAND. *Journal Research of Social Science, Economics & Management, 4*(10).

Ho, C. (2024). Circular economy education: Student feedback from five higher education institutions in the Asia Pacific. *Journal of Circular Economy Education, 10*(3), 123–145.

Hölzel, B. K., Lazar, S. W., Gard, T., Schuman-Olivier, Z., Vago, D. R., & Ott, U. (2011). How does mindfulness meditation work? Proposing mechanisms of action from a conceptual and neural perspective. *Perspectives on Psychological Science, 6*(6), 537–559. PMID: 26168376

Hoogendoorn, B., Guerra, D., & van der Zwan, P. (2015). What drives environmental practices of SMEs? *Small Business Economics*, *44*, 759–781.

Hosseinian, A., Ylä-Mella, J., & Pongrácz, E. (2021). Current status of circular economy research in Finland. *Resources*, *10*(5), 40.

Howe, N., & Strauss, W. (2000). *Millennials rising: The next great generation.* Vintage Books.

Hsieh, C.-C., Tai, S.-E., & Li, H.-C. (2023). A Bibliometric Review of Ethical Leadership Research: Shifting Focuses and Theoretical Insights. *AERA Open, 9*. https://doi.org/ (Original work published 2023)DOI: 10.1177/23328584231209266

Huang, M. H., Rust, R., & Maksimovic, V. (2019). The feeling economy: Managing in the next generation of artificial ıntelligence (AI). *California Management Review*, *61*(4), 43–65.

Huđek, I., & Bradač Hojnik, B. (2020). Impact of entrepreneurship activity sustainable development. *Problemy Ekorozwoju*, *15*(2), 175–183.

Hu, H., Parsa, H., & Self, J. (2010). The dynamics of green restaurant patronage. *Cornell Hospitality Quarterly*, *51*(3), 344–362. DOI: 10.1177/1938965510370564

Humphrey, C., O'Dwyer, B., & Unerman, J. (2016). Re-theorizing the configuration of organizational fields: The IIRC and the pursuit of 'Enlightened' corporate reporting. *Accounting and Business Research*, *47*(1), 30–63. DOI: 10.1080/00014788.2016.1198683

Iagăru, R., ipo , A., & Iagăru, P. (2023). Strategic Thinking and Its Role in Accelerating the Transition from the Linear to the Circular Economic Model—Case Study of the Agri-Food Sector in the Sibiu Depression Microregion, Romania. *Sustainability*, *15*(4), 3109. DOI: 10.3390/su15043109

Interface. (2021). Mission Zero: 2020 sustainability goals. Retrieved form https;// www.interface/sustainability/emea/ecometrics-2020/SustainabilityHighlights_2020 _EN.pdf

International Labour Organization (ILO). (2022). Youth Employment in Lebanon: Challenges and Opportunities. Geneva: ILO. https://www.ilo.org/resource/article/ilo-skills-training-key-unlocking-decent-employment-lebanon#:~:text=According%20to%20the%20ILO%2C%20Lebanon's,is%20essential%20to%20support%20employment

International Monetary Fund. (2023). IMF Executive Board Concludes 2023 Article IV Consultation with Lebanon. Retrieved from https://www.imf.org/en/News/Articles/2023/06/28/pr23245-lebanon-imf-executive-board-concludes-2023-article-iv-consultation-with-lebanon

International Monetary Fund. (2023). Lebanon: Article IV consultation report. IMF eLibrary. https://www.imf.org

Irwin, D. A. (2020). Innovation, obsolescence, and the environment: The unintended consequences of planned obsolescence. *Environmental Economics and Policy Studies*, *22*(1), 55–73.

Işkın, S. (2010). *Türk Bankacılık Sisteminde Alternatif Dağıtım Kanalları (Elektronik Bankacılık).* Hizmetlerinin Riskleri ve Denetimi. Marmara Üniversitesi Bankacılık ve Sigortacılık Enstitüsü.

Islam, Z., Gangat, S. A., Mohanan, P., Rahmat, Z. S., El Chbib, D., Marfani, W. B., & Essar, M. Y. (2021). Mental health impacts of Lebanon's economic crisis on healthcare workers amidst COVID-19. *The International Journal of Health Planning and Management, 37*(2), 1160.

Issa, H., Sun, T., & Vasarhelyi, M. A. (2016). Research ideas for artificial intelligence in auditing: The formalization of audit and workforce supplementation. *Journal of Emerging Technologies in Accounting, 13*(2), 1–20.

Issa, I. (2006). Impacts of political instability on tourism planning and development: The case of Lebanon. *Tourism Management Journal, 27*(3), 567–589.

Ivanović-Đukić, M., Rađenović, T., & Veselinović, N. (2022). Impact of entrepreneurship on sustainable development in emerging markets under the conditions of COVID-19. *Problemy Ekorozwoju, 17*(2).

Izzo, M., Ciaburri, M., & Tiscini, R. (2020). The challenge of sustainable development goal reporting: The first evidence from Italian listed companies. *Sustainability, 12*(8), 3494. DOI: 10.3390/su12083494

Jaksic, M., & Marinc, M. (2015). The future of banking: The role of information technology. *Bancni vestnik: Bankıng Sector At The Crossroads: Challenges For. Future, 64*(11), 68–73.

Järvinen, L., & Sinervo, R. (2020). *How to create a national circular economy road map: A guide to making the change happen* (Sitra Studies 170). Sitra. https://www.sitra.fi/en/publications/how-to-create-a-national-circular-economy-road-map/

Jefferson Research. (2022). The Heart's Little Brain. https://research.jefferson.edu/2022-magazine/the-hearts-little-brain.html

Jiao, W., & Boons, F. (2014). Toward a research agenda for policy intervention and facilitation to enhance industrial symbiosis based on a comprehensive literature review. *Journal of Cleaner Production, 67*, 14–25. DOI: 10.1016/j.jclepro.2013.12.050

Journals, A. H. A. (2003). Cardiac memory: Mechanisms and clinical implications. *Circulation, 108*(8), 950–955. DOI: 10.1161/01.cir.0000091402.34219.6c

Kadhila, T., de Wit, M. P., & Schenck, R. (2023). A conceptual framework for sustainable waste management in small municipalities: The cases of Langebaan, South Africa and Swakopmund, Namibia. *Environmental Science and Pollution Research International*, *30*(60), 125088–125103.

Kahneman, D. (2011). *Thinking, Fast and Slow*. Farrar, Straus and Giroux.

Kahneman, D., Sibony, O., & Sunstein, C. R. (2021). *Noise: A Flaw in Human Judgment*. Little, Brown Spark.

Kanda, W., Geissdoerfer, M., & Hjelm, O. (2021). From circular business models to circular business ecosystems. *Business Strategy and the Environment*, *30*(6), 2814–2829.

Kaplan, R. S., & Norton, D. P. (2004). *Strategy maps: Converting intangible assets into tangible outcomes*. Harvard Business School Press.

Kara, Ç. (2025). From Neural Processing to Pathos: The Neuroscientific Foundations of Persuasive Messages. Available at: https://neuroscience.org.uk/blog/f/n%C3%B6ral-i%CC%87%C5%9Flemeden-pathos%E2%80%99ai%CC%87kna-edici-mesajlar%C4%B1n-n%C3%B6robilimseltemeli

Karakulah, M., & Muneeza, A. (2024). Exploring the Role of Donation-Based Crowdfunding in Islamic Social Finance. International Journal of Islamic Economics and Finance Research, 7(1 July), 42-58.

Karyağdı, N. G. (2022). Bankacılık sektöründe dijital dönüşümün verimliliğe olan etkileri: TRB2 bölgesinde nitel bir çalışma. *Kahramanmaraş Sütçü İmam Üniversitesi Sosyal Bilimler Dergisi*, *19*(2), 852–870.

Käsner, S.-A., & Gihring, K. (2024, September). *ACEN – South Africa's Policy Framework*. African Circular Economy Network. Retrieved from https://www.acen.africa

Kataya, G., Cornu, D., Bechelany, M., Hijazi, A., & Issa, M. (2023). Biomass waste conversion technologies and its application for sustainable environmental development—A review. *Agronomy (Basel)*, *13*(11), 2833.

Katou, A. A., Kafetzopoulos, D., & Vayona, A. (2023). Investigating the serially mediating mechanisms of organizational ambidexterity and the circular economy in the relationship between ambidextrous leadership and sustainability performance. *Sustainability*, *15*(10), 7937.

Katz, J. (2019). The paradox of obsolescence: A study of the environmental impact of planned product obsolescence. *Environmental Sociology*, *5*(1), 35–45.

Khatter, A. (2023). Challenges and solutions for environmental sustainability in the hospitality sector. *Sustainability, 15*(15), 11491. DOI: 10.3390/su151511491

Khatter, A., McGrath, M., Pyke, J., White, L., & Lockstone-Binney, L. (2019). Analysis of hotels' environmentally sustainable policies and practices. *International Journal of Contemporary Hospitality Management, 31*, 2394–2410.

Khatter, A., White, L., Pyke, J., & McGrath, M. (2021). Stakeholders' influence on environmental sustainability in the Australian hotel industry. *Sustainability, 13*(3), 1351. DOI: 10.3390/su13031351

Khuntia, R., & Suar, D. (2004). A scale to assess ethical leadership of Indian private and public sector managers. *Journal of Business Ethics, 49*, 13–26.

Kim, I., Park, D., Kyung, D., Kim, G., Kim, S., & Lee, J. (2015). Comparative influences of precipitation and river stage on groundwater levels in near-river areas. *Sustainability, 8*(1), 1.

King, R., & Gëdeshi, I. (2024). The Albanian Scientific Diaspora from Kosovo: Prospects for Cooperation and Return. Sussex Centre for Migration Research, 1-35.

Kirchherr, J., Reike, D., & Hekkert, M. (2017). Conceptualizing the circular economy: An analysis of 114 definitions. *Resources, Conservation and Recycling, 127*, 221–232.

Kirkpatrick, S. A., & Locke, E. A. (2020). Direct and indirect effects of three core charismatic leadership components on performance and attitudes. *The Leadership Quarterly, 12*(3), 459–483. https://doi.org/10.10`16/j.leaqua.2001.02.002

Kirton, M. J. (1976). Adaptors and innovators: A description and measure. *The Journal of Applied Psychology, 61*(5), 622–629.

Kirton, M. J. (2011). *Adaption-innovation: In the context of diversity and change*. Routledge. (Original work published 2003)

Kirton, M. J. (2013). *KAI theory workbook*. KAI Distribution Centre.

Kisi, N. (2022). The role of collaborative leadership in the circular economy. [Elsevier]. *Circular Economy and Sustainability*, •••, 535–544.

Korhonen, J., Honkasalo, A., & Seppälä, J. (2018). Circular Economy: The Concept and its Limitations. *Ecological Economics, 143*, 37–46. DOI: 10.1016/j.ecolecon.2017.06.041

Korhonen, J., Nuur, C., Feldmann, A., & Birkie, S. E. (2018). Circular economy as an essentially contested concept. *Journal of Cleaner Production, 175*, 544–552. DOI: 10.1016/j.jclepro.2017.12.111

Kotler, P., & Keller, K. L. (2016). *Marketing management* (15th ed.). Pearson Education.

Kotter, J. P. (1996). *Leading change*. Harvard Business Press.

Koutroumanidis, T., & Tsironis, L. (2020). Predictive maintenance in circular economy: A systematic literature review. *Sustainability, 17*(19), 7830. DOI: 10.3390/su12197830

Kuhnert, K. W., & Lewis, P. (1987). Transactional and transformational leadership: A constructive developmental analysis. *Academy of Management Review, 12*(4), 648–657.

Kumar, R. (2022). Leveraging blockchain and smart contract technologies to overcome circular economy implementation challenges. *Journal of Circular Economy Technology, 15*(3), 89–102. DOI: 10.1016/j.jce.2022.03.004

Kuokkanen, H., & Sun, W. (2020). Companies, Meet Ethical Consumers: Strategic CSR Management to Impact Consumer Choice. *Journal of Business Ethics, 166*(2), 403–423. DOI: 10.1007/s10551-019-04145-4

Kusters, K. (2017). Participatory planning, monitoring, and evaluation of multi-stakeholder platforms in integrated landscape initiatives. *Landscape and Urban Planning, 165*, 1–10. PMID: 28324144

L'Orient Today. (2023a). Diaspora fatigue and diminishing hope._https://today.lorientlejour.com

L'Orient Today. (2023b). Remittances now fueling basic needs amid crisis._https://today.lorientlejour.com/article/1337950/remittances-fueling-food-and-rent-in-lebanon.html

Lam, C. K., Huang, X., & Chan, S. C. (2015). The threshold effect of participative leadership and the role of leaders' information sharing. *Academy of Management Journal, 58*(3), 836–855.

Lamming, R., Caldwell, N., & Harrison, D. (2000). An analysis of the sustainable supply chain. *The Journal of Supply Chain Management, 36*(3), 54–65.

Lara-Guerrero, L. (2020). Diasporas engaging during the pandemic: International global exchanges in response to the Covid-19 crisis. *HAPSc Policy Briefs Series, 1*(1), 177–182.

Lashitew, A. (2021). Corporate uptake of the Sustainable Development Goals: Mere greenwashing or an advent of institutional change? *Journal of International Business Policy*, *4*, 184–200. DOI: 10.1057/s42214-020-00092-4

Lenzen, M., Sun, Y., Faturay, F., Ting, Y., Geschke, A., & Malik, A. (2018). The carbon footprint of global tourism. *Nature Climate Change*, *8*(6), 522–528. DOI: 10.1038/s41558-018-0141-x

Lewandowski, M. (2016). Designing the business models for circular economy—Towards the conceptual framework. *Sustainability*, *8*(1), 43.

Lieberman, A. (2018). SDGs show slow progress, not on track to reach 2030 targets. *Devex*. https://www.devex.com/news/sdgs-show-slow-progress-not-on-track-to-reach-2030-targets-un-reports-92971

Lieder, M., & Rashid, A. (2016). Towards circular economy implementation: A comprehensive review in context of manufacturing industry. *Journal of Cleaner Production*, *115*, 36–51.

Linder, M., & Williander, M. (2015). Circular business model innovation: Inherent uncertainties. *Business Strategy and the Environment*, *26*(2), 182–196. DOI: 10.1002/bse.1906

Lit, F. C., Huijben, J. C., Cloodt, M. M., & Paredis, E. (2024). Business model innovation in circular start-ups: Overcoming barriers in the circular plastics economy. *International Small Business Journal*, *42*(4), 506–550.

Li, W. (2011). Comprehensive evaluation research on circular economic performance of eco-industrial parks. *Energy Procedia*, *5*, 1682–1688. DOI: 10.1016/j.egypro.2011.03.287

Li, X. (2016). Waste-to-profit policies in China: A pathway to circular economy. *Journal of Cleaner Production*, *112*, 1–10. DOI: 10.1016/j.jclepro.2015.07.123

Loiseau, E., Saikku, L., Antikainen, R., Droste, N., Hansjürgens, B., Pitkänen, K., Leskinen, P., Kuikman, P., & Thomsen, M. (2016). Green economy and related concepts: An overview. *Journal of Cleaner Production*, *139*, 361–371. DOI: 10.1016/j.jclepro.2016.08.024

Lowe, B. H., & Genovese, A. (2022). What Theories of value (could) underpin our circular future? *Ecological Economics*, •••, 195.

Lüdeke-Freund, F., & Dembek, K. (2017). Sustainable business model research and practice: Emerging field or passing fancy? *Journal of Cleaner Production*, *168*, 1668–1678. DOI: 10.1016/j.jclepro.2017.08.093

Lüdeke-Freund, F., Gold, S., & Bocken, N. M. (2019). A review and typology of circular economy business model patterns. *Journal of Industrial Ecology*, *23*(1), 36–61.

Lyle, J. T. (1994). *Regenerative design for sustainable development.* Wiley.

Lyndon, D., Gossling, R., & Kristensen, T. (2021). Designing for circularity in the fashion industry: A comparative analysis of circular design practices in SMEs and large companies. *Sustainability*, *13*(4), 2054. DOI: 10.3390/su13042054

Magnon, V. (2022). The heart to make the right choice: Vagal (re)activity and recovery predict advantageous decision-making. *Physiology & Behavior*, *249*, 113911. DOI: 10.1016/j.physbeh.2022.113911 PMID: 35820625

Majdalani, R. (2024). Dancing at the foot of a volcano: Bad governance, corruption, and ecological disaster in Lebanon. *Journal of Political Ecology*, *31*(2), 245–260.

Majed, R. (2021). In defense of intra-sectarian divide: Street mobilization, coalition formation, and rapid realignments of sectarian boundaries in Lebanon. *Social Forces*, *99*(4), 1772–1798.

Mak, A., & Chang, R. (2019). The driving and restraining forces for environmental strategy adoption in the hotel industry: A force field analysis approach. *Tourism Management*, *73*, 48–60. DOI: 10.1016/j.tourman.2019.01.012

Mak, A., Lumbers, M., Eves, A., & Chang, R. (2012). Factors influencing tourist food consumption. *International Journal of Hospitality Management*, *31*(3), 928–936. DOI: 10.1016/j.ijhm.2011.10.012

Malone, M. (2020). The Tres por Uno program: Diaspora engagement in Mexico's community development. *Migration Studies*, *8*(1), 56–74. DOI: 10.1093/migration/mnz045

Mangaroska, V. (2024). Circular built environment as international concept of sustainable innovation. In *Proceedings of the National Conference with International Participation* – (pp. 169–173). https://doi.org/DOI: 10.5937/greenb24022m

Manoj, M., Ram Das, A., Chandran, A., & Mandal, S. (2020). Antecedents of environmental engagement and environmental learning behaviour. *Journal of Hospitality and Tourism Insights*, *3*(4), 431–450. DOI: 10.1108/JHTI-01-2020-0001

Maolani, T. (2024). Governance and corruption: Evaluating anti-corruption policies and their effectiveness in strengthening institutional integrity. *Journal of Governance Studies*, *18*(4), 123–145.

Mariño, R., & Banga, R. S. (2016). UN Sustainable Development Goals (SDGs): A time to act. *Journal of Oral Research*, *5*(1), 5–6.

Marjamaa, M., Salminen, H., Kujala, J., Tapaninaho, R., & Heikkinen, A. (2021). A sustainable circular economy: Exploring stakeholder interests in Finland. *South Asian journal of business and management cases, 10*(1), 50-62.

Massoud, M. A., Mokbel, M., Alawieh, S., & Yassin, N. (2019). Towards improved governance for sustainable solid waste management in Lebanon: Centralised vs decentralised approaches. *Waste Management & Research*, *37*(7), 686–697. PMID: 30912714

Matiza, T., & Slabbert, E. (2025). Towards green hospitality: Exploring the consumer perceived value of pro-environmental star-graded accommodation. *Journal of Humanities and Applied Social Sciences*, *7*(2), 163–188. DOI: 10.1108/JHASS-07-2024-0123

Mayer, D. M., Kuenzi, M., Greenbaum, R., Bardes, M., & Salvador, R. (2009). How low does ethical leadership flow? Test of a trickle-down model. *Organizational Behavior and Human Decision Processes*, *108*, 1–13.

Mazur-Wierzbicka, E. (2021). Circular economy: Advancement of European Union countries. *Environmental Sciences Europe*, *33*(1), 111.

McCarville, M. (2019). Turning the Netherlands into a plastic circular hotspot. *Circular Economy Review*, *1*(2), 45–60.

McCraty, R., Atkinson, M., & Tomasino, D. (2003). Impact of a workplace stress reduction program on blood pressure and emotional health in hypertensive employees. *Journal of Alternative and Complementary Medicine (New York, N.Y.)*, *9*(3), 355–369. PMID: 12816624

McDonagh, K. (2023). Ireland's Foreign Relations in 2022. *Irish Studies in International Affairs*, *34*(1), 243–259.

McDonough, W., & Braungart, M. (2002). *Cradle to cradle: Remaking the way we make things (first)*. North Point Press.

McDowall, W., Geng, Y., Huang, B., Barteková, E., Bleischwitz, R., Türkeli, S., Kemp, R., & Doménech, T. (2017). Circular Economy Policies in China and Europe. *Journal of Industrial Ecology*, *21*(3), 651–661. DOI: 10.1111/jiec.12597

McLennan, M., Group, S., & Group, Z. (2022). *The Global Risks Report 2022* (17th ed.). World Economic Forum., https://www.weforum.org/reports/global-risks-report-2022

Meadows, D., Meadows, D., Randers, J., & Behrens, W. (1972). The limits to growth.

Melo, A., Azevedo, D., Silva, S., Silva, G., Figueiredo, A., & Melo, C. (2025). Circular economy in the restaurant sector: Do practices go hand in hand? In *Proceedings of the 8th International Conference on Tourism Research (ICTR 2025).* https://doi.org/DOI: 10.34190/ictr.8.1.3507

Merton, R. C. (1995). A functional perspective of the role of financial analysts. *The Journal of Finance*, *50*(4), 1413–1424.

Meyer, R., & Meijers, R. (2017). *Leadership agility: Developing your repertoire of leadership styles*. Routledge.

Michelini, G.. (2017). From linear to circular business models: The case of the mobile phone industry. *Sustainability*, *9*(9), 1–17.

Ministry of Land. Infrastructure, Transport and Tourism, Japan Tourism Agency. (2022). Case studies on the implementation of sustainable tourism content: Based on the FY2022 sustainable tourism content enhancement model project. https://www.mlit.go.jp/kankocho/content/001595025.pdf

Mitchell, R. K., Agle, B. R., & Wood, D. J. (1997). Toward a theory of stakeholder identification and salience: Defining the principle of who and what really counts. *Academy of Management Review*, *22*(4), 853–886.

Mohapatra, S., Roy, S., Upadhyay, A., & Kumar, A. (2024). Circular value creation through environmental entrepreneurship initiatives: A case-based exploration. *Business Strategy and the Environment*, *33*(5), 3811–3831.

Mok, Y. W., Arevalo, A., & Poon, C. S. (2020). Utilizing recycled materials in sustainable construction. *Sustainable Cities and Society*, *19*, 35–45. DOI: 10.1016/j.scs.2015.06.002

Molina-Azorin, J., Tari, J., Pereira-Moliner, J., Lopez-Gamero, M., & Pertusa-Ortega, E. (2015). The effects of quality and environmental management on competitive advantage: A mixed methods study in the hotel industry. *Tourism Management*, *50*, 41–54. DOI: 10.1016/j.tourman.2015.01.008

Montag, L. (2023). Roadmap to a Circular Economy by 2030: A Comparative Review of Circular Business Model Visions in Germany and Japan. *Sustainability*, *15*(6), 5374. DOI: 10.3390/su15065374

Mont, O. K. (2002). Clarifying the concept of product–service system. *Journal of Cleaner Production*, *10*(3), 237–245. DOI: 10.1016/S0959-6526(01)00039-7

Moreau, V., Sahakian, M., Van Griethuysen, P., & Vuille, F. (2017). Coming Full Circle: Why Social and Institutional Dimensions Matter for the Circular Economy. *Journal of Industrial Ecology*, *21*(3), 497–506. DOI: 10.1111/jiec.12598

Morseletto, P. (2020). Restorative and regenerative: Exploring the concepts in the circular economy. *Journal of Industrial Ecology*, *24*(4), 763–773. DOI: 10.1111/jiec.12987

Mouazen, A. M., & Hernández-Lara, A. B. (2023). Entrepreneurial ecosystem, gig economy practices and Women's entrepreneurship: The case of Lebanon. *International Journal of Gender and Entrepreneurship*, *15*(3), 249–274.

Mrówczyńska-Kamińska, A., Bajan, B., Pawłowski, K., Genstwa, N., & Zmyślona, J. (2021). Greenhouse gas emissions intensity of food production systems and its determinants. *PLoS One*, *16*(4), e0250995. DOI: 10.1371/journal.pone.0250995 PMID: 33930083

Muisyo, P., Su, Q., Hashmi, H., Ho, T., & Julius, M. (2022). The role of green HRM in driving hotels' green creativity. *International Journal of Contemporary Hospitality Management*, *34*(4), 1331–1352. DOI: 10.1108/IJCHM-07-2021-0833

Munana, F. A. (2025). Under What Conditions Does National Identity Contribute to National Stability in Rwanda and Burundi? (Doctoral dissertation, American Public University System).

Munir, A. (2025). The role of circular economy in green entrepreneurship: Sustainable business models. *Journal of Green Innovation*, *22*(1), 78–92.

Munoko, I., Brown Liburd, H. L., & Vasarhely, M. (2020). The ethical implications of using artifcial iin auditing. *Journal of Business Ethics*, *167*, 209–234.

Munonye, W. C., & Ajonye, G. O. Urban Policy and Governance for a Circular Economy: Opportunities and Challenges.

Muñoz, E., & Navia, R. (2021). Circular economy in urban systems: How to measure the impact? *Waste Management & Research*, *39*(2), 197–198.

Murakami, K. (2025). Policy approaches to sustainable and circular economy tourism: Comparative case studies of Japan and China. In *Proceedings of the 8th International Conference on Tourism Research*, *8*(1). https://doi.org/DOI: 10.34190/ictr.8.1.3405

Murray, A. (2014). The importance of sustainability in business. *Journal of Business Ethics*, *125*(1), 3–12.

Murray, A., Skene, K., & Haynes, K. (2017). The Circular Economy: An Interdisciplinary Exploration of the Concept and Application in a Global Context. *Journal of Business Ethics, 140*(3), 369–380. DOI: 10.1007/s10551-015-2693-2

Mutascu, M. (2021). Artificial intelligence and unemployment: New insights. *Economic Analysis and Policy, 64*, 653–667.

Mylan, J. (2018). The circular economy and consumer protection law: A case study of planned obsolescence. *Journal of Consumer Policy, 41*(1), 105–123.

Nasreddine, L., Akl, C., Al-Shaar, L., Almedawar, M. M., & Isma'eel, H. (2014). Consumer knowledge, attitudes and salt-related behavior in the Middle East: The case of Lebanon. *Nutrients, 6*(11), 5079–5102.

Nassar, A. (2021). Corruption in Lebanon: An exploratory study about Lebanese managers' and employees' perceptions. *Journal of Business Ethics, 34*(1), 78–92.

Nauffal, D. I., & Nasser, R. N. (2007). The American higher educational model in Lebanon: organisational cultures and their impact on student outcomes and satisfaction.

Ncube, T., Dlodlo, N., & Terzoli, A. (2023). Blockchain-based Peer-to-Peer Energy Trading through a Community-based Virtual Power Plant. In *2023 2nd Zimbabwe Conference of Information and Communication Technologies (ZCICT)* (pp. 1-6). IEEE.

Negnevitsky, M. (2005). *Artificial Intelligence: A Guide to Intelligent Systems*, 2. Ed., England: Pearson Education Limited.

Nelson, T., & Squires, V. (2017). Addressing complex challenges through adaptive leadership: A promising approach to collaborative problem solving. *Journal of Leadership Education, 16*(4), 111–123.

Nestor, J. (2020). *Breath: The New Science of a Lost Art.* Penguin Life.

Netter, S., Pedersen, E. R. G., & Lüdeke-Freund, F. (2019). Sharing economy revisited: Towards a new framework for understanding sharing models. *Journal of Cleaner Production, 221*, 224–233.

Nicolò, G., Zanellato, G., Tiron-Tudor, A., & Tartaglia Polcini, P. (2023). Revealing the corporate contribution to sustainable development goals through integrated reporting: A worldwide perspective. *Social Responsibility Journal, 19*(5), 829–857. DOI: 10.1108/SRJ-09-2021-0373

Nielsen, T. M., & Riddle, L. (2010). Investing in peace: The motivational dynamics of diaspora investment in post-conflict economies. *Journal of Business Ethics, 89*(4), 435–448. DOI: 10.1007/s10551-010-0399-z

Nike, Inc. (2025). Sustainability and circular economy initiatives. Retrieved from https:// www.nike.com/sustainability/

Nike. (2022). Move to Zero: A Journey toward zero carbon and zero waste. Retrieved from https;//www.nike.com/sustainability/move-to-zero

Northouse, P. G. (2022). *Leadership: Theory and practice* (9th ed.). SAGE Publications.

Note, C. (2022). Results and Performance of the World Bank Group 2022.

Nußholz, J. L. K. (2017). Circular Business Models: Defining a Concept and Framing an Emerging Research Field. *Sustainability*, *9*(10), 1810. DOI: 10.3390/su9101810

Nyakudya, P., Madushele, N., & Madyira, D. M. (2022, May). A Review of Industrial Symbiosis in Influencing Green Manufacturing. In *2022 IEEE 13th International Conference on Mechanical and Intelligent Manufacturing Technologies (ICMIMT)* (pp. 80-84). IEEE.

OECD. (2017). *Policy coherence for sustainable development 2017: Eradicating poverty and promoting prosperity*. https://www.oecd-ilibrary.org/development/policy-coherence-for-sustainable-development-2017_9789264272576-en

OECD. (2020a). *The circular economy in cities and regions: Synthesis report*. Organisation for Economic Co-operation and Development.

OECD. (2020b). The circular economy in Groningen, Netherlands. *OECD Urban Studies*. OECD Publishing.

OECD. (2021). *Entrepreneurship policies through a circular economy lens*. Retrieved from https://www.oecd.org/cfe/smes/entrepreneurship-and-the-circular-economy.pdf

OECD. (2023). *Digitalisation for the transition to a resource efficient and circular economy*. OECD Publishing. Available at: https://www.oecd.org/en/publications/digitalisation-for-the-transition-to-a-resource-efficient-and-circular-economy_6f6d18e7-en.html#:~:text=Digital%20transformation%20is%20increasingly%20recognised,way%20to%20scaling%20up%20circular

Okeke, O., & Asekomeh, A. (2024). A Systematic literature review on the UK's enterprise investment scheme and seed enterprise investment scheme and comparison with similar schemes in selected countries. *International Journal of Business & Economic Development*, *12*(02).

Omar, A. (2025). Engaging the Lebanese diaspora: Socioeconomic determinants, barriers, and opportunities for sustainable development. *Journal of Diaspora Studies*, *22*(4), 567–582.

Omar, M. H. (2025). Engaging the Lebanese diaspora: Socioeconomic determinants, barriers, and opportunities for sustainable development. *Edelweiss Applied Science and Technology*, *9*(2), 1784–1793.

Omar, M. H., Nehme, M., & Al Mohtar, L. (2025). The Lebanese expatriation: Between return and connection. *Edelweiss Applied Science and Technology*, *9*(2), 1636–1647.

Opiniano, J. M. (2020). The 'new'Philippine future "beside" the exodus. *Asian Education and Development Studies*, *10*(1), 53–68.

Ormazabal, M., Prieto-Sandoval, V., Jaca, C., & Santos, J. (2016). An overview of the circular economy among SMEs in the Basque country: A multiple case study. *Journal of Industrial Engineering and Management*, *9*(5), 1047. DOI: 10.3926/jiem.2065

Ozbay, B., & Koc, Y. (2022). Impact of Covid-19 lock-down period on variations of air pollutants around an industrialized city of Turkey, Izmit. *Environmental Forensics*, *23*(1-2), 198–207.

Özçetin, N. (2022). Muhasebe denetiminde yapay zekâ. *Uşak Üniversitesi Uygulamalı Bilimler Fakültesi Dergisi*, *2*(1), 29–41.

Packard, V. (1960). *The Waste Makers*. David McKay Company, Inc.

Palalić, R., Ramadani, V., Welsh, D. H., Dizdarević, A., & Đilović, A. (2021). Impact of networking and business environment on student leadership styles. *The International Entrepreneurship and Management Journal*, *17*, 447–475.

Pan, S.-Y., Du, M. A., Huang, I.-T., Liu, I.-H., Chang, E.-E., & Chiang, P.-C. (2015). Strategies on implementation of waste-to-energy (WTE) supply chain for circular economy system: A review. *Journal of Cleaner Production*, *108*, 409–421. DOI: 10.1016/j.jclepro.2015.06.124

Parida, V., Sjödin, D., & Reim, W. (2019). Reviewing Literature on Digitalization, Business Model Innovation, and Sustainable Industry: Past Achievements and Future Promises. *Sustainability*, *11*(2), 391. DOI: 10.3390/su11020391

Park, J., Sarkis, J., & Wu, Z. (2010). Creating integrated business and environmental value within the context of China's circular economy and ecological modernization. *Journal of Cleaner Production*, *18*(15), 1494–1501. DOI: 10.1016/j.jclepro.2010.06.001

Patagonia. (2022). Move to Zero: A Journey towards zero carbon and zero waste. Retrieved from https://www.patagonia.com/worn-wear/

Patwa, N., Paul, R., Dsilva, J., & Chadha, K. K. (2025). Enhancing circular economy practices in Asia through digitalization and infrastructure. *Academia Environmental Sciences and Sustainability, 2*(1).

Pearce, D. W., & Turner, R. K. (1990). *Economics of Natural Resources and the Environment*. Harvester Wheats.

Peng, J., Zou, Y.C., Kang, Y.J., and Zhang, X. (2021). Participative leadership and employee job well-being: perceived co-worker support as a boundary condition. *Journal of Psychological science*, 33, 873-880.

Perotti, F. A., Bargoni, A., De Bernardi, P., & Rozsa, Z. (2025). Fostering circular economy through open innovation: Insights from multiple case study. *Business Ethics, the Environment & Responsibility*, *34*(2), 390–408.

Petropoulos, G. (2018). The Impact Of Artificial Intelligence On Employment, Neufeind M., O'Reilly J. and Ranft F. (Eds.), *Praise for Work in the Digital Age*, Rowman & Littlefield International, 119-132.

Pierroni, M., McAloone, T., & Pigosso, D. (2019). Business model innovation for circular economy and sustainability: A review of approaches. *Journal of Cleaner Production*, *215*, 198–216. DOI: 10.1016/j.jclepro.2019.01.036

Pirim, H. (2006). Yapay zeka. *Journal of Yasar University*, *1*(1), 81–93.

Pitkänen, K., Karppinen, T. K. M., Kautto, P., Turunen, S., Judl, J., & Myllymaa, T. (2020). Sex, drugs and the circular economy: the social impacts of the circular economy and how to measure them. In *Handbook of the circular economy* (pp. 162–175). Edward Elgar Publishing.

Platt, M. L., ... (2024). Heart rate synchrony in teams: PNAS study linking physiological synchrony with group decision accuracy. Knowledge@Wharton. https://knowledge.wharton.upenn.edu

Platt, M. L. (2018). *The Leader's Brain: Enhance Your Leadership, Build Stronger Teams, Make Better Decisions, and Inspire Greater Innovation with Neuroscience*. Wharton School Press.

Plaza, S., & Ratha, D. (2011). Harnessing diaspora resources for Africa. Diaspora for development in Africa, 1-54.

Plotnic, M. (2024). Institutional barriers to circular economy in Lebanon: A governance perspective. *Journal of Environmental Policy*, *29*(3), 245–260.

Porter, M. E. (1985). *Competitive advantage: Creating and sustaining superior performance*. Free Press.

Porter, M. E., & Kramer, M. R. (2006). Strategy and society: The link between competitive advantage and corporate social responsibility. *Harvard Business Review*, *84*(12), 78–92. PMID: 17183795

Porter, M. E., & Kramer, M. R. (2011). Creating shared value. *Harvard Business Review*, *89*(1-2), 62–77.

Pouessel, S. (2017). Tunisia and its diaspora: Between protection and control. Emigration and diaspora policies in the age of mobility, 205-220.

Prakash, S., Sharma, V., Singh, R., Vijayvargy, L., & Nilaish, L. (2023). Adopting green and sustainable practices in the hotel industry operations: An analysis of critical performance indicators for improved environmental quality. *Management of Environmental Quality*, *34*(4), 1057–1076. DOI: 10.1108/MEQ-03-2022-0090

Preghenella, N., & Battistella, C. (2021). Circular business models for sustainable development: A "waste is food" restorative ecosystem. *Business Strategy and the Environment*, *30*(4), 1931–1945.

Prendeville, S., De Angelis, R., & Houghton, J. (2021). The Role of the consumer in the circular economy: Opportunities and challenges in understanding consumer behavior. *Journal of Consumer Behaviour*, *17*(3), 201–210. https://dor.org/10.1002/cb.1693

Priest, K. L., & Middleton, E. (2016). Exploring leader identity and development. *New Directions for Student Leadership*, *2016*(149), 37–47.

Prieto-Sandoval, V., Jaca, C., & Ormazabal, M. (2018). Towards a consensus on the circular economy. *Journal of Cleaner Production*, *179*, 605–615. DOI: 10.1016/j.jclepro.2017.12.224

Procter & Gamble. (2021). P& G and TerraCycle partner to create circular solutions for personal care and beauty products. Retrieved from https://www.recyclingtoday.com/news/procter-and-gamble-joins-loop-reuse-recycle-platforms/

Psarommatis, F., & May, G. (2024). Digital product passport: A pathway to circularity and sustainability in modern manufacturing. *Sustainability*, *16*(1), 396.

Purpose Brand. (2023). Sustainability Reports Track Fortune 500 Corporate Climate Action. Retrieved from https://purposebrand.com/blog/sustainability-report-examples-fortune-2023/

PwC. (2024). PwC's 2024 AI Jobs Barometer: How will AI affect jobs, skills, wages, and productivity? https://www.pwc.com.tr/tr/Hizmetlerimiz/dijital-hizmetler/ai-jobs-barometer.pdf (Access date: 20 September 2024).

Qi, X., Liu, H., Li, X., & Liu, H. (2021). The influence of flexiblework arrangements on innovative employee behaviour in China: A perspective of person-job fit. *Asia Pacific Business Review*, *29*(1), 1–22. DOI: 10.1080/13602381.2021.2001181

Quincey, J. (2019). Sustainability at Coca-Cola: A focus on the future. Retrieved from https://www.coca-cola.com/content/dam/journey/us/en/private/fileassets/pdf/2019-annual-report.pdf

Rabbi, M., & Amin, M. (2024). Circular economy and sustainable practices in the food industry: A comprehensive bibliometric analysis. *Cleaner and Responsible Consumption*, *14*, 100206. DOI: 10.1016/j.clrc.2024.100206

Rabiu, M., & Jaeger-Erben, M. (2022). Appropriation and routinisation of circular consumer practices: A review of current knowledge in the circular economy literature. *Cleaner and Responsible Consumption*, *7*, 100081. DOI: 10.1016/j.clrc.2022.100081

Ramakrishna, S., & Jose, R. (2022). Addressing sustainability gaps. *The Science of the Total Environment*, *806*, 151208.

Rashid, A., Asif, F. M. A., Krajnik, P., & Nicolescu, C. M. (2013). Resource Conservative Manufacturing: An essential change in business and technology paradigm for sustainable manufacturing. *Journal of Cleaner Production*, *57*, 166–177. DOI: 10.1016/j.jclepro.2013.06.012

Raub, S., & Martin-Rios, C. (2019). "Think sustainable, act local" – A stakeholder-filter-model for translating SDGs into sustainability initiatives with local impact. *International Journal of Contemporary Hospitality Management*, *31*(6), 2428–2447. DOI: 10.1108/IJCHM-06-2018-0453

Ray, S., & Hardi, I. (2024). Refining ESG Disclosure's Role in Corporate Economic, Environmental., and Social Sustainability Performance. *Indatu Journal of Management and Accounting*, *2*(1), 1–8.

Rizkallah, S. (2022). L'indépendance de la BDL Et Les Déterminants de la Crise Économique au Liban. *La Revue Internationale des Économistes de Langue Française*, *7*(2), 9–31.

Rizk, R., & Matta, J. (2025). The Impact of Green Finance and Green Consumption on Sustainable Economies: A Comparative Study of Lebanon and UAE. *Journal of Sustainable Economies*, *1*(1), 48–54.

Rodriguez-Anton, J., Alonso-Almeida, M., Celemin, M., & Rubio, K. (2012). Use of different sustainability management systems in the hospitality industry: The case of Spanish hotels. *Journal of Cleaner Production*, *22*(1), 76–84. DOI: 10.1016/j.jclepro.2011.09.024

Romano, O., & Akhmouch, A. (2019). Water governance in cities: Current trends and future challenges. *Water (Basel), 11*(3), 500.

Rosati, F., & Faria, L. (2019). Addressing the SDGs in sustainability reports: The relationship with institutional factors. *Journal of Cleaner Production, 251*, 1312–1326. DOI: 10.1016/j.jclepro.2018.12.107

Rosenbaum, E. (2022). Leveraging diaspora networks for circular economy: A global perspective. *Global Networks, 22*(4), 567–582. DOI: 10.1111/glob.12345

Rosenbaum, R. A., & Kehdy, J. F. (2022). Cultivating circular economies in the gaps of governance: Lessons from Lebanon's ecosystem of CE micro projects. *Local Environment, 27*(10-11), 1304–1320.

Rosvall, M. (2020). *Pursuit of Sustainability*. Decentralized Renewable Energy Services in India.

Ruiz-Real, J. L., Uribe-Toril, J., De Pablo Valenciano, J., & Gázquez-Abad, J. C. (2018). Worldwide research on circular economy and environment: A bibliometric analysis. *International Journal of Environmental Research and Public Health, 15*(12), 2699.

Ruohomaa, H., & Ivanova, N. (2019, November). From solid waste management towards the circular economy and digital driven symbiosis. []. IOP Publishing.]. *IOP Conference Series. Earth and Environmental Science, 337*(1), 012032.

Russo, I., Confente, I., Scarpi, D., & Hazen, B. (2019). From trash to treasure: The impact of consumer perception of bio-waste products in closed-loop supply chains. *Journal of Cleaner Production, 218*, 966–974.

Saad Alessa, G. (2021). The dimensions of transformational leadership and its organizational effects in public universities in Saudi Arabia: A systematic review. *Frontiers in Psychology, 12*, 682092.

Saam, M. (2024). The Impact of Artificial Intelligence on Productivity and Employment–How Can We Assess It and What Can We Observe? *Inter Economics, 59*(1), 22–27.

Sachs, J. D. (2015). *The age of sustainable development*. Columbia University Press.

Sadiq, M., Kannaiah, D., Yahya Khan, G., Ullah, R., & Mahfooz, Y. (2023). Does sustainable environmental agenda matter? The role of globalization toward energy consumption, economic growth, and carbon dioxide emissions in South Asian countries. *Environment, Development and Sustainability, 25*, 76–95. DOI: 10.1007/s10668-021-02043-2

Saidani, M., Yannou, B., Leroy, Y., Cluzel, F., & Kendall, A. (2019). A taxonomy of circular economy indicators. https://doi.org/DOI: 10.48550/ARXIV.1901.02709

Sakai, S., Yoshida, H., Hirai, Y., Asari, M., Takigami, H., Takahashi, S., Tomoda, K., Peeler, M. V., Wejchert, J., Schmid-Unterseh, T., Douvan, A. R., Hathaway, R., Hylander, L. D., Fischer, C., Oh, G. J., Jinhui, L., & Chi, N. K. (2011). International comparative study of 3R and waste management policy developments. *Journal of Material Cycles and Waste Management, 13*(2), 86–102. DOI: 10.1007/s10163-011-0009-x

Salloukh, B. (2025). The dynamics between banking performance and economic stability in Lebanon. *Middle Eastern Finance Review, 18*(1), 34–56.

Salvioni, D.M., & Almici, A. (2020). Transitioning toward a circular economy: The impact of stakeholder engagement on sustainability culture. Sustainability, 12920), 8641.

Salvioni, D., & Almici, A. (2020). Circular economy and stakeholder engagement strategy. *Symphonya, 1*, 26–44.

Samgerger, C. (2022). The role of water circularity in the food-water-energy nexus and climate change mitigation. *Energy Nexus, 6*, 100061. DOI: 10.1016/j.nexus.2022.100061

Sauvé, S., Bernard, S., & Sloan, P. (2016). Environmental sciences, sustainable development and circular economy: Alternative concepts for trans-disciplinary research. *Environmental Development, 17*, 48–56. DOI: 10.1016/j.envdev.2015.09.002

Savini, F. (2019). The economy that runs on waste: Accumulation in the circular city. *Environment and Planning A. Economy and Space, 51*(3), 1–15.

Saxena, A., Ramaswamy, M., Beale, J., Vázquez, C., & Shrivastava, P. (2021). Striving for the United Nations (UN) Sustainable Development Goals (SDGs): What will it take? *Discover Sustainability, 2*, 20. DOI: 10.1007/s43621-021-00029-8

Schaltegger, S., Hansen, E. G., & Lüdeke-Freund, F. (2017). Business models for sustainability: A co-evolutionary analysis of sustainable entrepreneurship. *Business Strategy and the Environment, 26*(4), 456–474.

Schaltegger, S., Lüdeke-Freund, F., & Hansen, E. G. (2016). Business models for sustainability: A co-evolutionary analysis of sustainable entrepreneurship, innovation, and transformation. *Organization & Environment, 29*(3), 264–289. DOI: 10.1177/1086026616633272

Schaltegger, S., & Wagner, M. (2017). Sustainable entrepreneurship and sustainable business models. In *Handbook of sustainable innovation* (pp. 229–255). Edward Elgar Publishing.

Schein, E. H. (2010). *Organizational culture and leadership* (4th ed.). Jossey-Bass.

Scholz, P. (2019). Green management implementation in accommodation facilities in Bulgaria. *Economics and Environment, 68*(1), 16. https://ekonomiaisrodowisko.pl/journal/article/view/108

Schramade, W. (2017). Investing in the UN Sustainable Development Goals: Opportunities for companies and investors. *Journal of Applied Corporate Finance, 29*(2), 87–99. DOI: 10.1111/jacf.12236

Schulte, U. G. (2013). New business models for a radical change in resource efficiency. *Environmental Innovation and Societal Transitions, 9*, 43–47. DOI: 10.1016/j.eist.2013.09.006

Schwager, P., & Moser, F. (2006). The Application of Chemical Leasing Business Models in Mexico. *Environmental Science and Pollution Research International, 13*(2), 131–137. DOI: 10.1065/espr2006.02.294

Scottish Parliament. (2024). *Circular Economy (Scotland) Act 2024*. Retrieved from https://www.legislation.gov.uk/asp/2024/2/contents SCP/RAC. (2020). Success Stories on Circular Economy in the Mediterranean: Case Studies from Jordan, Tunisia, Egypt and Lebanon. Regional Activity Centre for Sustainable Consumption and Production.

Sehnem, S., Lopes de Sousa Jabbour, A. B., Conceição, D. A. D., Weber, D., & Julkovski, D. J. (2021). The role of ecological modernization principles in advancing circular economy practices: Lessons from the brewery sector. *Benchmarking, 28*(9), 2786–2807.

Senge, P. M. (2006). *The fifth discipline: The art and practice of the learning organization*. Doubleday.

Serçemeli, M. (2018). Muhasebe ve denetim mesleklerinin dijital dönüşümünde yapay zekâ. *Electronic Turkish Studies, 13*(30), 369–386.

Shabir, M., Jiang, P., Wang, W., & Işık, Ö. (2023). COVID-19 pandemic impact on banking sector: A cross-country analysis. *Journal of Multinational Financial Management, 67*, 100784.

Shallal, A. (2021). Lebanon's economic collapse: A systemic review. *Journal of Global Health, 11*(3), 3052. DOI: 10.7189/jogh.11.03052 PMID: 33828836

Shen, Y., & Zhang, X. (2024). The impact of artificial intelligence on employment: The role of virtual agglomeration. *Humanities & Social Sciences Communications*, *11*(1).

Shibli, R. (2014). *Reconfiguring relief mechanisms: The Syrian refugee crisis in Lebanon*. Refugee Research and Policy in the Arab World.

Shi, X., Chen, Z., Wei, W., & Ni, B. J. (2024). Perspectives on sustainable plastic treatment: A shift form linear to circular economy. *Trends in Analytical Chemistry*, •••, 117631.

Silva, S. (2021). Corporate contributions to the Sustainable Development Goals: An empirical analysis informed by legitimacy theory. *Journal of Cleaner Production*, *292*, 125962. DOI: 10.1016/j.jclepro.2021.125962

Sitra. (2019). *Tackling root causes: Halving Finland's carbon footprint with circular economy*. Finnish Innovation Fund Sitra. Retrieved from https://www.sitra.fi/en/publications/tackling-root-causes/

Smith, J., & Gladstein, A. (2018). How the UN's Sustainable Development Goals undermine democracy. *Quartz*. https://qz.com/africa/1299149/how-the-uns-sustainable-development-goals-undermine-democracy/

Smith, R., Thayer, J. F., Khalsa, S. S., & Lane, R. D. (2017). The hierarchical basis of neurovisceral integration. *Neuroscience and Biobehavioral Reviews*, *75*, 274–296. PMID: 28188890

Smith, S. S. (2018). Digitization and financial reporting – How technology innovation may drive the shift toward continuous accounting. *Accounting and Finance Research*, *7*(3), 240–250.

Sobaih, A., Abdou, A., Alshamayleh, H., Alshebami, A., & Abu Elnasr, A. (2025). Greening minds before businesses: Navigating SDGs hurdles for micro and small hotels in Saudi Arabia. *Cogent Business & Management*, *12*(1). Advance online publication. DOI: 10.1080/23311975.2025.2459325

Solomon, N. O., Simpa, P., Adenekan, O. A., & Obasi, S. C. (2024). Circular economy principles and their integration into global supply chain strategies. *Finance & Accounting Research Journal*, *6*(5), 747–762.

Soni, S. (2023). Harnessing the power of collaboration to expand the coverage and equity of COVID-19 vaccinations in India: A community collaboration model. *Journal of Public Health Practice*, *18*(3), 245–260. DOI: 10.1016/j.jphp.2023.03.004 PMID: 37376411

Splash. (2019). Sustainable Products for a Better Tomorrow. Retrieved from www.splash.com

Stahel, W. R., & Reday, G. (1976). The potential for substituting manpower for energy, Report to the Commission of the European Communities.

Stahel, W. R. (1982). The product life factor. In Orr, G. S. (Ed.), *An inquiry into the nature of sustainable societies. The Role of the Private Sector*. Houston Area Research Centre.

Stahel, W. R. (2010). *The Performance Economy*., DOI: 10.1057/9780230274907

Stel, N. (2013). Diaspora versus refugee the political economy of Lebanese entrepreneurship regimes.

Stel, N. (2013). Governance and corruption in Lebanon: The role of sectarianism. *Third World Quarterly*, *34*(5), 705–722. DOI: 10.1080/01436597.2013.800747

Sterev, N. (2019). New Industrial Business Models: From Linear to Circular Economy Approach. *Trakia Journal of Sciences*, *17*(Suppl 1), 511–523.

Su, B., Heshmati, A., Geng, Y., & Yu, X. (2013). A review of the circular economy in China: Moving from rhetoric to implementation. *Journal of Cleaner Production*, *42*, 215–227. DOI: 10.1016/j.jclepro.2012.11.020

Sullivan, R., & Mackenzie, C. (2017). *Responsible investment: Guide to ESG data providers and relevant trends*. Springer.

Sullivan, R., & Mackenzie, C. (2020). *Sustainable business: Concepts, methodologies, tools, and applications*. IGI Global.

Supanut, A., Maisak, R., & Ratchatakulpat, T. (2024). Circular economy strategies in practice: A qualitative examination of industry adaptation and innovation. *Rev. Gestão Soc. Engenharia Ambiental*, *18*, e06723.

Susur, E., & Engwall, M. (2022). A transitions framework for circular business models. *Journal of Industrial Ecology*, *27*(1), 19–32. DOI: 10.1111/jiec.13128

Su, Y., Li, Z., & Yang, C. (2021). Spatial interaction spillover effects betwen digital financial technology and urban ecological efficiency in China: And empirircal study based on spatial simutaneous equations. *International Journal of Environmental Research and Public Health*, *18*(16), 8535.

Suzanne, T. (2020). Digital registries for circular economy: Case studies from China and the Netherlands. *Journal of Digital Innovation*, *15*(2), 89–102. DOI: 10.1016/j.jdi.2020.03.004

Szeiner, Z., & Balázs, K. (2023). The impact of digitalization on working and job roles in the banking sector. *Acta Oeconomica Universitatis Selye*, *12*(1), 68–78. DOI: 10.36007/Acta.2023.12.1.6

Tahulela, A. C., & Ballard, H. H. (2019). Developing the circular economy in South Africa: Challenges and opportunities. In Ghosh, S. K. (Ed.), *Sustainable waste management: Policies and case studies* (pp. 125–133). Springer., DOI: 10.1007/978-981-13-7071-7_11

Tanveer, M., Yusliza, M., & Fawehinmi, O. (2024). Green HRM and hospitality industry: Challenges and barriers in adopting environmentally friendly practices. *Journal of Hospitality and Tourism Insights*, *7*(1), 121–141. DOI: 10.1108/JHTI-08-2022-0389

Tarkett. (2020). Sustainable Innovation and Circular Economy. Retrieved from www.tarkett.com

Tendulkar, M., Tendulkar, R., Dhanda, P. S., Yadav, A., Jain, M., & Kaushik, P. (2024). Clinical potential of sensory neurites in the heart and their role in decision-making. *Frontiers in Neuroscience*, *17*, 1308232. PMID: 38415053

Thelle, M. H., Lundberg, A. T., Hovmand, B. E., Woltmann, H. H., Virtanen, L., Tranholm-Mikkelsen, N., Pedersen, S. T., & Oure, A. J. (2024). The economic opportunity of AI in Türkiye. Implement Consulting Group Study, May 2024, https://cms.implementconsultinggroup.com/media/uploads/articles/2024/The-economic-opportunity-of-generative-AI-in-T%C3%BCrkiye/The-economic-opportunity-of-generative-AI-in-Turkiye.pdf (Access date: 21 September 2024).

Toufaily, B., & Bou Zakhem, N. (2024). Drivers of Student Social Entrepreneurial Intention Amid the Economic Crisis in Lebanon: A Mediation Model. *Sustainability*, *16*(7), 2807.

Toufighi, S. P., Sahebi, I. G., Govindan, K., Lin, M. Z. N., Van, J., & Brambini, A. (2024). Participative leadership, cultural factors, and speaking-up bahaviour: An examination of intra-organizational knowledge sharing. *Journal of Innovation & Knowledge*, *9*(3), 100548.

Tr n, T. V., Phan, T. H., Lê, A. T. T., & Tr n, T. M. (2022). Evaluation of factors affecting the transition to a circular economy (CE) in Vietnam by structural equation modeling (SEM). *Sustainability*, *14*(2), 613.

Treviño, L. K., Hartman, L. P., & Brown, M. (2000). Moral person and moral manager: How executives develop a reputation for ethical leadership. *California Management Review*, *42*(4), 128–142.

Tukker, A. (2004). Eight types of product–service system: Eight ways to sustainability? Experiences from SusProNet. *Business Strategy and the Environment, 13*(4), 246–260. DOI: 10.1002/bse.414

Tukker, A. (2015). Product services for a resource-efficient and circular economy – a review. *Journal of Cleaner Production, 97*, 76–91. DOI: 10.1016/j.jclepro.2013.11.049

Tukker, A., & Tischner, U. (2006). *New business for old Europe: Product-service development, competitiveness, and sustainability*. Routledge.

Tversky, A., & Kahneman, D. (1983). Extensional versus intuitive reasoning: The conjunction fallacy in probability judgment. *Psychological Review, 90*(4), 293–315.

UNDP. (2022). *Integrating the circular economy in Lebanon's local governance: Pilot initiatives and lessons learned.* United Nations Development Programme.

UNEP,. (2011). Towards a Green Economy: Pathways to Sustainable Development and Poverty Eradication, Sustainable Development.

UNEP. (2019). *Global Resources Outlook: Natural Resources for the Future We Want.* United Nations Environment Programme.

UNEP. (2021). *Measuring circularity: Indicators for a circular economy transition.* United Nations Environment Programme.

UNESCO. (2020). *Education for Sustainable Development Goals: Learning Objectives.* United Nations Educational, Scientific and Cultural Organization. https://unesdoc.unesco.org/ark:/48223/pf0000247444

UNIDO. (2020). *Eco-industrial parks: Achieving the circular economy through industrial symbiosis.* United Nations Industrial Development Organization.

Unilever. (2021). Unilever's plastic commitments: Our vision for a waste-free world. Retrieved from https://www.unilever.com/news/news-search/2021/unilever-announces-commitment-to-reduce-plastic-waste/

United Nations World Tourism Organization. (2019). *Climate Change & Tourism.* https://sdt.unwto.org/en/content/climate-change-tourism

United Nations. (2019). *The Sustainable Development Goals Report 2019.* United Nations Department of Social and Economic Affairs. https://unstats.un.org/sdgs/report/2019/The-Sustainable-Development-Goals-Report-2019.pdf

Ushakov, D., & Shatila, K. (2022). The impact of agricultural sector on boosting the Lebanese economy throughout the economic crisis. *International Journal of Agricultural Extension, 10*(3), 377–385.

Usman, M., Ghani, U., Cheng, J., Farid, T., & Iqbal, S. (2021). Does participative leadership matters in employee' outcomes during COVID-19? Role of leader behavioral integrity. *Frontiers in Psychology, 12*, 646442.

Van der Waal, J., & Thijssens, T. (2020). Corporate involvement in Sustainable Development Goals: Exploring the territory. *Journal of Cleaner Production, 252*, 119625. DOI: 10.1016/j.jclepro.2019.119625

Velenturf, A. P., & Purnell, P. (2021). Principles for a sustainable circular economy. *Sustainable Production and Consumption, 27*, 1437–1457.

Veleva, V. (2018). The role of NGOs in fostering circular economy practices. *Sustainability, 10*(6), 2145. DOI: 10.3390/su10062145

Villiger, S., & Hämmig, O. (2023). Work Related Demands and Resources as Predictors of Well-being at Work Among Healthcare Workers in Switzerland. *Journal of Occupational and Environmental Medicine, 65*(8), 689–693. DOI: 10.1097/JOM.0000000000002885 PMID: 37193642

Vlaar, S. (2024). Applied neuroscience in supervision. *ANSE Journal, 8*(1), 27–32.

Votintseva, L., Andreeva, M., Kovalenin, I., & Votintsev, R. (2019). Digital Transformation Of Russian Banking Institutions: Assessments And Prospects. *IOP Conference Series. Materials Science and Engineering, 497*(1).

Walmart, Inc. (2025). Closed Loop Fund and community engagement in circular economy initiatives. Retrieved from https;//corporate.walmart.com/purpose/sustainability/planet/waste

Walmart. (2023). Sustainability Report. Retrieved from https://corporate.walmart.com/purpose/esgreport/esg-approach/about-our-reporting

Walmart: Walmart. (2021). Walmart's commitment to zero waste. Retrieved from https://corporate.walmart.com/newsroom/2021/10/06/walmart-announces-new-goals-to-reduce-packaging-waste-and-achieve-zero-waste-in-u-s-operations

Ward, B., & Dubo, R. (1983). *Only one earth*. Norton.

Wiedenhofer, D., Streeck, J., Wieland, H., Grammer, B., Baumgart, A., Plank, B., & Krausmann, F. (2024). From extraction to end-uses and waste management: Modeling economy-wide material cycles and stock dynamics around the world. *Journal of Industrial Ecology, 28*(6), 1464–1480.

Wilts, H., Von Gries, N., & Bahn-Walkowiak, B. (2016). From waste management to resource efficiency—The need for policy mixes. *Sustainability*, *8*(7), 622.

Winans, K., Kendall, A., & Deng, H. (2017). The history and current applications of the circular economy concept. *Renewable & Sustainable Energy Reviews*, *68*, 825–833. DOI: 10.1016/j.rser.2016.09.123

Wirtz, B. W., Pistoia, A., Ullrich, S., & Göttel, V. (2016). Business Models: Origin, Development and Future Research Perspectives. *Long Range Planning*, *49*(1), 36–54. DOI: 10.1016/j.lrp.2015.04.001

World Bank. (2021a). *Enabling the business of agriculture 2021: Lebanon profile*. World Bank Group.

World Bank. (2021b). *Lebanon Economic Monitor: The Deliberate Depression*. World Bank Group.

World Bank. (2023). Lebanon Economic Monitor, Fall 2023: In the Grip of a New Crisis. Washington, DC: World Bank. https://openknowledge.worldbank.org/entities/publication/1c302eca-bd1e-4751-9ebd-d425169ed161

World Bank. (2023, December 21). Lebanon's fragile economy pulled back into recession [Press release]. https://www.worldbank.org/en/news/press-release/2023/12/21/lebanon-s-fragile-economy-pulled-back-into-recession

World Commission on Environment and Development. (1987). *Our Common Future*. Oxford University Press.

World Economic Forum. (2020). Circular Economy in the Global Economy. Retrieved from www.weforum.org

World Economic Forum. Ellen MacArthur Foundation, & McKinsey Company. (2014). Towards the Circular Economy: Accelerating the scale-up across global supply chains. World Economic Forum.

World Tourism Organization. (2016). *UNWTO Tourism Highlights 2016 Edition*. https://www.e-unwto.org/doi/pdf/10.18111/9789284418145

World Travel & Tourism Council. (2017). *Global talent trends and issues for the travel and tourism sector*. World Travel & Tourism Council.

World Travel & Tourism Council. (2017). *Travel & Tourism: Economic Impact 2017*. https://www.wttc.org/-/media/files/reports/economic-impact-research/regions-2017/world2017.pdf

World Travel & Tourism Council. (2019). *Travel & tourism economic impact 2019*. Proceedings of the 8th International Conference on Tourism Research (ICTR 2025). https://wttc.org204

World Travel & Tourism Council. (2022). *Travel & tourism economic impact 2022*. World Travel & Tourism Council.

Xue, B., Chen, X., Geng, Y., Guo, X., Lu, C., Zhang, Z., & Lu, C. (2010). Survey of officials' awareness on circular economy development in China: Based on municipal and county level. *Resources, Conservation and Recycling*, *54*(12), 1296–1302. DOI: 10.1016/j.resconrec.2010.05.010

Yerkes, R. M., & Dodson, J. D. (1908). The relation of strength of stimulus to rapidity of habit-formation. *The Journal of Comparative Neurology and Psychology*, *18*(5), 459–482. DOI: 10.1002/cne.920180503

Yıldırım, H. U. (2019). *Bankacılık Sektöründe Yazılım Projelerinin Değerlendirilmesi ve Uygulamaya Yönelik Birer Örnek*. İstanbul Üniversitesi Sosyal Bilimler Enstitüsü İşletme Anabilim Dalı Muhasebe Bilim Dalı.

Yıldız, M. (2023). *Yapay Zekâ ve Yeni Sayı Sistemlerinin Muhasebe ve Finans Alanında Uygulaması*. İksad Yayınevi.

Yong, J., Yusliza, M., Ramayah, T., Farooq, K., & Tanveer, M. (2023). Accentuating the interconnection between green intellectual capital, green human resource management and sustainability. *Benchmarking*, *30*(8), 2783–2808. DOI: 10.1108/BIJ-11-2021-0641

Yong, R. (2007). The circular economy in China. *Journal of Material Cycles and Waste Management*, *9*(2), 121–129. DOI: 10.1007/s10163-007-0183-z

Youssef, S., Ramadan, M., Baydoun, H., Zakhem, N. B., Tahan, S., Diab, M. B., & Yassine, D. (2023). Entrepreneurial Intentions in Crisis: Shaping Through the Triad of Influence-Government, Education, and Environment. *Journal of Law and Sustainable Development*, *11*(6), e890–e890.

Yunis, M., El-Kassar, A. N., & Tarhini, A. (2017). Impact of ICT-based innovations on organizational performance: The role of corporate entrepreneurship. *Journal of Enterprise Information Management*, *30*(1), 122–141.

Yu, R. (2016). Stress potentiates decision biases: A stress-induced deliberation-to-intuition (SIDI) model. *Neurobiology of Stress*, *3*, 83–95. DOI: 10.1016/j.ynstr.2015.12.006 PMID: 27981181

Yusliza, M., Norazmi, N., Jabbour, C., Fernando, Y., Fawehinmi, O., & Seles, B. (2019). Top management commitment, corporate social responsibility and green human resource management: A Malaysian study. *Benchmarking*, *26*(6), 2051–2078. DOI: 10.1108/BIJ-09-2018-0283

Yusoff, Y., Nejati, M., Kee, D., & Amran, A. (2018). Linking green human resource management practices to environmental performance in hotel industry. *Global Business Review*, *21*(3), 663–680. DOI: 10.1177/0972150918779294

Zero Waste Scotland. (2014). *The Role of Local Authorities in a Circular Economy: Scotland's Zero Waste Taskforce Report*. Retrieved from https://www.zerowastescotland.org.uk/resources/role-local-authorities-circular-economy

Zero Waste Scotland. (2023, October). *Building a circular ecosystem for Scottish businesses: Supporting businesses on their circular economy journey*. Zero Waste Scotland.

Zero Waste Scotland. (n.d.-a). *What is the Circular Economy?* Retrieved May 14, 2025, from https://www.zerowastescotland.org.uk/circular-economy

Zhang, Z., Wang, M., & Fleenor, J. W. (2011, January). Effects of participative leadership: the moderating role of cultural values. *In Academy of management Proceedings* (Vol. 2011, No. 1. Pp 1-6). Briarcliff Manor, NY 10510: Academy of Management.

Zhang, L., Godil, D., Bibi, M., Khan, M., Sarwat, S., & Anser, M. (2021). Caring for the environment: How human capital, natural resources, and economic growth interact with environmental degradation in Pakistan? A dynamic ARDL approach. *The Science of the Total Environment*, *774*, 145553. DOI: 10.1016/j.scitotenv.2021.145553 PMID: 33611006

Zhidebekkyzy, A., Moldabekova, A., Amangeldiyeva, B., & Šanova, P. (2023). Transition to a circular economy: Exploring stakeholder perspectives in Kazakhstan. *Journal of International Students*, *16*(3).

Zhu, Q., Geng, Y., & Yin, H. (2020). Circular economy practices: A comparative study of Chinese manufacturing enterprises. *Journal of Cleaner Production*, *196*, 1004–1015.

Zhu, W., May, D. R., & Avolio, B. (2004). The impact of ethical leadership behavior on employee outcomes: The roles of psychological empowerment and authenticity. *Journal of Leadership & Organizational Studies*, *11*, 16–26.

Zou, Y. C., Peng, J., & Hou, N. (2020). Participative leadership and creative performance: A moderated dual path model. *Journal of Management Science*, *33*, 39–51.

Zreik, R. (2025). The factors driving Lebanon's medical brain drain. *Journal of Health Policy*, *34*(1), 78–92.

About the Contributors

Mohamad Saad El Dine Knio holds a PhD in Economics from Cardiff University in the United Kingdom. Currently, Dr. Knio serves as an Assistant Professor of Economics at the Lebanese International University. With a career in academia that began in 2011, Dr. Knio has taught at several well-reputed universities. Notably, he previously worked as an Assistant Professor and Head of Sustainability at City University Ajman in the UAE. Dr. Knio has made significant contributions to academic research and student mentorship. They have supervised numerous DBA students, guiding them to successfully complete their theses. His research primarily focuses on macroeconomics and sustainability, producing applied research aimed at addressing real-world problems. In addition to their academic endeavors, Dr. Knio was actively involved in an Erasmus project and has been a member of AACSB, where they contributed to strategic planning initiatives for their school. They have an extensive publication record in the areas of sustainability and macroeconomic variables, solidifying their reputation as a scholar committed to impactful research.

***

Aliaa Al Dirani is a Lecturer at Islamic University of Lebanon.

Amira Daouk is the Chairperson of the Business Management Department at the Lebanese International University (LIU) in Beirut, Lebanon. With over 10 years of experience in academia, leadership, and research, she holds a PhD in Business Management from Girne American University and an MBA and BS from the Lebanese American University. Dr. Daouk has published extensively on leadership, emotional intelligence, and digital transformation. She is known for her student-centered teaching and commitment to academic excellence.

Raouf Fadlallah is an Instructor and Coordinator in Management at the Lebanese International University (LIU), Lebanon. I hold a Master's degree in

Business Administration from the American University of Culture and Education, Lebanon, and currently pursuing a PhD in Management with a focus on Management & Hospitality. I have an extensive professional experience in the hotel industry, having served as a Front Office Manager, where he developed expertise in customer service operations, team leadership, and quality management systems. My academic interests center on sustainable business practices, customer engagement strategies, and digital transformation in the hospitality and tourism sectors. My recent research explores the intersection of circular economy principles and business model innovation within the hospitality industry.

Ghada Kalakesh is a professional academic and administrator with more than 15 years of experience in various industries such as the academic industry, the airline industry, the insurance industry and the computer industry. Former life insurance manager at Libano Suisse insurance, and a former Senior Commercial and Aero political manager at the Arab Air Carriers Organization (AACO), and lately a full_time faculty member in Business Management and International Business Management at the Lebanese International University (LIU). Holding a Ph.D. with high distinction in Entrepreneurship at the Ecole Superieure De Commerce (ESC) at Manouba University in Tunisia. Holding a Bachelor of Arts degree in Political Sciences and Public Administration at the American University of Beirut, and a Master degree in Business Management at the Lebanese International University. Dr. Ghada Kalakesh research interests include Intelligent leadership, Entrepreneurship, Emotional Intelligence and Digital Leadership.

Selma Kalkavan is a strategic advisor, facilitator, coach, and award-winning author with over 25 years of leadership experience in international companies. She specializes in strategic planning, organizational development, and human and cultural management, integrating neuroscience into workplace practices. Selma holds a Ph.D. in Management and Organization, a PCC-level coaching certification from the ICF, and the highest-level Master Neuroplastician® (M.npn) credential from the Institute of Organizational Neuroscience (2024). She is the author of five influential books, covering coaching, facilitation, recognition culture in the digital age, neuroscience in HR, and most recently, Neuroparenting—a guide for parents to understand and apply brain-based strategies for child development. As the founder of her consultancy practice, she supports leaders and organizations in cultural transformation and competency development across Turkey, the MENA region, and beyond.

Hala M. Koleilat Al Dilby is a PHD holder who pursued her studies at Girne American University in Kyrenia, Cyprus. Her academic and research endeavors are affiliated with Frontiers Media SA, a prominent academic publisher. Dr. Hala's research focuses on virtual and different leadership styles and their impact on job satisfaction through various mediating roles, like trust in leader and work life balance. Dr. Koleilat Al Dilby field of study started in marketing and pursued to cover business topics related to management, leadership, HRM, and digital marketing. She currently holds the position of a full timer, student advisor, coordinator and researcher at Lebanese International University.

Stelios Marneros is a Lecturer in Hotel Management at the Department of Tourism and Hospitality Management. He holds a PhD from Middlesex University in the development of competencies in hospitality management (Pedagogical Practices of Hospitality Management), an MSc in Hotel and Catering Management from Manchester Metropolitan University, and a BSc in Hotel, Restaurant and Tourism Administration from Southern Illinois University, Carbondale. Stelios taught as a faculty member at the European University Cyprus and served as the program coordinator in hospitality and tourism management program. He worked in the hotel and catering industry (Amathus Hotel Paphos, Pizza Hut, Anassa Hotel, Atlantica Hotels and Resorts) for several years before pursuing an academic career. His research interests focus on hotel industry education, hospitality management competencies, hospitality management programs, entrepreneurship, wine tourism, and gastronomy. His research papers have been published in academic journals such as Journal of Hospitality, Leisure, Sport & Tourism Education, Journal of Teaching in Travel and Tourism and Higher Education, Skills and Work-Based Learning.

Fatima Rahal has a PhD in Business Management Assistant Professor. Dr. Rahal is the Chairperson of the Management and Marketing across all branches of the Islamic University of Lebanon. I believe in continuous learning and love taking new challenges I'm passionate about storytelling, coaching, collaborating with an effective team.

Suha Tahan is the Chairperson of the Economics Department at the Lebanese International University. She has more than 12 years of both academic and professional experience. Her research mainly tackles sustainability, green practices, financial inclusion, and entrepreneurship.

Bassam Tarhini holds a PHD in Marketing from Bucharest University of economic studies, Romania in 2021. I earned my Master's degree in Marketing and Management Information Systems from Oklahoma City University, USA in December of 2004. My BS degree in Marketing was attained from the Lebanese University in 1998. In addition to being a faculty member at LIU, I have been holding the role of Chairman for the marketing department since Fall 2011- 2012 till Fall 2018-2019. Simultaneously, I held the role of Assistant Dean at the school of business for 14 years since Fall 2011 -2012. I have acquired 15 years of teaching experience at both the Graduate and Undergraduate University level and provided high standards of quality teaching. Prior to teaching I have managed the marketing and the daily operations for an Intercontinental Hotel Groups for 5 years in the USA I was also a corporate account manager and a sales trainer at Dell Inc. for 3 years in the USA. My research interests evolve around digital marketing, sustainable leadership, consumer and employee behavior.

Sonja Vlaar is a professional supervisor and coach for executive leaders and professionals, and a strategic advisor for organizational learning and development. Based in the Netherlands and working internationally, she has been operating independently since 2004 through her company Attune.nl. Sonja specializes in applied neuroscience, supporting clients in regulating their physiology, biology, and behavioral patterns to enhance relationships, health, wellbeing, performance, and leadership effectiveness. She holds a degree in Nutrition (Ir. MSc.) from Wageningen University & Research (1983), a Master's in Supervision and Coaching from HAN University of Applied Sciences (2003), and the highest-level Master Neuroplastician® (M.npn) credential by the Institute of Organizational Neuroscience (2024). Sonja is multi-certified in coaching, supervision, and applied neuroscience. She is co-author of the forthcoming handbook Supervision for Coaches, scheduled for publication in August 2025.

Index

I

L

N

P

R

S

www.ingramcontent.com/pod-product-compliance
Lightning Source LLC
LaVergne TN
LVHW081526300926
849161LV00006B/1319
9798337376554